# Selene

*The Moon Goddess
& The Cave Oracle*

Steve Moore

*For Selene, of course*

*Selene* by Steve Moore
First published by Strange Attractor Press, 2019
This Print on Demand edition 2023
ISBN: 978-1-913689-06-3

Front cover illustration shows *The Creation of the Starry Firmament*, 1924. Woodcut from Genesis, Paul Nash. Credit: Wellcome Collection. Back cover illustration shows *The Creation of Sun and Moon*, 1924. Woodcut from Genesis, Paul Nash. Credit: Wellcome Collection.

Edited by John Higgs
Indexing provided by Phil Baker

Steve Moore has asserted his moral right to be identified as the author of this work in accordance with the Copyright, Designs and Patents Act, 1988. All rights reserved. No part of this publication may be reproduced in any form or by any means without the written permission of the publishers. A CIP catalogue record for this book is available from the British Library.

Strange Attractor Press
BM SAP, London,
WC1N 3XX, UK
www.strangeattractor.co.uk

Distributed by The MIT Press, Cambridge, Massachusetts.
And London, England

# Contents

Foreword: *Steve Moore, Kouros* by Bob Rickard                     vii

Introduction: Selene, Who She Is, And Who She Isn't                  1
1. A Selene Compendium                                              13
2. Selene Herself                                                   33
3. The Minor Myths                                                  59
4. The Loves of Goddesses                                           85
5. Endymion                                                        111
6. Latmos and the Landscape of Myth                                129
7. Epimenides of Crete                                             143
8. Cave Initiations, Wisdom Traditions and Dwellers Under the Earth  159
9. The Oracle at Thalamae                                          173
10. Dream Oracles Elsewhere                                        189
11. Selene and Endymion: A Reprise                                 215
12. Selene and Pan                                                 233
13. Selene and the Oracle-Mongers                                  253
14. Mythical Afterlife: The Endymion Sarcophagi                    291
15. Conclusions: The Phases of the Moon                            301
16. Appendix: Selene, Endymion and Incest                          309

Bibliography                                                       319
Afterword: *At the Perigee* by Alan Moore                          343

Foreword

# Steve Moore, Kouros

## Moonrise

I had known Steve Moore since 1973. Throughout nearly five decades he was the best kind of friend and colleague I could have hoped for. It was not until after his death in 2014 that I realised he was so much more than that. This light dawned upon me after reading Peter Kingsley's profound reconstruction of the authentic legacy of the Pythagorean philosopher Parmenides, rooted in the Eleatic mysteries and their associated practice of incubation in a sacred place.[1] Please bear with me while I take a little detour to explain.

Quiet and solitude were highly valued by the Pythagoreans, and many of their associated hero-shrines had within their precinct a quiet place (often a cave under the shrine or on a nearby mountain), where, after appropriate rituals, consultants or supplicants slept in the hope of receiving divine guidance or healing in their dreams. As Kingsley shows, incubation was not simply to obtain healing or oracular guidance – those were practised widely – but wisdom-seekers (*kouros*) used this method specifically for meditation, inspiration and direct intercourse with the gods.

Parmenides flourished around the 6th century BC, in the Greek town of Elea in southern Italy. Recent scholars, such as Kingsley, place him in the Pythagorean tradition lineage, because of their reinterpretation of his single surviving work, the poem *On Nature*.

---

1 Peter Kingsley, *In the Dark Places of Wisdom*, 1999.

Long regarded as a supreme demonstration of precise logical analysis, the poem asserts the primacy of a universal unity of being, as distinct from the illusory world of appearances derived from imperfect sensation and thought. The strong rhetorical comparison between Parmenides' idea of the 'One Being' – (Greek: *aletheia*) – and its ancient Chinese equivalent – the Dao (or The Way) – was not lost on Steve; in fact it inspired him to accumulate a fine collection of books on both philosophies, and this in turn underpinned his studies of the I Ching (or *Yijing*), a prophetic almanac which interprets changes in the phenomenal world as tides or flows within the Dao itself.

Kingsley also illuminates another Pythagorean tradition, iatromancy, in which Parmenides stands in a lineage of healer-shamans going back to the legendary figures of Empedocles, Aristeas, Epimenides and Abaris (the Hyperborean skywalker who acknowledged Pythagoras as an incarnation of Apollo). Some of them were revered as cave-incubation oracles and had hero-shrines; some were said to be descended from Apollo and his son Asclepius. Those relevant to Steve's thesis fill section eight.

In the prologue of his poem, Parmenides describes a divine transportation into the underworld where he is greeted, intimately, by a goddess whose name he carefully – i.e. by ancient custom and with the respect an initiate should show his teacher – does not declare to the uninitiated. This was, most likely, Persephone (or Kore, the Roman Proserpina), the reluctant Queen of the underworld – who reveals to him the philosophy and its meaning. In other words, one of the great founding wisdom-teachings of Western civilisation was delivered to a man who slept in a dark, quiet place and communed with his goddess in a dream (or trance, or meditation).[2]

---

[2] Materialists of all stripes might like to consider this point; that out of something so unscientific came forth logical epistemology. The writer of the wiki on Parmenides mentions that the philosopher Karl Popper once likened Einstein's discourse on the paradox of 'Block Time' (in which past, present and future exist simultaneously implying that time itself can have no 'flow' or direction) to the way in which Parmenides used the deductive method, thus pre-figuring scientific methodology.

Bob Rickard

There are other links to the Pythagoreans within this, Steve's paean to Selene; circumstantial ones, but relevant nevertheless. For example, Steve and his long-time friend and writing partner Alan Moore (no relation) developed an interest in the second century 'prophet' Alexander of Abonoteichus and his human-headed snake-god 'puppet' Glycon for their forthcoming collaboration *The Moon and Serpent Bumper Book of Magic*. Steve's research into this Alexander – whom the Roman satirist Lucian had met and denounced as a boldly inventive conman – also figures in the appendix to section 13 in this book. This is in relation to the 'Mysteries of Selene', in which Alexander claims that he is the grandson of Asclepius, and that Glycon is the 'new Asclepius'.

The oracle shrines of Apollo and Asclepius were the main centres for incubation healing, but Alexander himself is said to have taken petitions from consultants and held them while he slept in an underground chamber so that Glycon could deliver the requested oracles to him in dreams. Furthermore, Alexander concluded his rites with re-enactments of the myth of Endymion and Selene; and even claimed that his daughter had been born because The Moon Goddess had fallen in love with him, having seen him asleep (as she had done with Endymion). Not only did Alexander teach Pythagorean precepts, such as the transmigration of souls, but, according to Lucian, often during the rites of the mysteries 'his thigh was bared purposely and showed golden'. This was a deliberate allusion to the legend that Pythagoras himself had been given a golden thigh by Apollo. By this sign, Alexander raised the idea that he might actually be a reincarnation of the great sage himself.[3]

## The Seleneum at Hilltop

This meander brings us to this book, as you'll find much herein

---

3 For the Pythagorean tradition and lineages generally, see Charles H. Kahn, *Pythagoras and the Pythagoreans: A Brief History* (2001). For how Alexander of Abonoteichus fits into it, see chapter 9 therein: 'The Pythagorean Tradition of the Occult and Paranormal'.

about the dream-oracles of different cults and their associated caves scattered across Magna Graecia. Indeed, in section 10 Steve concentrates on the widespread belief that dreams offered the possibility of encountering living gods. The shamanic elements of 'deathlike sleep' and 'descent into the underworld' – in particular, how these illuminate the stories Selene and her perpetually sleeping lover Endymion – form the concluding sections of Steve's book.

Kingsley's exposition affected me in a number of ways, the most relevant here is that it opened my eyes to something that had been in front of me in all my years of friendship with Steve and yet, until then, I had not noticed it or realised its meaning. Quietly, spontaneously and over time, Steve had worked out his own system of Pythagorean incubation to commune with his Muse through his study of the love between Selene and Endymion. Without deliberation, his routine evolved naturally, conforming to the strict definition of Classical Greek incubation (as formulated by Juliette Harrisson): 'a practice in which a person performs a ritual act and then sleeps in a sacred place, with the deliberate intention of receiving a divine dream'.[4] It is no coincidence, then, that in *Somnium* (2011), Steve's novel about an Elizabethan lunar romance, he placed the doorway into Selene's world deep beneath his home on the top of London's Shooters Hill.

Steve appointed Alan Moore and me as his executors. I had long known Steve kept a dream diary, but it was only when I began packing up his library – three metric tons of (mainly) books – that the extent to which he did this religiously became clear. His regular dream record, made over decades, which runs into many volumes is now in Alan's care. It is a unique resource and deserves its own study. Over time, Steve developed a remarkable level of recall and control over his dreams; once confirming to me that he was able, at times, to become conscious within them and direct them to some degree. This was one of the aims of Pythagorean incubation. We

---

4 Juliette Harrisson, 'The classical Greek practice of incubation and some Near Eastern predecessors' (2009), https://www.academia.edu/277934/

had been talking about his attempts to 'travel' in a dream – what used to be called 'astral projection' – but in retrospect I realise that he was more interested in the creative potential of dreams, both as inspiration for his story-telling and as a medium in which he could communicate intimately with Selene.

These dream diaries, alongside creating miniature icons of the goddess, were just some of his daily rituals. If, as Erich Neumann points out,[5] the making of a list of the variants of a deity's name and titles – as Steve does in the early chapters of this book – is in itself an act of worship, how much more is added to that when we apply the years of quiet scholarship, following the goddess's travels and exploring her relationships, acts, rituals, legends and mysteries?

His small office and bedroom were lined with sagging shelves and teetering stacks of ring-binders and file folders, each dedicated to some aspect of his research projects; each stuffed with his internet and other research, printed out and carefully filed. Uncovering earlier folders behind or beneath those was a kind of literary and philosophical archaeology, the ink tracing where Steve's curiosity had run far and wide, but always towards, his Goddess.

Steve's simple hermetic lifestyle (which included a few essential clothes and a regular vegetarian diet) also conformed to the Pythagorean formula. A chief characteristic of the wisdom-mysteries, as the Ancient Greeks knew it, was *kourotrophos*: the milieu in which initiates were brought into contact with the gods as living beings who would guide them. Although the modern use of the term *kouros* applies to Greek statuary depicting idealised youths, its more archaic usage, especially among the Pythagoreans, described any aspirant – even to aged philosophers like Parmenides and heroes like Herakles (as he made his own way into the underworld) – who quested, or stood before a teacher, or

---

5 Erich Neumann, *The Great Mother* (1974 edn.), p.275.

who lay down before a divine image and opened their innermost selves in quiet anticipation.

Upon each visit to his Hilltop home – once family full but, in the end, with only its sole occupant – the earthly traces of a stellar intellect was plainly evident. His book-lined bedroom was the quiet place in which Steve's daily acts of worship were devoted to illuminating the celestial entity in all her aspects. It was an analogue of Endymion's cave – a *temenos*, a sacred place where the boundaries of this and another world blurred, into which he placed his incubatory bed. He crafted an icon of Selene and kept it close to where he laid his head; gazing at it as he drifted off. Steve was a *kouros* in spirit and deed.

Throughout his regrettably short writing life, Steve was, innately, a consummate stylist, never straying from a narrow path between inspiration and professionalism. From his early career working in the UK's weekly comics industry until his last years, he wrote directly for his target audience. When he was, finally, free of his regular writing commissions and felt competent enough to give himself up to the muse that drew him ever onward, he wrote for her. In one of his many diaries is an entry for 3$^{rd}$ February 2005, in which he looks back over the three decades since he adopted Selene as his muse. He writes:

> *I've naturally interested myself, during that period, in all varieties of theurgy; and in particular the art of animating an image of the deity. As a result, my Selene manifests mainly through a small painting of her that I made in 1989 and, although I never made any particular attempt to 'ritually animate' the image, more than 15 years of love and adoration have gradually brought her to life nonetheless. And if that 'life' is a concept shared largely between myself and Selene, it remains a life nonetheless; and sharing it with her remains the great joy of my own.*
>
> *Many years ago, I began to sort through my change every time I arrived home and, if there were any twenty-pence pieces amongst*

*it, I would put them aside in an old, cracked-glass vase (given to me decades ago by another long-time object of my affection) as an offering to Selene. For long periods, I confess, this merely meant that when the vase was full, and cashed in at the bank, dear Selene would, in turn, 'buy me' a book that I couldn't otherwise afford.*

According to Hesiod, at least, there were nine Muses who were all Selene's siblings via their father Zeus. In a typical Greek paradox, Selene, herself, was elsewhere said to be pre-Olympian, a Titan, a daughter of Hyperion (Light, Wisdom) and Theia (Radiance) and a sister to Helios (Sun) and Eos (Dawn). The creative emanations of the nine daughters of Zeus and Mnemosyne (Memory) inspired epic poetry, history, lyric poetry, comedy and pastoral poetry, tragedy, dance, love poetry, sacred poetry and astronomy, and to be absorbed by their devotees. Mnemosyne is also noted for receiving sacrifices at incubation shrines, when the dreamers woke and recalled to the attendants details of their oneiric journey. They would have approved of Steve's diaries, I'm sure.

I'm not sure about his terpsichorean talents though – except that he did, once, have an interest in the tragic American dancer Isadora Duncan (1877-1927). But if I allow astronomy to correspond to his interest in Zhuge Liang (181–234 CE) – a philosopher, renowned inventor, and Prime Minister of the Three Kingdoms period in China, who developed successful military strategies based upon the trigrams of the I Ching and divinatory star patterns – then Steve was pretty much receptive to all these spheres of celestial influence.

## Moonbow

Steve was also one of those divinely-favoured creatures, an autodidact, with no university degree and no tutoring by academics. He conducted voluminous correspondences with those he regarded as friends, colleagues and fellow-travellers, and was always modest about his own accomplishments. Those who knew him only as a writer of comic strips will be surprised to hear that he devoted years to mastering Greek and Roman mythology; the literature of the late-19th century Decadent movement; Elizabethan culture; a variety of systems of magic both ancient and modern; to which he added a profound understanding of the I Ching and Daoism.

He built up an extensive collection of Chinese movies (matched only by his brother Chris's Japanese movie library), and could recite the plots and actors from most of them. With Alan Moore, he raised the bar on comic and graphic novel writing. With me, he'd discuss the work of Charles Fort (the American iconoclast and collector of reports of anomalies); and from its inception, guided the development of *Fortean Times*, making many valuable contributions to it. This includes the Herculean drudgery of compiling an index to its first 105 issues.

He tutored himself in written Mandarin. Following his own analysis of the I Ching and Zhuge Liang's strategies – published as *The Trigrams of Han* in 1989 – Steve collaborated with Gary Dickinson, Profs. Kidder Smith and Ed Hacker, and Lorraine Patsco, among other scholars of the I Ching, as editor of a dedicated periodical, *The Oracle*. He also co-authored *I Ching: An Annotated Bibliography* (2002); and translated the *Maquian Ke* (2012), a book of prophetic writings widely believed to be by the historical Zhuge Liang, but shown by Steve to be a more recent forgery.[6]

With Mike Crowley, he explored the mysteries of soma (an elixir which bestowed immortality upon the Hindu gods); and pursued China's mysterious Queen Mother of the West, Xiwangmu – possibly older, even, than the Greek deities – whose journey from the mists of antiquity into Daoist legend (she is credited in places as the original author of the Dao De Jing) has echoes in the shamanic processions of the ancient Greek supplicants to their slumbers in caves under mountains. What is relevant to us here is that Xiwangmu, a primordial immortal, is also said to have visited and tutored a

---

6 Available online at http://www.biroco.com/yijing/Maqian_ke.pdf

number of China's early historical emperors and kings, in intimate relationships that recall Selene's enchantment of Endymion.[7]

As Steve points out there is no single, coherent, or fully fleshed-out mythology of the Moon or its deities, only the steady accretion over time of fragments from different conquering or adjacent cultures (themselves barely animated skeletons after centuries of cultural erosion, acts of cultural vandalism, neglect and the passage of time). Unravelling this vast knot of Greek and Roman syncretism occupies most of the early part of this book.

The later sections deal with what French folklorist Michel Meurger calls the "mythical landscape" in which our *dramatis personae*, real and imagined, created their myths or enacted older ones. A good portion of this involves his own comprehensive survey of the various subterranean sites which had oracles or which were open to incubation (usually for healing and oracles, but also for initiation into the Mysteries); their oracular priesthoods and associated deities or heroes; and the stories or myths about them.

Finally we have a more detailed study of the most important of Selene's relationships, with a special focus upon the character and fate of Endymion who was quite a paradox in himself (despite being made immortal he was also eternally asleep). Two appendixes are added which tackle related but tangential topics: the Moon and its phases and their influence, and (the elephant in the room) the observation that so many of the pairs of lovers mentioned throughout the study are incestual. All of this is supported with an impressive bibliography.

Whether Steve wanted us to see Selene as he saw her, I cannot now tell; but clearly she was a real presence to him. As Alan records in his afterword here, Steve died precisely at the moment his earthly work was done.

---

7 Curiously, this correlation also appears in Dan Simmons' SF novel *The Rise of Endymion* (1997), which features a city named Xiwangmu on a planet named after China's holy mountain Tian Shan.

## Moonset

Steve's daily perambulation took several different routes around Shooters Hill. One favourite was into the ancient Oxleas wood – which dates back to the end of the last Ice Age – passing Severndroog Castle, one of the locations featured in *Somnium*. Another took him down Plum Lane to its junction with Mayplace Lane (both paved-over ancient tracks) and the low-lying Bronze Age barrow there. This location marks the last resting place of Steve's mortal remains. In one of the small anthologies of his writings that he'd produce occasionally for friends, he described what it meant to him:

> *Not long after I began to interest myself in the mound and its relation to the hill, a charming fantasy occurred to me (or intuition, if you will): that whoever had been reverently buried here, oh so long ago, to become one with the earth, had somehow become the tutelary deity of Shooters Hill as well, and would be still for as long as the mound survived. And so, in all the years that have drifted by since then, whenever I've passed the mound on one of my rambling walks, I've bid good morning to the local God; for to do anything less would seem to lack in courtesy.*
>
> *The courtesy was returned a few days after I began the practice. One March morning, after a light but recent snow (already melted everywhere else), I approached the mound, 'good morning' on my lips, and found a small snowman awaiting me, perhaps a foot high. A conical heap for a body, a snowball for a head ... but that head bristled with a 'hair' of little sticks, or perhaps some ancient cunning-man's antlered headdress made of twigs. I knew the God by sight, and paid him my respects. The following day he'd disappeared, never to be seen again. No further sight was necessary.*
>
> *Born high up on Shooters Hill myself, when I die I want my ashes scattered on the burial mound, by the light of a lovely full Moon. So just for a moment, I too can become an offering to the local Gods and Goddesses, and merge my essence with the native*

Bob Rickard

*soil ... before all that physically remains of me is blown away and scattered, like oak-leaves on the whirling wind.*[8]

And so they were; by the light of the full moon, on the 10th August 2014, attended, in good spirits, by a small company of friends and family.

Steve had no faith in the Mosaic or monolithic religions; his own personal *kourotrophos* offered him so much more. One of his favourite writers, Apuleius (although he liked the satirist Lucian more) described his own incubation thus: 'I approached the confines of Death; I trod the threshold of Proserpina; after being carried through all the elements I returned to earth [...] I penetrated into the very presence of the gods below and the gods above, where I worshipped face to face.'[9] In the best of all worlds, Steve will, by now, be enjoying his well-earned 'face to face'.

Steve's humble yet gloriously rich example and his unconditional friendship inspired many of his friends I'm sure; but it encouraged me to never feel daunted by the difficulty or exclusivity of a subject, or to chase the approval of established academia for its own sake, but always to aspire to authentic scholarship.

As I type, Steve's 'old, cracked-glass vase' is now close to my own desk and I have adopted his offertory ritual in his memory and to honour his goddess. It is my privilege to commend to you what follows here, his brightest and most public hymn to Selene.

Bob Rickard
Founding Editor, *Fortean Times*
London, May 8th, 2017

---

8 'The Burial Mound', being no.1. in *Sketches Of Shooters Hill*, written on '21st April 2004, in the evening, The first sight of the New Moon, The Old Moon in the New Moon's arms.'

9 Apuleius, *Metamorphoses* xi.23.

Introduction

# Selene, Who She Is, And Who She Isn't

Waxing and waning and reborn with each new month, the Moon has always been the supreme symbol of cyclical change in the western world. The Moon's Goddess too seems to undergo similar changes, each new century appearing to reinvent her in its own image. Considering the confusions of the late 20th century, with its conflicting academic interpretations and its proliferation of popular spiritual interests, it's not surprising that we've inherited a picture of an almost entirely synthetic 'Moon-Goddess' that is, to put it mildly, soft-focus and fuzzy round the edges, and which would hardly have been recognisable to anyone living in the ancient world.

Despite the importance of the Moon to those interested in such recent developments as the 'women's mysteries' and Neo-Pagan movements, it's not my intention in this book to present a 'Moon-Goddess for the 21st century', but rather to look at the myths of one specific Moon-Goddess, and how she appeared to the original creators of those myths. That Goddess is Selene, and the tellers of her tales were the ancient Greeks.

I use the word *tale* deliberately when talking about the myths of Selene. In recent years there has been much debate about the actual definition of the difficult word *myth*: its relationship to folktale, whether it should refer only to sacred matters, and so on.[1] Such are the variety of myths that have come down to us that this problem of finding a universally-applicable definition has largely defeated even the most learned of mythological scholars; there are some myths which contain folktale elements and some which do not, there are profane myths as well as sacred ones, and so forth. As a result, in trying to find something broad enough to apply without exception to *all* myths, we have ended up with very basic definitions. The one I shall be using here is that of Walter Burkert: '*myth is a traditional tale with secondary, partial reference to something of collective importance*. Myth is traditional tale applied; and its relevance and seriousness stem largely from this application. The reference is secondary, as the meaning of the tale is not to be derived from it – in contrast to fable, which is invented for the sake of its application; and it is partial, since tale and reality will never be quite isomorphic in these applications. And still the tale often is the first and fundamental verbalisation of complex reality, the primary way to speak about many-sided problems, just as telling a tale was seen to be quite an elementary way of communication. Language is linear, and linear narrative is thus a way prescribed by language to map reality.'[2] I would like to re-emphasise here what I said at the beginning of this paragraph, as it will be useful in trying to sort out some of the material relating to Selene, particularly with regard to modern interpretations. Myth is a *tale*; cultural relevance is important, but if there is no narrative element, there is no myth.

An attempt to uncover a 'Greek Selene' requires a certain amount of detective work, because the succeeding centuries have given us countless reinventions that have obscured her pristine glories. Even when these distorting images are stripped away we have further problems. Vast quantities of ancient literature have

---

[1] The current popular, American meaning of 'myth' as 'falsehood' or 'untruth' is, of course, completely inapplicable here.

[2] Burkert 1979: p.23.

been lost, owing to the destructive ravages of time and the book-burnings of religious zealots; that which does remain is incomplete, confusing and contradictory, and refuses to conform to our modern desires for neatness and order; indeed, it is far less easy to say what the mythology of Selene is than what it is *not*. The result, as will be seen from Chapter 1 where Selene's surviving myths are gathered together, is a frustrating collection of fragments that frequently lack structure or 'plot', with information completely lacking in some places, while in others there is a bewildering multiplicity of variants. Unfortunately, when the 'jigsaw-puzzle' is so obviously damaged and incomplete, there's often a tendency to 'fill in the missing pieces', and not always correctly. Given that Selene was later identified with other ancient Goddesses, the chances of constructing a false picture are all too obvious.

This synthesising identification began at an early period; almost as soon, indeed, as we have any written sources mentioning Selene. The first evidence we have of the process shows it beginning almost by accident: in the Classical period, around the 5$^{th}$ century BCE, Apollo, who seems originally to have been a God of young men, took on a number of solar aspects and became identified with the Sun-God Helios. The inevitable consequence was that Apollo's entirely non-lunar sister, the huntress-Goddess Artemis, became identified with Helios' sister, Selene; and, in turn, when Artemis was identified with the Roman Goddess Diana, so was Selene. In the Hellenistic and Roman periods, we find an astonishing syncretism, in which Selene is further identified with Hecate (also originally non-lunar, and only taking on lunar aspects in the Roman period[3]), Isis, Ishtar, Astarte and countless other Goddesses. Unfortunately, it's probably necessary to point out to the unwary reader that these identifications, although they may be justified in terms of religious, philosophical, symbolic or magical thinking (and so forth), are *not* mythological. There is no narrative strand involved in making an

---

[3] As demonstrated by Rabinowitz 1998: particularly at pp.43ff.

identification of Selene and Artemis, and the mythological stories told of Artemis remain resolutely non-lunar, no matter how much she might be said to represent the Moon.

Not only are the majority of these identifications far too late to be relevant to our understanding of Selenic mythology, they frequently result in downright distortion. As we'll see, the identification with Artemis/Diana has, on occasion, led to the misapprehension that Selene is a virgin Goddess. As the myths will show, this she certainly is not. Similarly, the original Selene has nothing whatever to do with a 'Triple Moon-Goddess' represented as Maiden, Bride/Mother and Crone. This is a 20th century invention largely propagated in the peculiar, poetic and misleading works of Robert Graves,[4] whose interpretations range from the idiosyncratic to the idiotic (his etymologies being so misleading that he has even been suspected of satirical intent[5]), and yet whose books continue to be influential in some circles. Apart from youthful 'dying-and-reviving-God' vegetation deities imported from the Middle East, such as Adonis, the ancient Greeks very definition of deity depended on the Gods being deathless, supernally beautiful and *ever-youthful*. It's true, of course, that certain deities such as Zeus are represented with a more mature appearance than other Gods, but this is simply a case of iconographically representing their greater *gravitas*; it in no way implies that they are more aged, because the Gods are eternal. The idea of a 'Crone-Goddess' would have struck the Greeks as absurd (unless it was some peculiar foreign deity, imported with all its imagery intact). Even Hecate, who modern interpreters frequently identify with the 'Crone' aspect, is always portrayed in Greek iconography as young and beautiful. Simply put, there are no ugly or aged Goddesses in Greek myth; such attributes are reserved for monsters and bogies.

---

4 Graves 1960: *passim*. Graves 1961: *passim*.
5 Peradotto 1973: pp.10-11.

The other point here, of course (particularly if the 'Triple Moon-Goddess' is claimed to be extremely ancient and tied in with other fantasies such as 'matriarchal society') is that it simply doesn't fit with the evidence. Among the Greeks, the earliest way of dividing the month that we know of is into *two phases*, 'rising' and 'waning'.[6] It is hard to see how this can be fitted together with a tripartite Goddess.

As Graves' 'Triple Moon-Goddess' appears to have become so ingrained in modern consciousness, it may be worthwhile taking a brief look at the somewhat similar lunar trinity we *do* find in late antiquity. This only appears after the syncretisation of Selene with the other Goddesses mentioned previously, and mainly in Latin authors such as Servius, writing in the 4th century CE.[7] Servius equates Diana with Hecate (often portrayed with either three faces or three bodies), and so arrives at a 'Triple-faced Diana', which he corresponds with Luna (Selene) in the celestial world, Diana (Artemis) in the terrestrial realm and Proserpina (Persephone) in the underworld; this, however, is a 'spatial' arrangement deriving from philosophy rather than mythology. Servius also tells us that Luna (Selene) has three phases, with Lucina (Eileithyia, the birth-Goddess) corresponding to the waxing (new-born) phase, the huntress Diana to the (strong) full Moon, and the underworld Hecate to the waning (dying) phase. Apart from the fact that we have here the virgin Diana corresponding to Graves' Bride/Mother phase, all these correspondences are easily explained in terms of the functions of the individual Goddesses; there is nothing here to suggest that the Goddesses correspond to particular ages or supposed 'aspects of womanhood'. And again, as no story is being told here, it should be emphasised that this is not mythology. Furthermore, absolutely none of these triple correspondences appear in the surviving stories of Selene, collected in Chapter 1;

---

6 Liddell-Scott 1996: *s.v.* Men.

7 Servius, commentary to Virgil's *Aeneid*, 4.509-514 (1826: Vol. 1, p.298).

neither do these correspondences appear in any of the myths of the other Goddesses brought into the triplicity, such as Diana or Hecate. To connect these triple-correspondences with mythology is a category error, like measuring the weight of one's purchases in miles-per-hour; they are the result of *religious and philosophical speculation about identities*, and they have nothing to do with *mythological stories*. They originated, besides, perhaps a thousand years after the original myth-making. I realise, of course, that the viewpoint expressed here may appear contentious, especially given the amount of opposing opinion to be found on the internet and in works about modern Neo-Pagan belief, so let me make myself clear here. As I see it, there is nothing wrong with a 21st century person with interests in modern Pagan belief or current interpretations of the deities working with the idea of, or holding the view that there is, a 'Triple Moon-Goddess', with all that that symbolises for contemporary beliefs. There is *everything* wrong in believing that such a notion can tell us how the ancients thought about Selene, and we cannot use the notion to interpret the myths about her.

The wide acceptance and popularity of such interpretations as Graves' (particularly in media such as the internet) tells us a great deal about modern attitudes to mythology and the deities that feature in it, but little else. So how have we arrived at this strange and distorted picture of the past and its beliefs? It seems to me that there are several reasons for this. We live in a world that would rather have neat-and-tidy versions of ancient myths and legends, rather than the 'difficult' complexity of having to deal directly with the ancient sources, even when they're available in translation. Obviously, a desire to impose some sort of order upon the disparate remnants of antiquity is understandable; but the problem is selecting the *right* order to impose, if that is actually possible. A far bigger problem is 21st century attitudes, particularly in the western world. We are naïve, narcissistic and arrogant enough to believe that we understand human nature, with the result that we tend to 'back-project' our own present-day concerns (political, psychological, anti-racist, humanitarian, gender-oriented, and so on) onto the behaviours and beliefs of the people of the past, as if people of 7th century BCE Sparta or Athens thought in the same way as those of 21st century CE New York. Or worse, as if they *should*.

This sort of fantasy-proneness may be forgivable in popular culture, but unfortunately it also applies to more academic studies, and particularly to what G.S. Kirk described as 'monolithic' theories of myth interpretation, where the proponents of the theories believe that they are in possession of the 'single key' which will unlock *all* the mysteries of the myths (for example, that *all* myth originates in ritual, or that *all* myths are 'nature myths', and so on).[8] As Kirk points out, such theories may go some way to explaining *certain aspects* of myths and, either individually or in combination, may provide us with useful insights, but explain *everything* they certainly do not. Since Kirk wrote, new approaches have been added to the interpreter's arsenal, such as Structuralism, Dumezil's theories of Indo-European social organisation, semiotics, cognitive theory, and so on.[9] Once again it has to be emphasised that these are *modern* theories being applied to ancient material. It may be possible to interpret a myth in Structural terms, but it is quite certain that the story was not composed with Structuralism in mind; and the net result of any such application is that we are likely to learn far more about the way Structuralism works than we are about myth. This is particularly true where such monolithic theories are mixed with political elements like Marxism or Feminism.

It's probably most apposite to discuss Feminist approaches to myth here, as we are dealing with the Moon. If one starts an investigation of lunar mythology from a Feminist viewpoint

---

8 Kirk 1974: pp.38-91.

9 For a summary treatment of these more recent approaches, with a critique of their defects, see Graf 1993: pp.35-56.

(especially at a popular, rather than an academic level), one is likely to bring to it a number of preconceived ideas that are current today: that at least on a symbolic level the Moon is associated with menstruation, and so with 'Women's Mysteries'; that, again, the Moon being the ultimate symbol of femininity, its phases can be correlated with virginity, reproduction and motherhood; that in ancient times there was a matriarchal culture, and so on. Given this set of beliefs about the Moon, one would naturally be predisposed to seek evidence for these interpretations.

However, once again, this is a modern *construction*. It has long been realised that there is no evidence for a universal, 'pre-patriarchal' matriarchal culture. This notion originated with J.J. Bachofen in the 19th century[10] who mistook indisputable evidence of *matrilineal descent* for evidence of *matriarchal rule*; thereafter it was taken over by Friedrich Engels and became an article of Marxist dogma, before making its way via the likes of the erratic Robert Graves into modern Feminism. Again, the Moon can hardly be seen as *universally* symbolising menstruation or women's interests when, as shown by the cases of the Sumerian Sin, the Egyptian Khonsu and the Indian Chandra, we frequently find that the lunar deity is masculine. Perhaps most crucially for this discussion, when we turn to the mythology of Selene collected in Chapter 1 (and, it should perhaps be remembered that we are dealing *only* with the mythology of *Selene* here, not 'Moon-Goddesses' in general), these aspects are, quite simply, absent. If we are going to argue a case from what the surviving evidence alone tells us (rather than what we believe the evidence *should* be telling us), then it becomes immediately apparent that such an interpretation does not fit the facts.

Of course, when we turn to religious worship and cult practices, there were Goddesses concerned with 'women's interests': Eileithyia with childbirth, Artemis with virginity and female initiation, Hera

---

10 Bachofen 1967: *passim*.

with marriage, and so forth. Although some of these Goddesses, particularly Artemis, have later, syncretic associations with the Moon, Selene herself is completely absent from this list. Similarly, we know a considerable amount about various religious festivals specifically celebrated by women, such as the Thesmophoria; once again, Selene is not present among the deities involved.

Indeed, when we look for archaeological and historical evidence for religious and cultic practices related to Selene, we find there is extraordinarily little material, particularly in the period when her mythology was being formed; and that which there is may prove to be of a somewhat different character to one's expectations. There is a small amount of, mainly magical, material from the late syncretistic period when Selene *was* equated with other 'Moon-Goddesses'; but again, this has little or nothing to do with her mythology. It would, of course, be possible to conjecture that since there's evidence of cult rites connected with the *other* Goddesses with whom Selene was identified, such as Artemis, similar rites were dedicated to Selene also. But these Goddesses are not Selene herself, and no matter how much we might like to believe that similar female-oriented practices 'must have' been carried out with regard to Selene, this is in no way a legitimate approach, and simply can't be justified by the evidence.

Of course, this is not to deny the *possibility* that there may have been particular feminine cult practices or interpretations of Selenic myth, or that the Moon, seen as the Goddess Selene, might have had a particular meaning for women. But the evidence for this is lacking, and so any speculation on the subject would, at best, be pointless or, at worst, pure fantasy.

The absence of any confirmation of such 'feminist' expectations is perhaps more comprehensible if we look not only at what the source material *says*, but also at *who wrote it*, and under what circumstances. Greek society was, to use the 20th century label, 'patriarchal'. Education for women was uncommon and, although there are a very few exceptions, such as the poetess Sappho, the material we have to work with (be it poetry, mythography, history or religious works) was almost entirely created and written down by men. The surviving written evidence, then, whether we would wish it or not, primarily reflects male attitudes, interests and concerns, and male interpretations, not female ones. This means, plainly, that we have to abandon the idea of looking at the mythology of Selene as if she was a preconceived 'woman's Goddess'. Naturally, this doesn't mean that we have to conceive her instead as a 'man's Goddess', but rather to leave *all* our preconceptions behind and simply follow where the evidence leads us.

Of course, this doesn't mean that we should, on principle, abandon all the approaches to myth that have been proposed in recent decades; there may be times when Structuralism, or semiotics, or whatever, prove themselves to be useful tools in understanding certain aspects of a particular myth. But they must be used with caution. As Charles Penglase remarks of his own approach to mythology (and in this his attitude is remarkably similar to my own): 'the purpose is to let the myths speak for themselves, as far as this is possible: to reveal the structures which reflect the abstract, or belief, system of the people concerned, rather than to impose one upon them from outside ... When a philosophical approach of this age is applied to the ancient material, the inherent belief system of a different people and a different age is automatically superimposed on the source. The effect is to rewrite the past and present it in terms which satisfy dogmas of the present day.'[11]

Lastly, there is the matter of asking the right questions. Asking 'how can this myth be interpreted?' implies that we are bringing to the problem a method of interpretation (such as Structuralism, psychology, etc.), and effectively means 'how are *we* (of the present day) to interpret this myth?' rather than 'what did it mean to those who told or heard the stories for the first time?' Even if we were to

---

11 Penglase 1994: p.10.

phrase the question in this way, it would still be pointless, given the evidence that we have. Without full and first-hand experience of the society, cosmology, belief-systems, etc., of those telling and hearing the stories, we cannot possibly know what *meaning* the stories had for them, and it is quite obvious that the authors of our various sources had varying purposes and engagements with the material they recorded. Even less can we ask the question that has become so popular in our rationalising times (especially in the lucrative 'ancient mysteries' genre): 'what is the historical truth behind this myth?', as if 'historical truth' was a concept any less nebulous than 'myth'.

If we are debarred from such questions, what can we look for? Instead of 'meaning', which is far too specific and materialistic an idea to apply to something as lovely, and fluid, and imagery-oriented as myth, we can try to discover to what a myth may *refer*, to place it in its *context*, to see how it *relates* to other stories, or to religious practices, or iconography, and so forth. The answers we receive will be nothing more than suggestions and hints which, we should realise, are all we *ever* get from the universe; but we shall try to avoid the mistake of building upon them such fallacious notions as 'truth' or 'meaning'. Our purpose, then, is not the linear penetration of a 'search for meaning' but rather a lateral view, in which we attempt to see the myth placed in, and part of, a much wider web of resonances and references. We cannot hope for explanation; instead our 'suggestive inquiry' will look for material that, appropriately enough, may provide some *illumination* of our subject matter, and so help us to see it in a new light. And when we apply such an approach to Selene and, particularly, to the myth of her love for the mortal Endymion, a rather unexpected picture emerges, as the following pages will show.

Chapter One

# A Selene Compendium: Myths, Stories And Sources

## 1.1 Introduction

This chapter collects, in fairly full summary form, and with references, the surviving myths of Selene. This is the core material we have to work with, and which we will refer to and attempt to illuminate in the following chapters. Only the myths that refer directly to Selene are given here, while myths of other Goddesses who were identified with her at a later stage are excluded. The compendium does not attempt to be exhaustive. Some of the surviving references to Selene, or to Selene and Endymion, are merely passing mentions, too fleeting to be useful; others are simply duplications of material given more fully elsewhere. Such minor references are omitted here.

There is little in the way of carefully-composed narrative here: no great symbolic story-cycles like that of the Rape of Persephone or the Labours of Heracles. Instead we have, on the one hand, a patchwork of brief fragments and incomplete tales, with gaps that we would dearly like to be able to fill; on the other hand we occasionally have multiple variants of the same story, which simply cannot be made to fit together. Unfortunately, Greek mythology is not a set of neat and discrete stories. We are dealing with survivals that have come down to us, mostly by pure chance, from more than two millennia ago. It should also be emphasised that myths are, primarily, *stories*; they are not records of actual events and, of course, stories are told in different ways at different times and places. It's in the duplications and mismatched variants, however, that we often find clues to what the myths' original narrators meant to imply, especially when we can identify the variants' places of origin.

Here the stories are simply presented as they survive; these fragments will be discussed in succeeding chapters.

## 1.2 Selene's Descent And Family

Right at the beginning, we run into the sort of problems discussed in the introduction to this chapter, for there is no agreement in our source material regarding Selene's lineage, and for further discussion see section 3.2. What is often regarded as the 'standard' version of the story first appears in Hesiod's long, systematising poem on the descent of the Gods, the *Theogony*, written in the 8th century BCE. This version also appears in the other major compendium of ancient Greek myth, the *Library* of Apollodorus, and runs as follows:

1.2.1 Selene's parents were Titans, the offspring of the primeval deities Ouranos (Sky) and Ge or Gaia (Earth); the Titans in turn being overthrown by Zeus and the Olympian Gods. Selene's parents were Hyperion ('The One Above') and his sister Theia ('The Goddess'), who together had three children: Helios (the Sun), Selene (the Moon) and Eos (the Dawn).[1]

There are, however, a number of variants to this story:

1.2.2 In the preface to his *Fabulae*, the Roman author Hyginus gives Hyperion's wife as Aethra (if this is not an error for Theia, either by Hyginus himself or by the copyist of the manuscript; Aethra is most commonly known as the human mother of

---

1 Hesiod, *Theogony*, ll.371-374 (1914: p.107). Apollodorus: *The Library*, 1.2.2 (1921: Vol. 1, p.13).

Theseus): 'From Hyperion and Aethra (were born): Sol (Helios), Luna (Selene), Aurora (Eos)'.[2]

1.2.3 *The Homeric Hymn to Helios* lists the same three offspring, Helios, Selene and Eos, but makes their parents Hyperion and his sister Euryphaëssa ('far-shining').[3]

1.2.4 Again, in *The Homeric Hymn to Hermes* we have another variant. Here there is no mention of Helios or Eos, nor of Selene's mother; however, she is said to be the 'daughter of the lord Pallas, Megamedes' son'. There are a number of mythological characters called Pallas, one of whom is of Titan descent, but Megamedes ('the very wise') is otherwise completely unknown.[4]

1.2.5 A further variant, appearing as early as the playwright Euripides, in the 5$^{th}$ century BCE, makes Selene the daughter of Helios, rather than his sister. Her mother is not mentioned here.[5] Nonnos, right at the end of the pagan period (5$^{th}$ century CE), repeats the story on more than one occasion, and once pointedly refers to the 'motherless Moon' as daughter of Helios, but the context here suggests that Nonnos is thinking astronomically rather than mythologically, as he refers to the Moon receiving its light from the Sun in the same sentence.[6]

1.2.6 Writing in the 1$^{st}$ century BCE, the historian Diodorus Siculus provides us with perhaps the most curious tale of Selene's origin. While collecting the myths of various countries of the ancient world, Diodorus turns his attention to 'the Atlantians'. Precisely where this story originated is far from clear, although as one of the characters, Basileia ('The Queen'), is partially-identified with the Asiatic Great Mother, Cybele, the story may have arisen in Asia Minor rather than 'Atlantis'. The story is euhemeristic, in

---

2 Hyginus, *Fabulae*, Preface (1960: p.25).

3 *Homeric Hymn XXI – To Helios*, ll.1-6 (in *Hesiod* 1914: p.459).

4 *Homeric Hymn IV – To Hermes*, ll.99-100 (in *Hesiod* 1914: p.371).

5 Euripides, *The Phoenician Maidens*, l.177-178 (*Euripides* 1912: Vol. 3, p.359).

6 Nonnos, *Dionysiaca*, 40.375-378, 44.191 (1940: Vol. 3, pp.181, 311).

## Selene

that it portrays its main characters as originally humans who were later deified, and runs like this:

The first king of Atlantis was Ouranos, who had 45 sons by a number of wives. Of these sons, 18 were by Titaea, and were called Titans after their mother. After their deaths, Ouranos and Titaea were deified, and Titaea's name was changed to Gaia. Ouranos also had daughters, the eldest of whom was Basileia ('Queen'), who was called the 'Great Mother' because she raised her brothers. After her parents' death, Basileia became queen and married her brother Hyperion, by whom she had two children, Helios and Selene, admired for their beauty and chastity. However, Basileia's brothers, fearful that Hyperion would take the throne himself, conspired and put Hyperion to the sword, while Helios was drowned in the River Eridanus (the Po, in Italy). Selene, who loved her brother very dearly, threw herself down from the roof, and died. Basileia, searching for her son's body, received a vision in which Helios told her that he and Selene would become immortal and that the Sun, which had been called the 'holy fire', would afterwards be called Helios; and the Moon, previously called Mene, would then be called Selene. Basileia thereafter became obsessed with those of her daughter's playthings that could make a noise, wandering the hills and imitating kettledrums and cymbals (symbols of Cybele), until she finally disappeared in a storm of thunder and lightning, and was afterwards considered a Goddess.[7]

1.2.7 Writing in late antiquity, the Latin poet Claudian (c.370-404 CE), while adding nothing to the genealogy of Selene, tells us that she was fostered by the sea-Goddess Tethys, the wife of Ocean. The passage is not well-known, so is given here in full. It describes the embroidered dress worn by Proserpine (Persephone) on the day of her abduction by Pluto/Hades. 'In it she had worked the birth of the sun [Sol] from the seed of Hyperion, the birth, too, of the moon [Luna], though diverse was her shape – of sun

---

7 Diodorus Siculus, *Library of History*, 3. 56-58 (1935: Vol. 2, pp.263-269).

and moon that bring the dawning and the night. Tethys affords them a cradle and soothes in her bosom their infant sobs; the rosy light of her foster-children irradiates her dark blue plains. On her right shoulder she carried the infant Titan, too young as yet to vex with his light, and his encircling beams not yet grown; he is pictured as more gentle in those tender years, and from his mouth issues a soft flame that accompanies his infant cries. The moon, his sister, carried on Tethys' left shoulder, sucks the milk of that bright breast, her forehead marked with a little horn.'[8]

## 1.3 The Offspring Of Selene

As pointed out in the introduction, Selene is far from virginal, although she does remain unmarried. Apart from the birth-stories, virtually all her myths retell her various amours, many of which resulted in offspring. These stories will be analysed in section 3.3.

1.3.1 Pandia. *The Homeric Hymn to Selene*, after describing Selene's nightly practice of bathing in the waters of the world-surrounding Ocean, dressing in shining clothing and driving her horse-drawn chariot across the night sky, goes on to briefly mention what sounds like a single encounter with Zeus, as a result of which she bore a beautiful daughter, Pandia ('All-bright').[9]

1.3.2 Ersa. A fragmentary quotation of one and a half lines from a poem by Alcman (7th century BCE) refers to Ersa ('Dew') as the 'Daughter of Zeus and Selene', but we have no further information than this.[10]

1.3.3 The Seasons (Horae). The poet Quintus Smyrnaeus, writing in the 5th century CE, mentions the four Seasons sitting by the throne of Hera in Olympus, and describes them as the

---

[8] Claudian, *De Raptu Proserpinae* 2.44-54 (1922: Vol. 2, pp.321-323).

[9] *Homeric Hymn XXII – To Selene*, ll.14-16 (in *Hesiod* 1914: p.461).

[10] Alcman fr.57P, quoted in Plutarch, *Quaestiones Conviviales*, 3.10.3 (in Boedeker 1984: p.50).

daughters of Selene and Helios. This is a variant on the more usual genealogy, which makes them daughters of Zeus and Themis.[11]

1.3.4 Narcissus. In a variant to the usual genealogy, which makes Narcissus the son of the river-God Cephissus and the Nymph Liriope, Nonnos (5th century CE) suggests in two passages that Selene is his mother. However, the passages are confusing and possibly contradictory. In the first, Nonnos is poetically describing the beauty of a young boy called Ampelos by comparing him with Narcissus: 'I recognise your blood even if you wish to hide it; Selene slept with Helios and brought you to birth wholly like the gracious Narcissus; for you have a like heavenly beauty, the image of horned Selene.' The second refers to the flower, the 'blooms which have the name of Narcissus the fair youth, whom horned Selene's bridegroom Endymion begat on leafy Latmos' (for Endymion, see below at 1.5). In both cases it appears that Selene is the mother; the first implies Helios is the father, the second Endymion. Why these variants should appear in the same work of a single poet is far from clear.[12]

1.3.5 Naxos. Stephanus of Byzantium, in his *Ethnics*, explains the name of the Cycladean island of Naxos as being 'called after Naxos, leader of the Carians. Others say it is called after Naxos the son of Endymion.' One suspects that the Carian Naxos and the son of Endymion are probably identical. No mother is mentioned, but the Carian Endymion is not recorded as having any other romantic engagements apart from the one with Selene, so we may conjecture that Naxos was thought to be the son of Endymion and Selene.[13]

1.3.6 Nemea and the Nemean Lion. According to a commentator on Pindar's *Nemean Odes*, the nymph Nemea was the daughter of Selene and Zeus;[14] however, Selene's offspring in

---

11 Quintus Smyrnaeus, *The Fall of Troy*, 10.334-344 (1913: p.443).
12 Nonnos, *Dionysiaca*, 10.214-216; 48.581-583 (1940: Vol. 1, p.343; Vol. 3, p.467).
13 Stephanus of Byzantium, *Ethnics*, s.v. 'Naxos' (1849: p.468).
14 Scholiast on Pindar, *Nemean Odes*, p.425 Boeckh. (quoted in Cook 1914:

this case is usually said to be the Nemean Lion, rather than the Nymph. A fragment of a poem by Epimenides (see below, 1.3.7) preserved by Aelian, says: 'For I am sprung from [*i.e.*, born of] the fair-tressed Moon, who in a fearful shudder shook off the savage lion in Nemea, and brought him forth at the bidding of Queen Hera.'[15] Another variant comes from Demodocus' *History of Heracles,* Book I, quoted in a work called *On Rivers* and attributed (almost certainly wrongly) to Plutarch. Referring to the mountain Apesantus, Demodocus says (rather confusingly): 'Apesantus was first called Selenaeus. For Hera, resolving to be revenged upon Heracles, called Selene to her assistance, who by the help of her magical charms filled a large chest full of foam and froth, out of which sprang an immense lion; which Iris binding with her own girdle carried to the mountain Opheltium, where the lion killed and tore in pieces Apesantus, one of the shepherds belonging to that place. And from that accident, by the will of the Gods, the hill was called Apesantus.'[16]

1.3.7 Musaeus and Epimenides. We have brief references to both these two noted legendary mystical poets as the offspring of Selene; although it may well be that their naming as 'sons of Selene' refers more to the source of their inspiration than their actual genealogy. The passage from Epimenides, preserved in Aelian, is given at 1.3.6 above; we shall have much more to say of him, and his prolonged sleep in a cave, in Chapter 7.

Although Musaeus is well known from other sources as the son of Orpheus, a variant tradition preserved by the 3rd century BCE historian Philochorus states that he was the son of Selene and Eumolpus, the founding figure of the Eleusinian Mysteries.[17] Again, the poet Hermesianax of Colophon, quoted by Athenaeus,

---

Vol. 1, p.456).

15 Aelian, *De Natura Animalium*, 12.7 (1958-1959: Vol. 2, p.19-23).

16 (Pseudo-)Plutarch, *De Fluviis*, 18 (Quotation slightly modified from the translation of R. White 1870: Vol. 5, pp.499-500).

17 Philochorus 328, FGrHist F208, quoted in Lefkowitz, p.326.

## Selene

says 'Nor did the son of Mene (*i.e.*, Selene), Musaeus, master of the Graces, cause Antiope to go without her meed of honour.'[18] Musaeus is also said to be the 'child of the Moon' (Mene) in an Orphic verse quoted by Clement of Alexandria.[19] For more on both Epimenides and Musaeus as offspring of Selene, see 13.3.3 and 13.3.4.

### 1.4 Selene And Pan

According to Macrobius, the primary source for this story of Selene's seduction by Pan appears to be the Greek author Nicander of Colophon (in Ionia, now western Turkey), who lived in the 2nd century BCE;[20] however the work concerned is lost, and we only know the story through Latin quotations and references from Virgil and his commentators, some of which are quite late. The 'Moon' referred to in the following passages is Luna, the direct Latin cognate of Selene. However, as our Latin authors obviously regard the story as scandalous, they are presumably confusing Luna with the virginal Diana in her lunar aspect. As usual, there are variants to this story, and there will be further discussion in Chapter 12.

1.4.1 The earliest reference we have to this story is in a poem by Virgil, written in the 1st century BCE. He says: "'Twas with gift of such snowy wool, if we may trust the tale, that Pan, Arcadia's God, charmed and beguiled thee, O Moon, calling thee to the depths of the woods; nor didst thou scorn his call.'[21]

The commentators to these lines, who are generally agreed that the story is 'impious' and a 'profanation of Luna', expand the story somewhat. Servius (4th century CE) tells us that the story of

---

18 Athenaeus, *Deipnosophistae*, 13.597 [13.71] (1937: Vol. 6, p.219).

19 Orphic fragment 5 (Abel), in Clement of Alexandria, *The Exhortation to the Greeks* 7.63p (1919: p.167).

20 Macrobius, *Saturnalia*, 5.22.9-10 (1969: pp.383-384).

21 Virgil, *Georgics*, 3.391-3 (1978: Vol. 1, p.183).

Endymion's love for the Moon has been changed to refer to Pan: 'as a despicable, trembling white sheep he seduced her to his embrace. The mystics find a secret meaning in this story.'[22] Phylargyrius expands the story: 'Pan burned with love for Luna, so in order to appear beautiful to her he surrounded himself with a snowy fleece, and in this way seduced her to the act of love. The originator of this story is Nicander. Only a Greek would think of such a thing.'[23] Lastly, regarding this version of the story, the anonymous scholiast of the *Interpretes Virgilii* presents a fragmentary comment: '... the gift of a beautiful ram from Pan to Luna to delude her ... seek for a fleece. Summon impudent Pan and the little Pans.'[24]

1.4.2 A rather different version of the story is given in the commentary attributed (perhaps falsely) to Valerius Probus of the 1st century CE. This says: 'Pan, son of Mercury, desired Luna and had the best flock of sheep. When she asked for them, he offered to divide his flock with her if she would lie with him. He divided the flock into two parts, where one of the two was whiter but the wool more coarse. Luna, deceived by the whiteness, took the worse flock.'[25]

## 1.5 Selene And Endymion

The romance of Selene and Endymion is undoubtedly the best-known of Selenic myths. However, we lack a major retelling of the story in the classical sources, presumably because the story was so well-known it could be referred to in passing without anyone thinking to preserve the full details. And so, as usual, we have gaps in the story and multiple variants. In some stories Endymion sleeps throughout the romance, though the reasons for this are

---

22 Servius, commentary to *Georgics*, 3.391 (1826: Vol. 2, p.281).
23 Phylargyrius, commentary to *Georgics*, 3.392 (1826: Vol. 2, pp.338-339).
24 *Interpretes Virgilii*, commentary to *Georgics*, 3.391 (1826: Vol. 2, p.309).
25 Probus, commentary to *Georgics*, 3.391 (1826: Vol. 2. p.369-369).

various; in others he is Selene's conscious lover. The variants will be discussed and interpreted below in Chapter 5 and throughout the book thereafter. Of these variants, the two main differences are to be found in the figure of Endymion: in one version he is a prince of Elis, in western Greece; in the other he is a shepherd of Mount Latmos in Caria (now south-western Turkey).

1.5.1 The Elean Endymion. The main sources for this version are Apollodorus and Pausanias, both of whom mention the story as part of longer discussions of the genealogies of various heroes and early rulers of Greece. Endymion was ruler of Elis and legendary founder of the foot-race at the Olympic games.

Apollodorus says: 'Calyce and Aethlius had a son Endymion who led Aeolians from Thessaly and founded Elis. But some say that he was a son of Zeus. As he was of surpassing beauty, the Moon fell in love with him, and Zeus allowed him to choose what he would, and he chose to sleep forever, remaining deathless and ageless. Endymion had by a Naiad nymph or, as some say, by Iphianassa, a son Aetolus ...'[26]

Pausanias' version of the story is as follows: 'The first to rule in this land, they say, was Aethlius, who was the son of Zeus and of Protogeneia, the daughter of Deucalion, and the father of Endymion. The Moon, they say, fell in love with this Endymion and bore him fifty daughters. Others with greater probability say that Endymion took a wife Asterodia – others say she was Chromia, the daughter of Itonus, the son of Amphictyon; others again, Hyperippe, the daughter of Arcas – but all agree that Endymion begat Paeon, Epeius, Aetolus, and also a daughter Eurycyda. Endymion set his sons to run a race at Olympia for the throne; Epeius won, and obtained the kingdom ... As to the death of Endymion, the people of Heracleia near Miletus do not agree with the Eleans; for while the Eleans show a tomb of Endymion,[27]

---

26 Apollodorus, *The Library*, 1.7.5-6 (1921: Vol. 1, p.61).
27 In Olympia, at the end of the stadium near the starting place for Olympic

the folk of Heracleia say that he retired to Mount Latmus and give him honour, there being a shrine of Endymion on Latmus.'[28]

1.5.2 The Carian Endymion. The version of the story set on Carian Mount Latmos was by far the best-known but, as mentioned above, was obviously such a mythological and literary commonplace that no major retelling of the story survives. Instead, we have to reconstruct the tale from its fragments, many of which are contradictory. Essentially, the most usual form of the story is that Endymion (for a variety of reasons) is cast into an eternal sleep; Selene, falling in love with him, descends each night to make love to him in the cave where he sleeps.

That Endymion's sleep was thought to be eternal was proverbial, and is referred to, in passing, by such comparatively early writers as Plato and Aristotle, in the course of broader philosophical arguments.[29] However, the myth itself is not explored further.

Probably the major collection of the fragmentary sources on which the story is built is to be found in the commentaries ('scholia') to a passage in the *Argonautica* of Apollonius of Rhodes (3rd century BCE), which is where we shall begin. These scholia possibly derive from the commentaries of Theon of Alexandria, of the 1st century BCE.

According to Apollonius, the sorceress Medea (amongst whose powers is that of 'drawing down the Moon') has fallen in love with Jason. Apollonius then has Selene appear and pass comment: 'And the Titanian Goddess, the moon (*Mene*), rising from a far land, beheld her as she fled distraught, and thus spake to her own heart: "Not I alone stray to the Latmian cave, nor do I alone burn with love for fair Endymion; oft times with thoughts of love have I been driven away by thy crafty spells, in order that in the darkness of night thou mightest work thy sorcery at ease, even the deeds dear

---

runners, according to Pausanias, 6.20.9 (1933: Vol. 3, p.123).

28 Pausanias, 5.1.3-5 (1926: Vol. 2, pp.381-383).

29 Plato, *Phaedo*, 45 (1848: Vol. 1, p.72). Aristotle, *Nicomachean Ethics*, 10.8.7 (1926: p.623).

to thee. And now thou thyself too hast part in a like mad passion; and some god of affliction has given thee Jason to be thy grievous woe. Well, go on, and steel thy heart, wise though thou be, to take up thy burden of pain, fraught with many sighs".'[30]

The commentator on this passage gathers up a number of quotations from various authors, many of whose works are otherwise lost, in a fairly random order. Several of these quotations attempt to rationalise the myths, although in doing so they provide us with valuable clues as to what the original myths actually were. As a direct translation of the original is hardly readable, I'll summarise, quoting as much of the text as possible. The passage begins by discussing Endymion alone, in a way that appears to be an attempt to integrate the Elean and Carian traditions. We're told that Latmos is a mountain in Caria, where there is a cave in which Endymion lived, and that the city of Heraclea is nearby. We then have a fragmentary quotation from Hesiod: 'Endymion was the son of Aethlius the son of Zeus and Calyce, and received the gift from Zeus: to be the keeper of death for his own self when he was ready to die.'

A second quotation from Hesiod tells us that: 'Endymion was transported by Zeus into heaven, but when he fell in love with Hera, was befooled with a shape of cloud, and was cast out and went down into Hades.' This sounds suspiciously like an error for the story of Ixion who, taken to heaven by Zeus, attempted to seduce Hera, but was fooled into making love to a likeness of Hera made of cloud, called Nephele. However, Epimenides is then quoted along similar lines: 'that spending time among the Gods Endymion fell in love with Hera; when Zeus was angry, he begged to sleep through all time.' For more on this, see section 5.5. We are also told that because of Endymion's great justice he was deified; then, having committed some offence he begged Zeus to let him sleep forever. His eternal sleep is rationalised in another

---

30 Apollonius Rhodius, *Argonautica*, 4.54-65 (1912: p.299).

source, where he is simply said to be a lover of sleep; the 'sleep of Endymion' being proverbial for those who sleep a great deal, or who are careless. And we are told that 'some say he was from Sparta, others from Elis.'

The compiler of this commentary has relatively little to say directly about Selene's involvement with Endymion; merely that Sappho and Nicander tell us 'that Selene went down to Endymion as he slept on Mount Latmos'. However, he then provides us with two further rationalisations. Both do away with Endymion's eternal sleep and the first tells us that, being fond of hunting, he hunted through the night by the light of the Moon, because that was the time when the wild animals were feeding; during the day he rested in a cave, and so seemed to be always sleeping. The other says that he was the first to undertake the study of the heavenly bodies, and the first to understand the phases and movements of the Moon; so devoting himself to these studies by night, he slept during the day. These, of course, are *explanations* of the myth, rather than mythical materials themselves.[31]

Another work, *On the Incredible*, almost certainly falsely attributed to the philosopher Heraclitus, gives a slightly more explicit version of the story, along with yet another different explanation. 'Regarding Endymion and Selene: it is said that while he was sleeping, Selene fell in love with him and coming down, slept with him. Endymion would have been a shepherd without experience of women; a woman, holding fast to him in her desire, when asked who she was replied "Selene".'[32]

The sexuality of the encounter between Selene and Endymion is confirmed by a slightly risqué satirical dialogue of Lucian's, written in the 2nd century CE, in which Selene and Aphrodite discuss the affair. Selene is said to stop her chariot every time she

---

31 *Scholia in Apollonii Argonautica*, 4.54-61 (1813: Vol. 2, pp.272-275, pp.576-577).
32 Heraclitus, *De Incredibilibus (Peri Apiston)*, 38 (1843: pp.319-320).

passes over Caria to gaze at Endymion, 'sleeping out of doors in hunter's fashion', lying on his cloak with his 'javelin' just slipping out of his left hand, and sometimes leaving her course to go down to him. Selene tells Aphrodite that she tip toes to him so as not to waken him, before continuing, 'but you can guess; there's no need to tell you what happens next. You must remember I'm dying of love.'[33] Like other relatively late writers, Lucian is prepared to ignore or alter various parts of the 'original' myth, such as the eternal sleep.

For the late poet Nonnos (5th century CE), Selene and Endymion are very much conscious lovers on Latmos, with Endymion frequently referred to as Selene's 'bedfellow' or 'bridegroom', and they are said to be 'inseparable'. Indeed, at one point Nonnos refers to Selene bathing, 'on her way to Endymion's bed on Latmos, the bed of a sleepless shepherd'. In a further variant, Endymion is said to be a 'neversleeping herdsman', the 'bridegroom of love-smitten Selene'. We have also seen (above at 1.3.4) that Narcissus was said to be the offspring of their union.[34]

Nonnos also hints at a curious variation, which would suggest that in one version of the story Selene and Endymion were regarded as sister and brother, and their love incestuous. Nonnos is mainly referring to another story, that of Caunos and his sister Byblis. Caunos and Byblis are normally taken to be the children of Miletos, the eponymous founder of the Carian city of Miletos that stands near Mount Latmos. There are various versions of their story: in some, Caunos conceives an incestuous passion for his sister, in others she for him; sometimes the affair is consummated, sometimes not. Nonnos makes Caunos a brother of Miletos, and the instigator of the affair. We are told that he was still young and: 'Not yet had he conceived a passion for his innocent sister, and

---

33 Lucian, *Dialogues of the Gods*, 19 (11) (1961: pp.329-331).

34 Nonnos, *Dionysiaca*, 2.325, 5.516-517, 7.237-240, 13.554-556, 47.283-284, 48.581-583 (1940: Vol. 1, p.69, p.205, p.263, p.471, Vol. 3, p.393, p.467) and *passim*.

composed that tricking love song; not yet had he sung of Hera herself joined with her brother Zeus in a harmonious bed of love like his own, the song about the Latmian cowshed of the neversleeping herdsman, while he praised Endymion, the bridegroom of love-smitten Selene, as happy in love's care on a neighbouring rock.'[35] What this song might have been, we have no idea; although obviously familiar to Nonnos, it is not preserved. That Zeus and Hera were incestuous was commonplace knowledge, though hardly given enormous emphasis. It has to be assumed, given that the story of Selene and Endymion was placed in the same sentence with this story, that it was somehow being used as a paradigmatic example to legitimise an act of sibling incest; from which it's tempting to infer a Carian tale placing Selene and Endymion in the same relationship. Unfortunately, as we have nothing more than this single reference from Nonnos, such an inference has to be seen as speculative. For more on this story, see the Appendix, Chapter 16.

Roman authors, however, confused Selene/Luna with the virginal Artemis/Diana and, as we've seen above (1.4) thought tales of Selene indulging in sexual intercourse scandalous. Cicero mentions Endymion's eternal sleep on Latmos while discussing the lack of sensation felt by those asleep or dead, and so he has no thought of the Moon 'by whom it is thought he was lulled to sleep, that she might kiss him in his slumber.'[36] Here we see another variant in that it is Selene herself who is responsible for Endymion's sleep. Cicero, however, is alone among the ancient sources in implying that Selene does no more than chastely kiss Endymion; and yet we should note that this version is the one that has become standard in the later western poetic and romantic tradition. That it is not the original tale should be obvious by now.

---

35 Nonnos, *Dionysiaca*, 13.545-556 (1940: Vol. 1, pp.468-471).
36 Cicero, *Tusculan Disputations*, 1.38.92 (1927: Vol. 18, p.111).

Even so, while still confusing Selene with Artemis/Diana ('Phoebus' sister'), Roman poets such as Propertius (1st century BCE) could still emphasise the sexuality of the encounter. Attempting to persuade his lover to have sex with him naked, he says: 'And it was naked that Endymion enraptured Phoebus' sister and naked, they say, lay with the Goddess.'[37]

### 1.5.3 Endymion of Arcadia (and elsewhere).

Elis and Caria are not the only locations given for the birth of Endymion, nor for his encounter with Selene. As we've seen above, in the commentary to Apollonius of Rhodes quoted in 1.5.2, Endymion is also said to come from Sparta. Elsewhere, the same commentator, after repeating the same story of Endymion's astronomical studies of the Moon, tells us that he came from Arcadia.[38]

Endymion's Arcadian origin is repeated in a passage from Plutarch's *Life of Numa*, of the 1st century CE, which, in what it denies, tells us much about the relationship between Endymion and Selene, as commonly thought of. The Goddess Egeria was said to have loved and married the almost legendary early Roman king Numa, with the result that he lived 'a life of blessedness and a wisdom more than human'. Plutarch says that the resemblance with other ancient tales, such as those of 'the Arcadians concerning Endymion, and other peoples concerning other mortals who were thought to have achieved a life of blessedness in the love of the Gods, is quite evident. And there is some reason in supposing that Deity, who is not a lover of horses or birds, but a lover of men, should be willing to consort with men of superlative goodness, and should not dislike or disdain the company of a wise and holy man. But that an immortal God should take carnal pleasure in a mortal body and its beauty, this, surely, is hard to believe.'[39]

---

37 Propertius, *Elegies*, 2.15.15-16 (1990: p.165).
38 *Scholia in Apollonii Argonautica*, 4.263-264 (1813: Vol. 2, pp.285-286, 586).
39 Plutarch, *Life of Numa*, 4.2-3 (1914: Vol. 1, pp.317-319).

## Steve Moore

Quintus Smyrnaeus (3rd century CE) preserves a story that sounds suspiciously like it was told to explain the reason for an actual mineral-spring, and transfers the tale to Phrygia (also in Asia Minor, but the province next to Caria – unless, indeed, Quintus is using 'Phrygia' poetically, to refer to Asia Minor generally). In telling of the end of the Trojan War, he mentions the death of Zechis: 'Who dwelt in Phrygia, land of myriad flocks, below that haunted cave of fair-haired Nymphs where, as Endymion slept beside his kine, divine Selene watched him from on high, and slid down from heaven to earth; for passionate love drew down the immortal stainless Queen of Night. And a memorial of her couch abides still 'neath the oaks; for mid the copses round was poured out milk of kine; and still do men marvelling behold its whiteness. Thou wouldst say far off that this was milk indeed, which is a well-spring of white water; if thou draw a little nigher, lo, the stream is fringed as though with ice, for white stone rims it round.'[40] It's notable here that Endymion sleeps in a cave of the Nymphs; this connection with caves and Nymphs will turn up repeatedly as we continue our investigation.

The location of the encounter between Selene and Endymion is moved again, in a commentary to Nicander's poem *Theriaca*. In lines 214-215, Nicander mentions a mountain called 'hoary Aselenus'. A scholiast places this in Locris, while the *Etymologicum Magnum*, a Byzantine lexicon, tells us that it was near Trachis. The latter source also says that Nicander 'asserted that the *Aselena ore* ('No-Moon mountains') were so called because when Selene slept there with Endymion the rest of the world went Moonless.'[41] For further discussion of this material, see 5.3.

A curious version of the Endymion story is given in the Greek *Alexander Romance*, falsely attributed to Alexander's companion Callisthenes, although our earliest version of the text dates from

---

40 Quintus Smyrnaeus, *The Fall of Troy*, 10.126-137 (1913: p.429).
41 Nicander 1953: pp.43, 174, 201.

the 3rd century CE. Here Selene is said to drive a chariot drawn by bulls (as in later astrological lore, the Moon being exalted in Taurus). Nectanebos, an Egyptian magician, is attending Alexander's mother Olympias at the time of his birth, and persuading her to hold back her labour until the astrologically correct hour. He tells her: 'Let the brief space of this hour pass. For the Moon, the horned, with the yoke of bulls left behind, was the last to descend to earth, and she embraced a fair lad, the cowherd Endymion. Because of the meeting, burned by fire, he perished. So he who is born under such conditions dies, smitten by fire.'[42]

Another curious variant of the Endymion story is preserved by Athenaeus: 'Licymnius of Chios, after explaining that Sleep (Hypnos) was in love with Endymion says that Sleep does not cover the eyes of Endymion when he slumbers, but lays his beloved to rest with eyelids wide opened, that he may enjoy the delight of gazing upon them continually. His words are: "Sleep, joying in the light of his eyes, was wont to lay the boy to rest with lids wide open".'[43]

## 1.6 Miscellanea

1.6.1 According to the Roman poet Statius (1st century CE), the personified Sleep (in Greek, Hypnos) is the charioteer of the Moon-Goddess.[44]

1.6.2 In the book *On Rivers*, attributed to Plutarch, we read a story unknown elsewhere, in a chapter on the river Indus: 'Near to this ... lies the mountain Lilaeus, so called from Lilaeus a shepherd; who, being very superstitious and a worshipper of the Moon alone, always performed her mysteries in the dead time of

---

42 Pseudo-Callisthenes, *The Life of Alexander of Macedon*, 1.12 (1955: p.19).
43 Athenaeus, *Deipnosophistae*, 13.564 [13.17] (1937: Vol. 6, p.49).
44 Statius, *Thebaid*, 12.307-308 (1928: Vol. 2, p.469).

the night. Which the rest of the Gods taking for a great dishonour, sent two monstrous lions that tore him in pieces. Upon which the Moon turned her adorer into a mountain of the same name.'[45]

1.6.3 There is another curious reference in Nonnos, to 'Dysis the nurse of Selene'.[46] Nonnos gives no story to explain who Dysis was or what actions she may have been involved in. Indeed, one rather doubts that Dysis actually has a mythological existence. Instead, she looks rather more like a personified 'poetic fancy'. *Dysis* is an ordinary word that can be translated as 'the sinking or setting of the sun'. With the onset of night, the Moon appears or, perhaps more specifically here, is 'born'. And so Dysis is an appropriate name for a 'nurse of Selene'.

Such are the stories that have been preserved, which, while varied, don't amount to a great deal. It's now time to start looking at the material in more detail.

---

45 (Pseudo-)Plutarch, *De Fluviis*, 25 (1870: Vol. 5, pp.509).
46 Nonnos, *Dionysiaca*, 41.284 (1940: Vol. 3, p.217).

Chapter Two

# Selene Herself

## 2.1 Introduction

Before moving on to examine the myths of Selene, it may be as well to take a closer look at the Goddess in isolation: her name, her appearance, and whatever small amount of religious worship it is possible to discover. This may give a better idea of the actual nature of the Goddess who appears in the myths, as well as giving a certain amount of context to the stories. Once again, we have to deal with evidence that is far from complete, often obscure, and filled with puzzling variants.

## 2.2 Selene And Mene – The Names Of The Goddess

As was mentioned in the introduction, the name *Selene* was applied to both the physical, astronomical body of the Moon, and to the Goddess of the Moon herself. To a certain extent, the two are indistinguishable: Selene was a 'visible Goddess', an aspect only really shared with her brother Helios, the Sun, and, to a lesser extent, with her sister Eos, the Dawn. As we'll see, this appears to have put Selene in a rather curious position with regard to the other Gods and to Greek mythology in general.

In talking of Selene, we also have to take account of the alternative name Mene, a name far less well-known in the modern era but used quite freely as a straightforward synonym by the Greeks. Again, *Mene* applies to both satellite and Goddess, in the same way that Selene does. The direct Latin cognate of Selene/ Mene is Luna, not Diana, who is associated with Artemis.

There is some confusion as to whether the name 'Selene' is actually a Greek or a pre-Greek word. It is possible to derive the first half of the word from the Greek word *selas*, 'light' or 'brightness'. The name would seem, from this, to be both Greek in origin and descriptive in nature: the name is drawn from the bright appearance of the Moon in the night sky. We might then perhaps render the meaning of Selene as 'the bright one', with a feminine ending.[1] This was how the origin of the name seems to have been understood by the Greeks themselves, and appears in a work *On Images* written by the Neoplatonist philosopher Porphyry in 3rd century CE.[2] Even so, Porphyry is not the most reliable of etymologists, and his *On Images* shows strong influences from Stoic philosophy; and like his Stoic sources and influences he proposes a large number of different meanings for the various names of the Gods, many of which are fanciful. By modern standards, Stoic etymologies tend toward the amateurish, being derived mainly from similar (and sometimes not too similar) forms of pronunciation.

However, there is also the possibility, as argued by Martin P. Nilsson, that the ending *ene* is pre-Greek. It appears in a number of place-names, such as Mitylene, which are generally regarded as being pre-Greek. It also appears, with the same accentuation, in the name of the Goddess Athene, who Nilsson also believes to be pre-Greek in origin.[3] The problem is, admittedly, compounded by the fact there is also an unarguably Greek word-ending *ene*; and also by the fact that Nilsson's proposal was made before the

---

1 Kerenyi 1951: pp.196-197.

2 Porphyry, *Peri Agalmaton (On Images)* 1903: p.123.

3 Nilsson 1950: p.489-490.

decipherment of the Linear-B writing used in early Greece and Crete, which turned out to be an extremely archaic form of Greek, rather than a pre-Greek language. The question as to whether 'Selene' is Greek or pre-Greek is, then, probably best left open (as is the possibility that if Selene *is* pre-Greek, of unknown meaning, then *selas*, 'brightness' may actually be a word derived from 'Moonlight'). Once again, we are very far from modern notions such as 'hard facts' or 'truth'; even discussions of something apparently so simple as the Goddess' name provide only glimpses of possibilities, as fleeting as Moonlight in the darkness of antiquity.

Be that as it may, it would seem possible to place Selene among a group of very early Goddess-names, including Athene and the barely-known Mykene, putative city-Goddess of Mycenae, which certainly go back to the Bronze Age Mycenaean period in the 2nd millennium BCE, if not to an even earlier pre-Greek period. As we progress with this investigation, such an early origin will assume greater importance, as well as finding confirmation in other related evidence.

The first of these confirmations comes when we turn to the word Mene, which is usually taken to be a feminised form of *men*, meaning 'moon' or 'month'. It appears on a clay-tablet excavated at Knossos, in Crete, and would seem to have been the name of the Moon-Goddess there, during the Greek-speaking Linear-B period.[4] In the syllabic Linear-B writing, the word appears as *Me-na*, and is identified in context by the translators as the name of the Goddess; elsewhere, *me-no* and *me-na* are used for 'month', both at Knossos and at Pylos on the Greek mainland. Again, we have variant possibilities. The first is that Mene was a pre-Greek Cretan Goddess whose name survived, via a Mycenaean transcription, into the classical period. A second is that Mene is simply an archaic Greek word of great antiquity, and is only used on the surviving tablet in a purely Greek context. A third is that the Greek name

---

4 Ventris & Chadwick 1973: p.309 [Tablet Gg717].

Mene is being used to identify a pre-existing Cretan Goddess of a similarly lunar function whose name is now lost to us. As usual, at this remove in time and with such slender evidence, we simply cannot say.

In later Greek, the ending of *Mene* uses the same spelling and accentuation as the ending of *Selene*. This evidence doesn't provide any further clues as to whether the name 'Selene' is Greek or pre-Greek, of course. It does, though, suggest that the Moon-Goddess we are dealing with goes back to the beginning of the Greek world: to the Mycenaean period in the middle of the 2$^{nd}$ millennium BCE at least, if not to the pre-Greek Minoan civilisation of Crete.

Can we say anything further that's meaningful about the relationship between Selene and Mene? The short answer is 'no', but that hasn't stopped various authors, both ancient and modern, making the attempt. It might be thought that Mene was the 'original', perhaps Cretan, Goddess and that Selene was a later development; or that Mene was Cretan and Selene Greek. But having a single tablet from Knossos mentioning Mene is insufficient evidence with which to make an argument. As always 'absence of evidence is not evidence of absence', and the fact that the Moon-Goddess is called Mene on our one surviving inscription does not mean that she was not *also* known as Selene at the same time. There is then a gap of several hundred years in the written record, until the Classical period, at which point Selene and Mene *are* used synonymously. One suspects, given that so much of the surviving source material mentioning Selene and Mene is in verse, that the choice of one name or another depends largely on metrical considerations: in some cases the trisyllabic 'Selene' fits the metre better, in others the disyllabic 'Mene'.

Among the moderns, Carl Kerenyi has suggested that Mene is the name of the visible, physical Moon, while Selene is that of the Goddess;[5] but the way the words are used in the literature provides

---

5 Kerenyi 1951: p.197.

no evidence that the ancients made such a distinction. Both names are used equally for both satellite and Goddess. Similarly, Kerenyi's vague hint that Mene is to be taken as a feminised form of the Phrygian Moon-God Manes or Mannes (known to the Greek-speaking world as Men, *i.e.*, 'The Moon-God')[6] appears to be speculative and without evidential support, particularly so as the Knossian tablet mentioning Mene pre-dates any evidence we have of Manes by several centuries.

The ancients, too were intent on having their say on the subject. We have seen in Chapter 1 (1.2.6) that Diodorus Siculus, in his euhemerising tale of Selene's origin, argued that the Moon was originally called Mene, and was later called Selene after the suicidal daughter of Basileia. This might be taken as suggesting a priority for the name Mene, but again the evidence is too far removed from the mainstream of Greek mythology and too slight for certainty. And, besides, it's not the only viewpoint.

A fragment of a poem attributed to Orpheus, known as the *Rhapsodies*, refers to the physical Moon as follows:

> *'And he contrived another vast earth: Selene*
> *The immortals call it, but men on earth Mene.*
> *Many mountains it has, many cities, many halls.'*[7]

M.L. West, reproducing this fragment, dates it in the pre-Hellenistic period (*i.e.*, 4th century BCE or earlier), but adds a note: 'The distinction made between the gods' and men's names for the moon has no religious significance but is a poetic mannerism.'[8] Once again all seems to be Moonlight and shadows, with nothing definite to grasp at.

---

6 Kerenyi 1951: p.197.
7 Orphic Fragment 91 Kern, in West 1983: p.92.
8 Orphic Fragment 91 Kern, in West 1983: p.92.

In summary, then, we seem to have two names, Selene and Mene, which, to all intents and purposes, refer to a single Moon-Goddess and who, hereafter, may generally be referred to simply as 'Selene', unless direct quotation of a source requires us to do otherwise. And, unsurprisingly for so obviously visible a Goddess, she would seem to be present from the earliest stages of Greek civilisation, thought and myth.

## 2.3 A Selenite Iconography

The way that Selene was depicted varied over the centuries, although these variations generally had less to do with her mythology and more with changing fashions and associations. So, for example, the advent of astrological thinking changed her iconography, and likewise in the Roman period Selene took on the appearance of Diana. None of these transformations in appearance, however, actually changed the stories told about her.

This section will not attempt to provide an exhaustive catalogue of Selene's iconography, although I hope the main variants in her depictions will be covered.

2.3.1 Literary Iconography. Regardless of dress, attributes or means of conveyance, Selene is always portrayed as a beautiful young woman. Indeed, as will be apparent to anyone who has gazed at the full Moon on a clear night, her beauty is her most obvious quality. Ovid, writing around the beginning of the Common Era, places only Aphrodite (Venus) before her in this; speaking in the 'voice' of Leander and referring to the beauty of his beloved Hero, he prays to the Moon and reminds her of Endymion, then places Hero's beauty third in line: 'After the beautiful face of Venus, and thine own [Selene's], there is none before hers.'[9]

Perhaps the most complete iconographic description of Selene in a literary form is to be found in the rather lovely (if late) *Homeric*

---

9 Ovid, *Heroides*, 18.69 (1914, p.249).

## Steve Moore

*Hymn to Selene*. The prose translation of H.G. Evelyn-White is perhaps the most literal to hand, although one or two of the details need a little further discussion. The iconographic passages begin with the poet invoking the Muses to 'tell of the long-winged Moon. From her immortal head a radiance is shown from heaven and embraces earth; and great is the beauty that ariseth from her shining light. The air, unlit before, glows with the light of her golden crown, and her rays beam clear, whensoever bright Selene having bathed her lovely body in the waters of Ocean, and donned her far-gleaming raiment, and yoked her strong-necked, shining team, drives on her long-maned horses at full speed, at even-time in the mid-month: then her great orbit [*sic*] is full and then her beams shine brightest as she increases. So she is a sure token and a sign to mortal men.' [...] 'Hail, white-armed Goddess, Bright Selene, mild bright-tressed queen!'[10]

The first puzzling aspect is the reference to the 'long-winged Moon' (Mene), as the Moon-Goddess is not normally portrayed with wings. There is no other known example of the application of this epithet to Selene, and its use here is also thought to imply that the hymn is a late composition; besides,[11] a 'winged Moon-Goddess' does not appear in the visual iconography of vases, statues, etc. However, as we'll see below, her chariot horses are sometimes winged; and it is this that gives us our clue. Selene's chariot and pair do not, of course, travel the surface of the Earth: they traverse the empty air. Wings are thus an obvious adjunct for them. In the same way Selene, as the Moon itself, takes a bird-like passage through the upper sky. Similarly, Hesiod refers to swift hawks as 'long-winged' so, again, we may have overtones of the Moon's swift path across the heavens, also suggested by her fleet winged horses.[12] There is, of course, another possibility, given

---

10 *Homeric Hymn XXII – To Selene*, ll.14-16 (in *Hesiod* 1914: pp.459-461). The more recent translation by West 2003: pp.217-219, is not substantially different.

11 Allen & Sikes, *The Homeric Hymns* [via *Perseus Project* web-page].

12 West 1983: p.191. *Hesiod* 1914: pp.29 & 459.

that the poem is thought to be of Hellenistic date and possible Alexandrian origin, and that is of iconographic influence from the Egyptian Goddess Isis, who is often portrayed with long wings; however, as the epithet seems explicable in Greek terms, such a supposition can be regarded as possible, but unnecessary.

Selene's 'crown', mentioned here, is a *stephane*, a diadem worn at the hairline on the forehead, having the greatest depth at the centre and narrowing to the rear of the head. The coronet surmounted by a crescent only becomes a standard feature in the Roman period. 'Golden' was as common an epithet as 'silver' in classical allusions to the Moon.[13]

While it may seem at first sight that Selene's crown is thought to be the source of her light, the fact that she also wears 'far-gleaming raiment' and is 'white-armed' would suggest that her light was thought to shine from all parts of her body.

'Ocean' (*Okeanos*) is not to be taken in the modern sense of the word: rather it was thought to be a vast river surrounding the edges of the flat Earth. As Selene is seen by all the peoples of the world, it is logical for her to begin and end her journey, literally, at the ends of the Earth. There is more here, however. The Ocean stream was thought to have its sources in the far west; and the Moon first appears, at nightfall on the 3rd day of the lunar month, in the western sky. Thereafter it makes its dusk appearance progressively further east as the Moon waxes. Unlike her brother Helios, the Sun, who was always thought to drive his chariot from east to west, Selene's apparent progress is from west to east. Thus, it is quite logical for her to start her journey from the western Ocean. Interestingly, in the *Odyssey* (24.12) we learn that beyond the Ocean stream is where the dreams live.[14] This is not only a suitably nocturnal place for Selene to commence her journey; her connection with the dream-world is something

---

13 Allen & Sikes, *The Homeric Hymns* [via *Perseus Project* web-page].
14 West 1966: p.227.

that will become progressively more important as we continue our investigation.

This may not exhaust the meaning here either. At the beginning of Hesiod's *Theogony*, we learn that the Muses bathe and dress before beginning their dances and songs of praise to the Gods.[15] This is their normal function, but it is one of great importance and holiness. Selene's bathing is probably to be seen less as a matter of personal cleanliness than as an expression of the sanctity of her nightly journey: this is the sky-crossing of a Goddess, whose every appearance is holy in itself.

It may be possible to read yet more into this passage, by turning our attention to parallels from slightly further afield. Charles Penglase has drawn attention to a number of parallels from Mesopotamian mythology, and its influence on that of the Greeks. He points out that Goddesses such as Ishtar, in dressing, are actually 'putting on their powers'.[16] Selene, in putting on her 'shining raiment' is, effectively, dressing herself in Moonlight; if today we would perhaps not think of this as a 'power', it's quite certain that illumination is her main function as a visible Goddess. Again, light and shining clothes appear, both in tales of Ishtar and in the Greek tale of Pandora, as enhancing the beauty and sexual attractiveness of the wearer.[17] Lastly, Penglase points out that both in tales of Ishtar and in the *Homeric Hymn to Aphrodite*, the Goddesses bathe and dress before consummating a sacred marriage.[18] While it is true that the *Homeric Hymn to Selene* implies that Selene indulges in this bathing and dressing every night before beginning her journey across the sky, this iconographic passage immediately precedes that in which the Moon-Goddess makes love with Zeus, with Pandia as the resultant offspring (a passage to be discussed in more detail below at 3.3.1.).

---

15 Hesiod, *Theogony*, l.5ff. (1914: p.79).
16 Penglase 1994: pp.167, 212.
17 Penglase 1994: pp.166-167, 214.
18 Penglase 1994: pp.170-171.

## Selene

The correspondence here may be coincidental, but it seems worth noting anyway. Similarly, Nonnos describes Selene bathing in the sea on her way to the bed of Endymion.[19]

Selene is here driving a horse-drawn chariot that, in the classical period, was her most usual form of transport. Her chariot was drawn by two horses, as opposed to the four that drew that of her brother Helios. Servius (admittedly a late commentator) divides the month into two halves and explains the two horses as representing the waxing and waning aspects of the month.[20]

'Her great orbit is full' is an odd expression, and it's tempting to imagine a translation error for 'orb'; but the Greek distinctly reads 'orbit'. A speculative interpretation might be that, the Moon being full, she rises with the dusk and sets with the dawn. If we regard the Moon as only being 'properly' visible at night (and 'invisible' by day) the night of the full Moon is that when the greatest ('fullest') extent of her 'orbit' is visible ... she is then seen making a hemispherical arc from one horizon to another.

The Greek words translated here by 'sign' and 'token' are *tekmor*, 'a sign, token or pledge', and *sema*, which means, among other things, 'a sign from heaven, an omen, a portent'. The poet may have had a number of things in mind here: that the Moon is a reliable source of nocturnal light, a reliable calendrical indicator, and so on. Allen and Sikes refer this to the latter meaning: 'men compute periods of time by the full Moon'.[21] The possibility that the poet may have intended to portray Selene as a source of omens and portents is, however, worth bearing in mind; her connection with divination is a subject to which we shall return.

Selene's white arms (and thus, by implication, her entirely pale skin) are appropriate to a nocturnal Goddess; and the colour of

---

19 Nonnos, *Dionysiaca*, 7.237-240 (1940: Vol. 1, p.263).
20 Servius, commentary to Virgil's *Aeneid*, 5.721 (1826: Vol. 1, p.343).
21 Allen & Sikes, *The Homeric Hymns* [via *Perseus Project* web-page].

the zenith Moon is, after all, much closer to silver-white than the golden light that appears nearer the horizon.

Lastly, 'bright-tressed' here translates *euplokamos*, literally 'of goodly locks'. Selene is here being referred to as 'lovely-haired', rather than there being an indication of hair-colour.

If, in the classical period, Selene is associated with horses and horse-drawn chariots, by late antiquity her favoured animal had frequently turned to the bull. The cause at work here is basically non-mythological, and comes from the influence of astrology, imported from Babylon and developed into a Greek form in the Hellenistic period, after 300 BCE.[22] In astrological lore, we are told by Ptolemy, writing in the 2nd century CE, the Moon was said to be 'exalted in Taurus', the constellation of the Bull.[23] 'Exaltation' refers to a sign of the Zodiac in which the influence of a particular planet was especially enhanced and so, iconographically, it became natural to associate Selene with bulls. This iconography, in turn, fed back into later poetry.

So Nonnos, writing his *Dionysiaca* in the 5th century CE, frequently refers to Selene driving a chariot drawn by bulls, or riding on a bull, or herself being 'horned' (another natural correlation with the 'horns' of the crescent Moon) or even 'bull-shaped'.[24] The essential mythological stories remain the same, but the imagery has changed.

Nonnos also provides us with a wealth of epithets for Selene and Mene, scattered throughout his lengthy poem: 'Titan', 'Cattle-driver', 'Endymion's bedfellow', 'Love-wounded', 'Bright-eyes', 'Bull-shaped, horned, driver of cattle', 'Round-faced', 'Bright', 'Horned', 'Bull-faced', 'Love-smitten', 'Desire-struck', 'Returning', 'Dewy', 'Unresting', 'Revolving', 'Circling', 'Of many turnings', 'Driver of the silver car', 'Golden-rein

---

22 Barton 1994: p.18-19, *passim*.
23 Ptolemy, *Tetrabiblos*, 1.19 (1940: Part 2, p.89).
24 Nonnos, *Dionysiaca* (1940: *passim*).

deity', 'Distracting', 'The nightly lamp of unresting Selene', and so on.[25]

2.3.2 Visual Iconography. We have two main sources for the ancient portrayal of Selene in art. The earlier of these is the Greek vase painting of the classical period, from about the 6th century BCE onwards; the later is the relief sculpture of the classical Greek period and the following Roman empire, although with the latter, of course, the imagery becomes influenced by other identifications, particularly with the Roman Diana.

Unsurprisingly, the most basic portrayal we have of Selene in Greek vase-painting is simply that of the Goddess' head, against the disc of the full Moon. This can be seen in a small decorative roundel that appears on a red-figured kylix that is now in Berlin.[26] Painted and signed by Sosias around 500 BCE, this was imported into Etruria, and was found at Vulci. Selene is portrayed in profile with dark hair, as her hair usually is portrayed on vases; one assumes that this is simply a natural outcome of painting in monochrome, but it is notable that no attempt is made to render her with golden or silver hair, as is so common in modern portrayals of 'Moon-Goddesses'. She wears earrings, a fillet and a necklace, and raises a hand near her chin.

Two further vase-paintings, each showing Selene driving her chariot are discussed and illustrated by L. Savignoni in an early article from 1899.[27] One is a well-known and splendidly executed painting from the interior of a red-figure kylix of the 5th century BCE, showing Selene's two-horse chariot coming directly toward the viewer. She wears a chiton with a mantle over her shoulders, and a decorated hat like a pelleus; the latter a fairly unusual feature, as she is more often shown crowned. Her hair is again dark. In her left hand she holds the horses' reins, in her right a lengthy rod

---

25 Nonnos, *Dionysiaca, passim*.
26 From the Perseus Project web-page. Vase catalog. Berlin F 2278.
27 Savignoni 1899: pp.265-272.

which is presumably used to control the horses. The body of the chariot is visible between the horses which, because of the limited, circular space, are shown with their heads turned to face in toward on another. The horses are winged, a feature which was discussed in the previous section. Above Selene's head, and overlapping the decorative border, is the disc of the full Moon, with two stars to either side; obviously these make clear that we are dealing with a nocturnal deity, and the disc above her head is that of the Moon, rather than the Sun.

Savignoni's second illustration comes from a red-figure bell-krater of the late 5th century BCE, found in Boeotia. Here the illustration is much cruder, and shows Selene in her chariot from a side-on viewpoint. She is again dark-haired, but this time wears a radiate crown appropriate to a deity of light. She is young, slim and wears a long flowing dress, and again holds the reins in her left hand, a rod in her right. The chariot is lightly-built for speed, and the horses are, again, winged. The Moon near her head is this time a crescent, and again is placed between two stars. Selene is here obviously just beginning her journey, rising from the waters of Ocean (as described in the *Homeric Hymn,* above), which are indicated by the curvetting dolphin below the horses' feet. Leading the way before the chariot is the figure of Hermes, whose connection with Selene is explained by Savignoni in terms of him being a God of sleep and dreams, often referred to as *oneiropompos,* 'leader of dreams'. When we recall that the dreams themselves dwell beyond the waters of Ocean, our set of correspondences is complete: with the onset of night come Selene, sleep and dreams.

The other main iconographic form, and apparently the most popular up to the 5th century BCE, shows Selene riding side-saddle on a single horse. The horse is never shown winged here, but this is natural enough; Selene's side-saddle posture would make it extremely awkward to show, even if it were thought necessary.

This motif is discussed by Cecil Smith,[28] although regrettably the particular vase he takes as his example is fragmentary, showing no more than Selene's head and right shoulder, and the head of her horse. The vase is again a red-figure work, of approximately the same date as the chariot picture discussed above. Here Selene is portrayed as a young woman or girl, with dark hair and a small, radiate crown, wearing a chiton. From Smith's discussion it is obvious that there are two versions of this motif: one shows, as here, Selene as a young girl, the horse lively and well-groomed, with the angle of the horse's body slanting upwards toward the head; the other shows Selene as a mature woman, the horse a tired old hack with bent knees and unkempt mane, its body angled with the head lowest. Obviously there are two possible interpretations here: that the first image represents the rising Moon, the second the setting; or that the first represents the waxing Moon, the second the waning. Without specific indicators from the context of the vase-painting, it would perhaps be unsafe to choose between these alternatives.

Fortunately, we do have a particular example that enables us to make just such a choice. An Attic red-figure bell-krater of c.430 BCE, shows a dawn scene featuring the whole trio of siblings, Helios, Eos and Selene, which is reproduced (and, unfortunately, misinterpreted) by Emily Vermeule.[29] All the figures are facing and moving toward the left and, starting from the right, we see Helios driving his quadriga, drawn by four winged horses. His horses are leaping upwards into the sky, while ahead of them (according to Vermeule, and the interpretation seems quite reasonable) the personified stars are diving into the waters of the ocean. Obviously this is a dawn scene, with the stars fading as the Sun rises. Appropriately enough, the next scene portrayed, ahead of Helios' chariot, is winged Eos, the Dawn Goddess, in the act of seizing the hunter Cephalus, portrayed with spears and

---

28 Smith 1888: pp.1-10.
29 Vermeule 1979: p.134.

a hunting dog, who she is about to carry off to heaven as her lover. She is the central figure of the three, and this primary position for Eos strengthens the view that we are dealing with a dawn scene. Unfortunately, Vermeule misidentifies Eos (frequently shown winged) as Selene (never winged in visual representations), and so declares this scene as showing 'Selene chases Endymion', which seems rather unnecessary when Endymion's primary function, especially at this early period, is to be asleep. As a result of this first misidentification, Vermeule would then appear to be forced to compound the error by identifying the following figure, furthest left, as the departing 'Night', when other commentators are agreed that it is Selene, portrayed using the second motif mentioned by Smith. The Goddess, looking somewhat more mature, rides side-saddle, wears a chiton and mantle, and has a veil drawn over her head. Her horse has a bedraggled mane, and is sinking up to its thighs in the waters of the Ocean, although it is here rather more horizontal than slanting downwards. Vermeule is not entirely to be blamed for interpreting this figure as Night, for as we shall see below, Night is occasionally portrayed on horseback; but as the horse is up to its thighs in the Ocean, we are surely intended to see this as Selene, returning to her starting point. And so we infer that with the dawn and the rising Sun, the Moon herself is setting. On this evidence then, it seems reasonably safe to assume that the varying portrayals of young and mature Selene, with her associated rising and declining horses, refer to the rising and setting Moon, rather than the waxing and waning phases.

Further confirmation of this may perhaps be found in a beautifully-rendered painting of Selene on her horse, from an Attic polychrome *pelike* of the 4th century BCE.[30] Here Selene's horse is being led by the figure of Hesperos, the personified Evening Star; the time, then, is obviously evening, and the Moon is making her first appearance. Similarly, Selene's sprightly horse is not only

---

30 Cook 1925: Vol. 2, Part 1. Plate XVI, opp. p.258.

portrayed with its head higher than its rump, it is quite obviously rearing, as if about to spring from the ground. Not surprisingly, Selene's youthful, nubile beauty is particularly emphasised here. She wears a veil that covers the back of her head, but her chiton is pushed down to her hips to expose the entirety of her upper body and breasts. The same vase shows Aphrodite in a similar state of partial undress, which may remind us of Ovid's description, given in the previous section: that Aphrodite and Selene were thought the most beautiful of the Goddesses.

The difficulties of differentiating between Selene and Night (Nyx) are shown by the lid of an Attic red figure pyxis. Three figures appear in a circular band round the central knob of the lid, usually identified as Helios, driving a quadriga; Selene, driving a biga; and Nyx, riding a horse, side-saddle.[31] Apart from the fact that Nyx here has her hands spread wide (perhaps signifying the horizon-to-horizon spread of night?), while Selene tends to hold the edges of her veil with her hands, there is little to help us choose which Goddess is which, except for context.

As with the myths themselves, so there are variants in the iconography. The neck of an Apulian red figure volute krater, shows Helios and Selene, each with a nimbus surrounding their heads and shoulders, but *both* are here driving identical four-horse chariots or quadrigae.[32] This nimbus may possibly be a variant specific to the Greek colonists of Italy. It turns up again on an amphora from Canosa, shown by Cook.[33] Here Selene is shown riding side-saddle on a prancing horse, her head circled with a nimbus which is painted red-brown and yellow. Selene has a similar nimbus in a wall-painting from Herculaneum of the 1st century CE: led by a small erote or cupid, she approaches the sleeping Endymion naked to the

---

31 Boardman 1989: plate 243.
32 Trendall 1989: plate 209.
33 Cook 1914: Vol. 1, p.250.

hip, her veil circling behind her shoulders and a blue nimbus around her head.[34]

A further variant on the nimbus appears in a Roman mosaic from Tunis, now in the Bardo Museum.[35] This shows a similar scene to the wall painting, with Endymion sleeping on a rock below a tree. Here Selene approaches, naked to the hip, but a crescent Moon appears behind her shoulders, with the horns pointing upwards; the space between them suggesting a nimbus behind her head.

There are a number of other wall-paintings from Pompeii, showing Selene and Endymion, and the subject appears to have been quite popular.[36] One shows, very faintly, Selene in her two-horse chariot, quite high in the sky but descending toward the sleeping Endymion, who reclines in the arms of Hypnos, the God of sleep, in a rural setting. A second shows what appears to be a seated Endymion, who may possibly be awake, holding two javelins and accompanied by a hunting dog. Selene, wearing a long dress and raising her right hand to hold a veil round her head, floats down from the sky, unsupported, a few feet away from him. A third shows a classically-posed sleeping Endymion, again with two javelins and hunting dog, while Selene floats down from the sky toward him. She holds a wedding torch in her right hand, and her left is raised to support the circling end of her veil, which may reflect the shape of the nimbus mentioned above. A crescent Moon, points upward, is placed behind her head, giving her a somewhat horned look, while two large stars appear on either side of the head. She is again naked to the waist, her veil appearing to arise from her dress, which is pushed down to her hip. Dating from the 1st century CE, these are relatively late portrayals, and by the hands of Roman artists, but they reflect a

---

34 Godwin 1981: p.55. Cook 1914: Vol. 1, pp.40-41.
35 http://www.vroma.org/images/mcmanus_images/Selenemosaic.jpg
36 Koortbojian 1995: figs. 33, 51, 66.

## Selene

surprising popular ubiquity for the myth, given its general lack of narrative.

When we turn to sculpture, the most obvious surviving relics are to be found among the Parthenon Marbles obtained by Lord Elgin. The figures of the east pediment, showing the birth of Athene, were framed by Helios at one end, driving his quadriga up from the horizon, while Selene descends at the other. Unfortunately, the only surviving fragments of Pheidias' portrayal of the Goddess are a damaged torso and a horse's head.[37] The horse has been described as tired-looking, while Helios' chariot horses are contrastingly sprightly.

Selene's torso, however, is extremely damaged, lacking arms, neck, head, and everything below the waist; what remains shows that she wore a sleeveless, belted chiton, with narrow straps crossing between her breasts. Regrettably, we have nothing else to tell us how Selene was portrayed in sculpture at such a specifically identifiable place and time, between 438 and 432 BCE. As a result, there has been a long-running dispute as to what exactly appeared on the pediment. Cecil Smith argued that Selene was riding side-saddle on her horse;[38] shortly afterwards Savignoni was arguing that she drove a quadriga, matching that of Helios at the opposite end of the pediment.[39] The latter interpretation appears to have become orthodox, in spite of the extreme rarity of representations of Selene in a quadriga. When all we have is but one horse-head and a torso, the question is perhaps best left open.

A.B. Cook, who describes Helios' quadriga rising from the sea and Selene's going down behind hills (which do not appear to be present among the remains of the pediment either) draws the interesting conclusion that as the Sun is rising at the same time that the Moon is setting, the birth of Athene is shown as

---

37 Perseus Project web-page. Sculpture catalog. Parthenon EP.O.
38 Smith 1888: pp.8-9.
39 Savignoni 1899: p.271.

taking place at full Moon. This sort of symbolism would appear to be typical of the usage made of these deities in art; they are present less because they are sacred than as temporal indicators.[40] However, if Cook's interpretation is right, it reinforces the view that 'young sprightly' Selene represents the rising Moon, 'mature and tired' the setting. In turn, we can now look anew at the bell-krater described by Vermeule, above: again we have a scene where, at dawn, the Sun is rising and the Moon setting. This scene, then, is also set at the Full Moon.

One of the arguments in favour of Selene riding on horseback at the Parthenon is that we know that Pheidias used this portrayal on the platform of his colossal statue of Zeus at Olympia, in Elis. Pausanias, the great travel-writer of the 2nd century CE, describes this as: 'the Moon (Selene) is driving what I think is a horse. Some have said that the steed of the Goddess is a mule and not a horse, and they tell a silly story about the mule.'[41]

Frazer, in his commentary on this passage, reproduces a story from the late writer Festus, explaining that: 'the Moon was supposed to ride a mule because she was barren as a mule; or because, just as a mule was not born of a mule but a mare, so the Moon shone not by her own light but by the light of the sun.'[42] Levi, commenting on Frazer, doubts that this story is silly enough, especially in view of the Elean prejudice against mule-breeding.[43] It should also be pointed out that in the Elean version of the Endymion myth, Selene bore 50 daughters, which hardly makes her barren.

Pausanias also mentions that in the market place of the city of Elis are stone images of the Sun and Moon (Selene), 'from the head

---

40 Cook 1940: Vol. 3, pp.718-719.
41 Pausanias: 5.11.8 (1926: p.443).
42 *Pausanias,* 1898: Vol. 3, p.544
43 Pausanias, 1971: Vol. 2, p.229.

## Selene

of the Moon project horns, from the head of the sun, his rays.'[44] If these are actual horns, rather than the points of a crescent Moon, it would have to be conjectured that the statue was late, after the advent of the astrological connection with Taurus.

This problem of identification becomes more difficult once the process of syncretisation among different deities becomes commonplace. A small relief from Attica, carved around 325 BCE, shows worshippers approaching two divinities.[45] The head of the male divinity is badly damaged, but the female, wearing chiton, himation and veil, appears to have a crescent on her forehead. Is this Selene, perhaps with Helios as a companion? Or Artemis (with lunar attributes) and Apollo? The latter seems most likely, but there is simply no way of being sure.

Such reliefs bring us to the carved sarcophagi of the Roman Imperial period, and their frequent depictions of the Selene and Endymion story. These will be discussed in more detail below, in Chapter 14, along with their particular applicability to funereal monuments. Here only a few words will be said about Selene's appearance in these sculptures, which by this time is influenced by her association with the Roman Diana. She is usually portrayed stepping down from her two-horse chariot and approaching the sleeping Endymion. She has a crescent on her brow, her long chiton pulled down to expose her right breast, and holds her veil so that it billows in a semi-circle above her head, perhaps representing the arc of the sky. Despite the relatively late period of these sarcophagi (2nd-3rd centuries CE), Selene's chariot is always drawn by horses, rather than bulls.[46]

There is one other iconographic source to discuss, which is Selene's extremely rare appearance on coins or, more often, medallions. A couple of examples can be found which date to the Roman period in the reign of Severus Alexander, 222-235 CE. The first is a bronze medallion minted at Smyrna in Ionia,

---

44 Pausanias: 6.24.6 (1933: Vol. 3, p.151).
45 Perseus Project web-page. Sculpture catalog. Boston 1977.171.
46 Koortbojian 1995: *passim*. McCann 1978: pp.34-45.

and shows confronting busts of Helios and Selene. Helios wears a radiate crown, while Selene is draped and has a crescent at her shoulders.[47]

The second example, from Perinthus in Thrace, is much more complex and, even at 4 centimetres across, is still an extremely miniaturised piece of work. At the centre sits an enthroned figure of Zeus, surrounded by Helios and Selene in their chariots, and, below by Gaia (Earth) and Thalassa (Sea). Around the rim are the signs of the Zodiac. Given the obvious astrological background, it's not surprising that Selene's chariot is here drawn by bulls.[48]

In summary then, this section has shown us Selene depicted in a wide range of media, from Greece, from Italy to the west, and eastwards to Asia Minor; and from the 5th century BCE to the 3rd century CE. Not surprisingly, given such a spread across both space and time, the iconography is very varied. Fashions change as the centuries pass; new influences and identifications alter the depictions. In the classical Greek period, Selene often appears in a pair with Helios and here, almost certainly, they are being shown as representations of the heavenly bodies. So Helios and Selene frame the pediment of the Parthenon; so on the Attic bell-krater, when the Sun rises, the Moon departs. At this early period we have no surviving images of the Selene and Endymion myth; although it does appear from a very early stage in the literature. Later, in the Roman period, the Selene and Endymion story becomes much more popular, as a subject for wall-paintings, mosaics and sarcophagi. This is to be attributed to renewed interest and a new way of interpreting the story, which will be examined in succeeding chapters. Like so much in the myths of Selene, so in the iconography it is very difficult to pin down a 'single, definitive version'. There are no fixed points here, only patterns that seem to shift even as we look at them.

---

47 Perseus Project web-page. Coin catalog. Boston 1984.6.
48 Perseus Project web-page. Coin catalog. Boston 62.629.

## 2.4 Selene In Greek Cult And Religion

Robert Parker, writing the entry for *Selene* in the *Oxford Classical Dictionary*, tells us that: 'Actual worship of Selene, as of Helios, is treated by Aristophanes as characteristic of barbarians in opposition to Greeks (*Pax* 406).[49] Like Helios, if in lesser degree, she seems to have infiltrated cult from the late Hellenistic period onwards. A more important way in which the moon had a place in religious life was through the identification with it (but not necessarily with the mythological Selene) of major goddesses such as Artemis or Hecate.'[50]

Parker's distinction is important. Cult practices of Artemis or Hecate are unlikely to tell us anything of those specific to Selene, still less of her mythology; indeed, they may possibly be misleading. Again, the later we get, with the composite 'Moon-Goddess' who appears in the Greek Magical Papyri of the Roman Imperial period, the further away we get from the Selene of myth. Similarly, we must be wary of Greek authors such as Strabo when they tell us of the cults dedicated to 'Selene' among the inhabitants of distant lands;[51] quite obviously these are local Moon-deities with no relation to the Greek Goddess.

What we have to look for, then, is material specifically relating to Selene herself, and preferably in an actual Greek setting; if we range beyond Greece it's necessary that the Goddess concerned is iconographically recognisable as Selene herself, and not as a local deity identified with her. Within these criteria, there is actually remarkably little evidence of cult worship to be found: no great city

---

49 Aristophanes, *Pax* ll.406-413 (Aristophanes 1998: p.481). Aristophanes' play, performed in 421 BCE, is a comedy, of course, but seems to reflect contemporary attitudes. Selene and Helios are also accused of plotting against the Gods to betray Greece to the barbarians, so they can take over the sacrifices for themselves.

50 Hornblower & Spawforth 1999: *s.v.* 'Selene', pp.1379-1380.

51 As a particular example, Strabo, 11.4.7, describing the lunar cult of the Albanian and Iberian dwellers between the Black and Caspian Seas, which includes possession and human sacrifice. Strabo 1917-1932: Vol. 5, pp.229-231.

festivals such as those of Artemis, Athena or Hera, no 'temples of Selene', no great epics. Indeed, Selene does not even appear as a Goddess in Homer, but only as the physical Moon. Undoubtedly part of the reason for this is to be found in the fact that she is a 'visible Goddess' to whom informal worship can be given by all without regard to time and place; even so, the absence still seems rather odd.

Hints of cult are to be found. Farnell discusses the *nephalia* or 'wineless' sacrifices, which did not include an animal victim, and were said to correspond to *melisponda*, or libations of honey. These sacrifices were offered to a number of deities, including Selene, Helios and Eos; the other deities on the list include Zeus Georgos ('agricultural Zeus'), Poseidon, the Winds, Mnemosyne (Memory), the Muses, Aphrodite Ourania ('of the sky'), Dionysus and the Nymphs.[52] It should be noted that this is a very rural collection of deities; these are, generally, not the Gods of city-dwellers.

Athenaeus, writing around 200 CE, quoting a number of authors of the 4th and 3rd centuries BCE (Philemon of Syracuse, Diphilus and Philochorus), mentions cakes called *amphiphon* offered to Artemis.[53] Selene herself is not mentioned, though by this period Artemis has become syncretised with Moon-Goddesses, and the context is plainly lunar. *Amphiphon* means 'shining all round', and refers to a flat, round cake surrounded by lights (literally 'torches', but likely to be something rather smaller, such as tapers), which was carried to the temples of Artemis, or to the crossroads (sacred to the equally lunar Hecate) on the night of the full Moon, when the Sun rises as the Moon sets, so the sky is 'doubly-lighted' (*amphiphos*). Whether such cakes were offered to Selene herself, prior to her

---

52 Farnell 1896-1909: Vol. 1, p.88, with collected references. See also Frazer's commentary to *Pausanias* (1898: Vol. 3, p.583), quoting Polemo. Polemo's list drops Zeus Georgos, Poseidon, Dionysos (perhaps not surprisingly) and the winds, and says these were the 'sober' sacrifices offered by the Athenians.

53 Athenaeus 14.53 (645a-b) 1937: Vol. 6, pp.481-483.

syncretisation with other deities, can only remain conjectural, of course.

Often, Selene appears (usually in association with Helios, so one gets the impression that this is simply a formalised pairing of 'Sun and Moon', rather than a reference to the Goddess as an independent deity) among lengthy lists of deities who are offered worship, or represented in temples. Thus there is an inscription from the seaport town of Gytheion in southern Laconia with refers to a 'priest of Zeus Boulaios, Helios, Selene, Asclepius and Hygeia'.[54]

Similarly, Selene appears among the associated deities having shrines at the great temple of Asclepius at Epidaurus: 'Within the *hieron* were several smaller and less elaborate, though beautiful, temples dedicated to Artemis Hekate, Aphrodite, and Themis, and the records indicate that there were shrines and chapels to Helios, Selene, Epione, Zeus, Hera, Poseidon, Athena, Leto, Akeso, the Eleusinian goddesses Demeter and Persephone, and others'.[55]

Again, there is an obscure and very late reference in the writings of Georgios Kedrenos (c.1100 CE) to a temple in Constantinople of 'Helios and Selene'; Kedrenos, however, tells us that it contained a statue of Zeus, attributed to Pheidias. Apart from the fact that this is extremely confusing and surprisingly late, if the temple was dedicated to *both* Helios and Selene, we might infer that they appeared here more as the 'celestial lights' rather than as individual deities. By the time Kedrenos was writing, of course, any worship would long have lapsed.[56]

Lastly, in Greece, there is the brief mention by Porphyry that in Arcadia there was a cave consecrated 'to Selene and Lycaean Pan.'[57] This will be of some import when we come to discuss

---

54 Farnell 1921: p.255.
55 Jayne 1925: p.264.
56 Georgios Kedrenos, *Hist. Comp.* 323c, Cook 1914: Vol. 1, p.92.
57 Porphyry, *De Antro Nympharum*, 20 1983: p.32.

the myth of Selene and Pan (Chapter 12), but unfortunately the classical sources give us absolutely no further details of the shrine, or what rituals may have been performed there, than this.

Strangely, the best evidence we have for a well-established Selenic cult comes not from Greece but from Etruria in Italy, from a city known to the Etruscans as Clevsin and the Romans as Clusium (modern Chiusi). Here, at the provocatively-named Sillene spring, was a cult which appears to have been dedicated to Selene. Apart from the name of the spring, archaeological excavation has revealed fragments of a bronze statue group of Selene and her *biga*, dating from the 4$^{th}$ century BCE; the presence of another statue identified as Apollo would suggest that, at least in its iconography, the cult revolved around imported deities, perhaps from the Greek colonies in southern Italy; the presence of Apollo might also suggest that Selene was on the way to being identified with Artemis/Diana here. We have to exercise caution here, of course; a votive bronze half-moon was discovered in the Sillene spring, while not far distant from Clusium another bronze half-moon has been found bearing an inscription to the Etruscan Moon-God, Tiur. It's possible, then, that what we have here is an ancient Etruscan lunar cult-site, which, with passing time, reinvented itself using the fashionable style of imported Graecism. Nonetheless, according to Sybille Haynes, we have here an important sanctuary dedicated to Selene and centred on the healing spring at Sillene, and possibly also an oracle of Apollo.[58] The site, a thermal spring said to have been visited by the Etruscan king Lars Porsena in the 6$^{th}$ century BCE, appears to have remained in constant use and, now known as Chianciano Terme, is still operating today. Etruscan bronze and stone model livers, used as guides to haruspicy, have also been found.[59]

---

58 Haynes 2000: p.343.

59 http://www.chiancianoterme.com/uk-storia.htm, http://www.

*Selene*

Even so, this is obviously a very short list indeed, and Philippe Borgeaud is undoubtedly right when he says that: 'Selene, the moon, remains a very marginal figure in urban religion.'[60] And yet there is more to be found, out in the countryside, and 'hiding in the houses of others'. These other traces of Selene will be uncovered as we turn our attention to the myths themselves.

---

termechianciano.it/legends.htm. Accessed 6 May 2002.
60 Borgeaud 1988: p.56.

Chapter Three

# The Minor Myths

## 3.1 Introduction

As will already be apparent from the material gathered together in Chapter 1, the major mythic stories of Selene centre on her involvement with Endymion. Our attempts to cast light on those stories will, for reasons that become plain as we progress, require us to handle the stories involving Pan and one or two of the less-developed tales at the same time, and that material will form the heart of what can be said about the Goddess. First, though, it is probably as well to deal with the lesser stories that have been preserved from Selene's 'biography'.

Unfortunately, it's necessary to handle the material here with a considerable amount of caution. Our sources cover a span of more than a thousand years, and are drawn from a wide variety of writers: mythographers, poets, playwrights, historians and so forth. Some of the material collected in Chapter 1 hardly qualifies as 'myth' at all, as the fragmentary references we have contain hardly anything in the way of narrative. Occasionally we have to deal with what are obviously nothing more than 'poetic conceits' or astronomical knowledge masquerading as personification. And, of course, the evidence is fragmentary, contradictory, and often lacking. Nonetheless, the difficulties and deficits in the material can often tell us as much as the better-preserved and more explicit passages. The important thing, though, is to let the evidence 'speak in its own voice', rather than attempting to impose later identifications, modern structures or belief-systems upon it.

## 3.2 Selene's Descent And Family

Even the briefest look at the material gathered together in section 1.2 will reveal that, despite the fact that we have an apparently 'canonical version' recorded by Hesiod and Apollodorus, we also have half a dozen variants. If we begin by looking at the Hesiodic version, we may find some clue as to why there is such variation in the other stories.

3.2.1 Hyperion's Daughter. Hesiod tells us that Hyperion and Theia are the parents of Helios, Selene and Eos, and we have seen that in Greek Hyperion means 'The One Above' while Theia simply means 'The Goddess'. Curiously, 'The Goddess' is also the meaning of Diana in Latin. Hyperion is used as the name of the Sun in Homer, in the latter half of the 8th century BCE, both in the *Iliad* and the *Odyssey*; but so are 'Hyperion-Helios' 'Helios' and 'Helios-Phaethon'.[1] In Hesiod (c.700 BCE) Hyperion has become the Sun's father. Again, the possibility has been mooted that a Linear-B tablet from Knossos, containing the word-ending '*-pe-ro-ne*', may be evidence that Hyperion was the name of the Sun-God there in the 2nd millennium BCE.[2] It has to be admitted that this is rather speculative, but taking these two pieces of evidence together, it might be possible to make an argument for Hyperion being an earlier name of the Sun-God, Helios a later one; if Mene was also known at Knossos, we might also argue, on this basis, that perhaps Mene is an earlier title of the Moon-Goddess than Selene. However, a single mention of each of these names in a Cretan context (that of

---

1 *E.g., Odyssey*, 12.133 (Homer 1919: Vol. 1, p.441). The alternative names are collected, with references, in Kerenyi 1951: pp.192, 194.

2 Ventris & Chadwick 1973: p.309 [Tablet E842].

Hyperion, especially, rather speculative), is hardly enough evidence to build any sort of convincing case upon.

According to Hesiod and Apollodorus, Hyperion and Theia are Titans, of the generation before Zeus and the Olympian Gods. Like the Olympians (and one cannot escape the notion that they have been assembled as a 'matching set'), Hesiod tells us that there are twelve Titans, six brothers and six sisters, all the offspring of Ouranos and Ge or Gaia. It has become commonplace among popular writers on mythology, especially among those influenced by Robert Graves and his ilk, to view the Titans as being the Gods of an earlier, possibly pre-Greek religion, 'overthrown' or replaced by the Greeks and their Olympian deities. Once again, we have here to deal with contemporary rationalist literalism: as Hesiod records a 'succession myth' whereby Zeus overthrows Kronos, and there is a subsequent war in which the Olympians defeat the Titans, so there *'must'* somehow be a 'real event' behind the story, and if we cannot believe in Gods fighting one another, we must rationalise it as being the overthrow of one religion by another. Curiously, the preceding myth of Kronos castrating Ouranos is rarely mentioned; nor is there any suggestion that Ouranos and Ge/Gaia represent an even earlier state of religious affairs.

Unfortunately, there are a number of problems with this notion. The first is that, apart from Kronos, who had the singular advantage among the Titans of being identified with the planet Saturn, there is no discoverable trace of religious cult devoted to the Titans.

The second problem is that large parts of the 'Titan succession myth' appear to have been either taken over wholesale from, or heavily influenced by, stories from Mesopotamia, either directly or through the intervening medium of Hittite myth. So, in brief, the Hittites had a generation of 'former Gods', while Zeus' imprisonment of the Titans in Tartarus has its parallel, if not its actual origin, in the way that Marduk treated the offspring of Tiamat in the Babylonian epic, *Enuma Elis*. And if the story of the Titans' overthrow can be shown to be, at least in part, non-Greek, it becomes difficult to see how the Titans can represent an autochthonous religion of Greece that was somehow superseded by 'incoming patriarchalists'. There is now a considerable literature about the Oriental influence on Greek myth,[3] and it really shouldn't be necessary any longer to spend time demolishing *modern* myths about ancient ones.

Lastly, the presence of the Titans in Greek myth is perfectly explicable without having to resort to 'earlier religion'. The idea of 'former Gods' is, like 'Chaos', a natural and necessary means whereby the current order is defined,[4] in the same way that to be 'Greek' is defined by comparison with being 'barbarian'. Both societies and religions define themselves as much by what they are not as by what they are; so the Olympian Gods are defined as much by being 'not-Titan' as anything else.

All this apart, if we look at Hyperion, Theia and their offspring purely in terms of the stories in which they appear, it is quite obvious that they do not 'fit' comfortably with their contemporaries and associates. Helios, Selene and Eos, although offspring of Titans, do not take part in the war between the Olympians and the Titans, on either side. Their continuing appearance in the skies makes it obvious that they have not been cast into Tartarus along with the other Titans (and if Homer continued to refer to the Sun as Hyperion, it's quite obvious that *he* wasn't cast into Tartarus either); while at the same time Helios and Selene are not numbered among the Olympians.

The problem with the Sun and Moon, of course, is that they are 'visible Gods'. They have quite plainly been with us 'since the world began' and will be here 'until the world ends'. As such, they do not fit easily into systematised 'families' of Gods, either Titan or Olympian, and their obvious, continual and predictable appearances in the sky make it difficult for them to appear in the sort of involved

---

[3] *Inter alia*, see Walcot 1966: *passim*. West 1966: p.19ff. Kirk 1974: pp.26-27, 116ff. Graf 1993: pp.86-96. Penglase 1994: *passim. Etc.*

[4] Dowden 1992: pp.135-136, and the same author's entry, *s.v.* 'Titan' in Hornblower & Spawforth 1999: pp.1531-1532.

mythical adventures that feature other Gods like Hermes or Apollo. So when we turn to Helios, we find little mythology that directly relates to the Sun-God as such, apart from the description of his chariot-drive across the daylight sky and his nocturnal return to his starting point, and his romances. However, these 'romances' are actually little more than compilations of genealogical information; there is very little *story* to them. It is his offspring, such as Circe and Pasiphae, and most notably his son Phaethon, who appear in the mythic stories. Even then, the Phaethon story is less a 'real' myth than a later aetiological explanation as to why certain parts of the world are hotter than others, and why some races of mankind have been 'sunburnt' black or brown. Similarly, when the sailors of Odysseus butcher the cattle on the Island of the Sun, the God (appearing in Homer as Hyperion) is unable to punish them himself, but has to call on Zeus to do so.[5]

The mythology of Selene has similarities to that of Helios, but also differences. Again, what myths we do have about her centre on her romances, but her offspring, as we'll see below, are little more than shadowy personifications, lacking stories of their own. Selene also has her chariot-drive across the sky, but there is a difference. While Helios' movements are fully accounted for (in the sky from dawn to dusk, returning to his starting point from dusk to dawn), there is only one night in the month when Selene is continuously visible from dusk to dawn: at the Full Moon. At all other times of the month, there are certain portions of the night when she is not to be seen, while around the period of New Moon she is simply not visible at all.

Thus while both Helios and Selene indulge their romantic inclinations, we can see a structural difference between them. Neither can be allowed the sort of adventures that involve the Olympian Gods, with the possible risks of destruction or imprisonment such as are involved in Titan wars or battles with the Giants, because the

---

5 Homer, *Odyssey*, 12.374ff. (1919: Vol. 1, p.459-451).

## Selene

outcome is always certain: whatever happens, Helios and Selene will *always* be at their posts when next they're due to appear. And yet, as mankind's light-bringers, they are obviously important Gods, about whom there is a natural desire for stories and information. Helios, then, whose actions are far more limited than Selene's, finds his place in mythical narration through his offspring. Selene, with somewhat greater freedom, does not need to express herself through her children; instead, what stories we have of her actually centre on her romances themselves.

Systematisers like Hesiod and Apollodorus have a problem, of course, in that their works are constructed primarily to provide a genealogy of the Gods and heroes of myth and legend. As a result, even deities who 'have always been there' such as the Sun and Moon have to have a genealogy too. It's hardly surprising, then, that the parentages of Helios and Selene are problematical; the logic involved here would be rather like pondering the hypothetical question 'does the eternally-existent Christian God have a navel?'

We have seen that, according to Hesiod and Apollodorus, the parents of Helios and Selene are Hyperion ('The One Above') and his sister Theia ('The Goddess'). In effect, the parents are doublets for the Sun and Moon. So, appropriately to a deity who has always existed, Helios becomes 'Sun, son of Sun'. Selene's case is a little more complex and takes us into some baffling, if suggestive, areas of Titanic genealogy.

If we were looking for a similar 'doublet' Titan Goddess to serve as Selene's mother, we might rather expect this to be Phoebe, whose name is a feminine form meaning 'pure, beaming, bright, radiant' (the Titan Goddess is to be distinguished from Artemis, who also takes the epithet Phoebe, as a counterpart to her brother Apollo's title Phoebus), which would correspond to the 'brightness' to be found in Selene's name (see above, 2.2). Instead we find her mother is called Theia, the Goddess, the Feminine Deity. This may at first seem puzzling, until we realise that 'theia', spelt exactly the same way in Greek, means 'aunt; one's father's or mother's sister'. The explanation then becomes much more obvious: Helios and Selene are, quite simply, the offspring of 'their father Hyperion and his sister', natural enough if the Sun and Moon are regarded as brother and sister, but a relationship which, because of its incestuousness, would not normally be described using the term 'aunt'. It is hardly surprising, then, that Theia is more often interpreted as 'The Goddess'.

As it happens, apart from the genealogy, there is almost no surviving literature on Theia except for a mention in the 5th Isthmian Ode of Pindar (c.520-440 BCE)[6]: 'Oh mother of the Sun-god, Theia of many names! For thy sake men even set a stamp upon gold, as mighty beyond all beside; because, for the sake of thy worth, O queen, not only ships racing on the sea, but also mares yoked to chariots in the swiftly-whirling struggles of battle, win wonder.'

Sandys' footnote to this passage offers the following explanation: 'Theia, "the goddess divine," is mentioned in Hesiod's *Theogony*, 371, as the mother of the Sun, the Moon, and the Dawn. She is thus the principle of Light, which gives brightness to all her offspring. She appears in many forms, and it is only for this reason that she is here said to have "many names." It is this Light that gives gold its brightness, and prompts men to stamp it as current coin.' It is, perhaps, possible to detect a circular argument in the first part of this note: because Theia is the mother of the celestial lights, so she is the principle of light, and thus gives light to her offspring. All this aside, given the singularity of Pindar's reference, it seems likely that we have here more a 'poetic fancy' on the name Theia, rather than a reflection of a sizeable body of tradition.

It is, perhaps, a fool's errand to delve too deeply into the morass of mythological genealogy (one suspects that even Hesiod was groping here), but the very confusion involved may help us map a larger pattern here, and some of the personages mentioned will reappear later. We shall not deal with *all* the Titans and their offspring

---

6 Pindar, *Isthmian Odes* 5.1-7 (1915, p.473).

## Selene

here; even so, the reader's patience is requested as we pick our way through this maze of names.

We shall begin with the radiant Phoebe. Her fraternal husband was Coeus, whose name, Kerenyi informs us,[7] had the same meaning as *sphairos*, a term used by Diodorus Siculus specifically for the celestial sphere.[8] Coeus was also called Polos, the (celestial) pole. Their offspring were two daughters, Asteria, whose name obviously suggests a star-Goddess, and Leto. Leto is well-known as the mother, by Zeus, of Apollo (most notable for his oracular function) and Artemis who, of course, in later times became identified with Helios and Selene, and received the epithets Phoebus and Phoebe. Asteria mated with Perses (of whom we shall have more to say below), and their offspring was Hecate. To Hesiod, Hecate was a Goddess who gave glory and victory, and increase of flocks; in the *Theogony* she had no lunar or underworld connections, even though her father Perses ('destroyer') might be seen as having the same connections to death and the underworld as Persephone ('destroyer-killer').[9]

Crius (whose name means a ram) married Eurybia, a daughter of Ocean and Gaia; Eurybia's name meaning 'wide-ruling' or 'of wide force', though Hesiod describes her as having a heart of flint.[10] He also describes her, however, as a 'bright Goddess', and Crius fathered on her Astraeus ('the starry'), Pallas and Perses (said to be 'eminent among all men in wisdom'), the father of Hecate mentioned above.

Astraeus mated with Eos, who gave birth to the three winds Zephyrus, Boreas and Notus, Eosphorus (the Morning Star) and the stars in general. Pallas mated with the underworld river Styx, a daughter of Ocean, though their offspring were four personifications:

---

7 Kerenyi 1951: p.130.
8 Diodorus Siculus, 3.60.2 (1935: Vol. 2, pp.278-279).
9 Hesiod, *Theogony*, ll.404ff (1914: pp.109-113).
10 Hesiod, *Theogony*, l.239 (1914: p.97).

Strength, Force, Emulation and Victory (Nike) of whom only the last entered the Greek pantheon.[11] We shall return to Pallas shortly.

Before summarising what can be learned here, one last genealogical discursus is necessary, to take in the wives and offspring of Helios. Hesiod tells us that his wife was Perseis (whose name, like Perses, signifies 'destroyer') and their offspring were Aeëtes ('the terrible') and Circe, the well-known witch-Goddess of the *Odyssey*.[12] Apollodorus adds another daughter, Pasiphae ('shining for all'), the mother of the Minotaur, but also a sorceress in her own right.[13] Aeëtes in turn married the Oceanid Idyia ('knowing'), and their daughter was another famous sorceress, Medea ('cunning' or 'wise').

Lastly, Kerenyi provides a convenient summary of Helios' other wives and offspring, which include, from the *Odyssey*, a wife Neaira ('The New One', apparently referring to the New Moon when, of course, Sun and Moon are in conjunction), and by her the daughters Lampetia ('the illuminating'), Phaethoussa ('the shining') and Aigle ('light'). Lastly, Helios's son by Clymene is Phaethon ('the brilliant').[14]

Before summing up here, it may be as well to deal with the genealogies contained above in 1.2.2 and 1.2.3. In the first of these Hyginus gives the parents as 'Hyperion and Aethra'. There are a number of difficulties with this text. We don't actually know who 'Hyginus' was, but the work bearing his name was written in Latin, apparently in the 2nd century CE, and seems to derive from Greek originals. It was then abbreviated by copyists, eventually surviving in only a single manuscript that was printed by Micyllus in 1535, after which the original manuscript was lost. 'Aethra' is otherwise unknown as the mother of Helios and Selene. We may have here a

---

11 Hesiod: *Theogony*, 1.375ff (1914: p.107)
12 Hesiod: *Theogony*, ll.956-962 (1914: p.151)
13 Apollodorus: *The Library*, 1.9.1, 3.15.1 (1921: Vol. 1, p.77, Vol. 2, p.105).
14 Kerenyi 1951: pp.193-194.

separate tradition, or Aethra could be an error for Theia, or perhaps for Aether; but whether such a putative error was made by Hyginus, his epitomisers, or later copyists, is quite beyond saying. Effectively, then, there is little we can do with Hyginus's genealogy, except to note it as 'uncorroborated'.

As we've seen, the *Homeric Hymn to Helios*, mentioned in 1.2.3, lists the parents as Hyperion and Euryphaëssa. The Homeric Hymns to Helios and Selene appear to form a pair, probably written in the Hellenistic period (post 300 BCE), and the genealogy given in the hymn to Helios obviously does duty for both hymns. Euryphaëssa means 'far-shining' or 'wide-shining'; once again we appear to be dealing with a title, rather more than a name, which would be easily applicable to a Moon-Goddess. We might also suspect that this is more of an Alexandrian poeticism than evidence of a separately-existing Goddess or cult-title.

There are, perhaps, two or three themes emerging from this web of intermarriages, personifications and duplications. The first is that the parents of the Sun and Moon, Hyperion mated with Theia, Euryphaëssa or whoever, appear to be doublets of their offspring, Helios and Selene. This marriage of the parents is portrayed as sibling incest, and with Helios and Neaira, mentioned in the *Odyssey*, we seem to have the same incestuous Sun-Moon marriage occurring. In the later poet Quintus Smyrnaeus (1.3.3) we find another incestuous pairing between Helios and Selene resulting in the birth of the Seasons.

Unlike the story appearing in Euripides and Nonnus (1.2.5), which makes Selene the daughter of Helios, a story that appears to be explicable in terms of the astronomical knowledge that the Moon receives its light from the Sun, this sibling incest story is intelligible in purely visual terms, without the necessity of any knowledge of celestial mechanics. The Sun and Moon, being celestial lights of equal size but of comparatively stronger (masculine) and weaker (feminine) brightness, are quite naturally interpreted as brother and sister. Coming together in conjunction at each New Moon, it's also natural to think of them as mating. So the Moon is renewed, and so the seasons of the year come to be.

The problem comes with the genealogists, with their insistence that the deities should have traceable parents. The Sun and Moon being visible deities who have 'always been there', the only real solution is to make their 'parents' the Sun and Moon themselves, if under slightly different names.

The second theme is perhaps less distinct, but it is notable that among the various offspring of the Titans discussed above we have a number of characters connected with night and the underworld. We have here the celestial sphere in Coeus, a number of stellar deities, and the stars themselves; while with Aeëtes ('terrible') and Perses and Perseis ('destroyers') we have obviously death-connected underworld deities. If the latter figures are seen, however, as also representing darkness (the 'death of the day', when the Sun is travelling back through the underworld from his western setting point to his eastern rising) we have a more obvious structural complementarity.

Lastly, the number of sorceresses included in the genealogies under consideration here is remarkable: Circe, Medea, Pasiphae. And while the connection is rather later than the Hesiodic genealogies, we have Hecate uniting both the last two strands, as Goddess of both the underworld and of magic. There is then, in this nexus of night/underworld/sorcery, a very definite underlying theme of 'the occult'; it is a theme that will reappear as we continue.

3.2.2 Pallas' Daughter. It's now time to turn our attention to the variant genealogy given in 1.2.4. This, it will be recalled, derived from the *Homeric Hymn to Hermes*, a work of the 6th century BCE, and made no mention of Helios or Eos: it merely says that Selene is 'the daughter of the lord Pallas, Megamedes' son'. This hymn,[15] referring to Hermes as the lord of Mount Cyllene in Arcadia, would

---

15 *Homeric Hymn IV – To Hermes* (in *Hesiod* 1914: pp.363-405).

seem then to represent an Arcadian tradition; the same tradition which makes the God Pan the son of Hermes. As we will be looking in some detail at the myth of Selene and Pan later in this work (Chapter 12), this reference is obviously of considerable interest, particularly if we can infer from this source that the story given here of Selene being the daughter of Pallas is an Arcadian tradition.

Who, then, is the Pallas referred to here as the father of Selene? Unfortunately, even a quick glance at the mythological dictionaries, such as that of Grimal,[16] reveals five different male personages called Pallas. Once again we are in the realm of multiple names, confused identities and variants.

There is little to indicate directly that the Titan Pallas mentioned above, son of Crius and Eurybia, is the 'Pallas son of Megamedes' concerned here, although Ovid, writing at the turn of the Common Era, calls Aurora (Eos) 'Pallantis' (the 'daughter of Pallas').[17]

There is, though, a Pallas with very definite Arcadian connections, and that is Pallas the son of Lycaon, king of Arcadia. According to the *Homeric Hymn*, Pallas' father is 'Megamedes'; and as this means 'greatly wise' or 'very cunning', we might conjecture that Megamedes is as likely to be a title as an actual name. Lycaon in turn was the son of the culture-hero Pelasgos, who is said by Pausanias to be the first inhabitant of Arcadia, cleverer than others, and who is credited with the invention of huts, sheepskin tunics and the diet of acorns for which the Arcadians were always noted in legend. Following this, Pausanias tells us that Lycaon 'made as many inventions even cleverer than his father.'[18] The Greek adjective used of Lycaon here derives from *sophos* rather than *metis*, but the English equivalents ('clever, cunning, skilled, wise') are the same in both cases. Another possible piece of corroborative evidence comes from a quotation preserved in Strabo's *Geography*. He quotes a

---

16 Grimal 1986: *s.v.* Pallas (pp.339-340).

17 Ovid, *Metamorphoses*, 9.421 (1916: Vol. 2, p.33).

18 Pausanias, 8.1.4-8.2.1 (1933: Vol. 3, p.349-351).

fragment of Hesiod, preserved by Ephorus: 'And sons were born of god-like Lycaon, who, on a time, was begotten by Pelasgus.'[19] The suggestive epithet 'God-like' here is *antitheoio*, where the prefix *anti* is obviously being used in the sense of 'equal to', 'like', 'matching'; it shouldn't be confused with *ante*, 'prior to', tempting as that may be in the circumstances. If Lycaon seems a likely candidate for the title 'Megamedes', then in his son we may have found our 'Arcadian Pallas'.

Having said that, we immediately run into a troublesome confusion, for Dionysius of Halicarnassus tells us that this Pallas son of Lycaon was the father of the Goddess Victory (Nike);[20] while as we've seen above, Hesiod makes Nike daughter of the Titan Pallas. Nonetheless, the interesting point here is that, at least to Dionysius, it was conceivable for a man to father a Goddess. Later Dionysius tells us that Pallas had another daughter with the suggestive name Chryse ('golden') who married Dardanus, one of the founders of Troy.[21]

It's true, of course, that we have no direct evidence that in Arcadian legend the father of Selene was Pallas son of Lycaon, but the evidence assembled so far is at least suggestive. It is perhaps of interest, though not directly relevant here, that in Greek tradition Lycaon was also the archetypal werewolf, having been transformed by Zeus as a punishment for offering a child as a human sacrifice; unlike later werewolf traditions, however, there is no link with the full Moon in the tale.[22] Yet the idea that Selene had a human father would require us to accept the idea that there were human beings in Arcadia, the offspring of Pelasgos, before the Moon was born. And this is precisely what the Arcadians claimed.

---

19 Strabo, *Geography*, 5.2.4 (1923: Vol. 2, p.345). The quotation is usually listed as Fragment 31 of Hesiod's *Catalogues of Women and Eoiae*.
20 Dionysius of Halicarnassus, 1.32.5-1.33.1 (1937: Vol. 1, pp105-107).
21 Dionysius of Halicarnassus, 1.61.2 (1937: Vol. 1, p.203).
22 Pausanias, 8.2.3-8.2.7 (1933: p.351-355).

*Selene*

As usual, the evidence here is fragmentary, and mostly consists of quotations from ancient historians collected in the commentaries to other works;[23] fortunately, however, Borgeaud gives an excellent discussion of the material.[24] The idea that the Arcadians were *proselenoi* ('Pre-Moonites') is first recorded only in the 5th century BCE, but this is hardly surprising, as this is also exactly the period when Arcadia was first coalescing into a single political entity, rather than a dispersed collection of small communities. Curiously some historians, however, actually refer to the Arcadians as 'Selenites', rather than 'pre-Selenites'; precisely why this should be so is unclear, unless it was believed that the inclusion of Selene in the genealogical line made Arcadians generally 'of the same family'. Pelasgos though, is said to be *proselenaios*, which would fit if his grandson Pallas was actually the Moon's father. More commonly, various sources tell us that the Arcadians generally were thought to be older than the Moon and stars, or older than Zeus and the Moon. A historian called Theodorus, quoted in the scholia to Apollonius Rhodius' *Argonautika*, tells us that the Moon first appeared just prior to 'Heracles' war against the Giants', which would put her birth very much within the human period; and Pan, the other major God born in Arcadia, was also said to have a human mother. When we discover that Lycaon is said to have had, according to one source, a wife, and according to another, a daughter, called Dia, a name meaning 'Goddess',[25] we may start to feel a sense of familiarity: we are back in the world of wife-and-daughter doublets we discovered in the Hesiodic genealogy. There is no evidence to suggest that Dia was the mother of Selene by her brother Pallas; though by now it would hardly be surprising if there was.

What we have here, again, are hints that suggest a more fully developed mythology, now lost; indeed, perhaps even lost in antiquity

---

23 *Scholia in Apollonii Argonautica*, 4.263 (1810, 1813: Vol. 2, pp.285-286, pp.586-587). *Scholia in Lycophronis Alexandra*, 1.482 (1908: Vol. 2 p.174-175).

24 Borgeaud 1988: pp.6-8.

25 Borgeaud 1988: p.7.

by the time our sources were written down. As such, a number of rationalisations were put forward for the term *proselenoi*: Aristotle speculated that the Arcadians received the name because they attacked the barbarians occupying the country one night 'before the Moon rose'. Others derived *proselenoi* from *proselein*, 'to attack', and so explained the epithet as 'the violent ones'. Yet others thought the *proselenoi* were people living before the Moon's phases were understood, resulting from observations which were often said to have been first made by figures associated with Arcadia, including Endymion and Pan. As for the last rationalisation, it is of a type we shall find occurring repeatedly throughout this investigation; it always appears in late authors, when euhemerisation and allegorisation had become fashionable, and long post-dates the mythic stories themselves.

Before summing up this section, there is one last curious diversion to make. Pausanias tells us that there was in Arcadia a town (ruined in his time) called Nonacris, which was also the name of a wife of Lycaon; and that not far from there was a high cliff and a waterfall. This stream, he says, is the River Styx; and it was quite obviously thought to be identical to the underworld River Styx, because it was said that the waters were deadly to drink, and capable of dissolving any vessel that it was held in, except for a horse's hoof.[26] While this is undoubtedly a surprising notion to modern minds, which make a sharp distinction between the world of daily life and the otherworld, the ancients made few such distinctions. We read of 'gateways to the underworld' in various parts of Greece, and the distance between upper and lower worlds was as narrow as the skin of the Earth's surface itself; so offerings to the underworld deities could be made by simply sacrificing an animal over a pit, and letting the blood drain straight down through the surface to the infernal deities below. The idea, then, that the identical River Styx ran in both Arcadia and the underworld should no more surprise us than the idea of a Titan deity marrying a personified river. And, as Pausanias himself

---

26 Pausanias, 8.17.6-8.18.6 (1933: p.431-435).

remarks, Hesiod tells us that the River Styx, daughter of Ocean, was the wife of the Titan Pallas, as we've seen above.

As usual, we have no definite story here, but some suggestive and tantalising fragments. It seems likely that there was an Arcadian tradition that Selene was born in that country after the advent of human beings (this would seem to be presupposed by the Arcadians' claim to be *proselenoi*) and possibly to a human parent. Her father Pallas may have been the son of Lycaon, and so once again gives us a connection to a stream of otherworldly wisdom. And it seems quite possible that the Arcadian Pallas has in turn become confused and identified with the Titan Pallas, husband of the Styx and father of Eos. Or perhaps the two were identical from the start, and only became separated in the hands of later authors.

3.2.3 Basileia and Tethys. Of the last two genealogical stories (1.2.6, 1.2.7) there is little that can be added. Diodorus' story of Selene and Helios as offspring of Basileia is one of the many stories that he obviously took from another author to use in his compilation but, as is often the case, he gives no details of his source. From the fact that the story is both euhemerising (*i.e.*, it propounds the view that 'gods' were once normal human beings who, because of their achievements or outstanding characteristics, were later deified) and allegorising, we can perhaps place its time of origin between about 300 BCE and 30 BCE when Diodorus finished his *Library*. Similarly, the fact that the story takes place in 'Atlantis' means that it must post-date Plato, who died in 347 BCE. In other words, the story is from the Hellenistic period, long after Selene's mythology originated, and might possibly even derive from an Alexandrian novel. That the character of Basileia herself is connected with the Anatolian Goddess Cybele could (though not necessarily) point to an origin among the Hellenistic cities in Asia Minor; although by this time Cybele was becoming an international Goddess. We might also note that the story gives us another attempt to explain the difference between Mene and Selene, and the relative priorities of the two names.

One would have thought it transparently obvious that this late story had little relevance to the original mythology of Selene, but that hasn't stopped it causing confusion. Savignoni mentions an ancient relief from Attica representing Echelos and Basile, and refers to Basile as 'the mother of Helios and Selene'.[27] Basile is also known as Basileia, and one has to assume that Savignoni (and his sources) is attempting to identify her with the Basileia mentioned by Diodorus. The identification is unsupportable: Echelos and Basile are of that class of semi-deity known as hero and heroine and, as Larson points out, the inscription accompanying the relief actually reads 'Iasile', not 'Basile'. Furthermore, while there was a Basile who was known to have a cult in Attica, it has been argued that Basile and Basileia are not identical either.[28] This notion is perhaps best regarded as one of those interesting but fruitless side-tracks.

Lastly, Claudian's very late (4th century CE) variant, making the sea-Goddess Tethys the nurse of Helios and Selene, adds nothing to our knowledge of the genealogy: they are the offspring of Hyperion by an unidentified mother. Yet the tale is of some interest because Tethys is the wife of Ocean; and we have already seen a connection between Selene and the world-encircling Ocean stream. This tale may be seen as strengthening that connection.

## 3.3 Selene's Offspring

The first three tales of Selene's children (1.3.1–3, Pandia, Ersa and the Horae), while not without interest, are probably more to be seen as 'poetic fancies' than true mythological stories.

3.3.1 Pandia. Pandia's tale is very briefly told, in the *Homeric Hymn to Selene*, a hymn which has already been discussed in some detail in section 2.3.1. This is the standard source, and other versions of the story appearing later in the literature which has come down to us in the normal way (such as the very abbreviated reference in

---

27 Savignoni 1899: pp.265-272. The story is discussed on page 271, with further references.

28 Larson 1995: pp.38, 149, 169, 171.

Hyginus' *Fabulae*²⁹) quite obviously derive from this. The tale, in its entirety, is this: 'Once the Son of Cronos [Zeus] was joined with her in love; and she conceived and bare a daughter Pandia, exceedingly lovely amongst the deathless gods'.³⁰

Kerenyi tells us that the meaning of Pandia is 'the entirely shining' or 'the entirely bright',³¹ so the name is appropriate enough for a daughter of Selene. However, Allen and Sikes were rather more ruthless with the material, telling us that Pandia is elsewhere unknown as a daughter of Selene, that the point of introducing her here is not apparent, and that she seems to be merely an abstraction of 'all-shining Selene' herself. They also point out, quite properly, that there is no connection between Selene's daughter and the Attic festival of Zeus known as the Pandia (another false trail over which a certain amount of ink has been spilled).³²

Charles Boer suggests that the *Homeric Hymns* to Helios and Selene are very late, perhaps the latest of all of the hymns, and may well date to the Alexandrian period (post 300 BCE).³³ We know that by this time it had also become feasible to identify Zeus with the Sun,³⁴ so it seems quite possible that the story of Pandia is to be explained as a 'poetic way' of saying that when the Moon is 'impregnated' with the light of the Sun, so the Moonlight (the 'all-bright' Pandia) shines out as a result; in other words, the simple astronomical principle that the Moon shines by the Sun's reflected light, here personified.

---

29 Hyginus, *Fabulae*, Preface 1960: p.26.

30 *Homeric Hymn XXII – To Selene*, ll.14-16 (in *Hesiod* 1914: p.461).

31 Kerenyi 1951 pp.197.

32 Allen & Sikes, 1904 [via *Perseus Project* web-page]. West 2003 p.19, points out that a woman called Pandia was the wife of Antiochus, eponymous hero of the Antiochid *phyle* at Athens, and thus conjectures an Attic origin for this story. Given the probably Hellenistic, Alexandrian origin of the hymn, this seems far less likely than a simple coincidence of names.

33 Boer 1979: p.iii.

34 Numerous references to Zeus' identification with the Sun are collected in Cook 1914: Vol. 1, pp.186-195.

As usual, of course, there is a complicating factor here, which is a recently discovered papyrus fragment of the poet Philodamus. This contains a quotation attributed to Musaeus who, as we have seen (1.3.7, and further discussion at 13.3.4) was said to be a son of Selene. In this fragment, though, Musaeus claims to be the son of Pandia, daughter of Zeus and Semele.[35] 'Semele' need not detain us here; it is a very common scribal or copyist's error, both in antiquity and more recently, for Selene. The only known offspring of Zeus and Semele is Dionysus, and there is no other record of Pandia in such a context. As an example of a similar error, we find that Cicero, discussing the various genealogies of Dionysus, mentions one where he is the offspring of 'Jupiter and Luna', where Luna, translating Selene into Latin, is obviously an error for Semele, who is otherwise not mentioned at all by Cicero, despite appearing as the mother in the most famous Dionysiac story of all.[36]

If we then read the story as 'Musaeus, son of Pandia, daughter of Zeus and Selene', there are two points of interest here. The first is the literal text, which provides us with a variant genealogy (otherwise unexplained) of Musaeus, and a meagre expansion to the tale of Pandia. The second is the date, for if there is one certain dating in the life of Philodamus, it's that one of his poems was written around 340 BCE. This would thus take the story of Pandia, daughter of Selene, back before the Alexandrine period; but how far back seems impossible to say.

3.3.2 Ersa. We seem to have a similar process in operation with Ersa (or Herse) as with Pandia. Again we have little more than this fragment of 'poetic fancy', describing Ersa as the daughter Zeus and Selene, and no reason to connect this Ersa with the daughter of Cecrops, of the same name and spelling, mentioned in relation to the ritual of the Arrhephoria at Athens. Our Ersa here seems to be

---

35 Parke 1992: p.188.

36 Cicero, *De Natura Deorum*, 3.23 (58) (1933: p.343). Similar confusions of Selene and Semele in other ancient authors, including Ulpian and Eusebius, are listed in Cook 1914: Vol. 1, p.457.

nothing more than a personification of the dew itself. Taking Zeus as the God of the sky, what Alcman seems to be expressing is simply that on clear nights when the Moon is shining, dew can be expected to fall.

3.3.3 The Seasons (Horae). As was pointed out at 1.3.3, this tale connecting the Seasons with Selene and Helios is a very late variant on the usual tale of their origin. As with the previous cases, we seem once again to have a 'poetic' description of natural phenomena. Time is basically measured according to the movements of the Sun (days) and the Moon (months): as such, they are obvious 'parents' for the four Seasons, for without the movements of time there are no seasons. This parentage fits well enough with the same sort of incestuous relationship we have previously seen posited between the Sun and Moon, but it seems more likely that Quintus Smyrnaeus was simply thinking in astronomical and temporal terms here.

A similar concept is found in Plutarch, although here the incestuous tale is directed more to the monthly growth of Moonlight than the birth of the Seasons, and the context makes it plain that the notion is poetical: 'natural philosophers assert that the Sun loves the Moon and that they unite and propagate.'[37]

3.3.4 Narcissus. The best known form of the story of Narcissus is that given by Ovid, which makes him the son of the river-God Cephisus and the Nymph Liriope. Narcissus was said to be extremely handsome, but rejected the advances of girls and Nymphs (and in some versions men as well); in particular those of Echo, whose rejection caused her to fade away until she was nothing but a voice. One of his rejected lovers prayed to heaven, and the Goddess Nemesis arranged that Narcissus should see his own image reflected in a stream and fall in love with it. Thereafter he became indifferent to everything else and died, the flower bearing his name springing up on the spot where he had passed away.[38]

---

37 Plutarch, *Of Love*, 24 (770A) (1961: Vol. 9 p.433).
38 Ovid, *Metamorphoses* 3.339-510 (1916: Vol. 1, pp.149-161).

We've seen above (1.3.4), however, that Nonnos, writing in the 5th century CE has two passages suggesting that Narcissus was the son of Selene and Endymion, and it's now time to examine these references in more detail. The second of these passages is the most interesting, and probably gives us a better insight into the way that Nonnos thought.

The context of this passage is that Dionysus, wishing to seduce the prudish maiden Aura (a follower of Artemis), magically creates a fountain of purple wine in the mountains, and surrounds it with flowers, particularly the narcissus. It's in the description of the spring that Nonnos gives us the passage 'There were the clustering blooms which have the name of Narcissus the fair youth, whom horned Selene's bridegroom Endymion begat on leafy Latmos, Narcissus who long ago gazed on his own image formed in the water, that dumb image of a beautiful deceiver, and died as he gazed on the shadowy phantom of his shape.' Aura arrives at the spring at midday, drinks, and as a result falls into a deep sleep. Dionysus then ravishes her while she sleeps, and we are told: 'Sleep [Hypnos] embraced the body of Aura with overshadowing wings, and he was marshal of the wedding for Bacchos [Dionysus], for he also had experience of love, he is the yokefellow of the Moon [Selene], he is companion of the Loves in nightly caresses. So the wedding was like a dream.'[39]

It has to be recalled, of course, that Nonnos is not an ancient mythographer but an extremely late and highly baroque poet; nonetheless, he obviously has a compendious store of mythological motifs to hand, and there are a number of interesting contextual features surrounding the actual material on Narcissus. We may note that the encounter of Aura and Dionysus takes place on a hill, out in the wild countryside, and that Aura drinks and falls asleep at midday; we will see this to be a liminal point when 'time stands still' in our discussion of the 'hour of Pan' (12.3.1), and also that in certain versions of his tale, Epimenides fell asleep at noon (7.3). Again, our

---

39 Nonnos, *Dionysiaca*, 48.570-645 (1940: Vol. 3, p.467-471).

second quotation from this passage unites Sleep (Hypnos) with Selene, dreaming and nocturnal sexual activity in ways that remind us very much of the Endymion story. Undoubtedly these resonances were consciously intended by Nonnos, particularly after his mention of Selene and Endymion in relation to Narcissus.

The question remains, though, as to why Nonnos makes particular mention of the narcissus flower, and mentions its eponym Narcissus as the Latmian offspring of Endymion, 'Selene's bridegroom'. The answer seems to be that Nonnos is deriving the meaning of the word *narkissos* (to give it the original Greek spelling) from the verb *narkao* (to grow stiff, numb or dead) or the noun *narke* (stiffness, numbness, equivalent to the Latin *torpor*), and is thus referring to the plant's *narcotic* properties. Whether this is a legitimate etymology is perhaps open to question. As L.R. Palmer points out, names and place-names ending in *–issos* are taken to be indications of a pre-Greek, Anatolian origin.[40] *Narkissos*/Narcissus may thus not be an Indo-European Greek word, and deriving its meaning from Greek words such as *narkao* or *narke* may be erroneous. Admittedly, such questions may not be particularly relevant here, as Nonnos is engaged in poetic invention rather than etymology.

Pliny, in the 1st century CE, illustrates the point further in his *Natural History*, where he says that, used as medicine, the narcissus 'causes a dull headache, its name being derived from the word "narce", torpor, and not from the youth (Narcissus) in the myth.' He also tells us that 'the root of each variety has the taste of honey wine.'[41] All this makes it a very appropriate plant to be growing by the wine-spring that Dionysus is going to use to put Aura to sleep.

Given all this, it is perhaps not surprising that Nonnos chooses to make Narcissus the offspring of Endymion. Although, in Nonnos' lengthy work, it is often hard to tell whether he is thinking of Selene and Endymion as conscious, married lovers, or treating Endymion

---

40 Palmer: 1980 p.9.
41 Pliny, *Natural History* 21.75 (128-129) (1951: Vol. 6, pp.255-257).

as asleep, in this case it is obviously the latter scenario that he has in mind. Narcissus, mentioned here for the resonance of his 'narcotic' name, is very appropriately portrayed as the son of Endymion, the embodiment of eternal sleep.

In this passage, it's not absolutely explicit that Selene is the mother of Narcissus, though as Endymion is mentioned as 'Selene's bridegroom' and Narcissus is begotten on Latmos it is at least heavily implied. Nor is it absolutely explicit that Selene is the mother in Nonnos' other reference to Narcissus, and in this case Endymion is not mentioned as the father either. In this passage, Dionysus approaches a young boy called Ampelos and is so impressed by his beauty that he questions him as to his parentage, listing a number of possible divine parents before concluding 'I recognise your blood even if you wish to hide it; Selene slept with Helios and brought you to birth wholly like the gracious Narcissus; for you have a like heavenly beauty, the image of horned Selene.'[42]

Again, this passage is a little confusing. There seems to be an implication that Selene is the mother of Narcissus, who has inherited her beauty; however the passage has to be read that 'Selene slept with Helios and brought *Ampelos* to birth'. This, of course, is primarily flattery rather than mythology (neither Nonnos nor Dionysus intend this parentage of Ampelos to be taken seriously; it's simply a conceit), and Selene and Helios are being cited here as types of beauty. It's hardly likely that Nonnos intended us to think here that Helios and Selene were the parents, *together*, of Narcissus, even if Selene may be implied as his mother. Additionally, it has to be remembered that Endymion was also regarded as a type of masculine beauty, and thus would be a suitable candidate as Narcissus' father.

Taking these two passages together, and bearing in mind the above qualifications, we can perhaps argue that, to Nonnos, Selene was the mother and Endymion the father of Narcissus. Whether anyone else believed the same, or even whether Nonnos himself

---

42 Nonnos, *Dionysiaca*, 10.213-216 (1940: Vol. 1, p.343).

took such an idea seriously, rather than a poetic conceit, is perhaps a moot point. There is, however, one small piece of corroborative evidence, though again it is from a very late, Byzantine source. A.B. Cook quotes a poem by Konstantinos Manasses of the 12th century CE which discusses the various minerals and flowers attributed to the planetary deities. The relevant lines are: 'Clear as crystal was Selene's light' and 'Selene, a narcissus with fair petals'. This mention of the narcissus as the flower of Selene is also, apparently, repeated by other Byzantine authors.[43] It may not demonstrate that the Byzantines regarded the mythological Narcissus as the son of Selene, but the connection is at least of interest.

3.3.5 The Nemean Lion. The first of the 12 Labours of Heracles was the destruction of the Nemean Lion, the hide of which was invulnerable to weapons. Heracles squeezed the beast to death and then skinned it with its own claws, after which he used the skin as a form of armour.[44]

As we've seen above (1.3.6), Selene is said to have either given birth to the Nemean Lion, or to have magically created it from a chest of foam and froth. 'Foam of the Moon' (*aphroselenos*) was a notorious magical ingredient in the ancient world, most often said to be gathered by witches during nights of the eclipsed Moon. I have examined the subject of *aphroselenos* in considerable detail elsewhere;[45] however, much of the evidence discussed in that article is not strictly mythological, and only the material relevant to the Nemean Lion will be reproduced here. It is, indeed, the story that Selene created the Lion from foam that gives us our clearest clue as to her relationship with the beast, rather than the more simplified tale that she actually gave birth to it. However, let us deal with the latter story first.

---

43 Cook 1914: Vol. 1, pp.625-626 (quoting Manasses, *Comp. Chron.* 113-114).
44 Kirk 1974: p.184.
45 Moore 1995: pp.216-245.

Steve Moore

The tale that Selene gave birth to the Lion comes from a verse, quoted above at 1.3.6, attributed to Epimenides, who lived (if he lived at all – we shall have more to say on Epimenides below) in the 7th century BCE. It might be thought that the story could be interpreted astronomically, as some of the previous tales have been: that we have to do here with a 'horror-story' hinging on an unnatural reversal of fact. Such an allegorising interpretation would run along the following lines: that instead of being passively illuminated by the Sun, the Moon is here bringing forth her own light in the form of a lion, an animal of known solar attributes. The true nature of the Moon as a solid body illumined by the Sun, however, was not known until the 5th century BCE. Such an allegorical interpretation would, of course, be possible if the poem attributed to Epimenides was actually a later creation 'fathered' on the earlier poet; particularly if the later, actual author was attempting a 'simplified' explanation of an earlier tradition that had Selene construct the Lion from foam.

Unfortunately, we have no real way of dating the 'foam' tradition. The work *On Rivers* that contains the story is thought to be falsely attributed to Plutarch, of the 2nd century CE; which means that we have no idea of the real author and so cannot date the work as a whole. The story itself is quoted from the *History of Heracles* by Demodocus, but the only other Demodocus we know of is a fictitious minstrel mentioned by Homer in the *Odyssey*, and although it appears that attempts were made to attribute the *History of Heracles* to that same minstrel, this is hardly reliable evidence, and insufficient grounds for arguing that the 'foam' tradition is anywhere near as early as the Homeric period. Nonetheless, it does provide us with the most satisfactory explanation of Selene's connection with the Lion.

As we have seen above, Selene was also said to be the mother of Ersa, the dew. However, moving away from the actual personification, we find that the Greeks used two words to refer to normal, physically-occurring dew: *erse (ersa)* and *drosos*. I have argued that there are connections between the conception of *aphroselenos* and

## Selene

dew.[46] However, the words *erse* and *drosos* were also used to refer to young animals, and in particular to young lions. In this story, then, we seem to have a case of magical magnification. Normally, Selene is productive of dew and, by punning association, lion-cubs; here, dew is replaced by the virulent, magical Moon-foam and, associated with this, we find springing forth a full-grown, monstrous lion.[47]

The remaining 'minor' myths regarding Selene's offspring listed in section 1.3 are best discussed in the context of her most important tales, concerning Endymion and Pan. It's now time to turn our attention to these.

---

46 Moore 1995: pp.227-228.
47 Moore 1995: p.228, with the references collected there.

Chapter Four

# The Loves Of Goddesses

## 4.1 Introduction

The story of Selene's love for Endymion, whatever unique elements it may contain, is far from standing alone among the Greek myths. Although less common than tales of Gods seducing human women, there are a number of stories where Goddesses took mortal lovers, and these deserve our attention for whatever light they may shed on the major myth regarding Selene, her encounter with Endymion on Mount Latmos (1.5.2).

Encounters with Goddesses could have their dangers, of course. The hunter Actaeon, having spied upon Artemis bathing in a spring, was devoured by his own hunting dogs; the seer Tiresias was struck blind (in one version of the tale) for having seen Athene naked. And, as we'll see below, Tithonus the lover of Eos fared none too well. It would be easy to jump to a gender-related conclusion here, that these stories reflect masculine fears of the fatal or emasculating consequences of female sexuality; but this would be rather too simplistic. Actaeon and Tiresias were punished as much for breaches of divine protocol than anything else; Tithonus' tale highlights the differences and intersections between mortality and immortality. Gods could be just as dangerous to human women (so Semele, tricked into asking to see Zeus in all his glory, was burned to death as a result); but equally, men could have perfectly safe and productive relationships with Goddesses, as Odysseus did with Athene throughout the *Odyssey*, or the Latin king Numa did with the Nymph/Goddess Egeria. As always, such 'monolithic' theories (rarely fashionable for more than a decade or two), while useful in one or two cases, have to be used with caution; otherwise they simply throw light on the theory and its users, rather than the subject-matter in hand.

While it's useful to look for common factors in the following stories, each of them should be treated individually, and examined for the particular illuminations they can provide us with; for to see how the story of Selene and Endymion is *unlike* the story of, say, Eos and Tithonus, may be as useful an insight to us as what they *do* have in common.

If, at this early stage, there is any one conclusion to be drawn from the tales of Actaeon, Tiresias and Tithonus, then probably the safest is one that is simple and basic, yet none the less important. It is that, to the Greeks, the deities (both male and female) could be capricious and had agendas of their own; that their actions and morals were not necessarily subject to the same evaluations that we, as humans, would make of other humans (the idea that God, or Gods, should be 'good' is rather a late development); and that they had the superior powers to carry out their whims regardless of human desires. In a word, the Gods and Goddesses were not human but *'other'*; and that, given our tendency to look back on the classical tradition and see the Greek Gods as 'made by man in his own image', is a point that deserves to be emphasised repeatedly.

## 4.2 Eos And Her Lovers

Being generally regarded as the sister of Selene and Helios, it's appropriate to begin this survey with Eos, the Goddess of the Dawn; particularly so as the tale of Eos and Tithonus offers the most significant parallels with that of Selene and Endymion. With these two points in mind, it may be well to afford Eos a slightly deeper treatment than the other Goddesses in this chapter.

4.2.1 Eos Herself. As we've seen, Hesiod makes Eos the sister of Helios and Selene, and so the daughter of Theia and Hyperion.[1] He then continues the genealogy by uniting Eos with Astraeus ('Starry'), the son of the Titans Crius and Eurybia, by whom she bore the three winds, Zephyrus, Boreas and Notus, and then Eosphorus (the Morning-Star) and all the stars.[2] Apollodorus follows suit.[3] However, as seen above at 1.2.3, *The Homeric Hymn to Helios* lists the same three offspring, Helios, Selene and Eos, but makes their parents Hyperion and his sister Euryphaëssa.[4] Unsurprisingly, we're back in the world of multiple variants. Again, Ovid, calls Aurora (Eos) 'Pallantis', *i.e.*, the 'daughter of Pallas'.[5] One's immediate thought here would be that this would be that Pallas mentioned by Hesiod, the son of Crius and Eurybia and brother of Astraeus. As this would result in Eos marrying her uncle, it's perhaps better to leave these as variant traditions, rather than attempt an identification; besides, we've already seen the confusion surrounding 'Selene daughter of Pallas' (3.2.2) and here we have even less material with which to attempt any clarification. However, it seems possible that Ovid may be referring to the same Arcadian tradition that makes Selene the daughter of Pallas; for if Eos is the sister of Selene, one has to think that her father would also be Pallas. Whether Pallas or Hyperion is the father, though, the fact remains that Selene and Eos are sisters, and so we may not be too surprised if they share certain elements of their stories.

Naturally, Eos is portrayed, like all the Goddesses, as a beautiful and eternally youthful woman. Her favoured epithets

---

1 Hesiod, *Theogony*, ll.371-374 (1914: p.107).
2 Hesiod, *Theogony*, ll.378-382 (1914: p.107).
3 Apollodorus, *The Library*, 1.2.2-4 (1921: Vol. 1, p.13).
4 *Homeric Hymn XXI – To Helios*, ll.1-6 (in *Hesiod* 1914: p.459).
5 Ovid, *Metamorphoses*, 9.421 (1916: Vol. 2, p.33).

in Homer are 'rosy-fingered' and 'saffron-robed', both of which undoubtedly refer to the colours of the Sun-illuminated clouds at dawn. Like Helios and Selene, she is also shown as a chariot driver, and like Selene, her chariot is a *biga*, drawn by two horses (colts, not mares). Homer gives us the horses' names: Lampus and Phaethon ('Shiner' and 'Blazer').[6] In Greek vase paintings she often appears driving a chariot, particularly when her appearance is purely representational; that is, when she appears as representing 'Dawn', in the same way that Helios and Selene appear as representing 'Sun' and 'Moon'. In narrative pictures, particularly those that show her abducting handsome young men, the chariot is frequently discarded, and Eos appears winged, carrying off her lovers in her arms.[7]

4.2.2 Eos the Nymphomaniac. Merely from the Hesiodic genealogy given in the previous section, we see that Eos is credited with considerably more in the way of offspring than Selene. Like Selene, though, virtually all of Eos' stories revolve around sexual encounters of some sort. Both Goddesses have visible, cosmological functions: Goddess of the Moon or Bringer of the Dawn-light, but when we look at the actual narratives in which they appear, these functions appear to be virtually irrelevant.

Apollodorus tells us that a vengeful Aphrodite caused Eos to be perpetually in love, because she'd discovered Eos sleeping with Ares.[8] As a result, Eos became notorious for carrying off handsome young men and sleeping with them (and the tales always centre on the abduction of mortals, rather than Gods). She carried off the hunter Orion to Delos, where he was ultimately slain by Artemis (for variant reasons, and by variant methods); Cephalus (son of Hermes and Herse, the daughter of Cecrops, not Selene), by whom she had a son Phaethon (obviously not the same Phaethon who

---

6 Homer, *Odyssey* 23.246 (1919: Vol. 2, p.391).

7 See, for example, Vermeule 1979: pp.165-166.

8 Apollodorus, *The Library*, 1.4.4 (1921: Vol. 1, p.33).

was son of Helios, and drove his father's chariot with disastrous results) who, as a boy, was carried off in turn by Aphrodite to be a 'keeper of her shrine by night' (Apollodorus gives a much more genealogical variant, where the son of Eos and Cephalus is Tithonus, whose son in turn is Phaethon). And, most notably, Eos carried off Tithonus to the land of 'Ethiopia' (where the Sun rises), and by him had two sons, Memnon (later king of the Ethiopians) and Emathion.[9] Memnon, according to a fragment of the epic, *The Aethiopis*, was eventually slain by Achilles during the Trojan War, after which Eos obtained from Zeus the gift of immortality for him; presumably in the afterlife.[10]

Homer, in the *Odyssey*, mentions another of Eos' abductees, Cleitus, whose lineage ties in with the seer-tradition that will often be seen in the material under discussion here. Homer's genealogy is a little confusing and (unsurprisingly) shows variants to other sources. It begins with the seer Melampus, who had two sons, Antiphates and Mantius. Antiphates was the father of Oicles, who in turn fathered Amphiaraus (for discussion of whose dream oracle, see **10.3**) who, in turn, fathered Alcmaeon and Amphilochus (also the possessor of a dream oracle). Mantius, whose name obviously derives from *mantis*, a seer or prophet (although confusingly said by Homer to be Amphiaraus' brother, rather than uncle) was the father of Polypheides and Cleitus: 'Now Cleitus golden-throned Dawn [Eos] snatched away by reason of his beauty, that he might dwell with the immortals; but of Polypheides, high of heart, Apollo made a seer, far the best of mortals, after that Amphiaraus was dead.'[11] Cleitus, in turn, was the grandfather of another famous seer, Polyidus. While these genealogies obviously deal with

---

9 Apollodorus, 1.4.4-5 (1921: Vol. 1, p.33); 1.9.4 (Vol. 1, p.79); 3.12.4-5 (Vol. 2, p.43); 3.14.3 (Vol. 2, p.83). Hesiod, *Theogony*, ll.984-991 (1914: p.153).

10 Proclus, *Chrestomathia*, 2 (in *Hesiod* 1914: p.507). For Eos mourning Memnon (but without mention of his immortalisation), see also Quintus Smyrnaeus 2.549-666 (1913: pp.107-115).

11 Homer, *Odyssey* 15.240ff (1919: Vol. 2, p.93).

mythical characters, there was a long-standing tradition, existing until at least the 3rd century BCE, of seers claiming a direct lineage from Melampus and other soothsayers. The main 'families' of seers were the Melampodidae (descended from Melampus), the Clytiadae (from Cleitus, himself descended from Melampus), the Iamidae (from Iamus, son of Apollo), and the Telliadae (from Tellias). Strangely, the last three of these families originated in Elis, the scene of one version of the Endymion myth.[12]

The most notable mythological narrative we have of Eos and her lovers, though, is the story of the Trojan Tithonus, son of Laomedon. Homer, our oldest source, while mentioning Eos' abduction of Cleitus and Orion,[13] has no actual narrative of Tithonus' abduction or its consequences. Instead, we have what sounds like a poetical commonplace for daybreak: 'Now Dawn [Eos] arose from her couch beside lordly Tithonus, to bear light to the immortals and to mortal men ...'[14] When we turn to the *Homeric Hymn to Aphrodite*,[15] however, we get a rather fuller version. Here we learn that Eos abducted Tithonus and asked Zeus to free him from death and give him eternal life, which was granted. Eos, though, forgot to ask for eternal youth as well. So while Tithonus remained young he lived rapturously with Eos 'by the streams of Ocean, at the ends of the earth'. But when the first grey hairs appeared, Eos kept away from his bed, though she cherished him in her house, fed him ambrosia and gave him rich clothing. But when he grew extremely aged, and could no longer move his limbs,[16] she decided to place him in a room and shut the doors, where now,

---

12 Flower 2008: pp.39, 42.

13 Homer, *Odyssey* 5.121ff (1919: Vol. 1, p.179).

14 Homer, *Odyssey* 5.1ff (1919: Vol. 1, p.171).

15 *Homeric Hymn V – To Aphrodite*, ll.218-238 (in *Hesiod* 1914: pp.421-423).

16 Thus Evelyn-White's translation in *Hesiod* 1914: p.423. Emily Vermeule points out that the Greek is rather more coarse: rather than Tithonus being unable to 'move his limbs' the original tells us Eos abandoned him when he could no longer 'get it up'. Vermeule 1979: pp.164.

completely lacking in strength, he simply lays there and babbles endlessly. Later authors, such as Hellanicus and Servius provide us with a tailpiece, whereby Tithonus becomes so shrunken that he's transformed into a cicada, his babbling similarly transformed into the insect's chirruping.[17]

There are variants to all these tales, of course. Late authors such as Ovid and Antoninus Liberalis bring Eos' abduction of Cephalus (son of Hermes and Herse) into what was probably a completely separate tale of another Cephalus (son of Deion). Here, although carried off, Cephalus rejects the love of Eos in favour of his wife Procris; angry, Eos returns him to earth, but proposes a test of Procris' fidelity, with unhappy results for all concerned.[18] The story of Orion's death, and its cause, has multitudinous variants, most of which centre on his amorous intentions toward Artemis. Homer, however, attributes the death more to the abduction by Eos, when he has Calypso claim that, loose-moralled though the Olympian Gods might be, they were outraged at Eos' conduct in sleeping with Orion, and so persuaded Artemis to shoot him.[19] Again, it's been pointed out that, at least in representations on vase-paintings, there seems to be a certain amount of iconographic confusion between the characters of Orion and Cephalus anyway.[20] Nonetheless, we've now covered the essential mythic narratives, and it's time to turn our attention to their significance.

4.2.3 Interpretations of Eos. Eos is sometimes 'explained' as being the Indian Vedic Dawn-Goddess, Ushas. Philologically, Eos and Ushas do appear to be cognate, and there are a number of details common to the iconography and function of both Goddesses that suggest a common, Indo-European origin.[21]

---

17 Gantz 1993: Vol. 1, pp.36-37.

18 Ovid, *Metamorphoses*, 7.690ff (1916: Vol. 1, pp.391ff). Antoninus Liberalis, 41 (1992: p.101-102).

19 Homer, *Odyssey* 5.121ff (1919: Vol. 1, p.179).

20 Griffiths 1986: p.58-70 (p.66).

21 West 2007: pp.217-227.

Such an origin, it appears, cannot certainly be demonstrated for Selene, and it's notable that in India the Moon is represented by a masculine God, Chandra. If then, the trinity of Helios, Selene and Eos is a conglomeration of deities who may not share their origins in the same tradition, we may wish to treat the Eos/Ushas material with slightly more caution than otherwise.

Ushas is said to be the daughter of Heaven and sister of Night; she is also said to be the sister or wife of the Sun. Clad in crimson robes and veiled in gold (again, we have the colours of the dawn, and in this we have an iconographic similarity to Eos), she is portrayed as a beautiful bride. She wakes sleepers from seeming death and brings light and wealth. Ever young herself (being born every day), she is immortal yet brings age to men, who disappear one after another while she remains undying (and this may have some relevance to the Tithonus story). She drives a shining chariot drawn by seven ruddy cows or horses. Actual mythological narratives, however, appear to be lacking for Ushas; and, as Wilkins remarks, 'in the later writings we find merely the name of Ushas'.[22] There are certainly no Vedic narratives regarding Ushas that could be equated with those of Tithonus or Cephalus,[23] so these tales may well have originated in the Greek world.

Perhaps this 'Indo-European' conception (Sun-God paired with Dawn-Goddess, Moon-God masculine) is reflected in Homer, where there are mentions of the personified Sun (Hyperion, rather than Helios) and the dawn (Eos), but where 'Selene' refers only to the physical Moon, rather than the personified Goddess. The Homeric poems, of course, were written in the Ionic dialect, while the vast majority of the material discussed here about Selene and related matters appears to originate in a different cultural area: the Cretan-Carian-Arcadian area. Disentangling cultural, linguistic

---

22 *Inter alia*, see Dowson 1972: *s.v.* Ushas, pp.327-328. Ions 1967: pp.21-22. Wilkins 1882: pp.48-52.

23 West 2007: pp.224-225.

or racial elements in the spaghetti of Greek society is difficult, of course, but the variant terminology and emphasis in Homer is at least suggestive.

Before turning our attention to the essential meaning of the most developed Eos story, that of Tithonus, we should, perhaps, look at the cicada element. As mentioned above, this 'tailpiece' to the story survives only in a fragment of Hellanicus, and in Servius; not appearing in the major retellings of the story, it might be thought of less relevance, or simply an example of Greek playfulness in likening Tithonus' babbling to the chirruping of a cicada. But the cicada is rather more interesting than this.

In a lengthy and fascinating article on the cicada in ancient Greece,[24] Rory B. Egan collects a number of ancient beliefs about the insect and its symbolism. As the cicada spends its nymph stage (lasting months or years) burrowing in the earth, and then emerges to shed its original skin and sprout wings for the final, grasshopper-like stage of its life, it was regarded as being either 'born from the earth' or capable of resurrection, and thus an appropriate symbol of immortality. Again, in the final stage of its life-cycle, it was thought to live on dew, or dew and air. As Boedeker points out, the cicada was thought to pass no excrement, and this, in turn, is said to be a characteristic of men of the Golden Age, reflecting their closeness to the Gods, who also abstain from terrestrial food.[25] And both Boedeker and Egan draw attention to Plato's dialogue, *Phaedrus*, where (besides making it plain that the cicada represents the soul) we find a story that when the Muses first introduced music to men, the first musicians devoted themselves entirely to the art and forgot to eat or drink, with the obvious result that they wasted away; the Muses rewarded their devotion by turning them into cicadas.

We have a complex of beliefs here, with considerable relevance

---

24 Egan 1994.
25 Boedeker 1984: p.44.

to our subject-matter. While there is an obvious, surface linkage between the babbling of Tithonus and the call of the cicadas, we also see that transformation into a cicada can be interpreted as reinforcing the idea of Tithonus' immortality. The cicadas' diet of dew and lack of excrement, along with their implicit immortality, will have some relevance when we come to examine the story of the longevitous Epimenides, who also existed without mortal food and lacked excrement (7.5). And, as Egan points out, the tale of the musicians who became cicadas suggests 'that they are disembodied souls who have achieved a higher level of knowledge than the needs of their physical bodies would normally allow for.' This matter of supernal knowledge obtained from the deities is another area we shall have cause to examine in more detail as we progress.

Emily Vermeule makes a number of interesting comments on Eos and her abductions.[26] To summarise briefly, she points out that dawn represents the end of sleep, and the awakening to a new day; but that Eos' abductions also represent 'waking to a new life' among the immortals. More importantly, she also points out that Greek funerals (whether cremation or inhumation) took place at night, so as not to pollute the living and the day, and were timed to conclude at dawn, at which point the Dawn Goddess carried off the soul 'on the wings of the morning'; an idea reflected in the tales of the abduction of young men like Tithonus or Cephalos who, once carried off, are 'no longer of this world'.[27] This may at first seem an interesting insight, and brings to mind the tale of Selene and Endymion as, being asleep forever and never waking, Endymion is also, to all intents and purposes, in precisely the same condition as being dead.

However, while it must be admitted that there is a comforting overtone to the notion that the dead man has been transported, not to the grey underworld of Hades, but to the loving embrace of

---

26 Vermeule 1979: pp.162-165.
27 Vermeule 1979: pp.165, 166, 176.

a Goddess, Lefkowitz rightly points out that the tales of Tithonus and Cephalos do not end happily.[28] Indeed, as we'll see from the following tales, being loved by a Goddess is frequently a risky business. Among the lovers of Eos, Orion ends up being killed, while Tithonus ends up immortal but impotently aged. Regarding the fate of Cephalos son of Hermes and Herse we have no details, though Cephalos son of Deion, rejecting the love of Eos, escapes with his life but with his marriage ruined (and in one variant, with a dead wife). Of Cleitus we hear nothing bad, which may in itself merely reflect an absence of evidence; yet it's notable that Cleitus is of the family of Melampid seers, and our investigation of the myth of Selene and Endymion will lead us deeply into the area of seers and oracles. As we'll see, one possible conjecture, suggested by the case of Cleitus, is that a 'safe and productive relationship' with Goddesses is to be found through visions and oracles; but this is a subject to which we'll return below.

Obviously Vermeule's 'funerary insight' hardly provides a complete explanation for everything going on in the tales of Eos' abductions, however. Similarly, her witty if rather frivolous portrayal of the story of Tithonus as a 'sexual joke' (the 'witless Dawn' seeking an immortal lover, while forgetting to keep him young, and discarding him when he can no longer 'get it up'), while true in one sense, surely misses a much more important point, as do modern interpretations influenced by contemporary concerns regarding sexual politics that interpret the story as providing a strongly negative message about (human) female sexuality (comprehensively refuted by Lefkowitz[29]).

The main subject matter of the story of Eos and Tithonus would appear to me to be the apparently unbridgeable gulf between mortal mankind and the immortal Gods. The essence of deity for the Greeks was that the Gods and Goddesses were *both* immortal

---

28 Lefkowitz 2002, pp.334-335.
29 Lefkowitz 2002, *passim*.

and ageless, in contrast to men, who were neither. Some mortals, such as Heracles and Dionysus, did indeed cross the boundary and become Gods; but in such cases it's notable that while they may have been born mortal, of a mortal mother, the father was a God (in both these examples, Zeus). Tithonus had no such divine parentage; nor did Endymion.

Both Tithonus and Endymion had 'intercourse' with Goddesses, and in both cases the relationship is represented in sexual terms. But neither man was able to permanently cross the unbridgeable gulf. Tithonus obtained eternal life, but not eternal youth; and so, after a normal human span of conjugal bliss with Eos, was cast aside into an eternity of progressive deterioration. Endymion, whether immortalised at Selene's instigation or by other means, obtained both eternal life and eternal youth, but at the cost of conscious existence, being eternally asleep. The stories are, in many ways, doublets of each other, with only slight differences in emphasis, and one would rather suspect the influence of one on the other (though deciding which came first would be difficult and probably pointless). Either way, they point us toward notions of the inescapability of mortality, while at the same time emphasising the desirability of interaction with the divine. And both stories operate in those liminal areas between life and death, between mortal and immortal; such liminal areas will figure largely in the material we will have to examine in future chapters.

## 4.3 Aphrodite And Anchises

The story of Aphrodite's love for Anchises appears as early as Homer and Hesiod,[30] though it is found in its fullest form in the slightly later *Homeric Hymn to Aphrodite*.[31] Here we learn that, with

---

30 Homer, *Iliad* 2.819-821, 5.247-248, 5.311-313 (1924: Vol. 1, pp.111, 213, 217). Hesiod: *Theogony*, ll.1008-1010 (1914: p.153).

31 *Homeric Hymn V – To Aphrodite* (in *Hesiod* 1914: pp.407-427).

the exception of the virgin Goddesses Athene, Artemis and Hestia, all the Gods are subject to Aphrodite's love-inducing powers, including Zeus. However, so that she wouldn't be able to boast of immunity to her own powers, Zeus caused Aphrodite to fall in love with the handsome Trojan herdsman Anchises, at that time tending cattle on 'many-fountained' Mount Ida. Despite herding cattle, Anchises was of the royal house of Troy, and a cousin to Tithonus. Finding him playing the lyre in his mountain shelter, while the other herdsmen were out with the cattle, Aphrodite came to him disguised as a human maiden rather than a Goddess, so he would not be frightened, claiming to have been carried off from Phrygia by Hermes to be Anchises' wife. It's notable, however, that she wore a shining golden robe which 'shimmered like the moon' (*selene*)[32] and that Anchises, on first seeing her, immediately thought she was a Goddess. Only after they had slept together, though, did Aphrodite actually reveal her divine form to him. At this point Anchises makes an interesting request: 'leave me not to lead a palsied life among men, but have pity on me; for he who lies with a deathless goddess is no hale man afterwards.'[33] Aphrodite then reassures him that no harm will come to him, and that she will bear him a son, Aeneas, who will be raised by the Nymphs on Ida. She also explains that he's been chosen as her lover because of the beauty of the Trojan royal house, telling how, from the same house, Ganymede was carried off by Zeus (with obvious homoerotic overtones) to be his cup-bearer, and Tithonus carried off by Eos, as discussed above. Aphrodite says that, if he could remain as youthful as he now is, she'd take him as her husband; but as she refuses to see him age like Tithonus, she will not make him deathless; she also tells him, rather ungraciously, that their affair has caused her much misery and disgrace among the Gods, and warns him not to boast of the affair, or Zeus will strike him

---

32 *Homeric Hymn V – To Aphrodite*, 1.89 (in *Hesiod* 1914: p.413).
33 *Homeric Hymn V – To Aphrodite* ll.188-189 (in *Hesiod* 1914: p.419).

down with a thunderbolt (which, in some later versions of the story, actually happens, resulting in Anchises being made lame or blind).[34]

Again, we have a number of parallels with the story of Selene and Endymion here: the Asiatic setting, the herdsman, the liminality of the mountain-top encounter, even the Selenic appearance of Aphrodite, and one is tempted to imagine that there are influences, one way or the other, between the two stories; or at least that they draw on a common stock of imagery and narrative motif. There are also significant differences as well, of course. On the surface, at least, the major narrative point of the story is quite obviously the come-uppance of the Goddess of love, suffering from love herself, to the point where she bears the child of a mortal. Similarly, the story also explains the divine origin of the hero Aeneas and his line, an origin exploited by the Julian emperors of Rome, who claimed descent from Aeneas, and thus directly from Venus/Aphrodite. Underlying this, however, are further explorations of themes that we've already come across before: the dangers and difficulties for mortals interacting with Goddesses and the frequently unpleasant aftermath, even for the innocent mortal (palsy, eternal sleep, eternal ageing, and so on); and the gulf between mortals and immortals. Here, the gulf is drawn back from, despite its discussion through the tale of Eos and Tithonus; the mortal/immortal interaction is effectively closed after the single encounter, neither partner wishing to extend it into regions of the eternal or the divine.

It's notable, perhaps, that in these tales of the mortal/immortal divide, the protagonists generally are mortal man and immortal Goddess, rather than woman and God. Woman's role seems to be to bear the children of the Gods and then (barring accidents such as that of Semele) to raise them while carrying on a relatively normal human life; the encounter is 'closed' and of brief duration, like that of Anchises. For men such as Endymion and Tithonus,

---

34 Grimal 1986: *s.v.* 'Anchises'.

we have an enduring (if imperfect) relationship with a Goddess. It's possible, of course, that this may, once again, reflect the fact that our sources were written by men, with a masculine viewpoint. For such authors, it may have been inconceivable that women could have any other relationship with the divine than the passive one, symbolically represented by child-bearing, and that only the masculine sex was worthy of 'meaningful' interaction with the divine. Yet there may also be a suggestion that, for such authors, 'the divine' (rather than a specific deity) was, like the soul, personified as feminine.

## 4.4 Dying Gods And Asiatic Goddesses

Given the obviously Asiatic connection of some of these stories (Endymion asleep on the Carian Mount Latmos, Tithonus and Anchises both being members of the Trojan royal house), it might be thought the tales reflect the influence of the major Asiatic myths of Goddesses and their human lovers, such as that of Ishtar and Tammuz (Dumuzi) or, in a form more familiar to the Greeks, Aphrodite and Adonis. A closer examination reveals, however, that such tales might not be as relevant as first thought.

As Vermeule points out, it was by no means uncommon for the Greeks to displace perfectly Hellenic stories, such as those of Andromeda, Ganymede, and the like, into the realm of 'foreigners',[35] so the mere geographical setting of a story is not necessarily an indication of Asiatic influence. And when we look more closely at the narrative construction of such tales, and the concerns they seem to reflect, we find the correspondences with such tales as those of Selene and Endymion or Eos and Tithonus aren't actually very close.

4.4.1 Aphrodite and Adonis. Unsurprisingly, the story of Aphrodite and Adonis is complex, and has several variants; over

---

35 Vermeule 1979: p.164.

the course of time a number of authors seem to have added to and 'improved' the story, providing solutions for previously unexplained aspects and generally complicating the narrative. In essence, it can be summarised as follows:

Theias (or Cinyras), king of Syria, had a daughter Myrrha (or Smyrna) who incurred the wrath of Aphrodite and was thus stricken with an incestuous passion for her father. Having slept with him by subterfuge, she became pregnant. Her father discovering what had happened, pursued her with a knife, whereupon she appealed to the Gods, who transformed her into a myrrh tree. In due course, the tree split open to give birth to the infant Adonis. Taken with the child's beauty, Aphrodite gave him to Persephone to bring up and she, in due course, refused to give him back. The Goddesses took their dispute to Zeus, who ruled that Adonis should spend a third of the year with Persephone in the underworld, a third with Aphrodite, and a third wherever he chose, with the result that Adonis chose to spend two-thirds of the year with Aphrodite. Eventually, due to the anger of Artemis, Ares or Apollo (according to different variants), Adonis was gored by a boar while hunting, and fatally injured. The tale is set sometimes on Mount Idalion, sometimes in Lebanon.[36]

4.4.2 Vegetation Gods. The above tale appears to have Semitic roots, the name 'Adonis' deriving from the Hebrew word *adonai*, meaning 'Lord'. As such, it falls into a similar class as the story of Ishtar and Tammuz (Inanna and Dumuzi) where the Goddess' mortal/immortal lover died and was taken to the underworld, but was then brought back to spend half the year in the upper world, half in the underworld.[37] Tammuz's death was ritually mourned and his revival celebrated. An obvious parallel from Greek myth is the story of Persephone, daughter of the corn Goddess Demeter;

---

36 Grimal 1986: *s.v.* Adonis (and refs collected there). Gantz 1993: Vol. 2, pp.729-731.

37 *Inter alia*, Wolkstein & Kramer 1983: pp.124-125.

abducted to the underworld by Hades, she was later allowed to split her time between the lower and upper worlds, spending six months in each, or a third in the underworld and two-thirds in the upper world, according to various versions.

These stories, and the rituals often associated with them, seem to reflect the vegetation cycle, where the seed lies hidden beneath the earth for a part of the year and the plant then lives, reproduces and dies above ground. Their concerns are thus entirely cyclical, with the Goddess' 'mortal husband' continually crossing and recrossing the borderland between life and death, being *either* in one state or the other. As such, they seem to have little relevance to stories such as those of Endymion or Tithonus, who continually occupy that liminal state *between* life and death. With this negative conclusion, we can perhaps pass on.

## 4.5 Other Man/Goddess Encounters

Although most of the comparative material we need to look at has been discussed in the preceding sections, for completion's sake some other, similar encounters with the feminine divine need to be summarised briefly.

4.5.1 Odysseus and Calypso. The voyages in the *Odyssey* are, perhaps, the ultimate exploration of the liminal regions of the world preserved for us in ancient Greek literature for, despite the usual and ultimately pointless attempts to identify various locations mentioned in the epic with actual places in the Mediterranean, it is quite obvious that both for 'Homer' and his audience, Odysseus and his men were sailing to places at or beyond the edge of the world we know. Among these locations is the island of Ogygia, where Calypso lived.

Calypso, whose name means 'she who conceals', is one of those characters difficult to place in the scheme of things, being sometimes referred to as a Goddess, sometimes as a Nymph. Homer refers to her as both: 'the queenly nymph Calypso, that bright goddess'[38], and tells us that she was a daughter of Atlas who, in turn, was a son of Iapetus; Calypso is thus the granddaughter of a Titan and, while a generation 'younger' than Selene, of the same Titan stock, which may have some relevance to her ambiguous position. Homer refers to her as the child of 'Atlas of baneful mind' and talks of her 'beguiling' Odysseus with 'soft and wheedling words', (interpreted by E.V. Rieu, in his translation, as referring to her as a 'wizard's daughter', which may perhaps remind us of Selene the daughter of Pallas, Megamedes' ['the very wise'] son).[39]

Calypso lived in a great cavern on the well-wooded island, with a garden of vines and four springs near the entrance, a loom, furnishings and a fireplace within.[40] There she lived, sang and wove with her maids, until Odysseus was washed up on her island. She kept him with her for seven years (according to Homer, later sources vary the duration),[41] refusing to let him go and trying to persuade him to stay and marry her, offering him both immortality and eternal youth. Odysseus refused, spending his days on the shore longing for his home on Ithaca, though he slept with Calypso at night. Finally, Zeus sent Hermes to Ogygia with instructions for Calypso to release him, and, given our interest in parallels to figures such as Endymion and Epimenides, who sleeps in caves, Homer tells us that Hermes was carrying 'the wand wherewith he lulls to sleep the eyes of whom he will, while others again he awakens even out of slumber'.[42] Upon his arrival, Calypso voiced the complaint mentioned above (4.2.2) about the jealous Gods who would not let a Goddess sleep with a man, citing Eos' ill-fated affair with Orion, and Demeter's passion for the mortal Iasion in a ploughed field; Iasion was duly struck dead by one of Zeus'

---

38 Homer, *Odyssey* 1.14 (1919: Vol. 1, p.3).

39 Homer, *Odyssey* 1.52ff (1919: Vol. 1, p.7). See also Homer, *Odyssey* (1946: p.26).

40 Homer, *Odyssey* 5.55ff (1919: Vol. 1, p.175).

41 Homer, *Odyssey* 7.259 (1919: Vol. 1, p.251).

42 Homer, *Odyssey* 5.47ff. (1919: Vol. 1, p.173).

thunderbolts.[43] Calypso, however, obeys Zeus' order and releases Odysseus, though he has to build his own boat in order to escape.

Again, there are a number of facets of interest here. Odysseus effectively lives in a cave (of which we will have much more to say in Chapter 8) even if his days are spent outside, for a protracted period (seven years) with a non-Olympian, Titanic (and thus to a certain extent non-orthodox) Goddess, while enjoying a sexual relationship with her. His release comes with the intervention of a God specifically said to hold the key to sleep and waking. Immortality is a factor in the relationship, offered though not accepted; unsurprisingly as the relationship is not going to be allowed to be permanent. And Odysseus, noted above all for his wisdom, is in a relationship with a 'wizard's daughter'; he receives little in the way of advice or increase of wisdom from her, but the conjunction of the two is at least worthy of remark. As we delve more into the stories of Endymion, Epimenides and the like, these resonant facets will reappear repeatedly.

4.5.2 Numa and Egeria. Being a Roman, rather than a Greek tale, this story may at first seem inadmissible, although as we'll see, its handling by Plutarch is of considerable interest. Numa was traditionally the second king of Rome, after Romulus, and noted for both his wisdom and for founding a number of Roman religious practices. He was said to have had the Nymph or Goddess (again, the terminology is confused) Egeria as a wife, and the Muses as his guides and companions (Livy adds the interesting detail that Numa consulted Egeria in 'a grove watered by a perennial spring which flowed through the midst of it, out of a dark cave',[44] a tale confirmed by Lactantius[45]). Plutarch's treatment of the story, reflecting as it does the views of a rational, 2nd century CE Greek

---

43 Homer, *Odyssey* 5.116ff (1919: Vol. 1, p.179).

44 Livy, *History of Rome* 1.19.5, 1.21.3 (1919 : Vol. 1, pp.69-73). Ovid, *Metamorphoses* 15.480ff (1916: Vol. 2, p.399ff.). Ovid, *Fasti*, 3.273ff (1951: p.141ff). Dionysius of Halicarnassus, 2.60-61 (1937: Vol. 1, pp.487-489).

45 Lactantius, *Divine Institutes* 1.22 (1871, p.65).

Platonist, is worth quoting at length. After telling us how Numa preferred to spend his time outside the city, alone, he continues:

'This, more than anything else, gave rise to the story about his goddess. It was not, so the story ran, from any distress or aberration of spirit that he forsook the ways of men, but he had tasted the joy of more august companionship and had been honoured with a celestial marriage; the goddess Egeria loved him and bestowed herself upon him, and it was his communion with her that gave him a life of blessedness and a wisdom more than human. However, that this story resembles many of the very ancient tales which the Phrygians have received and cherished concerning Attis, the Bithynians concerning Herodotus, the Arcadians concerning Endymion, and other peoples concerning other mortals who were thought to have achieved a life of blessedness in the love of the gods, is quite evident. And there is some reason in supposing that Deity, who is not a lover of horses or birds, but a lover of men, should be willing to consort with men of superlative goodness, and should not dislike or disdain the company of a wise and holy man. But that an immortal god should take carnal pleasure in a mortal body and its beauty, this, surely, is hard to believe.

'And yet the Aegyptians make a distinction here which is thought plausible, namely, that while a woman can be approached by a divine spirit and made pregnant, there is no such thing as carnal intercourse and communion between a man and a divinity. But they lose sight of the fact that intercourse is a reciprocal matter, and that both parties to it enter into a like communion. However, that a god should have affection for a man, and a so-called love which is based upon affection, and takes the form of solicitude for his character and his virtue, is fit and proper. [Plutarch then gives examples of a number of poets said to be beloved of various deities, before continuing:] Is it worthwhile, then, if we concede these instances of divine favour, to disbelieve that Zaleucus, Minos, Zoroaster, Numa, and Lycurgus, who piloted kingdoms and formulated constitutions, had frequent audience of the Deity?

Is it not likely, rather, that the gods are in earnest when they hold converse with such men as these, in order to instruct and advise them in the highest and best way, but use poets and warbling singers, if at all, for their own diversion?[46] Similar comparisons with Minos and Lycurgus are to be found in Dionysius of Halicarnassus' treatment of Egeria as well (although it should be pointed out that Lycurgus appears simply to have consulted the oracle at Delphi, and so had his laws confirmed by Apollo, rather than receiving them directly from the God).[47]

As noted, this is a fairly rationalising interpretation, but there are a number of points worth emphasising here. The first is Plutarch's discussion of the 'Aegyptian distinction' which, while not immediately obvious, probably refers to the unlikelihood of a mortal man making a Goddess pregnant; we have seen a number of cases where the opposite is true, although apart from the tale of Anchises and Aphrodite, the offspring are generally insignificant when compared with heroes fathered by the Gods. Whether that be the case or not, this discussion certainly highlights the general difference in relationships between men and Goddesses, and women and Gods, discussed above.

The second point would be that a relationship with a deity, and in Numa's particular case, with a Goddess, is a source of super-human wisdom; this, again, is something we shall return to. And finally, it's notable that Numa's relationship with Egeria is directly compared to Endymion's with Selene. The implication, then, seems to be clear: if we look beyond the simple, surface tale of a sexual relationship between Endymion and Selene, we may find something of greater interest besides. Indeed, Lactantius provides us with another interesting tale regarding Numa: that during the consulship of Cornelius and Bebius (180 BCE), two stone chests were discovered buried in a field below the Janiculum

---

46 Plutarch, *Numa* 4 *passim* (1914: Vol. 1, pp.317-321).
47 Dionysius of Halicarnassus, 2.60-61 (1937: Vol. 1, pp.487-489).

(one of Rome's seven hills). One contained the body of Numa, the other 'seven books in Latin regarding the laws of the pontiffs, and the same number written in Greek respecting systems of philosophy'.[48] If Numa received his wisdom from Egeria, a Goddess associated with a cave and a spring, these writings would be of considerable interest.

4.5.3 Ixion and Hera. This tale is perhaps rather marginal, compared to the other themes explored in this chapter, but should probably be discussed due to the confusion in the Hesiodic fragment (1.5.2) which makes Endymion the hero of the story usually told of Ixion. The major early source for the story is Pindar's second *Pythian Ode*,[49] although this already presupposes that the hearer will know some details of the story that Pindar glosses over. The full story (and its variants) can be compiled from other sources.[50] In essence, the narrative is as follows:

Ixion married Dia (a name meaning 'Goddess-like'), but murdered his father-in-law rather than give him the wedding gifts he expected. Neither man nor God would purify Ixion for this crime, until Zeus took pity on him, not only purifying him but inviting him to Olympus. There Ixion attempted to rape Hera, but Zeus substituted a woman made of cloud (Nephele) with Hera's appearance. The result of their intercourse was a son, Centaurus, who mated with mares on Mount Pelion, from whom were bred the race of Centaurs. Ixion was punished for his presumption by being bound to a wheel, sometimes said to be winged, fiery or decorated with snakes, and this wheel spins forever, either in the sky or the underworld. One of the commentators to the *Odyssey* states that Ixion was given nectar and ambrosia on Olympus, thus making him immortal; as he cannot be killed, his punishment on the wheel is eternal.

---

48 Lactantius, *Divine Institutes* 1.22 (1871, pp.64-65).
49 Pindar, *Pythian Ode* 2.20ff (1915: pp.173-175).
50 Collected in Gantz 1993: pp.718-721.

The correspondence of Ixion's story with the others discussed in this chapter would seem to be slight. Essentially, this is a 'breach of protocol' story, similar to those of Actaeon and Tiresias mentioned at the beginning of this chapter. There is no actual relationship between man and Goddess, only an attempted rape, diverted to a substitute, and the mention of Ixion's immortalisation seems to be merely an *ad hoc* explanation for the fact that he is eternally punished, rather than simply killed. That the story is so widely different from the other narratives that interest us here not only suggests that we can pass over it, but also that the version of the Endymion tale which appears to be confused with it is probably no more than that: an error of confusion.

4.5.4 Hylas and the Nymphs. The last area we need to touch on here is that of the abduction of mortal men by Nymphs, of which the most notable example is that of Hylas, the young companion of Heracles. This tale is most well known from Apollonius Rhodius, though there are many variants.[51]

Jason and the Argonauts having reached the Mysian coast (NW Turkey) Heracles set off for the forest to cut wood for a new oar, while his beloved young companion Hylas set off to collect water. However, the Nymph (or Nymphs) of the spring, enamoured of his beauty, carried off Hylas below the water to live with her as her husband (or as lover in common with the several Nymphs). Leaving Heracles still searching for Hylas, the Argonauts sailed on to Colchis.

While it's possible that this is a local Mysian legend which has been taken up and preserved in the *Argonautika*, and so perhaps trimmed of further detail, essentially, the narrative concludes with the abduction. There is no exploration of the later life of the abductee or discussion of his immortalisation or otherwise. Beyond the fact that the particular story of Hylas is another with an Asiatic setting,

---

51 Apollonius Rhodius, *Argonautica*, 1.1207-1239 (1912: pp.85-87). Antoninus Liberalis, *Metamorphoses* 26. (1992: p.85). Etc.

and that such stories add to our notions that interactions between mortal men and divine females were rather more common than generally thought, there are only really two factors of interest here. The first is that in later antiquity 'abduction by Nymphs' became a sentimental euphemism for death in epitaphs and sarcophagus decoration, especially with regard to drowned children; we shall see similar developments in the sentimental use of the Selene and Endymion story, where Endymion represents the deceased 'not dead but sleeping' (see Chapter 14). The second is the whole concept of 'nympholepsy', a word of multiple interpretations, ranging from literal abduction by Nymphs to a frenzy caused by them, to simple devotion to their cult (7.4).

## 4.6 Summary

Taking this selection of stories and, for the moment, including that of Selene and Endymion among them, what do we have in the way of common or uncommon factors between them?

One obvious factor is geographical, with a surprising percentage of stories taking place in what is now western Turkey. Endymion's tale (usually but not always) takes place in Caria; Tithonus and Anchises are Trojan princes, and Hylas is carried off by Mysian Nymphs. It has to be remembered, though, that these areas were all colonised by Greeks from an early date (well before any of our surviving written sources) and even where we have evidence of cult, such as the sanctuary of Endymion at the foot of Latmos, it has to be pointed out that this is found in the Graecised refoundation of the city, as Heraclea-under-Latmos, rather than in the original Carian city of Latmos. Equally, despite the Asiatic settings of the stories mentioned here, they quite obviously are of a completely different type to those Asiatic/Semitic tales of Goddesses and their dying lovers, such as Aphrodite and Adonis or Ishtar and Tammuz. Thus there's no reason to think that these stories are not 'Greek' in either structure or origin. The fact that many have an Asiatic setting may reflect a predilection for this type of story among colonial Greeks or, equally as likely, this might be part of a 'liminalisation' procedure. We have seen that such stories are often set in liminal areas such as mountain-tops and, relative to the Greek mainland, colonies on the Asiatic shore could similarly be seen as lying 'on the borders of the world' where strange things, or interactions with the divine, were more likely to occur.[52] Whatever the cause (Asiatic influence, colonial predilection or liminalisation), the actual geographical setting is perhaps not a major factor; there are, after all, a considerable number of tales that have either purely Greek or non-specific locations.

We have also seen sufficient variety among the various stories collected here to realise that the interactions between man and Goddess take a number of different forms and that the stories often have differing concerns and points to make. However, the fact that we have a group of stories which, despite the differing emphases placed on individual encounters, also frequently take time out to discuss the encounters of other individuals in a comparative fashion (Calypso's and Aphrodite's digressions on Eos and the like) would suggest that such stories have a tendency to circle round areas of common concern, approaching them from differing viewpoints. One of these clusters of concerns seems to centre on the divide between man and the divine, between mortality and immortality, between life and death; this too is a liminal area, so it's perhaps hardly surprising that the tales are placed in such liminal areas as caves and mountain-tops. Another is on the wisdom to be obtained through interaction with the divinity. Both these concerns will reappear frequently as we continue our exploration of the myth of Selene and Endymion.

---

[52] A parallel case might be found in the 19th century USA, where the legendary 'Wild West' was largely an invention of East Coast writers such as Ned Buntline, retailing stories of the 'wild frontier' for an urban audience.

Chapter Five

# Endymion

## 5.1 Introduction

In many ways, the 'essential' myth of Selene is that of her love for Endymion, as represented by the story in its Carian setting, while the other stories, such as that of her amour with Pan, are more easily understood in relation to the Carian tale and, in turn, throw further light upon it. Before getting to grips with that story, however, it's probably as well to prepare the ground by looking more closely at Endymion himself.

## 5.2 The Name 'Endymion'

One of the more puzzling aspects of attempts to 'explain' the name Endymion is the tendency, on the part of the explainers, to embellish the meaning with reference to the myth of his encounter with Selene.

So Robert Graves, whose etymological speculations are, to put it mildly, untrustworthy, lists 'Endymion' in his index as meaning 'seduced native'.[1] When we turn to his (fancifully embroidered) main entry on Endymion, we find a note explaining as follows:

'The name Endymion, from *enduien* (Latin: *inducere*), refers to the Moon's seduction of the king, as though she were one of the

---

1 Graves 1960: Vol. 2, p.390.

## Selene

Empusae [...]; but the ancients explain it as referring to *somnum ei inductum*, "the sleep put upon him".[2]

Carl Kerenyi, with a little more restraint, gives us:

'The name Endymion means one who "finds himself *within*", encompassed by his beloved as if in a common garment.'[3]

Let's strip away some of the embellishments here. Both authors appear to be deriving the name from the Greek root *enduo*, meaning 'to put on, to wear', 'to go in, to enter' and 'to implicate oneself in'. This is, to a certain extent, cognate with the Latin *induco*, meaning 'to put on', although rather than 'to go in', *induco* means 'to bring in', 'to lead, to induce, to persuade, to introduce'. With *enduo*, '*one* goes in'; with *induco*, 'one *brings another* in'. From this pairing we derive the English word 'endue' (or 'indue'), meaning 'to put on, to clothe, to invest with'. However, even when treating of the English word, the *Everyman English Dictionary* shows the distinction in the derivatives from the root, giving an origin from 'L. *inducere*, draw + association with *induere*, put on'.

Graves, following his own peculiar programme of etymological interpretation, thus proceeds to derive his meaning of 'Endymion' *not* from the Greek *enduien*, as he says, but from the Latin *inducere*, with which it is only partially cognate. From 'induce' he then makes the speculative but completely unjustified leap to 'seduce', and on this basis implies that Selene is cognate with the demonic, succubus-like beings known as Empusae. If ancient Goddesses could sue dead authors, one would rather expect a libel-case in the hereafter; the interpretation starts from false premises and results in a completely unjustified conclusion.

Graves, unfortunately, gives no reference for the 'ancients' who derived the name from *somnum ei inductum*, but deriving from the same Latin root, it's obviously as inapplicable as Graves' explanation. Interpretations that use the meanings of three words to explain that of one are hardly likely to convince.

---

2 Graves 1960: Vol. 1, p.211.
3 Kerenyi 1951: p.198.

## Steve Moore

Kerenyi is more obviously restricting himself to the Greek *enduo* in his interpretation, but again we have problems. 'One who "finds himself *within*"' has overtones of self-discovery; and considering the overall thrust of Kerenyi's work and his association with Jung, one suspects such overtones may not be entirely unintentional. They are, of course, unjustified by the original Greek. It's possible that, by adding to this the phrase 'encompassed by his beloved as if in a common garment' Kerenyi is attempting to imply that Endymion finds himself *within the love* of Selene; but this not only attempts to use two different meanings of *enduo* at the same time, it also implies a 'beloved' (Selene) deriving from mythology rather than etymology. In other words, for both Graves and Kerenyi (and the unidentified 'ancients') there is no meaning possible for the name Endymion without the presence of Selene. This is a rather peculiar state of affairs.

The possibility has to be admitted, of course, that the name Endymion originated quite separately from the myth; in which case any quest for a meaning that has mythological relevance would be a false trail. That said, it's also obvious that such a possibility merely leads us to a dead end. However, there may be a 'halfway house' here; a meaning which has a certain, perhaps limited, relevance to ancient myth or ritual practice, without buying into the full-blown 'Endymion and Selene as an inseparable pair' story in the same way that Graves and Kerenyi do. So, without letting our imaginations run away with us, let's see what it's actually permissible to infer, if such relevance is to be assumed.

In spite of Kerenyi's rather stretched attempt to bring in the meaning of 'to wear', this doesn't really seem to have any relevance to the material under discussion. The far more likely meaning of Endymion would seem to derive from interpreting *enduo* simply as 'to go in' or 'to enter', and so to be 'he who is within' or 'the one inside'; we've already seen a similar construction with Hyperion, 'the one above'.

## Selene

If Endymion's name actually has a meaning similar to 'the one within', then the obvious mythical reference-point would seem to be that he sleeps within a cave, as he does in the version of his story that finds its most archetypal form associated with the Carian Mount Latmos. If story and name came into existence at the same time, then we may perhaps feel justified in assuming that the Carian version of the story is the original one. We'll explore this idea further as we progress. However, as we'll see in due course, there are in the Greek tradition a number of other figures who sleep in caves; if we were to regard 'Endymion' as a *descriptive name,* in the same way that 'Hyperion' ('the one above') can be seen as a descriptive name of the Sun, then we can find a relevant meaning for 'the one within' that does not necessarily presuppose the story of 'Endymion and Selene as an inseparable pair'. Obviously, in the following pages we shall be concentrating largely on Endymion in his relationship with Selene; but the possibility that the name 'Endymion' can be seen as a general title for 'cave sleeper' will have some relevance to the arguments to be developed later on.

Returning briefly to the notion that the Carian version of the Selene and Endymion story is the original one, there is, of course, one more possibility that needs to be borne in mind. That is that the story itself may well have a Carian, rather than a Greek origin, and that the original story, now lost, told how a Moon-Goddess had an affair with a sleeping human male. In this case, the names of the principles concerned would have been in Carian; and when the story transferred to Greece, the Moon-Goddess would have been identified, naturally, as Selene ... while the Carian name of the sleeping male, presumably being meaningless to Greek speakers, would have had to have been replaced. In such a case we might expect the name to be composed to fit the meaning: the Carian 'one *within*' would then be given the self-explanatory name 'Endymion'. This is, of course, speculation; no such Carian original of the story appears to exist, and even if it did, the Carian language is currently undeciphered; we simply have no idea what the Carian word for 'one within' might have been. However, we do know that, at least from the 5th century BCE onwards, Carian personal and place-names became increasingly Graecised: thus Carian place-names such as Syangela and Uromos take on the Greek forms Theangela and Euromos, while the city of Latmos itself is renamed Heraclea. Similarly, there is a growing tendency for personal names in Caria to take the form of a Greek forename with a Carian patronymic.[4] There may be no evidence for original Carian names of Selene and Endymion, that were later renamed with Greek forms, but there is certainly historical precedent and context which makes such a transformation not inherently impossible.


5.3 Who Is Endymion?
As we've seen in section 1.5, we have a number of variants of the Selene and Endymion story, which occurs in a wide variety of geographical locations. The most important is undoubtedly the tale attached to Carian Mount Latmos, but we also have variants from Phrygia (if that is not simply a poeticism for 'Asia Minor' [*i.e.,* what is now Asiatic Turkey, including and, ultimately, referring to Caria]), Elis, Arcadia, Locris and Trachis. We're also told that Endymion was Spartan.

For the most part these sources are so fragmentary that there is little to be done with them except to note them in passing, though we might conjecture that the root of the story placing Endymion in Arcadia lies in the variant genealogy of Selene that makes her the daughter of Pallas, son of Megamedes, discussed above at 3.2.2. If Selene was thought to be an Arcadian Goddess and known to have Endymion as a lover, it would be natural to place Endymion in Arcadia as well.

---

4 Hornblower 1982: pp.63, 346-350.

With regard to the variant locations, perhaps the most interesting is Nicander of Colophon's mention that Selene slept with Endymion on Mount Aselenus (*Aselena Ore*).[5] This mountain is mentioned in Nicander's *Theriaca*, without reference to Selene and Endymion, where a scholiast places it in Locris. However, it is the 12th century CE *Etymologicum Magnum* (153.4),[6] which tells us that Nicander said, in an otherwise lost work, the *Aetolica*, that Selene and Endymion slept on Mount Aselenus, and that the mountain is to be found in Trachis. Steven Jackson, in a frequently problematic article,[7] adduces this location in Trachis as evidence for his construction of an 'original Peloponnesian' version of the Endymion story, discussed below at 5.6. Unfortunately, Trachis is actually in Phocis, in northern Greece, a considerable distance from the Peloponnese.

However, the location in Trachis is not without interest. As we know, the standard 'Carian' version places Selene and Endymion on Mount Latmos, near the city of Heraclea-under-Latmos. Trachis was actually a region of northern Greece whose main town was originally also called 'Trachis'. However, in 426 BCE, during the Peloponnesian War, the Spartans attempted to settle the area, and the town of Trachis, now in ruins, was rebuilt and renamed Heraclea Trachinia.[8] One is tempted to conjecture that Nicander, writing in the 2nd century BCE, may have simply placed Selene and Endymion at 'Heraclea' (his hometown of Colophon was, after all, only 50 miles from Heraclea-under-Latmos), and that the *Etymologicum Magnum* may have misidentified this as Heraclea Trachina; in which case the location at 'Trachis' could be interpreted as a long-standing error.

---

5 Nicander 1953: pp.43, 174, 201.

6 Nicander 1953: p.174.

7 Jackson, 2006: *passim*.

8 Pausanias, 1971: Vol. 1, pp.263, 460.

With the exception of the Elean version of the story, these lesser variants (vague as they are) seem to be simply recast versions of the Carian tale. In other words, the essence of the story, that Selene descends to sleep with Endymion, appears to remain the same, but the location changes. These recast versions can thus be considered with the Carian story, beginning in the next chapter. Here, we can perhaps dispose of some of the lesser items: 'Endymion the astronomer', Endymion and Hera, and the Endymion story from Elis.

## 5.4 Endymion The Astronomer

We've seen above (1.5.2) that the scholiast on Apollonius Rhodius 'explained' the story of Endymion and Selene by supposing that Endymion was an early astronomer who was the first to undertake the study of the heavenly bodies, and the first to understand the phases and movements of the Moon; so devoting himself to these studies by night, he slept during the day. We find the same rationalisation, *inter alia*, in the anonymous work *De Incredibilibus*,[9] in Pliny the Elder,[10] and in Lucian.[11] Germanicus Caesar, in the commentary to his Latin translation of the *Phaenomena* of Aratus, informs us that this story goes back to the 3$^{rd}$ century BCE writer Mnaseas of Sicyon.[12]

George E. Bean (without naming his sources) gives us further strange variants: 'A later account rationalizes the story. According to this, Endymion was the first man to discover the true orbit of the moon; having done nothing with his life but study for this, he was said to have slept for thirty years. Let other scientists take note. Later still, certain Christian writers declared that Endymion was

---

9 Anon. *De Incredibilibus (Peri Apiston)*. 12 (1843: p.324).
10 Pliny, *Natural History*, 2.6 (43) (1949: Vol. 1, p.195).
11 Lucian, *Astrology*, 18 (1936: Vol. 5, p.361).
12 Lucian, *Astrology*, 18 (Harmon's footnote, 1936: Vol. 5, p.361).

a Carian mystic who desired to learn from the moon the name of God; on learning it he died, and his mortal remains were preserved to that time in Caria, where his coffin was opened every year and the bones were observed to emit a humming sound – presumably in an effort to communicate the name of God to man.'[13]

We'll return to the late, Christian interpretation in due course, as it is, in fact, more interesting than it looks. Similarly, Bean's version of the 'astronomer' story has a certain interest in that it limits the period of Endymion's sleep. For now, though, we can merely regard these tales as interesting variants on what seems to have been a commonplace rationalising explanation in the Hellenistic and Roman periods. Indeed, this sort of rationalising explanation remains common today, particularly in popular 'ancient mysteries' books that seek to reveal 'the truth' behind ancient myths and legends.

Of course, that there were problems with this sort of explanation must have been apparent from a very early date, if only because exactly the same form of explanation is applied to Phaethon, the dangerous-driving son of Helios 'who marked out the course of the Sun, as Endymion that of the Moon; not accurately, but dying before he accomplished the calculation'[14] and also to Hyperion, a name of the Sun-God himself: 'Of Hyperion we are told that he was the first to understand, by diligent attention and observation, the movement of both the sun and the moon and the stars, and the seasons as well, in that they are caused by these bodies, and to make these facts known to others; and that for this reason he was called the father of these bodies, since he had begotten, so to speak, the speculation about them and their nature.'[15]

In other words, this is an 'off-the-shelf' explanation, easily adapted to different persons and circumstances. It also has to be

---

13 Bean 1979: pp.212-213.
14 Anon. *De Incredibilibus*. 13 (1843: p.324).
15 Diodorus Siculus, 5.67 (1939: Vol. 3, pp.277-279).

noted that none of these passages quoted here date before the 1st century BCE. They are all 'posterior explanations', given many centuries after the stories first appear, and obviously influenced by late trends toward allegorisation and euhemerism.

Fritz Graf, while dealing more with modern historical reductionists, is particularly scathing about this sort of rationalisation.[16] As he points out: 'the historical reductionist usually explains away essential features of the myth – the elements of its plot and the details of its narrative – as if these features were a mere nuisance; moreover, the procedure whereby myth is traced back to historical reality is highly arbitrary.' It might also be felt, more generally, that one of the main objections to historical reductionism would, quite simply, be its sheer banality; the essence of myth is its wonder and imagination, and, where it intersects with religious concerns, the interaction with the divine. Thus its characters are Gods and heroes; so its stories are displayed in 'Widescreen and Technicolor'. To reduce myth to a collection of misunderstood natural events or exaggerated memories is, bluntly, a lamentable failure of the imagination.

That said, let's look again at the notion of 'Endymion the astronomer'. The essential features of the myth, in Graf's terms, are simply ignored. Endymion carries out his astronomical observations while, presumably, being both asleep and inside a cave. The Moon is treated wholly as an astronomical, physical body, rather than a Goddess, and there is neither an amorous nor a sexual relationship between deity and mortal. The sleep, the cave, the mountain and the sheep have all disappeared. In concentrating on explaining only one feature of the myth, this interpretation, ultimately, explains nothing at all.

## 5.5 Endymion And Hera

---

16 Graf 1993: pp.30-31.

## Selene

As was pointed out in 1.5.2, the scholiast on Apollonius Rhodius includes a curious tale about Endymion and Hera, which he quotes as a fragment from Hesiod's *Great Eoiae*. In Evelyn-White's translation, this passage runs as follows:

'In the *Great Eoiae* it is said that Endymion was transported by Zeus into heaven, but when he fell in love with Hera, was befooled with a shape of cloud, and was cast out and went down into Hades.'[17]

We also have the quotation attributed to Epimenides: 'that spending time among the Gods Endymion fell in love with Hera; when Zeus was angry, he begged to sleep through all time.'[18]

These are the only sources for this story, surviving only as quoted by the scholiast, and any later quotations derive from them alone. It's notable here that in neither of these quotations are we given any background information about Endymion's descent or place of habitation: we simply don't know if these stories refer to the Endymion of Elis or Latmos. The problem, of course, is that this tale is completely out of context with the rest of the material we have about Endymion. The story is, however, extremely close in content to that of Ixion (4.5.3), and the following excerpt from Apollodorus should be compared with the quotation from Hesiod given above:

'Ixion fell in love with Hera and attempted to force her; and when Hera reported it, Zeus, wishing to know if the thing were so, made a cloud in the likeness of Hera and laid it beside him; and when Ixion boasted that he had enjoyed the favours of Hera, Zeus bound him to a wheel, on which he is whirled by winds through the air; such is the penalty he pays. And the cloud, impregnated by Ixion, gave birth to Centaurus [the father of the centaurs].'[19]

---

17 Hesiod, *Great Eoiae* fragment 10, from Scholiast on Apollonius Rhodius, *Argonautika*, 4.57 (1914: p.261).

18 Scholia in Apollonii Argonautica, 4.54-61 (1810, 1813: Vol. 2, pp.272-275, pp.576-577).

19 Apollodorus, Epitome 1.20-21 (1921: Vol. 2, p.149).

The story of Ixion was widely known, and appears in numerous ancient authors. The same story is told at greater length (but without significant addition) by Pindar[20] and, again, by Diodorus Siculus;[21] it is also referred to in passing by Apollonius Rhodius, Ovid and others.

One might suspect, then, that there has been a confusion of Endymion with Ixion, and what we have here is the Ixion story with Endymion's name attached to it, although the fact that Epimenides also records Endymion's desire for Hera makes it difficult to simply write this off as an error. However, we should perhaps not go as far as Steven Jackson does,[22] when he assumes this to be a Peloponnesian story (Endymion being variously said to have come from Elis, Arcadia, Sparta and so on; see 1.5.3 and below at 5.6) in which he 'reconstructs' the story as follows: that Endymion was in fact taken up to heaven, attempted to force himself on Hera, was also tricked with a cloud and then cast into an eternal sleep by Zeus, who thereafter gave him to Selene as her beloved, and that this is a deliberate doublet of the Ixion story. Ixion's fiery wheel is taken as cognate with the Sun, while Endymion is said to somehow have a similar relationship with the Moon, and that both have become part of the 'operating mechanism' of the universe. This is conjectural and cannot be supported by the evidence. It should be noted that in neither the quotation from Hesiod, nor from Epimenides is there any mention of Selene or the Moon, and the hypothesis asks us to believe that two identical stories of a mortal taken to heaven and tricked with a cloud-likeness of Hera were told about entirely separate characters. Whether this is more likely than that one story has been confused with the other, we can only let the reader decide.

---

20 Pindar, *Pythian Ode*, 2.20ff (1915: pp.173ff).
21 Diodorus Siculus, 4.69.3-5 (1939: Vol. 3, pp.39-41).
22 Jackson, 2006: *passim*.

## 5.6 Endymion Of Elis

We've seen, at 1.5.3, that the version of the Selene and Endymion story from Elis differs considerably from the Carian version. Indeed, we might go so far as to simply call this an 'Endymion story', for Selene's role here is comparatively minor, and the mentions of her involvement tend to be prefaced by phrases along the lines of 'but some say ...' We have also seen that, in Pausanias' telling of the story,[23] and in the discussion of the scholiast to Apollonius Rhodius,[24] attempts are made to link the Elean and Carian stories together. When Endymion is a King of Elis in one tradition and a Carian shepherd in the other, such linkages rather stretch our credibility, particularly as no reasons are offered as to why a single person should occupy both such widely contrasting roles; also, Selene's role in the variant stories is equally dissimilar.[25]

Lee Patterson makes the interesting suggestion that the citizens of Heraclea under Latmos and the Aetolians were united by supposed kinship ties (the Aetolians deriving their name from Aetolus, son of Endymion), who agreed that Endymion was their common ancestor, despite having variant stories about him.[26] However, his suggestion that Heraclea was a colony of the Aetolians, founded by Endymion, is perhaps taking historicising

---

23 Pausanias, 5.1.3-5 (1926: Vol. 2, pp.381-383).

24 Scholia in Apollonii Argonautica, 4.54-61 (1810, 1813: Vol. 2, pp.272-275, pp.576-577).

25 These attempts at synthesis are extremely persistent. A late but very full, Latinised version is quoted by Leland, in translation, from the *Dizionario Storico Mitologico*, by Pozzoli *et al*: 'Now it is fabled that Endymion, admitted to Olympus, whence he was expelled for want of respect to Juno, was banished for thirty years to earth. And having been allowed to sleep this time in a cave of Mount Latmos, *Diana*, smitten with his beauty, visited him every night till she had by him fifty daughters and one son. And after this Endymion was recalled to Olympus.' [Leland 1899: p.51] This probably tells us less about the mythology than the human desire to tie up loose ends, as if somewhere amid all these variants there was actually a single 'true story' which just needed to be disentangled from the errors of transmission and ignorance.

26 Patterson, 2004: p.349.

too far, particularly as it seems that Heraclea was originally a Carian foundation, only receiving its Greek name subsequent to the 5th century BCE.[27]

D.L. Page[28] 'suggests in fact two separate Endymions, a Western king of Elis taken up to Olympos (where he falls in love with Hera) and an Eastern youth of Asia Minor visited by Selene as he sleeps.'

This suggestion has both good points and bad points. The major problem with it is that neither of the two main sources discussing the Elean Endymion (Apollodorus and Pausanias) make any mention of the Hera story, while the scholiast to Apollonius Rhodius, who is our only source for the Hera story, does not actually give it a fixed geographical location. The Endymion who attempted to seduce Hera is neither said to be the Elean King nor the Carian shepherd; and, as has already been suggested, the whole story sounds suspiciously like a confusion with that of Ixion, anyway.

On the other hand, Page's suggestion that the Elean and Carian Endymions were in fact separate figures has much to commend it, although it probably doesn't go far enough. Let's examine the Elean story in more detail, see what it actually represents, and how it contrasts with the Carian story.

If we look at the Endymion figure in the Carian version of the story (and its close variants), it's quite obvious that he's portrayed as little more than a cipher: he's the handsome young man asleep in the cave who's loved by Selene. He has no known ancestry, and the tales of any progeny are, as we'll see, fairly tenuously connected with him. The part he plays in the story is, effectively, all that there is to his character. This is a mythical tale, with no specific time of occurrence and, as we've seen that the tale also appears at other locations besides Latmos, fairly non-specific geographically as

---

27 Bean, 1979: pp.211-212.
28 Page 1955: pp.273-274 (quoted in Gantz 1993: Vol. 1, p.lvi).

well (unless those other locations are, in fact, errors for Latmos, as suggested for Trachis, above). This is, in effect, 'pure storytelling', with only the slightest direct connection, within the story itself, to the 'real, human world'.

By contrast, the Elean version of the Endymion story is very specific in both spatial and temporal terms and, with its strong genealogical setting, very much connected with the human world. Both our main sources for the story, Apollodorus and Pausanias, are obviously drawing on a common tradition with very different aims to that which preserves the Carian story. This is the tradition of 'legendary genealogy', whereby families, clans and states trace their line back to include famous ancestors and, quite often, to an ultimate 'founding father' who is numbered among the Gods. This is hardly what we could call 'history' as understood in the 21st century, but there is no doubt that, when first composed, it was thought to be more historical than mythical. The characters appearing in the genealogies were thought to be real human beings who had once lived in real time. And if absolute chronology was lacking, at least a rough time-frame could be established by counting the generations, or placing figures in relation to specific temporal landmarks (*e.g.*, 'before or after the Trojan War'). Again, the Elean story is very specific geographically, particularly in Pausanias' version, where the story is told as part of the lore surrounding Olympia, its temple of Zeus, and the founding of the Olympic Games.

According to this genealogical version, Endymion is the son of Aethlius, and we've seen above, at 1.5.2, that the scholia to Apollonius Rhodius also give a fragment from an unidentified work by Hesiod confirming this story of Endymion's descent. The same scholia inform us that this story also appears in now-lost works by Pisander of Rhodes, Acusilaus of Argos and Pherecydes of Athens. Steven Jackson is correct in pointing out that these are all early sources, from the 8th to the 5th centuries BCE, and there may be some merit in his suggestion that this version originates earlier than the Carian one.²⁹ However, his argument that this is the 'original', Peloponnesian story and that the Carian version is a poetic invention originating in Alexandria is largely dependent on the fact that we have no surviving sources for the Carian story earlier than the Hellenistic period, and that during this period Caria was under the control of the Ptolemaic dynasty, who ruled from Alexandria. It's true that this Ptolemaic occupation would give a greater opportunity for the Carian story to become known throughout the Greek world, but this hardly rules out the fact that the story may be older than the surviving sources. Besides, as we've seen above, at 5.3, Jackson's co-opting of Mount Aselenus in Trachis, in support of his contention for a 'Peloponnesian Endymion' story, appears to be fanciful.

Let's examine this Elean genealogy in a little more detail. We start with a very specific temporal landmark: the Greek story of the great flood, of which the only survivors were Deucalion and Pyrrha. Amongst their children was a daughter, Protogeneia ('Firstborn'), on whom Zeus fathered Aethlius.³⁰ Aethlius and Calyce then had a son, Endymion, who led the Aeolian people (named after Aethlius' cousin, Aeolus) from Thessaly to Elis; but we are also told that 'some say' that Endymion was a son of Zeus.³¹ Pausanias is in broad agreement with this version of Apollodorus, although he makes Aethlius the first ruler of Elis, and makes no mention of Endymion himself as a son of Zeus.

The importance of portraying Endymion as son or grandson of Zeus becomes obvious when Pausanias tells us that he instituted the footrace (or at least provided the legendary aetiology for it) which was an important event in the Games celebrated at Olympia for Zeus. We are also told that his tomb was placed near the starting

---

29 Jackson, 2006: pp.11-12.
30 Apollodorus, 1.7.2-3 (1921: Vol. 1, p.57).
31 Apollodorus, 1.7.5-6 (1921: Vol. 1, p.61).

place for the runners.³² Similarly, Pausanias informs us that there was a statue of Endymion, 'all in ivory except for the clothes' at Olympia in the Metapontine Treasury (which contained offerings to Zeus from Metaponton in Italy). All this (particularly the tomb and the descent from Zeus) suggests that Endymion was actually a minor local deity at Olympia, who received offerings appropriate to a hero (a figure of somewhat similar standing to a local saint in the Christian religion). He is both a political founding-figure of the state of Elis, and a cultural founding-figure of the Olympic games.

Apollodorus tells us that Endymion married either an unnamed Naiad Nymph or Iphianassa; Pausanias that he married Asterodia, or Chromia, or Hyperippe. All these ladies are quite unknown, except as the wife of Endymion, and appear to have no other surviving stories attached to them. Most notable among his sons was Aetolus, who gave his name to the land of Aetolia. Regardless of the confusion as to his wife's identity, this material places Endymion in a very solid genealogical tradition, and Pausanias even goes so far as to tell us that there were six generations between Endymion's son Aetolus and the Trojan War.³³

It is to this material that Apollodorus adds: 'As he was of surpassing beauty, the Moon fell in love with him, and Zeus allowed him to choose what he would, and he chose to sleep forever, remaining deathless and ageless.' Pausanias says (and gives the story less probability than the genealogy): 'The Moon, they say, fell in love with this Endymion and bore him fifty daughters.'

Levi points out that 50 is not merely a round number, but also the number of several other heroic broods, such as those of Priam, Aegyptus and Danaus.³⁴ However, Kerenyi's interpretation may be more relevant here, pointing out that the 50 daughters correspond to the 50 lunar months that make up the four-year

---

32 Pausanias, 5.1.3-5, 6.20.9 (1926: Vol. 2, pp.381-383; 1933: Vol. 3, p.123).
33 Pausanias, 5.3.6 (1926: Vol. 2, p.395).
34 Pausanias 1971: Vol. 2, p.198.

period between the holding of each Olympic Games.[35] Considering the strong connection in Pausanias' summary of the Endymion material with the lore of the Olympic Games, this seems the most likely interpretation.

There is one further matter that needs to be considered here, and that is the geographical position of Elis, on the western coast of Greece. As will be further explored below in the following pages, the 'Carian version' of the Endymion story, and the related material that needs to be examined with it, comes from an area that occupies the central Peloponnese, Eastern Greece, Crete and Caria. This is an area that, in Bronze Age times shared common linguistic and cultural traits and, unsurprisingly, a common mythological view of the Endymion story. Elis is outside this area, and has an extremely *un*common version of the Endymion story, and no amount of ancient scholarly effort will actually link the two versions in any convincing way.

We might thus suggest a simple solution to the problem of the differences between the Elean and Carian Endymion stories: that it is the Carian version which centres on the amour of Selene and Endymion, while the Elean version centred on a quite separate figure, a local Olympian hero portrayed as a king of Elis, who coincidentally happened also to be called Endymion. Then, given the correspondence of names, attempts would have been made to integrate the two and attach the tale of Selene's love to the Elean king, where it never really belonged. It is, perhaps, dangerous to make any sort of definite statement where the surviving material is so fragmentary, but for now we can perhaps take this as a working hypothesis, and move on.

---

35 Kerenyi 1951: p.198.

Chapter Six

# Latmos And The Landscape Of Myth

## 6.1 Introduction

We can now begin to turn our attention to the archetypal version of the myth of Selene and Endymion, set on Mount Latmos, in Caria. This is a complex investigation, and not the easiest to organise, for the trail will lead us into some fairly obscure corners of the Greek religious and mythological worlds. As such, it's necessary to break the story down into parts and examine them individually, and then, as we gain a greater insight into the individual aspects of the myth, to put them back together again in what will I hope be a more comprehensive, and comprehensible, whole. We'll begin at the scene of the action, and examine both the physical and mythological landscape of Mount Latmos (also frequently spelled 'Latmus').

## 6.2 The Physical Landscape: Latmos, Heraclea-Under-Latmos, & The Sanctuary Of Endymion

Mount Latmos lies in Caria, in SW Turkey, just south of the Maeander river, and only a short distance from the ancient city of Miletus. In former times, an inlet of the sea ran to the western foot of Latmos, and the city of Heraclea (also spelled Heraklea, Heracleia, Herakleia) stood at the head of the inlet, spreading

*Selene*

up the slopes of the mountain. Today, the Maeander river has silted up the mouth of the inlet, and it has become a fresh-water lake, the modern name of which is Lake Bafa.[1] According to the Carian version of the Selene and Endymion myth, Endymion was a shepherd or hunter on Latmos, and Selene slept with him in a cave on the mountain.

I have yet to find a convincing explanation of the name Latmos, and the name may be of Carian origin. If the word is Greek, then considering the craggy and boulder-strewn appearance of the mountain, a derivation from *laas (las, lat-)*, 'a stone, a rock, a crag', might be conjectured, but the speculativeness of this should be emphasised. Richard Stoneman conjectures a connection with the Semitic name for the Moon, *al-Lat*, but offers no evidence for this.[2] Jean Richer mentions a Lycian Goddess, Lada, 'herself probably a form of the Semitic Alilat'.[3] Lycia being the land immediately east of Caria, this may provide more of a connection. However, there seems to be no evidence of the Carians having Semitic connections, and their language, while as yet undeciphered, is thought to be Indo-European.[4] More than this, Perrot & Chipiez inform us that 'proper Carian appellatives, whether of individuals or places, have naught that is Semitic about them.'[5] That being the case, it is perhaps best to treat a possible connection with a Semitic Moon-Goddess as speculative; similarity of sound, and the lunar function of the deity, may be suggestive but hardly conclusive.

Freya Stark, who visited the area in 1952, remarks that modern Turks call Latmos 'Besh Parmak, the hill of the Five Fingers, from its many summits', and offers the following observation: 'Here [from the Maeander], as the moon increased, I watched her

---

1 Levi 1980: p.221.
2 Stoneman 1991: p.69.
3 Richer 1994: p.46.
4 Hornblower & Spawforth 1999: *s.v.* 'Caria'.
5 Perrot & Chipiez 1892: p.303.

climbing in the south, hidden by the five crests and re-emerging as she went from one to another, and appearing, by a trick of the light, to stoop between them as she did so ... For what else did some shepherd see in his earlier day, but the Goddess bending from rock to rock as I saw her, till in that high and barren chaos above the height of trees she looked down on a more fortunate shepherd, Endymion asleep? So the legend began.'[6] This hardly 'explains' the myth, but it does provide an interesting sidelight on the way myth and geographical features mesh together at significant locations.

The classical city of Heraclea,[7] which contains the sanctuary of Endymion, is a re-foundation, possibly by Mausolus (r.377/6-353 BC), or possibly by Artemisia I of the 5$^{th}$ century BC.[8] The old city, which is generally said to have been originally called simply 'Latmos', lies somewhat to the east of Heraclea, and was perhaps a third of the size of the later city. However, Stephanus of Byzantium, writing in the *Ethnika*, informs us that the original name of the city was 'Bolbai', 'a city of Caria by the river Bolbaiotes, now called Herakleia. There is also by the city an inlet, Bolbe. The ethnic is Bolbaios.'[9] If Greek, the name appears to derive from *Bolbos*, bulb, or bulb-shaped; perhaps a reference to the shape of the inlet.[10]

The shrine of Endymion is mentioned by both Pausanias and Strabo. Pausanias says: 'As to the death of Endymion, the people of Heracleia near Miletus do not agree with the Eleans; for while the Eleans show a tomb of Endymion, the folk of Heracleia say that he retired to Mount Latmus and give him honour, there being

---

6 Stark 1956: pp.185-6.

7 Said to be 'allegedly founded by Endymion', according to Hornblower & Spawforth 1999: *s.v.* 'Heraclea by Latmus'. I have yet to find the source upon which this statement is based.

8 Reger: 98.11.19, note 23.

9 Stephanus of Byzantium 1849: p.174, *s.v.* 'Bolbai'. The date of Stephanus' work is unknown. The original is lost and only an epitome survives, written between the 6$^{th}$ and 10$^{th}$ centuries CE.

10 See also: Arkwright 1918: p.57.

## Selene

a shrine of Endymion on Latmus'.[11] Strabo, describing Latmos, says: 'This mountain lies above Herakleia, and at a high elevation. At a slight distance away from it, after one has crossed a little river near Latmos, there is to be seen the sepulchre of Endymion, in a cave.'[12]

There is some confusion here: Pausanias refers to a sanctuary, Strabo refers to a tomb in a cave. The confusion is made worse when Stark[13] refers to both the city's council house and the sanctuary of Endymion as lying 'across a brook', while no such brook appears on the map of the city given by George E. Bean.[14] Perhaps there was *both* a sanctuary in the city and a cave-tomb on the mountain; if so, no such cave-tomb on the mountain appears to have been identified. Or perhaps Pausanias and Strabo have confused their interpretations of the same, single site.

The sanctuary is described by Bean[15] who also provides a plan and a photograph. He too remarks on this confusion: 'Endymion had a sanctuary on Mt. Latmus; either this is a second shrine, or the spot is counted as being on the mountain.' The sanctuary is in the south of the city, near the shore. Bean describes it as follows:

'The accompanying plan shows the form of the structure: the main chamber is rounded at the back, and its wall fills in the spaces between large outcrops of rock which project into the interior. The wall was originally higher than it is now; beds for the blocks are cut into the surface of the rocks where it ran over them. A cross-wall with originally a door in the middle divides this chamber from an entrance porch with a row of unfluted columns in front; the row consists, most unusually, of a square pilaster at each end and five columns in between. An odd number of columns, giving

---

11 Pausanias, 5.1.5 (1926: Vol. 2, p.383).
12 Strabo, *Geography*, 14.1.8 (1929: Vol. 6, p.209).
13 Stark 1956: p.192.
14 Bean 1979: p.213.
15 Bean 1979: pp.214-215.

a column in the middle instead of a space, is exceedingly rare, and the whole form of the building is exceptional in the extreme. Two other column bases are visible in the interior; as they are not symmetrically placed, there may originally have been others. The identification of this strange building as a sanctuary of Endymion is very attractive; the entrance on the south-west suits the shrine of a hero or demi-god such as Endymion was; temples of gods and goddesses were entered from the east.'

From the scale on Bean's plan, it appears that the sanctuary is some 37 feet wide and 68 feet deep. With the rounded inner section being built amongst outcrops of rock, one is tempted to wonder if this was intended to represent the cave in which Endymion slept; if this is the case, it may perhaps explain the discrepancy in the descriptions of Pausanias and Strabo. From the source material available, there do not seem to be inscriptions or other evidence which make the identification of the shrine as being connected with Endymion absolutely certain; nor, unfortunately, is there any evidence of what the sanctuary may originally have contained, or what rites were performed there.

## 6.3 The Mythological Landscape: The Edges Of The Otherworld

Fascinating as the physical landscape of Carian Latmos may be, we mustn't allow ourselves to be misled, as Freya Stark appears to have been, into thinking that an 'explanation' for the myth is to be found in such simple observations as the way in which the Moon seems to linger about the mountain peaks. Similarly, the presence of a putative Endymion sanctuary at Heraclea (particularly as we know nothing of the rites performed there) really establishes little more than that this mountain was thought by the local populace to be the particular place in the physical world where the mythological event occurred. As that event appears to be transferable to other locations, we should suspect that perhaps mythological events, and mythological space, are of a rather different nature to the physical. As such, we need to pay more attention to the landscape that appears in the stories and written sources, rather than that which appears on the ground. If a cave is obviously important to the mythical event, but no corresponding physical cave has been found on the mountain itself, this should indicate that the cave is *more* important than might otherwise be thought, rather than something to be written off as 'just a fiction'. It is *so* important that it *has* to be in the story, regardless of whether it has a physical correlate in the 'real world'.

If we look back at the myths collected in Chapter 1, and at the material about Selenic cult in 2.4, it should be immediately obvious that Selene is not an urban Goddess, nor are her myths placed in urban contexts; Earthly Selene-temples are lacking, and in myth she does not even reside with the other Gods and Goddesses on Mount Olympus. Again, this is probably because she is a visible Goddess, and if she can be seen in the zenith sky she is quite obviously not resident in any particular 'home town' or temple. She begins her journey across the night sky from the Ocean stream, and returns to it at the journey's end; and the encircling Ocean stream defines the outer limits of the world. Indeed, she's hardly 'in the world' at all, and when she does descend to earth it tends to be in out-of-the-way places such as mountain-tops, or the 'backwoods' areas of Arcadia.

Greek civilisation was essentially urban. Its central organisational unit was the city, and society existed and was organised within those city-walls. Here were the palaces, the temples, the assemblies, the market-places and, most importantly, the relatively secure homes of the inhabitants. Within the city walls was Culture, with its knowable structures, familiarity and safety: the controlled and trustworthy 'inside'. Beyond the walls was Nature, far less known, unstructured, unpredictable and often dangerous: the 'outside' that defines 'civilisation' by *not* being civilised.[16] 'Civilised people' (soldiers, priests, merchants, etc.) move *through* this non-urban countryside; it's the 'outsiders' who actually *dwell* there, and amongst this non-urban class are shepherds, herdsmen and hunters. It may be recalled that the Carian Endymion is variously described as a shepherd, a herdsman or a hunter. It's not actually necessary to our analysis to believe that he was *literally* a shepherd or a hunter, or to try to decide which occupation better suited him; the point is that these various occupations define him as a person who is, or has gone, *outside* of what would be regarded as normal, predictable everyday life.

When we turn our attention more specifically to the scene of the actual encounter between Selene and Endymion, we find it occurs in what is known as a 'liminal area'. This is a boundary area where normality butts up against abnormality, where things change from one to another, or are both at once, or neither, and where time is often distorted and, ultimately, where contact with the otherworld becomes a possibility. We might quote a couple of simple examples for those unfamiliar with the concept. The tideline on the beach is a liminal area: it's where the sea meets the land, and it becomes hard to say whether that particular spot is one or the other. Noon is a similar 'liminal time': the Sun is directly overhead, and neither rising or setting, it's neither morning nor afternoon; in the tropics, at least, shadows disappear when the Sun is overhead which, particularly in an era of sun-dials, effectively means that time stands still. Looking at the Latmian tale of Selene and Endymion, we'll discover that, in fact, several aspects of liminality intersect with one another here.

Obviously, mountains and caves are 'outside' areas compared to the normal life of the city-dweller. As Buxton remarks, mountains are 'outside and wild'. They are also 'before': they were mankind's first home before he built cities, and they have always existed and

---

16 For this notion, and for much of the background that follows, see Buxton 1994, particularly p.80ff.

always will; as such, they are outside time in a way that the cities of men are not. Lastly, Buxton tells us, a mountain is a place for reversals, where things normally separate are brought together.[17] In particular, he says, they are places where men and deities encounter one another. We can perhaps go a little further than Buxton here: mountains are actually in a liminal area between earth and heaven. They rise up above the rest of the earth and, as anyone will know who has climbed to one of their peaks, heaven, or the sky, seems very close. It's perhaps not surprising that men meet the Gods here.

Buxton's summarised thoughts on caves are also worth quoting. 'A cave is defined by its anomalous and ambiguous shape: it is both inside and outside. It may also be simultaneously above and below ground, and be located either in the wilds – on a mountain, near the sea, under the sea – or in the heart of a human settlement ... A cave is both like and not like a house: unlike because natural; like, because sheltering. Caves are also open, yet impenetrable. They give access to the sacred or, ultimately, to the dead ...'[18] It's already been mentioned how close the 'underworld' was thought to be by the Greeks, in that it was possible to sacrifice to the underworld Gods by simply digging a hole in the ground and letting the blood of the sacrifice run straight down to the deities below. A cave, then, is another ambiguous, liminal area: it's the border-crossing between upper and lower worlds, and also between the world of the living and the dead.

It's perhaps of less importance to our thinking here that the physical Mount Latmos was on the coast, another liminal area where the land meets the sea (and, interestingly, at the head of an inlet, where the sea was effectively 'out of place', having come inland to meet the mountain). However, the conjunction of the cave and the mountain (the 'low' underground cave being high up

---

17 Buxton 1994: pp.88-91.
18 Buxton 1994: p.108.

the mountain) is of particular importance: here we have a nexus of all three aspects of a triple universe: heaven, earth and underworld ... the worlds of the Gods, the living and the dead. Selene and Endymion in the Latmian cave, then, are at the absolute centre of the mythical universe in all its aspects. Such is the ambiguity of such liminal areas, however, that they can also be seen as being outside it, in a timeless world of their own. This, then, is a liminal area *par excellence*; we might almost say it is a 'mythically-enhanced' liminal area, or a truly archetypal representation of one. Or, to put it more simply, we can read this as code: 'there is something *supremely special* about this cave'.

Having examined the place of their encounter, it's now time to turn our attention to the spatial and temporal co-ordinates of Selene and Endymion themselves. We'll begin with Endymion.

We've seen that Endymion, as hunter, herdsman or shepherd, is already 'outside' of normal, urbanised society, and ultimately he's found residing in a cave, a liminal area we've discussed above. He is usually said to be eternally asleep, and sleep itself is a liminal state: it is halfway between wakefulness and death, when the body is paralysed but the mind may still be active, in dream. As was remarked above, the cave itself can be seen to be archetypal, and the eternal sleep can be seen in the same way: this is 'mythically-enhanced' sleep, and once again we can read the code: 'this is *supremely special* sleep'. In one variant, where it is Hypnos ('Sleep', the brother of Thanatos, 'Death') who is responsible for his slumber, Endymion sleeps with his eyes open, which indicates yet another ambiguity: this is sleep simulating wakefulness, neither really the one or the other. Again, we may read the fact that there are variants where Endymion can either be asleep in Selene's arms, or Selene's conscious lover, as indicating the possibility of both. This is a very ambiguous sleep indeed. There are two ways of reading the 'eternal sleep' as well. One is the obvious, and literal, idea that the sleep lasts forever; the other is that this is sleep that is eternal because time itself has stopped. In the ambiguous, borderland area of the cave on the mountain, Endymion is outside of the timestream that flows on for normal people in the 'real world'. That in some very late versions the sleep is limited to 30 years, while less relevant to the discussion here, becomes more meaningful in this context: the sleep is 'eternal' in that it is outside the normal flow of time, but is seen to be limited to 30 years when viewed from a real-world perspective. This 'limited eternity' of the sleep also gives us a link to the material to be presented in the next chapter.

If Endymion is a 'liminal figure', on the borderline between life and death, sleep and dream, and such-like, we should recall that Selene herself is also very much the same. Selene is, after all, *both* the Goddess and the physical Moon, a 'cross-over position' if ever there was one, so it's not surprising to find Plutarch telling us that: 'The moon, in fact, is both earthly and heavenly, a place where the immortal is blended with the mortal.'[19] It's hardly surprising then, that Selene is the perfect partner for the similarly mortal-immortal, earthly-heavenly figure of Endymion.

Selene is also, as we've seen, an 'outsider' to urban society. In this story she's well outside her normal domain as well. No longer in the sky, and not even at the 'edges of the world' where she begins and ends her journey in the Ocean stream, she's descended to Earth; and more, she's in a cave below the surface as well. The stories we have of her amour with Endymion don't actually state a time when this occurs, although obviously this is a nocturnal encounter. Night, too, is a time for 'outsiders': the day's activities, which define urban society, such as work, trade and worship, are concluded; night is for the activities of entertainers, thieves, drinkers, lovers, sleepers and dreamers ... precisely the people that Shakespeare referred to as the 'minions of the moon'.[20]

Given that Endymion's sleep is eternal, it would not be surprising if his amour with Selene was thought to be continued

---

19 Plutarch, *Of Love* 19 (764D) (1961: Vol. 9, p.399).
20 Shakespeare, *Henry IV*, Part One, Act 1, Scene 2.

on a nightly basis; and perhaps that is why the stories don't actually name specific times for the encounters. There may be a reason for this, for except at the time of the Full Moon, when the Moon rises with the dusk and sets with the dawn, there is always some part of the night when the Moon is not visible: toward morning when she is waxing, in the evening when she is waning. Such times of darkness would, of course, provide opportunities for Selene to be with Endymion. One should also mention that, with a knowledge of the Moon's phases and its position in the sky, it is possible to use the Moon to tell the time: for example, when the Moon is Full and at its zenith in the south, the time is midnight. When the Moon has set or not yet risen, there is no temporal indicator: we are once again in a liminal period, outside time.

When looking for more specific liminal points in the Moon's course, however, there are two times of the month of particular interest: the New Moon (*i.e.*, specifically the Dark of the Moon, rather than the first appearance of the crescent 'New' Moon) and the Full Moon. Regarding the New Moon, we've seen at 1.5.3 that Nicander is said to have stated that '*Aselena ore* ('No-Moon mountains') were so called because when Selene slept there with Endymion the rest of the world went Moonless'. This suggests the fairly obvious thought that the time when Selene visited Endymion was when she was completely invisible in the sky: at the New or Dark of the Moon, the perfect liminal point between the old and the new months.

The Full Moon, while obviously another liminal point between the waxing and waning half of the months, provides a more interesting problem for, as mentioned above, this is the one time of the month when we would expect Selene *not* to be with Endymion. It will be recalled that the scholia to Apollonius Rhodius, which provide so much of our information on Selene and Endymion, referred to a passage of Apollonius that had Selene saying to Medea: 'How many times when I was bent on love, have you disorbed me with your incantations, making the night Moonless …' (see above

## Selene

1.5.2). While Apollonius' intention here is obviously to imply that Medea has *interfered* with Selene's love-life by the witchcraft practice of 'drawing down the Moon', the fact that this is another reference to the Moon descending to Earth makes it worthy of our attention.

When we examine the ancient literature on this subject,[21] it becomes apparent that one of the stereotypical 'powers' of witches, especially the witches of Thessaly, who were archetypally the most potent of them all, was to 'draw down the Moon with spells', with the result that the Moon would then shed a 'foam' (*aphroselenos*) on certain herbs, which could then be collected and used as a magical ingredient. The nature of this foam, and its uses, is too complex a subject to go into here; the point that interests us for the present is *when* this occurred: which was during a lunar eclipse. Indeed, that 'witches were drawing down the Moon' became a folkloric *explanation* for eclipses, with the result that it was customary to assist the Moon to recover by beating copper pots and making loud noises, in order to drown out the sound of the witches' spells. The point here, of course, is that lunar eclipses only occur when the Moon is full. The Moon may be descending under compulsion, and by 'artificial' rather than 'natural' means; yet this still defines another point in the monthly cycle when it is *possible* for the Moon (who, it will be recalled, is always Selene as well as the physical Moon) to descend to Earth. In the case of an eclipse, of course, the Moon is unnaturally darkened and the cause is apparently wicked witchcraft; what we have here is an evil reversal of the natural process which still demonstrates the possibilities of this liminal moment by showing its abnormal twin. And, it must be remembered, lunar eclipses occur on average only twice a year; the rest of the year, the Full Moon may well have been seen 'stooping' between the peaks of Latmos, just as Freya Stark described.

Whether we think it more likely that Selene descended to

---

21 Moore 1995: pp.216-245, with collected references. See especially pp.217-221.

## Steve Moore

Latmos on a New Moon than a Full is perhaps beside the point. Both New and Full Moon are liminal zones: times of change-over when the Moon is *neither* waxing *nor* waning ... when, effectively, time stands still. Each is an appropriate occasion, then, for Selene to encounter Endymion, for whom, being eternally asleep, time also stands still.

It is in this timeless time, this eternal moment, that Selene and Endymion consummate their relationship, whatever that relationship might signify. It is a moment that may at first seem to be nothing more than 'ever-now', but in the 'ever-now' the past and the future merge with the present moment. Sequential time may have ceased to flow, but concurrently *all* of time's flow, from beginning to end, becomes simultaneous; and being simultaneous, become accessible to those who have the means to experience it.

Chapter Seven

# Epimenides Of Crete

## 7.1 Introduction

At the end of the previous chapter (6.3) we outlined a number of features regarding the mythical space-time in which the Carian story of Selene and Endymion takes place. So far, however, we have yet to discover exactly what was going on, under the surface of the story, in the Latmian cave, and to what this interaction between deity and human actually refers. The search for clues will now take us away, temporarily, from Latmos and across physical time and space, to the island of Crete. Arriving there, however, we may well find that the mythical space-time co-ordinates have a rather familiar feel to them. It's now time to examine the story of the other great cave-sleeper of Greek antiquity, Epimenides.

## 7.2 Who Was Epimenides?

Whether Epimenides was a historical person around whom a number of legends gathered, or an entirely mythical figure, has long been a matter of dispute. As with Endymion, it seems worth taking a closer look at his name, which appears to derive from *epimeno*, 'to abide still, to continue, to await', in turning deriving from *meno*, 'to abide, to linger, to continue, to be lasting, to be unchanged'. Given that Epimenides is said to have slept for several decades in a cave, and to have lived well into a second century (or even beyond), we might suspect that, as with Endymion, there's a possibility that the name is simply too conveniently fitting to the stories told about him to be entirely coincidental. Fortunately, whether Epimenides was 'real' or not is a matter of little consequence to the development of the argument here; what's important are the *stories* told about him. However, a short 'biographical' sketch will help set the scene.

Our main source of material on Epimenides from antiquity is a work by Diogenes Laertius called *Lives and Opinions of Eminent Philosophers*, probably written in the early part of the $3^{rd}$ century CE.[1] Diogenes Laertius, in turn, seems to draw most of his material about Epimenides from Theopompus of Chios, who lived in the $4^{th}$ century BCE. However, as one of the philosophers who is sometimes included in the varying lists of the 'Seven Sages of Greece', Epimenides appears in a number of other sources which, almost inevitably, means that there are a number of variant tales about him.

Assuming him to be historical, Epimenides is generally thought to have lived about 600 BCE, although as always, there is disagreement here. All our sources seem to agree that he was Cretan. Theopompus says he was a native of Knossos, and names his father as Phaestius; Diogenes Laertius also mentions the names Dosiadas and Agesarchus for his father. Plutarch makes him a native of Phaestus, but perhaps here we have a confusion with the possible paternal name Phaestius; Plutarch names no father, but simply says that Epimenides' mother was a Nymph named Balte. He also describes Epimenides as 'a man beloved of the gods, and endowed with a mystical and heaven-sent wisdom in religious matters'.[2]

Leaving aside the matter of his legendary sleep for the moment, Epimenides is mainly famed as a purificatory priest, and is

---

1 Diogenes Laertius, 1.10 (1.109-115) (1925: Vol. 1, pp.115-121).
2 Plutarch, *Solon*, 12.4. (1914: Vol. 1, p.433).

particularly noted for his purification of Athens[3]. This is said to have occurred in the 46th Olympiad (595-592 BCE) when Athens was suffering from a plague, supposed to have been connected with the attempted coup of Cylon. When this failed, Cylon escaped, but certain of his friends were slaughtered while suppliants at an altar on the Acropolis; and this pollution of the right of sanctuary was thought to have been punished with pestilence. Epimenides was brought by ship from Crete, and purified the city by releasing a number of sheep, some black, some white; wherever the sheep lay down, they were duly sacrificed to the local divinity. A variant story, however, has Epimenides offering two young men as human sacrifices. He returned to Crete and is said to have died shortly thereafter, at an age variously given by Diogenes Laertius as 154, 157, or 299. As we'll see, for a number of these years, he was thought to have been asleep in a cave.

Plato has a variant story of Epimenides' visit to Athens, which he places 10 years before the Persian invasion of Greece (*i.e.*, Epimenides' arrival was c.500 BCE). Plato says that Epimenides made certain sacrifices and predicted the Persian invasion, but when the Athenians were alarmed by this, added: 'They will not come for ten years, and when they do come, they will return back again with all their hopes frustrated, and after suffering more woes than they inflict'.[4] It's possible that the story of Epimenides' long life may originate in the century-wide differences in dating; it's even possible that the tale of his long sleep may have a similar origin, in an attempt to correlate differing dates. This is unprovable, of course, and one suspects that, whatever its origin, the story of the long sleep is actually far more important than concerns with absolute dating.

Epimenides was said to have written a number of works, including a poem *On the Birth of the Curetes and Corybantes*, a

---

3 Diogenes Laertius, 1.10 (1.109-115) (1925: Vol. 1, pp.115-121). Plutarch, *Solon*, 12.4. (1914: Vol. 1, p.433).

4 Plato *Laws, Book 1* (642D-E) (1926: Vol. 9, pp.61-63).

*Theogony*, and a poem on Jason and the Argonauts; prose works included *On Sacrifices and the Cretan Constitution* and *On Minos and Rhadamanthus*. Whether such works were actually authored by Epimenides, or were otherwise anonymous works that had his name attached to them, is impossible to say; they have not survived, and we only have a few fragments of verse attributed to him.

## 7.3 The Sleep Of Epimenides

While there are variants, the 'standard' (*i.e.*, most complete and unitary) version of the story of Epimenides' long sleep, as given by Diogenes Laertius, is as follows:

'One day he was sent into the country by his father to look for a stray sheep, and at noon he turned aside out of the way, and went to sleep in a cave, where he slept for fifty-seven years. After this he got up and went in search of the sheep, thinking he had been asleep only a short time. And when he could not find it, he came to the farm, and found everything changed and another owner in possession. Then he went back to the town in utter perplexity; and there, on entering his own house, he fell in with people who wanted to know who he was. At length he found his younger brother, now an old man, and learnt the truth from him. So he became famous throughout Greece, and was believed to be a special favourite of heaven.'[5]

Naturally, the length of the sleep varies in other sources, as we might have come to expect. So Tertullian, Varro and Plutarch time the sleep at 50 years (Plutarch adding the curious detail that he went to sleep a youth and woke an aged man, which may simply be reference to the length of his sleep; if it implies that he went to sleep as a physical teenager and woke up grey-haired, this is a notion

---

5 Diogenes Laertius, 1.10 (1.109-110) (1925: Vol. 1, pp.115).

not reflected in other sources);[6] Pausanias at 40.[7] When we come to unreferenced secondary sources, there is even more variation: so Lempriere has 40, 47 or 57 years,[8] while Halliday gives 40, 50, 57 or 60 (the last figure apparently drawn from Hesychios).[9] According to the Greek lexicon known as the *Suda*, he lived 150 years, but slept 90.[10]

Another relatively complete treatment of the sleep of Epimenides is given by Apollonius Dyscolus (2nd century CE). Although claiming Theopompus as his source, Apollonius provides a couple of significant variants: that Epimenides led a flock of sheep belonging to his father and brother out into the country, and lost one; and that he fell asleep when overtaken by night. Otherwise, the story proceeds as normal (though it lacks some details; there is, for example, no mention of the cave) and the length of sleep is once again given as 57 years.[11]

Naturally, this doesn't exhaust the references to the sleep of Epimenides (and we shall refer to others as we proceed), but these give us sufficient material for a preliminary discussion. It's notable also that, in all our sources, the sleep of Epimenides appears at the beginning of his life-history; it's only *afterwards* that we hear of his activities as a priest, seer or poet with particular knowledge of, or contact with, the deities. This is an aspect we shall return to below.

To start with, though, we can begin to draw some preliminary comparisons with the story of Endymion. First, it appears to be obvious that the young Epimenides, prior to his sleep, was a shepherd, whether he's associated simply with a single missing sheep, or whether he has a flock with him. As is usual with such multivalent material, there may, possibly, be a punning reference here. Diogenes Laertius

---

6 Tertullian, *De Anima*, 44 (1874: Vol. 2, p.511). Varro: De Lingua Latina, 7.3 (1951: Vol. 1, p.269). Plutarch: Aged Men, 1 (1936: Vol. 10, p.81).

7 Pausanias, 1.14.4 (1918: Vol. 1, p.73).

8 J. Lempriere, *A Classical Dictionary* (n.d.): *s.v.* 'Epimenides'.

9 Halliday 1967 (Rpt: 1913): pp.91-92.

10 Suda, *s.v.* 'Epimenides'.

11 Apollonius Dyscolus, *Historiae 1* (1792: pp.35-39).

lists a small amount of material that connects Epimenides with the Nymphs, including a quotation from Theopompus' *Mirabilia*, informing us that he was building a temple to the Nymphs, when a voice came from heaven saying: 'Epimenides, not a temple to the Nymphs but to Zeus'[12] and we have also seen above that Plutarch says his mother was a Nymph. Perhaps this relation arises from a punning association between Epimenides and a class of Nymphs known as the Epimelides, who were particularly associated with flocks of sheep;[13] however, our sources simply refer to 'Nymphs' without specifying a particular class. The connection with sheep may be rather more important than that with the Nymphs, however, for in this we find a close parallel with Endymion, and the significance of the sheep to both stories is one we will return to in due course (see below, 11.2). Similarly, both Epimenides and Endymion sleep in a cave. According to the version of the story presented by Maximus Tyrius (2nd century CE), this was the cave of Dictaean Zeus, a Cretan sanctuary placed high up on a mountain.[14]

Apollonius Dyscolus tells us that Epimenides retired to sleep at night. This may simply be an assumption; it is, after all, more logical for him to have retired at night; and yet in this, again, we see some parallel with Endymion's nocturnal sleep. Diogenes Laertius, however, has Epimenides retire to the cave at noon. This is not so surprising as it may first appear.

Carl Kerenyi makes an interesting point about the significance of noon in this story: 'It is the time of noon when the shadows of things cease by their length and direction to serve as a measure of time. The shadows withdraw. The culmination of the Sun makes it seem as if time had stopped. The actual time-measurer, the Sun,

---

12 Diogenes Laertius, 1.10 (1.115) (1925: Vol. 1, p.121).
13 For the Epimelides, see Antoninus Liberalis 31 (1992: pp.90, 196-197).
14 Maximus Tyrius 28 (1994 (Rpt. 1805): p.221).

stands at its peak and really does seem to 'stand still'.[15] This is undoubtedly a valid point, and correlates particularly well with was said above (6.3) about the 'timeless' aspects of the new and full Moon, discussed in relation to the story of Endymion. Once again, we have the young man in a cave, associated with sheep, sleeping in a 'timeless instant'; the liminal space and time correlates may well sound familiar.

Kerenyi's further discussion of the story is rather less satisfactory and depends (as unfortunately seems rather too frequently to be the case with Kerenyi) on selective use of the source material. His quoted source for the story is Theopompus fragment 67, presumably deriving through Diogenes Laertius, and he continues: 'Epimenides woke up fifty-seven years later ... It was three times the nineteen years of the Metonic cycle, the greatest unit of time among the Greeks. Fifty-seven years are time *itself*, increased threefold. Epimenides lived to be a hundred and fifty-seven. Thus, he lost out of his lifespan (rated, in the view of antiquity, at a hundred years), by the insertion of timelessness symbolised by the fifty-seven years, nothing.'

While it may seem that there is nothing inherently objectionable here with regard to the development of an argument comparing the Endymion and Epimenides stories, Kerenyi's handling of the topic is open to criticism. The first is the handling of sources.

Kerenyi quotes only Theopompus and, indeed, both Diogenes Laertius and Apollonius Dyscolus quote Theompompus likewise for a sleep of 57 years. However, as we've seen, a number of different lengths for Epimenides' sleep are given: 40, 47, 50, 57 and 60 years. Kerenyi takes no account of any of these differing figures. Similarly, the statement that Epimenides lived to be 157 years is open to question. Apollonius Dyscolus quotes Theopompus as saying that, according the Cretans, Epimenides lived 150 years.

---

15 Kerenyi 1975: p.32.

## Selene

Pliny quotes Theopompus and says he lived to be 153.[16] Valerius Maximus, however, quotes Theopompus for 157 years.[17] Diogenes Laertius does give a lifespan of 157, but *not* from Theopompus; for this figure he quotes Phlegon of Tralles' *Long-Lived Persons* (although no mention of Epimenides remains in Phlegon's fragmentary text).[18] However, he also quotes 'the Cretans' as saying that he lived 299 years, and Xenophanes of Colophon for 154 years. Given the conflicting nature of the evidence, it seems unsafe to build upon it such definitive arguments as Kerenyi does.

Putting aside Kerenyi's selective use of the material, what can we make of his interpretation of the '57 year period'? Meton of Athens introduced to the Greek world the 19-year luni-solar calendrical cycle, which brings the lunar and solar years into conjunction (19 solar years equalling 235 lunar months), probably basing this on Babylonian astronomical work. He lived in the 5$^{th}$ century BCE, and so before Theopompus; thus there's nothing inherently unlikely in Theopompus taking a 19-year cycle and multiplying it by three. However, to speak of the 19 years of the Metonic cycle as the 'greatest unit of time among the Greeks' while, in the same paragraph, referring to a 'lifespan' rated in antiquity at 100 years, seems contradictory, to say the least. If Theopompus wished to triple the 'greatest unit of time' one would expect him to triple the century. Besides, by Theopompus' day, the Metonic cycle was being replaced by the more accurate 76-year Callipic cycle of Theopompus' contemporary, Callipus. If Epimenides had slept for 19 years only, then an interesting argument for timelessness might be made, in that 'time had returned to its starting point', as the Moon would then be both in the same phase, and in the same position in the zodiac, for the first time since the sleep began. In this case, though, tripling the cycle would appear to be pointless;

---

16 Pliny, *Natural History* 7 48 (154) (1942:Vol. 2, p.609).

17 Valerius Maximus, *Memorable Doings and Sayings* 8.13.ext.5 (2000:Vol. 2, p.269).

18 Phlegon of Tralles 1996: p.183.

and indeed, Kerenyi offers no explanation as to *why* Theopompus might have wished to triple it. If multiplying by three had any particular significance to the Greeks in terms of indicating 'the largest expansion possible', Kerenyi offers nothing to back this up.

We do know, however, that Meton's contemporary Oinopides (using inaccurate lengths for the lunar months and solar years) proposed a 'Great Year', bringing the lunar and solar calendars into conjunction after 59 years.[19] If Theopompus had a similar notion in mind, of a 'Great Year' of 57 years (perhaps based on a tripling of the Metonic cycle), then Epimenides' sleep of 57 years, rather than representing Kerenyi's 'three times time itself', would simply represent a 'long cycle of time'.

This may seem like a harsh critique of Kerenyi's handling of the material, but there is an important distinction to be made. Endymion's sleep is timeless, eternal and, effectively, outside the measurable world we know. Epimenides' sleep may temporarily take him outside of the normal progression of time, but it is *not* eternal; it is measurable in terms of this earthly world and, most importantly, it ends when he wakes. In that Epimenides enters the cave at noon, when 'time stands still', his sleep has a qualitative similarity to that of Endymion; in terms of quantity, however, it is quite different.

Nonetheless, G.H. Huxley pointed out a number of connections between Epimenides and Endymion.[20] We've seen above, at 1.5.2, that Epimenides is credited as one source of the story about Endymion's attempted seduction of Hera, and also that he claimed to be the offspring of Selene (1.3.6-7); he also points out the parallels between their lengthy slumbers. Given these connections and similarities, it's now time to look at the effects of Epimenides' lengthy sleep.

---

19 Dicks 1970: pp.88-89.
20 Huxley 1969: pp.82-83.

## 7.4 The Revelations Of Epimenides

If it appears that the sleep of Epimenides has similar qualities to that of Endymion, it then becomes of some interest to discover what we can about the nature of those qualities. It's already been remarked, in the previous section, that Epimenides only appears to have taken on the roles of priest and poet upon his return to the world *after* his lengthy sleep; Endymion, of course, makes no such return.

Talking of Epimenides, Anna Strataridaki states, forthrightly, that 'a dream was believed to have transformed him into a seer'.[21] This appears to be confirmed by Maximus Tyrius who, referring to Epimenides' handling of the Athenian pollution mentioned above, tells us that 'he was skilful in divine concerns ... not from having learnt them, but a long sleep narrated them to him, and a dream was his preceptor'.[22]

Elsewhere, Maximus returns to Epimenides, and says that, lying in the cavern of Dictaean Zeus 'in a profound sleep for many years, he saw the gods, and the offspring of the gods, together with Truth and Justice'.[23]

Like Strataridaki, Halliday justly interprets these passages from Maximus as referring to initiation in dreams[24], and also brings to our attention a passage from Porphyry's *Life of Pythagoras*: 'Going to Crete, Pythagoras besought initiation from the priests of Morgos, one of the Idaean Dactyls, by whom he was purified with the meteoric thunderstone, during which he lay, at dawn, stretched upon his face by the seaside, and at night, beside a river, crowned with a black lamb's woollen wreath. Descending into the Idaean cave, wrapped in black wool (translated by Eliade

---

21 Strataridaki 1991, p.209.
22 Maximus Tyrius 22 (1994 (Rpt. 1805): p.163).
23 Maximus Tyrius 28 (1994 (Rpt. 1805): p.221).
24 Halliday 1967 (Rpt: 1913): p.92.

as a 'black fleece', which seems rather more likely[25]), he stayed there 27 days, according to the custom; he sacrificed to Zeus, and saw the couch which there is yearly made for him.'[26] There are a number of interesting points about this passage, of which we will have more to say in the next chapter. The seaside, the river and the cave are all liminal areas, as discussed above (6.3), and the Idaean Cave is another sanctuary-cave placed high on a mountain; it is, besides, often confused with the Dictaean. And, again, we have the connection with sheep, through the black lamb's fleece. This passage doesn't tell us the nature of the initiation conferred on Pythagoras, but when we turn to the section on initiations in Diogenes Laertius' *Life of Pythagoras*, we're told that: 'while in Crete he went down into the cave of Ida with Epimenides'.[27] This linking of the two names would seem to suggest that the initiation of Pythagoras was similar to that of Epimenides; and Maximus Tyrius has told us that Epimenides, sleeping and dreaming, saw the Gods and their offspring, and Truth and Justice (which, here, we might take as code for 'Wisdom'). There is a further connection between the two men: Diogenes Laertius tells us that Epimenides claimed his soul had passed through many incarnations,[28] and this is a distinctly Pythagorean tenet.

There is, though, a further tale connected with the cave of Zeus, recorded by Plato in the *Laws*[29] and again in the (Pseudo-Platonic?) *Minos*[30]. *Which* cave of Zeus is unclear; in the *Laws*, Plato has his group of dialogists begin their walk to the cave from Knossos, but as Knossos is more or less equidistant from both the Idaean and the Dictaean Caves, there seems to be no way of choosing between

---

25 Eliade 1972: p.26.
26 Porphyry, *Life of Pythagoras* 17 (1987: p.126).
27 Diogenes Laertius, 8.1. (8.3) (1925: Vol. 2, p.323).
28 Diogenes Laertius, 1.10 (1.114) (1925: Vol. 1, p.121).
29 Plato, *Laws* 1.1 (624B-625B) (1926: Vol. 9, pp.3-5).
30 Plato, *Minos* 13-14 (319B-E) (1927: Vol. 8, pp.413-415).

them. Plato then tells us that in ancient times, the legendary king Minos of Crete, noted as a wise lawgiver, would enter the cave of Zeus every ninth year to confer with him and, as he says in the *Laws*, 'according to the oracular responses given by him', would then lay down the laws. The *Minos* tells us that 'each ninth year, Minos went to the cavern of Zeus, to learn some things, and to show forth others'. Again then, we have a tradition where wisdom is gained in a cave and, perhaps more interestingly, a reference to 'oracular responses' ... a subject to which we'll return in Chapter 8. That these oracular responses are obtained in the cave where Epimenides is thought to have slept is of particular interest.

Whether we regard this material as initiatory or not, what we seem to have here, underlying the tales of Epimenides, Pythagoras and Minos (all of which are stories 'writ large' in a legendary or mythical fashion), is a tradition of gaining wisdom, 'occult knowledge' or oracles by sleeping in a cave on a mountain, at least two of the stories also being connected with sheep. Cicero is more explicit regarding Epimenides: he discusses divination by those 'under the influence of mental excitement, or of some free and unrestrained emotion. This condition often occurs to men while dreaming and sometimes to persons who prophesy while in a frenzy – like Bacis of Boeotia, Epimenides of Crete and the Sibyl of Erythraea. In this latter class must be placed oracles [...] uttered under the impulse of divine inspiration.'[31]

If divine inspiration is involved here, it has to be said that the sources quoted above give us very little idea as to which particular divinity, or divinities, are associated with Epimenides. However, W.R. Connor, in a fascinating article on nympholepsy (possession by the Nymphs), provides a possible explanation.[32] We have seen above (7.3) that Epimenides was building a temple to the Nymphs when a voice commanded him to build it to Zeus instead. As

---

31 Cicero, *De Divinatione* 1.18 (34) (1923: Vol. 20, p.263).
32 Connor 1988: 164-165 & *passim*.

Connor points out, a common practice at other cave-shrines to the Nymphs was that the main nympholept, apart from spending much time in the cave where he would be possessed, would also carve the cave itself into a shrine. We've also seen that Epimenides' mother was said to be a Nymph (7.2) and, as discussed below (7.5), he received food from them as well. Connor therefore suggests that Epimenides himself may have been nympholeptic, and that the story of his long sleep reflects a withdrawal from the world to spend time in the Nymphs' cave-shrine, a known practice at other such locations. If this is the case, Theopompus' story about the voice commanding him to dedicate the shrine to Zeus may, in fact, represent a change of emphasis in the story, whereby Epimenides originally slept in an unidentified Nymph's cave, while later tradition connected him with the rather more noteworthy caves of Zeus on Mounts Ida and Dictae.

Connor also makes a number of other interesting points about nympholepsy: that the encounters between nympholept and Nymph(s) usually take place in caves, and that the relationship is often described in erotic terms; that the state of nympholepsy is often brought on by looking at springs or fountains (and we shall see that both springs and Nymphs are common at the oracular shrines to be discussed below in Chapter 10); that nympholepsy itself is not a state of frenzied possession but one that brings heightened awareness, eloquence, prophecy and, occasionally, speech in metrical verse; it also brings enhanced social status.[33] As we'll see below (13.3.3), Epimenides was credited with producing oracular texts, and these were, of course, written in metrical verse.

Diogenes Laertius, while not telling us *how* Epimenides made his predictions, tells us that he had 'superhuman foresight' and lists two or three military defeats that he is supposed to have foretold.[34] The *Suda* is perhaps more interesting still, in that

---

33 Connor 1988: *passim*, with collected classical sources.
34 Diogenes Laertius, 1.10 (1.114-115) (1925: Vol. 1, p.121).

it tells us Epimenides' soul could leave his body and enter it again at will; that he wrote 'certain mystery-writings and spells and other riddling works'; and that after death his skin was found to be tattooed with letters, giving rise to a proverb about '"Epimenidean skin", in reference to "secrets".'[35] Whether we are to read the mention of his soul leaving his body as referring to an out-of-the-body experience, as we understand it today, or simply as a visionary encounter in an altered state of consciousness is, perhaps, a moot point. However, the 'Epimenidean Skin' has been explained, firstly by Leahy[36], and enthusiastically taken up by Bremmer[37], as actually being a parchment or leather scroll, perhaps of actual human skin, kept at Sparta, which also claimed to be the site of Epimenides' tomb (interestingly, we have seen above at 1.5.2 that a minor tradition preserved by the Scholiast to Apollonius of Rhodes makes Endymion of Spartan origin); and that this scroll was actually a collection of oracles. From Herodotus we know that among the Ionian Greeks of what is now the Turkish mainland, papyrus books were still referred to as *diptherai* or 'skins', this being a survival of the name of earlier books written on parchment, and that as late as the 5th century BCE oracle books were still referred to as *diptherai*.[38] Nonetheless, it has to be said that the matching of such *diptherai* and 'Epimenides' skin' is no more than conjectural and Strataridaki suggests the story of the letters tattooed on the seer's skin has become confused with that of the Spartan king Cleomenes, who flayed the founder of Anthana and inscribed oracles on his skin.[39] Given Epimenides' connections with oracles and oracular texts, and the *Suda*'s reference to the skin referring to 'secrets', one is very inclined

---

35 *Suda: s.v.* 'Epimenides'.
36 Leahy, 1958: p.155.
37 Bremmer 1993 [1]: pp.235-236. Bremmer 1993: [2], p.156.
38 Burkert 1992: p.31.
39 Strataridaki 1991: p.213.

to follow Leahy and Bremmer; but there's no actual proof of the connection.

We have seen above (1.3.6-7) that Epimenides claimed, in a poem attributed to him, to be a 'sprung from the fair-tressed Moon', and that in this he was similar to Musaeus; and that the pair of them, along with Orpheus, were noted for the promulgation of oracles, a subject we'll return to below in Chapter 13. We seem, then, to have a growing collection of material suggesting a pattern of lunar-related oracles, received in dreams, in caves, along with an ongoing tradition of revelation related to it. We shall explore this revelatory tradition and its parallels further in the next chapter.

## 7.5 Appendix: Epimenides' Diet

Diogenes Laertius quotes a certain Demetrius (perhaps Demetrius of Phalerum), who said that Epimenides 'received from the Nymphs food of a special sort and kept it in a cow's hoof; that he took small doses of this food, which was entirely absorbed into his system, and he was never seen to eat'.[40] If the long-lived Epimenides 'entirely absorbed' the food, and did not evacuate, as seems to be implied here, this resonates strongly with what we have seen above (4.2.3) regarding cicadas and the immortality of Tithonus. However, this same lack of excretion is similarly recorded about the putative inhabitants of the Moon, who also did not evacuate;[41] again, this ties in with Epimenides as 'Moon-Man'. Plutarch emphasises the minimal size of the meals in his *Face which Appears in the Orb of the Moon* where he tells us, without giving any indication of the recipe, that Epimenides' meals were no larger than the size of an olive.[42] We might also note that Porphyry, in his work on vegetarianism, puts forward the idea that the less we

---

40 Diogenes Laertius, 1.10 (1.114) (1925: Vol. 1, p.119).

41 A topic of Pythagorean speculation, satirised by Lucian in his *True History*. Moore, 1990.

42 Plutarch, *Concerning the Face which Appears in the Orb of the Moon* 25 (940C) (1957: Vol. 12, p.177).

eat, the more we become immortal; an idea of some relevance to Epimenides' alleged longevity.[43] We've also seen above, at 4.2.3, that passing no excrement and abstaining from normal food was a sign of closeness to the Gods.

Rohde quotes Theophrastus' *History of Plants*, to the effect that Epimenides' diet consisted of asphodel, mallow and squill, and points out that these plants are sacred to the underworld deities.[44] Interestingly, there is actually a variety of squill known as 'Epimenides' squill', which was used both medically and apotropaically (*i.e.*, magically).[45] However, when we turn to Plutarch's *Dinner of the Seven Wise Men* we find asphodel and mallow mentioned as part of a vegetarian diet, but no mention that Epimenides ate them; instead he is said to have eaten his 'potent "no-hunger" [*alimon*]', which he himself compounded (rather than it being given to him by the Nymphs), and which enabled him to go all day without eating.[46] Plutarch goes on to explain that *alimon* is a 'drug' composed of honey, a cheese found among barbarians, and a great many seeds of a sort hard to procure, and contrasts this strongly with a diet of mallow and asphodel. This sounds rather like the cheesecakes (*amphiphon*) offered to the Moon mentioned by Athenaeus (above at 2.4). As is so often the case, we have a group of tantalising hints that seem to indicate a connected whole, but are not quite enough to give us the complete picture. They are, however, small pieces of a jigsaw that will continue to be put together as the book progresses.

---

43 Porphyry, *On Abstinence From Animal Food* 4.20 (1965: p.179).
44 Rohde 1966 (Rpt. 1925): Vol. 2, p.331.
45 Stannard 1974: p.689.
46 Plutarch, *Dinner of the Seven Wise Men* 14 (157D-F) (1928: Vol. 2, pp.411-413).

Chapter Eight

# Cave Initiations, Wisdom Traditions And Dwellers Under The Earth

## 8.1 Introduction

It has been pointed out above (7.4) that the sleep of Epimenides has been interpreted as referring to a form of initiation in dreams, in which the person to be initiated sleeps in a cave. In that initiation confers knowledge and wisdom, there is some parallel here with consultation of a dream oracle (of which we will have more to say in Chapters 9 and 10). However, religious initiation also implies rather more than this: that the person initiated is entering into an intimate relationship with a particular deity (or group of deities), spirit or wisdom-source, and that this 'higher source' (however conceived), will provide the initiate with knowledge, wisdom, status and the like, or in such cults as the Eleusinian Mysteries, salvation in the afterlife.

Endymion's relationship with Selene could hardly be more intimate, of course, in that it overwhelms his entire consciousness. As there are a number of tales of underground or cave initiation, they obviously deserve our attention for whatever light they may throw on our subject. As Graf remarks: 'A higher knowledge always results from the subterranean meeting with a superhuman being.'[1]

---

1 Graf 1997: p.91.

## 8.2 Pythagoras

We've seen two stories of Pythagoras' cave initiation in Crete, at 7.4, above. This took place in the Idaean Cave, a sanctuary of the Cretan Zeus and, according to Diogenes Laertius, he was accompanied into the cave by Epimenides.[2] This would seem to suggest that whatever the 'initiation' might have been that Pythagoras underwent, it at least shared its essence with the experience of Epimenides. We've also seen that Porphyry's biography of Pythagoras tells us that he sought initiation from one of the Idaean Dactyls, and spent 27 days in the Idaean Cave, wrapped, according to Guthrie's translation, in 'black wool'.[3] However, Mircea Eliade[4] translates this as a 'black fleece', an item which we'll see (10.3.3) plays a considerable part in the consultation of dream oracles. The black colour here is particularly appropriate to dealings with the underworld, symbolically represented by the cave. What is also of interest here is that Diodorus Siculus, discussing the Idaean Dactyls (minor deities associated with magic, metalwork and mystery religions), tells us that 'Orpheus, who was endowed with an exceptional gift of poesy and song, also became a pupil of theirs, and he was subsequently the first to introduce initiatory rites and mysteries to the Greeks.'[5] And Orpheus, as we've seen, appears to have been 'married' to Selene (1.3.7), and was certainly closely connected with her tradition (13.3.4).

In Chapter 7, this material about Pythagoras was mentioned with the intention of showing that the sleep of Epimenides was suggestive of gaining wisdom through dream, a subject to which we'll return in Chapters 9 and 10; here, our interpretation takes a slightly different (but not mutually exclusive) emphasis. That going underground, or into a cave (both of which are symbolic of entry

---

2 Diogenes Laertius, 8.1 (8.3) (1925: Vol. 2, p.323).
3 Porphyry, *Life of Pythagoras* 17 (1987: p.126).
4 Eliade 1972: p.26.
5 Diodorus Siculus, *Library of History*, 5.64.4. (1939: Vol. 3, p.271).

into the underworld/otherworld) for a ritual or religious purpose is a method of gaining higher knowledge, or an intimate relationship with a deity. These are not the only stories of Pythagoras spending time underground. Indeed, the same passage of Diogenes Laertius that mentions his descent into the Idaean Cave with Epimenides is immediately followed by a sentence describing how, when in Egypt, Pythagoras descended into crypts (*adyta*) and learned the secrets of the Gods.[6] The satirist Lucian of Samosata has one of his characters make a similar claim; of having visited Egyptian sanctuaries (again, *adyta*) and learned the books of Horus and Isis by heart.[7] Lucian, of course, is both a rationalist and a writer of fictions, so this is by no means to be taken as veritable account, and the 'knowledge' obtained is here in the form of books; yet the story obviously suggests that it was a commonplace notion that wisdom was to be gained underground.

Diogenes Laertius also tells that when he was in Italy, Pythagoras made a chamber underground, and lived in it for some time. He asked his mother to record everything that happened in the upper world, and when it occurred, and she passed the messages down to him (presumably in secret). Eventually he reappeared, emaciated and skeletal, went to the local assembly and said he had been in Hades; he then informed them of everything that had happened. The locals were so impressed that they regarded him as divine. It has been suggested that this may well be a rationalising account of a story, like those already given, of Pythagoras gaining divine knowledge from a Goddess in the underworld, and that 'Pythagoras' mother' should actually be read as 'The Mother' (possibly Demeter), who gave Pythagoras prophetic knowledge.[8]

Whether coincidentally or not, the next figure we have to deal with here was also associated with Pythagoras.

---

6 Diogenes Laertius 8.1 (8.3) (1925: Vol. 2, p.323). Ogden 2002: p.10.

7 Lucian, *The Dream* 18 (1915: Vol. 2, p.209).

8 Diogenes Laertius 8.1 (8.41) (1925: Vol. 2, pp.357-359). Ogden 2002: p.10.

## 8.3 Zalmoxis

The stories we have of the Thracian Zalmoxis (also known as Zamolxis and Salmoxis; generally only the first form will be used here) are often of the same rationalising type as the tale given above, of Pythagoras and his 'mother'. Our major source for this confused and confusing story is Herodotus although, as usual, there are many variants; here we not only have to pick our way through Greek rationalising, but also a probably-less-than-perfect Greek understanding of their Thracian neighbours and their religion. Herodotus' tale, in brief, is this:

The Getae, a Thracian tribe, believe themselves immortal, and that after death they go to join the divine being Zalmoxis, who some call Beleizis or Gebeleizis. Every five years they select a messenger to Zalmoxis, by lots, who is to pass on their requests. The messenger is then hurled into the air so that, falling, he's impaled on the points of three spears. If he dies, the deity is propitious; if he survives, another messenger is selected and sent by the same method.

So far, then, we would appear to be dealing with a deity (variously described in the range of sources as a God or a daemon). However, Herodotus then provides us with an alternative story, which he's heard from Greeks living on the fringe of Thracian territory. According to this, Zalmoxis was once a slave of Pythagoras, on the island of Samos. He was eventually freed, acquired considerable wealth, and returned to Thrace, where the inhabitants were poor and witless. He then built a hall and lavishly entertained the local notables, and taught them that he, and all who drank with him, and their descendants, would not die, but instead go to a place where they'd live forever and enjoy all conceivable blessings. While teaching this, he was also constructing an underground chamber (*adytum*), into which he then disappeared and lived for three years. The Getae mourned him as dead, but at the end of this period he reappeared, and so they believed his claims. Herodotus is non-committal about whether he believes the story, and also as to whether Zalmoxis was a man or a local God.[9]

Strabo[10] tells a similar rationalising story to Herodotus. Again, Zalmoxis is a slave of Pythagoras, who had learned both astrology and Egyptian wisdom. Returning to the Getae he was courted by the ruler because he could make predictions from celestial signs and could report the will of the Gods, and became a priest of the God 'most honoured' in Thrace, later being addressed as a God himself. Rather than constructing an underground chamber, however, he took possession of a cavern in a mountain and spent his life there, only meeting with the king and his own attendants, and providing the royal decrees with a priestly sanction. Strabo suggests that such a priestly position, with the counsellor described as a God, persisted down to his own day, around the beginning of the Common Era, and that Pythagorean vegetarianism survived, as taught by Zalmoxis; but whether this counsellor continued to live in the cave is far from clear. The fact that Zalmoxis obtained his communications from the Gods in a cave on a mountain is certainly worth remarking upon, however.

Other sources expand the story further. Diogenes Laertius knows Herodotus' tale, but adds that the Thracians worshipped him as Kronos (being the deity who presided over the blessed dead in the Elysian Fields, the connection would seem obvious).[11] Iamblichus recounts the same tale of Zalmoxis being Pythagoras' slave, mentions him teaching the Getae the immortality of the soul (rather than simple immortality), and giving them laws, though he omits the underground chamber; he then tells us that the Getae considered Zalmoxis the greatest of the Gods.[12] Diodorus Siculus, treating Zalmoxis more as a man, concentrates on his law-giving aspect, saying he obtained these laws from the Getae's

---

9 Herodotus 4.93-96 (1921: Vol. 2, pp.195-297).

10 Strabo 7.3.5 (1917-1932: Vol. 3, pp.185-187).

11 Diogenes Laertius 8.1 (8.2) (1925: Vol. 2, pp.321-323).

12 Iamblichus, *Life of Pythagoras* 30 (1987: p.100).

'common Goddess', Hestia; Hestia, presumably, is here the Greek Goddess whose function and attributes most closely correspond to an otherwise unnamed Thracian deity.[13] As we'll see (at 13.3.4), Strabo puts Zalmoxis in some very interesting company, mostly noted for purveying oracles and wisdom teachings: 'Such, also, were Amphiaraus, Trophonius (see 10.3), Orpheus, Musaeus and the god among the Getae, who in ancient times was Zalmoxis, a Pythagorean.'[14] Plato describes Zalmoxis as both a king and a God of the Thracians, whose physicians make men immortal; Zalmoxis is also said to purvey medical incantations, which cure both the soul and the body.[15] Porphyry adds a few more interesting details, describing Zalmoxis firstly as a disciple of Pythagoras who was named Zalmoxis because he was born wrapped in a bear's skin, which is called *zalmon* in Thracian, and that he was worshipped by the 'barbarians' as Heracles. He then gives another version where Zalmoxis was a servant of Pythagoras who was carried off by thieves and branded by them, and bound up his forehead on account of the scars. Lastly, he says that others say the name Zalmoxis signifies 'stranger' or 'foreigner'.[16] And finally, there is a lexicon entry in the *Suda* under 'Zamolxis', which simply says 'name of a Goddess'.[17]

It would, of course, be a fool's errand to try to disentangle these variants and form a coherent narrative from them; or to try to uncover the 'truth' as to whether Zalmoxis was a man or a God; he's obviously a figure that moves between the human and the divine. However, there are a number of elements in the stories that seem worth pointing out, as they are shared with other stories we've examined. As we'll see when examining the case of

---

13 Diodorus Siculus 1.94.2 (1933: Vol. 1, p.321).
14 Strabo, 16.2.39 (1917-1932: Vol. 7, p.289).
15 Plato, *Charmides* 9.13 (156D-157A, 158B-C) (1927: Vol. 8, pp.19-21, 25).
16 Porphyry, *Life of Pythagoras* 14-15 (1987: p.125).
17 *Suda, s.v,* 'Zalmoxis'.

Orpheus (13.3.4), Thrace itself was a liminal area as far the Greeks were concerned, and this liminality is further reinforced by the interpretation of Zalmoxis' name as 'stranger' or 'foreigner'. He is said to be a law-giver, an attribute shared with Minos, who descended into the Cretan cave to commune with Zeus every nine years, and received laws from him (7.4); Zalmoxis' laws, however, come from a Goddess, 'Hestia'. The three years spent underground (for whatever reason that might have been) reminds us of both Epimenides and Pythagoras, while Strabo puts him in the company of subterranean oracles such as Amphiaraus and Trophonius. In this context, the reference to him being 'wrapped in a bear's skin' takes on rather more interest, considering that to sleep wrapped in an animal's skin was a common procedure at dream oracles such as that of Amphiaraus. Lastly, there is the branding on the forehead, which may remind us of Epimenides' tattoos. All these elements are nebulous in themselves, but again they are suggestive of the same sort of pattern we've seen develop throughout this inquiry.

Eliade[18] regards the cult of Zalmoxis as a Mystery tradition, teaching the immortality of the soul and promising its adherents a happy afterlife, which was interpreted in the Greek sources as being similar to Pythagoreanism; the link being reinforced by the tale that he was a slave of Pythagoras. This may be extrapolating a little too much on the basis of fragmentary evidence; but the connection with teachings, interpreted by the Greeks as 'Pythagorean', certainly fits into a recurring pattern which will be explored further in Chapter 13. More interestingly, Eliade also points out that *adytum* and cave are essentially cognate, and both signify the 'otherworld', and that 'the ritual cave sometimes imitates the night sky. In other words, it is an *imago mundi*, a Universe in miniature. Living in a cave does not necessarily imply going down among the shades; it can as well imply living in a different world – a world that

---

18 Eliade 1972: p.24.

is vaster and more complex because it incorporates various modes of existence (gods, demons, souls of the dead, etc.) and hence is full of "riches" and countless virtualities (cf. the desacralized myths of caves containing treasure, etc.)'[19]. Such an interpretation will prove of considerable importance.

Before leaving Thrace, however, we might re-emphasise the importance of caves to the stories of its semi-divine heroes. We'll see, Orpheus was thought to be conceived in a cave, and his severed head gave oracles from a cave in Lesbos (13.3.4). Furthermore, it's from Orpheus that the initiatory rites of Demeter and Persephone at Eleusis derived their authority; and these rites, of which we know so little, except they offered some form of salvation in the afterlife, took place in the dark, enclosed chamber of the Telestrion, the 'House of Initiation'.[20] Again, we have the case of the Thracian king Rhesus who, like Orpheus, was the son of a Muse, Terpsichore, and the river God Strymon; he was also raised by Nymphs. He went to Troy as an ally against the Greeks but was butchered in his sleep by Diomedes and Odysseus on the night of his arrival. However, according to Euripides' play, *Rhesus*, his mother is said to have persuaded Persephone to release his soul from the underworld, so he could take up residence after death in a cave on Mount Pangaeus as a 'God-man' (*anthropodaimon*); there he became an oracle of Dionysus.[21] We're not told what procedure was followed at this oracle, so we can't legitimately describe it as a dream-oracle (see below, Chapters 9 & 10); however, the fact that a God-man returns from the underworld to give oracles from a cave certainly fits the story into the usual pattern.

---

19 Eliade, 1972: pp.24-25, 29-30.

20 Ogden 2001: p.125.

21 Homer, *Iliad*, 10.434-504 (1924: Vol. 1, pp.469-473). Euripides, *Rhesus*, ll.917-930, 962-973 (1912: Vol. 1, pp.235, 237-239). Rhode 1925 (Rpt: 1966): p.143. Fol & Marazov 1977: pp.26, 48.

## 8.4 Demosthenes

Although only touching on the fringes of our subject here, there is a curious tale told of the Athenian orator Demosthenes (384-322 BCE). Early in his career, Demosthenes struggled as an orator, until the actor Satyrus showed him how much a graceful delivery could add to the words themselves. After this, Demosthenes built an underground chamber and 'into this he would descend every day without exception in order to form his action and cultivate his voice, and he would often remain there even for two or three months together, shaving one side of his head in order that the shame might keep him from going abroad even though he greatly wished to.'[22]

This is obviously very far away from stories of initiation or encounters with deities, yet Demosthenes could just as easily have practised his art in a room of his house, or in the country outside the city. The notion that one may improve one's art (not too dissimilar to gaining wisdom through a spiritual practice) by spending lengthy periods, effectively, 'in the underworld', remains a striking one, even if no more than oratory is the end result.

## 8.5 Thessalus Of Tralles

The next two tales, though still of Greek origin, take us to Egypt, which was then regarded (as it still is today) as the archetypal land of ancient wisdom and magic. Thessalus was a noted physician of the 1st century CE, although it's doubtful if the treatise on the virtues of herbs attributed to him is actually by his own hand; speculative dates for this treatise range from the 1st to 4th centuries CE. It opens with a first person narrative, in which 'Thessalus' describes his unsuccessful medical studies in Alexandria. He thereafter moved to Egyptian Thebes, with its many temples, where he befriended the priests, one of whom

---

22 Plutarch, *Demosthenes* 7.6 (1919: Vol. 7, pp.17-19).

he eventually persuaded to arrange a face-to-face conversation for him with Asclepius. For this the priest prepared a purified crypt or chamber containing a throne for the God. The priest then summoned Asclepius using a series of secret names, then left the chamber and shut Thessalus within. The God then appeared on the throne in full sight, and he and Thessalus commenced a conversation on the virtues of medicinal plants, which are then presented as revealed mysteries in the remainder of the book.'[23]

This tale is a peculiar mixture. It has elements of a dream-oracle story, such as those we hear of elsewhere concerning Asclepius (see 10.2), though the encounter with the deity is made while fully conscious; it takes place in an underground chamber, and revealed wisdom is passed on, though the encounter is brief by comparison with the months or years involved in other tales; and it also has elements of magic. It also has to be pointed out, of course, that there are doubts that the author is Thessalus, or that he was involved in any such event. The story may just be a way of claiming divine authority for the material to be presented in the following pages; in effect, the story may simply be a fiction. That said, of course, it would hardly be attached to a serious medical work if it was not thought to be a *convincing* fiction; in other words, such a story would have been considered by no means outlandish. We can thus assume that such tales were relatively commonplace, and include this one (with this proviso, of course) amongst our evidence for underground initiation.

## 8.6 Lucian's 'Pancrates'

Our last story from the ancient world is undoubtedly fictional, for it comes from the satirist Lucian (c.120-190 CE), and is part of his

---

[23] Thessalus of Tralles, *De virtutibus herbarum* 1-28 (Ogden 2002: p.52-54).

collection of tall tales about magic, *The Lover of Lies*. The character Pancrates is, in fact, the sorcerer in this earliest version of the well-known story of 'The Sorcerer's Apprentice'. The apprentice here is one Eucrates who, travelling up the Nile by boat to see the Colossi of Memnon, makes the acquaintance of the wonder-working Egyptian priest, Pancrates. Pancrates is said to have lived for 23 years underground in the temple sanctuaries (*adyta*), where he learned magic from Isis.[24]

The rest of this well-known tale, of animated brooms and pestles fetching water, need not concern us here. And, as already mentioned, the story, being satirical, is undoubtedly an exaggerated fiction. Yet there would be no point to the satire if similar tales (and probably far more than are collected here) were not abundant in the Graeco-Roman world. As Graf remarks, the story 'is grounded in precise information about contemporary beliefs and rituals.'[25] Perhaps most interesting is that, while in his lengthy underground existence, Pancrates was receiving wisdom from Isis, a Goddess who (particularly by the Greeks) was often associated with the Moon.

## 8.7 Toledo

Although rather far removed from these ancient tales, we find that legends of magical knowledge gained in caves endure well into the Middle Ages and beyond, particularly at Toledo, in Spain; although in Christian times this magic is generally damned as Satanic. After the Moorish invasion of Spain, Toledo became a great centre of Islamic and Jewish learning, but was widely regarded in the mediaeval period as a hotbed of necromantic teaching. According to legend, the city was founded by Hercules, and 'caves of Hercules' were reputed to lie beneath the city, though

---

24 Lucian, *The Lover of Lies 33-34 (1921:Vol. 3, pp.371-373)*.
25 Graf 1997: p.92.

what are supposed to be the surviving remains of these appear to be nothing more than the entrance to a short section of Roman sewer.[26] These 'caves' appear to have attracted their share of tales.

According to Francesco Maria Guazzo's 17th century *Compendium Maleficarum* (quoting Ferdinand of Castile),[27] a certain Egidius (1185-1265), a talented Portuguese from Vouzella, was persuaded by a demon in human form to visit the caves below Toledo, where he remained for seven years, making a pact with the Devil and studying the black arts, as a result of which he became a supremely talented doctor. Eventually he reformed and joined the Dominican Order, after which he took the name Giles and was eventually beatified. No sleep is involved here, but the length of time spent underground is notable, although 'seven years' may just be traditional for 'a long time'. Other tales, by the 14th century storyteller Don Juan Manuel and the 17th century historian Cristóbal Lozano, speak of sorcerers with underground workshops and libraries, or even of a vast palace of Hercules where magic was studied, eventually collapsing to be rediscovered, and hurriedly closed again, in 1543.[28] Martin del Rio (1551-1608), in his *Investigations into Magic*, tells a similar tale of forbidden knowledge being taught in caverns under Salamanca, another Spanish town notorious for necromancy, having allegedly seen, in person, a secret vault that had been blocked with rubble on the orders of Queen Isabella.[29]

Finally, the poet Virgil, who mediaeval fancy had transformed into a sorcerer,[30] was also said to have studied necromancy at Toledo. According to the 16th century *Virgilius Romance*, Virgil entered a cave in the mountains and journeyed within so far that all

---

26 Davies 2009: pp.27-28.
27 Guazzo, *Compendium Maleficarum*, 3.4.8 (1988 (Rpt. of 1929): pp.194-195).
28 Davies 2009: pp.27-28. Waxman 2007 (Rpt. of 1916): pp.1-42.
29 Del Rio 2009: p.28.
30 Moore 2006: pp.108-125.

light was extinguished; at which point he met and tricked a demon into giving him books and instruction in the black arts.[31] Again we are very far removed from the ancient stories given above, and no time at all is spent in the cave, but we have a cave in the mountains, and the complete absence of light, which seems to be a prerequisite for such revelations.

## 8.8 Summary

Obviously, none of the stories collected here actually relate directly to Selene, though certain of the personnel mentioned, such as Epimenides and Orpheus, were said to claim a relationship with her. Nor do they *directly* throw any light on stories such as that of Selene and Endymion.

What they do demonstrate, however, is a continuity ranging through a number of areas of interest to us. As always, the stories are prone to confusion, rationalisation, variants and differences of emphasis. However, taking the whole collection together, we can see a considerable overlap between areas such as dream oracles, initiation and the gaining of knowledge, wisdom or magical incantations, seclusion underground (effectively in the underworld), 'long sleeps', encounters with deities, and the gaining of immortality or salvation. These stories obviously represent an underlying stratum of what might perhaps be called 'deliberate interaction with the numinous', and thus provide us with a background context for the other material under discussion here; they also offer us various different ways in which the ancients could have 'read' such an apparently simple story as that of Selene and Endymion.

---

31 Anon, *The Wonderful History of Virgilius the Sorcerer of Rome* 1893: pp.24-25.

Chapter Nine

# The Oracle At Thalamae

## 9.1 Introduction

In previous chapters the similarities have been pointed out between the stories of Endymion, sleeping with Selene, and Epimenides, sleeping with less specific deities and obtaining wisdom or oracles from them. We have also seen that a tradition of seeking wisdom underground, across a spectrum of legendary and historical figures, can be traced as late as the classical period and beyond. There is a descent of scale here. Endymion sleeps forever, and none know what he dreams or learns; his sleep may thus be seen as a mythical archetype. The quasi-historical Epimenides sleeps for a limited time, reveals what he learns in his dreams, and puts it to use in the real world; his story thus might be seen as legendary. Other figures, from the legendary to the real, spend varying amounts of time in caves or subterranean chambers in search of wisdom. To complete the pattern, and bring it back to the subject in hand, we now need to look for a truly historical case, where ordinary men slept for perhaps no more than a single night in search of oracular dreams and guidance, in a context associated with Selene. This we find in the shrine of Pasiphae at ancient Thalamae, originally in Messenia, though by Spartan conquest it came to be thought of as being in Laconia.

## 9.2 Thalamae In The Classical Sources

There are a number of references to Thalamae, virtually all of which date from the Roman period, even if the events they refer to took place some centuries previously. This is by no means helpful, as it's far from clear exactly what was going on at Thalamae at the time the references were written; the stories are, as usual, contradictory; and the one eyewitness description of the shrine that we do have is confused.

Pausanias, in his *Description of Greece*, remarks: 'From Oetylus to Thalamae the road is about eighty stades long. On it is a sanctuary of Ino and an oracle. They consult the oracle in sleep, and the goddess reveals whatever they wish to learn, in dreams. Bronze statues of Pasiphae and Helios stand in the unroofed part of the sanctuary. It was not possible to see the one within the temple clearly, owing to the garlands, but they say this too is of bronze. Water, sweet to drink, flows from a sacred spring. Pasiphae is a title of the Moon [Selene], and is not a local goddess of the people of Thalamae.'[1]

Cicero, in his work *On Divination*, tells us: 'Moreover, the Spartan rulers, not content with their deliberations when awake, used to sleep in a shrine of Pasiphae which is situated in a field near the city, in order to dream there, because they believed that oracles received in repose were true.'[2]

Plutarch makes two references to the shrine, in his *Lives* of the Spartans Cleomenes and Agis, both of whom lived in the 3rd century BCE. The first relates to Cleomenes' attempt to seize sole power for himself: 'Now it came to pass about that time that one of the ephors [magistrates], who was sleeping in the precinct of Pasiphae, had an astonishing dream. He dreamed that in the place where the ephors were wont to sit for the prosecution of business, one chair only stood, but the other four had been taken away; and

---

1 Pausanias, 3.26.1 (1926: Vol. 2, p.163).
2 Cicero, *On Divination* 1.43 (96) (1923: Vol. 20, p.327).

that in his amazement at this a voice came to him from the temple saying that this was better for Sparta.'³

Plutarch's discussion in *Agis* is more detailed, and far more confusing. This begins with a reference to 'earlier oracles' (of uncertain provenance) warning Sparta against the love of riches, 'as well as the oracles which had lately been brought to them from Pasiphae. Now there was a temple of Pasiphae at Thalamae, and her oracle there was held in honour. Some say that Pasiphae was one of the daughters of Atlas, and the mother of Ammon by Zeus, and some say that Cassandra the daughter of Priam died at Thalamae, and was called Pasiphae because she *declared* her oracles *to all*. Phylarchus, however, says that she was a daughter of Amyclas, Daphne by name, and that, fleeing the embraces of Apollo, she was changed into a tree of like name, after which she was honoured by the god with the gift of prophetic power. Be this as it may, it was now said that the oracles brought from this goddess ordained that all Spartans should be on an equality according to the original law made by Lycurgus.'⁴

This is all extremely confused and confusing, with the result that the shrine is often referred to in modern sources as that of 'Ino-Pasiphae' or 'Selene-Pasiphae', rather than simply of 'Pasiphae' (and that without taking into account Plutarch's multiple candidates for the shrine deity). All that seems clear is that consultants would sleep in the temple of 'Pasiphae', and receive oracular dreams. Yet where was the shrine? Cicero places it in a 'field near the city' of Sparta, which sounds as if it was within a short walking distance; while most of our sources place it at Thalamae which, assuming its modern identification with the village of Koutiphari is correct, lies some 25 miles from Sparta. However, Cicero was, of course, a Roman author and, for all that it's known he visited Athens, it seems likely that he had no first-hand knowledge of the oracle of

---

3 Plutarch, *Cleomenes* 7.2 (1921: Vol. 11, p.65).
4 Plutarch, *Agis* 9.1-3 (1921: Vol. 11, pp.21-23).

Pasiphae, and may have used secondary sources in his account of it. While noting the discrepancy, it is probably legitimate to accept the majority of the Greek sources and place the shrine at Thalamae. Even so, we are still left with the question: why was a shrine of such obvious importance to the ruling classes of Sparta so far from the city itself and, originally, in the foreign territory of Messenia?

And who was the presiding deity? The first thing to notice is that Pausanias says that on the road from Oetylus to Thalamae 'is a sanctuary of Ino *and* an oracle'. He does *not* say that these two places are identical, although this is frequently assumed. Shortly before this (at 3.23.8 & 3.24.4) Pausanias has mentioned other sites connected with Ino, and we know that she was a popular deity in this coastal area; it would thus not be surprising if there was a sanctuary of Ino on the Thalamae road. That doesn't necessarily mean, though, that sanctuary and oracle are identical, or that Ino was the presiding deity of the oracle. Essentially, what Pausanias says about the oracle is: 'there are statues of Pasiphae and Helios; the statue in the temple couldn't be identified; and that Pasiphae is a title of the Moon (Selene)'. There is, then, nothing specific here to connect Pasiphae with Ino, or the oracle with Ino's shrine.

There is an alternative reading here, as given by Rohde: that the shrine *originally* belonged to Pasiphae, but that by Pausanias' time it had been rededicated to Ino.[5] Such being the case, the primary deity would still be Pasiphae.

All the other sources given above simply refer to the oracle of Pasiphae, and to this we can add two other brief references. The Christian Tertullian, writing in the early 3rd century CE and discussing divination by dreams, gives a list of dream-oracles and their presiding deities, concluding with 'Pasiphae in

---

5 Rohde 1925 (Rpt. 1966): p.152.

Steve Moore

Laconia'.[6] Apollonius Dyscolus, meanwhile, quotes the treatise on *Music* written by Aristoxenus (4th century BCE) that 'the oracles of Pasiphae and Delphi' both declared that music restored the city of Thebes with the sound of trumpets.[7] Again, as we'll see below, inscriptions from the site refer only to 'Pasiphae'. If Pausanias' mention of Ino can at least be queried, and perhaps entirely discounted, then our sources are generally in agreement that the presiding deity was Pasiphae. Which brings us back to the question, who was *she*?

It should be noted, to begin with, that not a single one of our classical references makes any attempt to correlate the Pasiphae of the oracle with Pasiphae the wife of King Minos of Crete and mother of the Minotaur. Given that, in a previous chapter (7.4), we have seen Minos as another figure who, like Epimenides, slept in caves and received oracles, this may seem unexpected. However, we should not try to force a connection if the evidence isn't there to support it. There was a common tendency in the early 20th century to see all figures of myth and legend as 'degraded deities', which led to a number of fantastic constructions being forced onto ancient history and religion; as there's nothing to suggest an identity between the queen of Crete and the deity of Thalamae, the only safe course is to assume that they're separate personalities.

As Pausanias remarks, Pasiphae is a 'title of Selene', and if we look at the meaning of the word as a title, rather than a name, his reasoning becomes clear. Pasiphae derives from *pasi*, 'for all', and from *phaino* 'to bring to light, to make clear, to disclose; to give light, to shine forth'. Pausanias is obviously thinking of the latter meanings: Pasiphae is a title of Selene because she 'gives light for all'. It seems, however, that Spartan usage preferred the earlier meanings, even to the point of making *phaino* and its derivative, *phainein*, mean 'to proclaim'. Thus we have the meaning given

---

6 Tertullian, *De Anima, 46. (1874: Vol. 2, p. 516)*.

7 Apollonius Dyscolus, *Historiae 49. (1792: pp. 98-101)*.

by Plutarch, that Pasiphae *'declared'* her oracles *to all'*. Both are legitimate derivations, in the same way that, in English, 'to enlighten' can mean both 'to shed light' and 'to explain'. As we'll see below (9.3), there is some evidence to suggest that Thalamae was operative as an oracle long before the Spartan occupation of the area; in that case there may be no reason to give particular weight to the Spartan interpretation ('declares to all') rather than the more normal one ('gives light for all').

The argument for 'Pasiphae' being a title rather than a name would, of course, be strengthened if we could find a parallel case where this is known to have happened. There is such a parallel and, interestingly, it refers both to a Goddess presiding over a dream-oracle, and also to one that comes from Caria. The location is Castabus (modern Pazarlik) in the Carian Chersonese, some 65 miles to the south-east of Latmos and under Rhodian domination through much of its history; whether the cult was originally Carian or Rhodian, we have insufficient information to decide. Summarising from Diodorus Siculus, writing in the first century BCE, the story is as follows:[8]

Staphylus and Chrysothemis had three daughters, Molpadia, Parthenos and Rhoeo. Rhoeo was seduced by Apollo and when her father found out, he placed her in a chest which was washed up on Apollo's holy island, Delos, where she had a son called Anius, who was taught divination by Apollo himself. Molpadia and Parthenos, left behind, were watching their father's wine, when they fell asleep and allowed some pigs to break in and destroy the wine jar. They woke and fearing their father's wrath, hurled themselves off some rocks into the sea. Apollo is said to have rescued them out of affection for their sister, but Diodorus is unclear about what actually happened; there is no further mention of them living earthly lives, but Apollo is said to have established them in temples of their own, Parthenos in Bubastus (Bybassus; modern Hisaronu) and

---

8 Diodorus Siculus, 5.62-63 (1939: Vol. 3, pp.265-269).

Molpadia in nearby Castabus. This uncertain transition between life and death (did they die, or were they instantly translated into deities?) is a common attribute of the deities presiding over dream-oracles; see below at 10.3.1. Of Parthenos we hear no more, but Molpadia is said to have been given the name Hemithea ('Half-Goddess'). Because of the circumstances surrounding her deification, she was worshipped with libations of milk and honey rather than wine, while pigs and pork were tabooed (for similar 'wineless' and bloodless sacrifices offered to Selene, see above at 2.4). Her shrine was a healing dream oracle, like that of Asclepius, and Diodorus says that 'she appears in visible shape in their sleep to those who are suffering and gives them healing'.

Hemithea's sanctuary was apparently so popular, but in such a constricted area, that attendance exceeded the shrine's capacity, as we know from inscriptions found at the site, and it remained operative for at least two centuries.[9] Here, then, we have a dream oracle where the presiding deity's name not only *is* transparently a title, but which our original Greek source *tells us* is one as well. This would seem to give us a reasonable model on which to interpret the name 'Pasiphae'.

If Pasiphae is primarily a title, rather than a personal name, this may go some way to explaining the immense confusion reflected in Plutarch's discussion of the name in his *Life of Agis*, given above. All the material he assembles there attempts to add a 'real person' to the title, with their own history and descent. However, none of these stories is commonplace or supported by other references.

Pasiphae is said to be 'one of the daughters of Atlas', and Atlas is said to have had three groups of daughters: the Pleiades and Hyades by Pleione, and the Hesperides by Hesperis; however, the name Pasiphae does not appear on any of the standard lists of these ladies. Again, we have no other mention of her being the mother of

---

9 For a description of the archaeological remains, and historical discussion, see Bean 1989: pp.136-138.

Ammon by Zeus; Ammon is, of course, the Egyptian God Amen, and 'Zeus Ammon' had an oracular temple at Siwa, to the west of Egypt, which famously declared Alexander the Great to be a God. However, this oracle did not operate using dreams, but gave yes/no answers according to the apparent movements of the God's statue when carried on the shoulders of his priests.

Cassandra, the daughter of the Trojan king Priam, was given prophetic powers by Apollo but then refused to let him have his way with her, as she'd promised in return; the result being that, while Apollo could not take back his gift, he then cursed her to never be believed. The usual story of her demise is that Agamemnon brought her to Mycenae on his return from the Trojan War, where Agamemnon's adulterous wife Clytemnestra murdered both of them. The story that Cassandra died at Thalamae appears only here.

Daphne, in the version of the story that makes her daughter of Amyclas, was a Spartan huntress who, attempting to escape rape by Apollo, was turned into a laurel tree by Zeus. Daphne's name means 'laurel', and the laurel is the sacred and oracular tree of Apollo. Again, though, there seems to be no specific reason why she should be connected with Thalamae; and it might be noted that Phylarchus (3rd century BCE), to whom this tale is credited, was regarded as an unreliable source, even in antiquity. Polybius referred to him as a writer of sensationalism rather than history.[10]

What we have in this collection of explanatory stories from Plutarch, then, are a number of ladies with vaguely oracular connections that at least give them some slight grounds for identification with Pasiphae; but no corroborative evidence, and an appearance with most of the tales of having been 'made up on the spot' specifically to provide a 'background story' for the otherwise unknown name Pasiphae. If Pasiphae never was an individual, but simply a title, these difficulties disappear.

---

10 Casson 2002: p.67.

Added to this, we have Pausanias' statement that 'Pasiphae is a title of Selene', and this does have the corroborative evidence of the pair of statues he mentions, of Helios and Pasiphae. If Pasiphae is Selene, this pairing is quite natural. Of course, it may be argued that, while statues of Helios and Pasiphae stood in the sanctuary grounds, we still have no name far the main statue, inside the roofed part of the temple, which was hidden by garlands.

This discussion actually highlights a possible problem with Pausanias' description of the shrine. As H.W. Parke remarks, Pausanias was obviously particularly interested in oracles,[11] and we shall see that he is a major source for descriptions of other dream-oracles to be discussed in Chapter 10. He gives us our only actual eyewitness account of the shrine at Thalamae, and as the statues of Pasiphae and Helios were visible, in the open, in the temple precinct, we may take his word for this part of his account. He says, though, that the statue within the temple itself was too covered with garlands for him to see it clearly; this suggests that, although the temple was obviously still functioning, it may have been closed at the time of his visit, and that the statue was perhaps only visible at a distance through something like a window or grating. If that was the case, it would also suggest that there was no-one on the premises to give Pausanias detailed information. Pausanias, therefore, has no hard evidence to offer us about the main deity of the shrine, and even if his text is read as suggesting that it was Ino, it may be only supposition on his part. Against this, however, we have the other sources, all of which are united in describing the shrine as belonging to Pasiphae.

That Pasiphae was Selene, and thus that Selene was the presiding deity of the dream-oracle at Thalamae, is obviously not susceptible to absolute proof. On the basis of the discussion here, however, we may at least admit it as a reasonable possibility. The pattern of material that builds up as we explore the subject further may well be seen to increase that likelihood.

---

11 Parke 1988: p.37.

## 9.3 Thalamae In The Archaeological Record

Regrettably, there is not an enormous amount of useful information to be gleaned from archaeological investigations at Thalamae, as the shrine has not survived. Furthermore, much of the early archaeological investigation and reportage was coloured by early 20th century preconceptions, and this has to be sifted carefully if we don't wish to go astray.

E.S. Forster first identified the site in 1903.[12] Working from Pausanias' description and road distances, he identified the village of Koutiphari as the most likely location and, in the village itself, found two ancient inscriptions mentioning the people of Thalamae. To the east of the village, he found ancient remains of columns and walls at a place called Palaiochora, and near to this two springs, the larger of which he thought to be the spring mentioned by Pausanias. A stone that had been built into a nearby schoolhouse bore an inscription from an 'Elder' (presumably a Spartan Elder) called Nikosthenidas, which thanked Pasiphae for a 'good oracle'. We thus have reasonably good evidence for Koutiphari being Thalamae, and for the oracle of Pasiphae being in the area.

The next investigation of the site was by Guy Dickins, the following year.[13] Trial excavations centred round the larger of the two springs mentioned by Forster (the one still in use by the local populace), and Dickins was again of the opinion that this was the one connected with the sanctuary, mentioned by Pausanias. This wellhouse included some walling of 'Hellenic' date (*i.e.*, of the Classical period). Dickins surmised that the town of Thalamae had been on rising ground above the open space surrounding the two springs. The ground had apparently been so well turned over, and so much stone removed for later building purposes, that there was little hope of finding substantial remains. Dickins mentioned finding a 'Neolithic object', the upper part of a large jar he believed

---

12 Forster 1903-4: pp.158-189 (specifically pp.161-2, 173-4, 188-189).
13 Dickins 1904-5: pp.124-136.

to be Cretan, Doric capitals, marble pilasters, some coins and pottery from the Hellenic period, and lamps, pins and Samian pottery from the Roman period. It is possible that the Doric capitals and pilasters came from the sanctuary (such was Dickins' belief) but so little remains that we have nothing really to indicate the size or appearance of the shrine itself.

Dickins returned to the subject in a later article.[14] He then proposed that Epimenides, who he says was known to have visited Athens about 594 BCE, and also to have visited Sparta, founded the shrine of 'Ino-Pasiphae'. While admitting that 'we know nothing' of the date when the sanctuary was founded, he went on to say that 'two things are well-established': that it 'is Cretan', and that it was directly connected with the Spartan ephors. He continued: 'Obviously then, the cult belongs to the period of growth in power of the ephorate, for we know that the ephors' business in Thalamae was concerned with the depositions of kings.' He placed the rise of the ephorate between 620 and 550 BCE, and stated that the most obvious moment for consulting a cult-specialist (*i.e.*, Epimenides) would be during the reverses of the Tegean War, after 580 BCE; thus bringing Epimenides into relation with Chilon, who raised the ephorate to a level with the kingly power. He also points out that the kings of Sparta had a strong relationship with Apollo's oracle at Delphi, and suggests that the ephors built a parallel relationship with Thalamae.

Attractive as the idea may be of relating Epimenides with Thalamae, unfortunately it has to be said that Dickins' proposal is simply a fantasy of an all-too-common type, where attempts are made to unite physical archaeological remains with figures from the written historical or religious record (a problem which continues to plague the more popular reaches of 'Biblical Archaeology', in particular). From the pottery that he believed to be Cretan (though this would presumably have been Minoan-Cretan, some 600 years

---

14 Dickins 1912: pp.1-42 (see p.21).

before Epimenides) and, one assumes, the name of Pasiphae being that of the wife of King Minos, he'd decided that the site was 'well-established' as 'Cretan'. Thus it was appropriate that a Cretan should found the site, and having found an appropriate Cretan, he then looked for appropriate historical circumstances to justify his proposal. There is, of course, no evidence at all that Epimenides ever visited the site, or that it began to operate around the turn of the 7$^{th}$ and 6$^{th}$ centuries BCE; whether the shrine was consulted exclusively by the ephorate or was open to all remains a moot point.[15]

R. Hope Simpson re-examined the site in the late 1950s, and also Dickins' finds.[16] He swiftly disposed of Dickins' evidence, declaring the 'Neolithic object' to be half a stone hammer which could have dated to any period during the Bronze Age, and was almost certainly not Neolithic. The 'Cretan' jar was said to be 'now known' to be of mainland origin, and dating from the Late Helladic III period (1400-1100 BCE). Simpson also found some Mycenaean sherds from Late Helladic IIIB-C (1300-1100 BCE). He also mentioned the (then recently-found) head from a broken clay statuette, which he thought most likely to be of local Late Helladic manufacture, though admitting its similarity to Sub-Minoan statuettes from Crete, of a century or two later. However, in spite of this more considered view of the evidence, Simpson remains in thrall to the same sort of Cretic speculations as Dickins, undoubtedly influenced by the Cretan connections of the name Pasiphae, remarking that 'we should expect the Cretan influence suggested by the Oracle of Ino-Pasiphae to have originated in the Bronze Age'. It should already have become apparent that there is considerable doubt about a connection between the Pasiphae of the oracle and the Queen of Crete. It can be argued that all the material we have to deal with here originates in a 'common

---

15 Wardle 2006: pp.335-336.
16 Simpson 1957: pp.231-259 (see pp.232-3).

cultural area' of Bronze Age south and eastern Greece, Crete and the Aegean, and south-western Anatolia; if such be the case, whether specific items of evidence are 'Cretan' or 'Mycenaean' becomes considerably less important.

Summing up these archaeological reports, so far, the safest thing we seem able to say is that the sanctuary of Pasiphae at Thalamae appears to have been in the area of the modern village of Koutiphari, and that there is evidence that the site was occupied at least as early as the Late Helladic III period, from 1400 BCE onwards. There is, however, some rather more interesting evidence found in the clay-tablets, written in Linear B, discovered at the ancient palace of Mycenaean Pylos, some 40 miles from Thalamae. Preserved by the burning of the palace at the end of the Late Helladic III period, these would obviously be contemporary with early occupation at Thalamae.[17]

These tablets are virtually all administrative records, rather than literary works, and written in the syllabic Linear B script. Here we find a lease-holder and owner of sheep or cows called Ta-ra-ma-ta, alphabetised as Thalamatas, which is interpreted as an 'ethnic' deriving from Thalamae; *i.e.*, the name means 'inhabitant of Thalamae'. Also listed is a woman's name, Ta-ra-mi-ka, Thalamika, which also derives from Thalamae; she is said to be a 'servant of the god', but which deity is unclear; the term is commonplace in the tablets, and appears to simply mean 'temple-slave'.

Slender as this evidence may seem, if we put it together with the evidence of Late Helladic III occupation of the site given above, we can see that not only was there activity at Thalamae in the Late Helladic III period, but that, at the same period, it was called by that name as well.

If we now look at the meaning of the word 'Thalamae', we find results of similar interest to those discovered in the meanings

---

17 Ventris & Chadwick 1973: pp.94, 169, 170, 240, 258.

of Endymion and Epimenides. Thalamae derives from the word *thalamos*, which means, firstly, 'an inner room or chamber', which in turn is cognate with the women's apartments of the house; secondly and, it would seem in this case, more importantly, it means a 'bed-room or a bridal-chamber'. Again we have a transparently obvious and appropriate name when applied to the oracle: this place is the 'bed-room' where one sleeps to obtain an oracle. By extension, we may speculate that, because of the connection with 'bridal-chamber' and women's apartments, this can be seen as the 'bed-room where one sleeps with the Goddess who gives the oracle'. Such being the case, it would seem far more logical that the town of Thalamae was named after the oracle, than that the town was given an otherwise-meaningless name and that an oracle was founded there because 'the place-name was appropriate'. Admittedly, we are in the realms of conjecture here, but if this is the case, there would appear to be a suggestion that the dream-oracle at Thalamae, presided over by a Goddess (whether that was Selene or not), was in operation from the Late Helladic III period, and survived (undoubtedly with various restorations) for some 1500 years until the time of Pausanias. This long-established history may go some way to explain its importance to Sparta: its reputation was hallowed by antiquity, even if it was originally in Messenia. As such it would have been worth making the journey to and, eventually, including in Spartan territory. This may not be as attractive a suggestion as that of Dickins, that the oracle was founded by Epimenides (and this evidence is obviously disastrous to Dickins' thesis), but it is perhaps of greater interest, in that it pushes the origins of these practices back into the Minoan-Mycenaean period.

In summary, then, what we have at Thalamae is an extremely ancient dream-oracle, with at least a reasonable likelihood that the presiding deity, under the local name of Pasiphae, was actually Selene. What we don't yet have is any idea of the specific procedures used at Thalamae (these may, indeed, never be known for certain) and, while 'sleeping and dreaming with Selene' may indeed seem to have some broad relevance to the Endymion myth, we still need more details to make the connection secure. For this we'll have to turn to parallel evidence from other dream-oracles, where we have more complete information.

Chapter Ten

# Dream Oracles Elsewhere

## 10.1 Introduction

Tertullian, writing in the 2nd or early 3rd century CE and discussing the soul, provides us with a very interesting list of dream oracles: 'Epicharmus, indeed, as well as Philochorus the Athenian, assigned the very highest place among divinations to dreams. The whole world is full of oracles of this description: there are the oracles of Amphiaraus at Oropus, of Amphilochus at Mallus, of Sarpedon in the Troad, of Trophonius in Boeotia, of Mopsus in Cilicia, of Hermione in Macedon, of Pasiphae in Laconia. Then, again, there are others, which with their original foundations, rites, and historians, together with the entire literature of dreams, Hermippus of Berytus in five portly volumes will give you all the account of, even to satiety.'[1]

Unfortunately, Hermippus' 'five portly volumes' (written at the beginning of the 2nd century CE) have not survived (and we only have fragments of Epicharmus, 5th century BCE, and Philochorus, c.340-260 BCE); even so, this single quotation from Tertullian will give some idea of how widespread, and how important, dream oracles were in the ancient pagan world. There is, besides, no mention in Tertullian's list of the numerous temples of Asclepius where incubation ('temple-sleep') was practiced, and

---

1 Tertullian: *De Anima*, 46. (1874: Vol. 2, p.516).

in their dreams patients would receive either miraculous cures or medical prescriptions from the God. Such practices were by no means restricted to the Greek world, but were widespread throughout ancient civilisations, often preceding their appearance in Greece. Jayne provides a broad survey of such incubation oracles, particularly with reference to healing incubation, not only from Greece, but also from Egypt, Babylon and elsewhere.[2] When we also consider the large number of oracle-centres where the Gods answered questions by other means than dreams, such as the numerous oracles of Apollo and Zeus, various Sibyls, and so forth, we realise that the practice of directly consulting the Gods was almost universal in pre-Christian times.

This is a notion which contemporary western society seems to find difficult to accept, for a number of reasons. One is, obviously, the influence of Christianity, which has declared the deities involved to be either demonic or 'false gods'; the latter denomination being the more damaging in that it implies that, if the Gods are 'false', then similarly the experience itself is false, and can thus be discounted as unimportant and, ultimately, unreal. Similarly, modern rationalism (which regards 'Greek rationalism' as its founding paradigm and so feels particularly uncomfortable with such evidence of 'irrationality'), in denying any form of deity and the practices associated with it, can only regard such practices in the ancient world as 'primitive', 'superstitious' or 'aberrations'. As such, Classical studies have tended to treat subjects such as oracles, divination and the practice of magic as 'irrational' and puzzling, and so swept them under the carpet. It's only since the latter part of the 20th century that they have begun to be seen as legitimate areas of scholarly interest. Unfortunately, the corollary of this attitude is that when such 'irrational' practices as the consultation of oracles do turn up, there is a tendency to 'explain

---

2 Jayne 1925: *passim*. For a briefer but broader view of dream-oracles, including some beyond the ancient Mediterranean and Middle East, see Trubshaw 2003: pp.24-27.

them away' in terms of drugs or fraud ... because to the modern mind, there is simply no way they can be accepted as, in any way, *real* experiences of encounters with deity.

Fortunately, for our purposes we don't have to worry about such questions as 'were the Pagan Gods "real"?' or 'was what happened at a dream oracle a "valid spiritual experience"?' In order to uncover what the Selene and Endymion story refers to, we can confine our inquiries to such areas as what the Greeks *believed* and what they *practised*.

The subject of Greek oracles is too vast for any sort of comprehensive treatment; even a general survey of dream oracles alone would extend far beyond the space that can be devoted to it here. Instead we need to concentrate on two main areas: the possibility of encountering Gods during dream-oracle consultations, and those elements of dream-oracle practice which throw some light on stories such as those of Endymion and Epimenides.

## 10.2 Encountering Asclepius (And Other Deities)

We are particularly fortunate in having a considerable amount of surviving material regarding the healing God Asclepius (though, as always, this is never as much as one would have liked). Amongst other material we have the 'Sacred Tales' of Aelius Aristides,[3] which is pretty much a 'journal' of his treatment and encounters with Asclepius at the sanctuary at Pergamum; and also the collected testimonia of Asclepius' cult and practice from antiquity, put together and interpreted in two sizable volumes by the Edelsteins.[4]

To summarise briefly, Asclepius had sanctuaries (often large temple complexes which developed, particularly in later antiquity, into sacred hospitals and nursing homes) across the length and

---

3 Aristides, 'Sacred Tales' 1-6, *Orations XLVII–LII* (1986, 1981: pp.278-353).
4 Edelstein & Edelstein 1945 (Rpt. 1998).

breadth of the ancient world, the most notable being at Epidaurus, Pergamum, Cos, Tegea, Tricca, Lebena and, eventually, at Rome. The sick would travel to these sanctuaries in order to sleep there and encounter the God in dream, with the result that the God would either provide a miraculous cure while they remained asleep, or would give them a 'prescription' (which could be either a course of drugs or one or more actions to be carried out).

There are two features about the Asclepia that we should note which, while not seeming of immediate importance, are worth discussing because similar features recur at other dream oracles. The first is the presence in most of the sanctuaries of sacred snakes, and the fact that Asclepius himself was thought to sometimes take on the form of a snake; indeed, statues of Asclepius frequently show him either with a snake or with a staff with a snake winding round it.[5] The snake, shedding its skin, is a symbol of survival, renewal and rebirth, and thus quite appropriate to a medical deity who brings the patient back 'from the dead', or at least the borders of death. It is also, though, a chthonian animal, living in holes is the ground and sliding on its belly on the earth. In both these aspects, then, it lies athwart the borderland between life and death, this world and the underworld. It is also, of course, associated with oracles; one merely has to think that the presiding deity at Delphi, before the arrival of Apollo, was the snake Python and that, Apollo having destroyed it, his own oracular priestess was called the Pythia in its memory. As we'll see, the snake reappears in connection with other oracles.

The second feature is the presence of Hygieia, the personification of Health, usually said to be the daughter of Asclepius, though sometimes his wife. She too is frequently portrayed with a snake, and seems to have been an indispensable presence in the sanctuaries, along with a sacred spring.[6] Naturally, being

---

5 Kerenyi 1959: pp.9-15, 18-20, *etc.*

6 Edelstein & Edelstein 1945 (Rpt. 1998): p.89-90. Kerenyi 1959: pp.5, 57.

primarily a personification, Hygieia can hardly be considered a major Goddess; she seems instead to fill the niche that, at other oracles, is taken by a Nymph. Regardless of who the actual presiding deity (usually male) may be at an oracle, it seems to have been necessary that there was a female presence involved as well, whether she be Nymph, Muse or Goddess, and we'll see further evidence of this below. We may also recall that Quintus Smyrnaeus informed us that Endymion himself actually slept in a cave of the Nymphs (1.5.3).

Obviously some of the testimonia we possess of Asclepius' cures (particularly those inscriptions found at the sanctuaries themselves) are highly propagandist in nature, but the simple fact is that the sanctuaries remained in operation for several centuries, surviving from at least as early as the 5$^{th}$ century BCE to beyond the Christianisation of the Roman empire, when the practices were taken over and reconsecrated in the name of Christian saints. Quite obviously, then, there was some form of 'real experience' occurring in these sanctuaries (whatever the exact nature of that may have been) and, even if it were but psychological, at least some form of healing and comfort. If this was not the case, such sanctuaries would have withered away long before a thousand years had passed.

Regrettably, the notion that it is possible to dream of Gods and to receive instructive prescriptions from them while asleep appears to be anathema to some authors of the present day, who are then forced to provide us with alternative 'explanations' which show an unforgivable unfamiliarity with the subject matter. Thus Norman MacKenzie tells us (entirely without references to back up his assertions) that in incubation temples the sleep was 'induced by drugs, herbs, or other potions' and that 'evidence suggests that often the priests returned later in the night, dressed as gods, to give medical treatment.'[7] This is entirely suppositious

---

7 MacKenzie 1965: pp.43, 45.

and is, in fact, contrary to all the evidence we do have. It is also entirely unnecessary.

It is true that we now have good evidence of the use of cannabis and opium in the Mediterranean area, from the Bronze Age onwards, with the result that it has become fashionable among some interpreters to 'explain' a variety of religious phenomena (including, for example, the Eleusinian Mysteries) in terms of drug-induced experiences. There are a number of problems with this notion. One is that, in cases such as the Eleusinian Mysteries, we have so little knowledge of what the participants actually experienced that the 'religious phenomenon' being explained is a highly speculative reconstruction anyway. Even if we were to accept that such a reconstruction represents what actually happened, we are then left with the problem that, although it may be possible to reproduce similar, or even identical, effects through the use of drugs, this doesn't actually *prove* that drugs *did* produce the phenomenon, rather than some other means of achieving ecstasy. And lastly, evidence of the use or trade of drugs in itself does not imply ritual usage, any more than an empty wine bottle implies that the person drinking it was involved in Bacchic religious rites; quite obviously a large amount of ancient opium was simply used for its painkilling effects. Perhaps the most judicious summary of the evidence is presented by such scholars as Richard Rudgley who, discussing the export of Cyprian opium to Egypt during the Bronze Age suggests that this was 'for medical reasons and probably also as a means of inducing altered states of consciousness – although in a secular rather than a religious context – and perhaps even as an aphrodisiac.'[8] The words 'probably' and 'perhaps' should be noted in this quotation.

The main problem with the 'drug hypothesis' (especially when appearing in such poor presentations as that of MacKenzie, given above, where it is stated as a bald fact, rather than even as

---

8 Rudgley 1993: p.28.

a hypothesis), is that it is ultimately reductionist and materialist, effectively denying the possibility that any form of religious or metaphysical phenomena can be produced by any means other than chemical. As such, it can only be seen as a lamentable failure of the imagination, and one has to suggest that its proponents should attempt to gain some first-hand knowledge of devotional or meditational practices and the experiences they bring, before providing rationalising alternatives. Unfortunately, having become fashionable in recent years thanks to some highly vocal proponents, the drug hypothesis is rarely subjected to the sort of critical scrutiny it deserves.

It is, of course, difficult if not impossible to prove a negative, and one is mindful of the cliché that 'absence of evidence is not evidence of absence'. However, in his *Life of Apollonius of Tyana*, Philostratus provides us with a lengthy discussion, in words credited to the neo-Pythagorean mage Apollonius, which baldly states that dreams received under the influence of wine or 'sleeping-draughts' are useless for divination. As such, Apollonius only drank water, so that, dreaming, he could receive oracular dreams with his 'soul in a condition of utter transparency'.[9] And as an example, he goes on to mention the dream-oracle of Amphiaraus (more of which below, at 10.3.2), where we know that consultants were required to fast completely for one day beforehand, to abstain from wine for three days, and to avoid beans. Beans contain a substance called levodopa or L-dopa, which can induce either insomnia, nightmares or waking hallucinations. Beans were thought harmful to dreaming and to fog perception.[10] There are, perhaps, two points to emphasise here. The first is that the ancients were well aware of the effects of certain substances on dreaming, and that the use or prohibition of such substances survives in the historical record in a way that one would expect references to other drugs

---

9 Philostratus, *The Life of Apollonius of Tyana*, 2. 36-37 (1912: Vol. 1, p.211-217).
10 Ogden 2001: pp.79, 86.

(such as opium or cannabis) to survive also. And secondly, with the prohibition of both beans and wine, the inference must surely be that the dreams received in incubation-practices were required to be 'pure' and unaffected by the influence of diet, alcohol or drugs.

All that said, let us return to the procedures used at the sanctuaries of Asclepius, about which, as was said above, we have considerably greater information than a number of other ancient religious procedures. As the Edelsteins point out, all that was required was that the patient bathe and offer sacrifice, the main sacrifices being honey-cakes, cheesecakes and figs (and we may note here the similarity to the cakes offered to Selene, mentioned above at 2.4). No fastings or abstentions were required, nor were there solemn ceremonies or purificatory rites. Without special garments or anything else unusual, the patients then slept, as a group, on pallets within the familiar temple or halls set aside for incubation.[11] There is absolutely no mention of 'drugs, herbs or potions' here.

Turning to more specific, first-hand evidence, Publius Aelius Aristides (117-c.180 CE) provides us with our most complete record of an individual user of dream-oracles, in his 'Sacred Tales' (*Orations* XLVII – LII). Aristides was an aristocratic orator living near Smyrna in what is now western Turkey, who also suffered from prolonged ill-health. As such, he was an extremely pious devotee of Asclepius, spending up to two years at the God's famous temple in Pergamum where, as a patient, he engaged in incubation, receiving advice, prescriptions and medical instructions in his dreams. He continued his worship in the temple at Smyrna, and at home. On some occasions he would be addressed directly by the God in dreams; on others he would interpret seemingly more commonplace dreams as if they were more discursive messages from the deity. His submission to the God's instruction was absolute, giving it precedence over the doctors who he also consulted, and

---

11 Edelstein & Edelstein 1945 (Rpt. 1998): Vol. 2, pp.149-150, 186-187.

often, at the God's apparent command, undertaking long journeys while in poor health. There is no mention in his record of narcotic or hallucinatory drug use, and absolutely nothing to suggest that it was in any way involved in the operation of the dream oracle. It would appear that, given sufficient devotion to the deity concerned, belief in the efficacy of the oracle, and enough willingness and flexibility to interpret the dream-messages, dream-oracles were capable of working perfectly well without the necessity for drugs. Drugs are not *necessary* to an explanation of dream-oracles, nor are they the simplest answer.[12]

For, as the Edelsteins remark: 'That people who came to the Asclepieia dreamed in the sanctuaries seems understandable. They came with this aim in mind, and if some did not succeed in having visions, as the testimonies candidly admit [...], they must have been in the minority. It is equally well comprehensible that the sick dreamed of Asclepius and of their diseases, that they saw the god, as he was represented in his statues, assisting them or giving them counsel. Coming in quest of the god's help, excited by the long journey which sometimes they had undertaken for this selfsame purpose, preoccupied with their suffering as they must have been, having seen the sights of the sanctuary and having stayed in these surroundings at least for a number of hours, having read the tablets on which the reports on portentous dreams and successful cures were inscribed–how could the supplicants fail to dream as they did? It is hardly exaggerated to say that anybody who in a world in which the gods were still alive should visit a temple and wait for a divine vision would have such dreams. In the given circumstances these visions were quite natural.'[13]

Similarly, the suggestion that 'often the priests returned later in the night, dressed as gods, to give medical treatment' cannot be substantiated. As the Edelsteins remark, the ancients were well

---

12 Aristides, 'Sacred Tales' 1-6, *Orations XLVII–LII (1986, 1981): pp.278-353.*
13 Edelstein & Edelstein 1945 (Rpt. 1998): Vol. 2, p.163.

enough aware of, and frequently exposed, pious frauds, but '...  the Asclepieia remained free of all charges of fraud. The priests of Epidaurus, of Cos, of Pergamum were never accused of being impostors, of having themselves fabricated the miracles ascribed to their god; not even those who were sceptical of the healings went so far.'[14] There is, besides, the logistical problem: given that perhaps 20 or 30 patients were sleeping in the same hall, apparently awake enough to see the priests at work, and so to misinterpret them as 'dreams of the Gods', how is it that no one ever reported seeing Asclepius at work on someone else, but not them? Or simply seeing through the whole fraud? A further difficulty is that Aristides on occasion dreamt of Asclepius with three heads, which would perhaps have tested the ingenuity of even the most fraudulent priesthood.

Perhaps the main problem for 21$^{st}$ century rationalists who wish to propose drugs or fraud as explanations for ancient dream-oracle practice is their difficulty in conceptualising 'a world in which the gods were still alive', particularly when they start with a viewpoint that the Gods never even existed in the first place. That the world before the Common Era was full of Gods, and that they were 'still alive' seems hardly worth pointing out, even if we have difficulty now imagining what that may have been like. That people dreamt of them on a day-to-day basis (even without resorting to dream oracles) can also be shown, simply by turning to the one surviving dream-book that we have from antiquity, the *Oneirocritica* of Artemidorus, of the 2$^{nd}$ century CE. Artemidorus devotes considerable space to what it means to dream of particular Gods and Goddesses (including Selene), often tailoring his explanations to fit various types of persons or profession.[15]

That, in the ancient world, people dreamt of Gods, and in particular that they dreamt of specific Gods at their oracular

---

14 Edelstein & Edelstein 1945 (Rpt. 1998): Vol. 2, p.160.

15 Artemidorus, *The Interpretation of Dreams*. (1975: see especially 2.34-39 (pp.112-124), 4.71-77 (pp.214-216)).

shrines, or received meaningful dreams thought to have been sent by those same deities in those shrines, would seem to have been amply demonstrated. Asclepius has given us our specific 'case-study', while Tertullian's listing, given at the beginning of this chapter, has demonstrated how widespread the practice was, and how many different deities were involved. It's now time to turn our attention to some of those other deities and their shrines, in order to gather some more details of practices carried out at them.

## 10.3 Dream Oracles: Places And Practices

Obviously, considering the number and variety of dream-oracles, it would be impractical here to provide a general survey of the entire subject. Instead we have to select those features and practices of the oracles that seem most relevant and concentrate on those, mentioning the rest only in passing, as necessary.

10.3.1 Diviners and their 'deaths'. As can be seen from Tertullian's list, dream oracles in the Greek world were very numerous, and the presiding 'deities' were similarly numerous. 'Deities' is deliberately put in quotation marks here, for those presiding over dream oracles were, for the most part, 'heroes' rather than Gods. Heroes occupied a position similar, in some ways, to Christian saints: they were figures believed to have been originally human, who were then deified or given semi-divine status, and as such received cult-worship, though usually on a fairly local basis. Even Asclepius himself was believed to have been originally 'human', though like several other heroes one of his parents was divine: he had Apollo as father and the human Coronis (usually) as mother; nonetheless, he lived a life in the human world before Zeus struck him down with his lightning, in punishment for raising a man from the dead. Most heroes, whether of half-divine parentage or not, lived before or during the Trojan War, which was said to have been stirred up by Zeus as a way of ridding the Earth of the race of heroes. Besides this, a number of the heroes presiding over dream oracles (Amphiaraus, Amphilochus, Calchas, Mopsus, etc.) were diviners during their lifetimes. As such, it's perhaps not surprising that attempts were made to provide a similar 'back-story' for Pasiphae (see above, 9.2); given that most dream-oracles were centred on once-human heroes or heroines, it would be natural to attribute the same status to Pasiphae, and in particular to try to tie her in with prophetic figures such as Cassandra. Nonetheless, let us be clear here: not all the heroes or heroines who presided at dream oracles were diviners or prophets in their former lives, and dream-oracles were occasionally given by deities rather than heroes (such as Gaia, the Earth[16]). If Pasiphae was a title of Selene, and gave dream-oracles, this would perhaps be an uncommon state of affairs, but by no means unique or unheard of.

There is, however, another interesting facet to a number of the heroes given in Tertullian's list, which is the manner of their 'deaths'. Asclepius, as just mentioned, was struck by lightning.[17] As Rohde remarks, Zeus' lightning here 'did not destroy life, but translated the person affected to a higher existence outside the visible world.'[18] Similarly, some of the heroes presiding over dream oracles were removed to an existence 'outside the visible world' without suffering a 'normal death'.

Amphiaraus, although being a seer, was tricked into becoming one of the seven chieftains who made an attack on Thebes in Boeotia, even though he could foresee that it would end in disaster. In the ensuing rout, Amphiaraus fled in his chariot; then Zeus hurled a thunderbolt that split the earth and Amphiaraus drove, still alive, into the underworld and was deified. Here, though not struck himself, the lightning

---

16 Euripides, *Iphigenia in Tauris*, 1259-1269 (1999: p.291). See also Rohde 1925 (Rpt. 1966): p.290, and Farnell 1896-1909: Vol. 3, pp.8-9.

17 Edelstein & Edelstein 1945 (Rpt. 1998): Vol. 1, pp.53-56, collects the ancient testimonies.

18 Rohde 1925 (Rpt. 1966): p.100.

opened the way for Amphiaraus to pass into the beyond without dying.[19]

Amphilochus and Mopsus, though suffering death, actually killed each other in combat, rendering them both murderers and murdered at the same time and in the same incident; certainly an ambivalent way of passing into the beyond.[20]

There is some confusion about Sarpedon, who appears to have been a brother of King Minos of Crete, before removing to Lycia; he was later worshipped as a hero by the Lycians. Whether this was the same Lycian Sarpedon who fought for Troy in the Trojan War isn't clear, but the fact that Tertullian mentions Sarpedon having a dream oracle in the Troad would suggest that he was the one who fought on the Trojan side. Homer's *Iliad* tells us that when Sarpedon was slain by Patroclus, Zeus commanded Apollo to remove his body from the battlefield, to 'bathe him in the streams of the river, and anoint him with ambrosia, and clothe him about with immortal raiment, and give him to swift conveyers, even to the twin brethren Sleep [Hypnos] and Death [Thanatos], who shall set him speedily in the rich land of wide Lycia.'[21] Although Sarpedon suffers violent death, to be anointed with ambrosia is a form of deification and immortalisation, and *both* Sleep and Death carry him away.

For Trophonius, most noted in life as a builder and architect, we have variant stories. Pausanias tells us that he and his brother Agamedes built Apollo's temple at Delphi, and also the treasury of Hyreus at the same place. However, they left a secret entrance in the latter, through which they could return and steal the treasure. Agamedes eventually fell into a trap, and Trophonius, unable to extricate him, cut his head off to prevent identification. Afterwards, the earth split open and swallowed Trophonius in the sacred wood

---

19 Apollodorus, 3.6.8 (1921: Vol. 1, p.371). Philostratus (the elder): *Imagines*, 1.27 (332-333K) (1931: p.105-107).

20 Apollodorus, 6.19 (1921: Vol. 2, p.265).

21 Homer, *Iliad*, 16.667-675 (1925: Vol. 2, pp.213-215).

at Lebadea, at a place later called 'the pit of Agamedes'; this is an obviously similar tale to that of Amphiaraus.[22] Cicero, on the other hand, tells us that when Trophonius and his brother Agamedes had completed Apollo's temple, they prayed to the God for 'what was best for man'. Apollo promising to grant this on the third day following, they then died in their sleep.[23]

Tertullian appears to be confused about 'Hermione in Macedonia', which seems to be untraceable. One has to conjecture that he's actually referring to a *place-name* Hermione (rather than to the daughter of Menelaus and Helen, who was not noted for oracular abilities), but this Hermione is presumably the one in Argolis where there was a chasm in the ground that was believed to lead into the underworld. While we have no other sources suggesting a dream oracle here, Rohde remarks (referring to Strabo) that the Hermioneans felt that the underworld of the dead seemed so close that they didn't bother to put the usual coin in the mouth of the dead to pay Charon, the ferryman of the dead.[24]

Pasiphae's oracle has already been discussed above (Chapter **9**); regrettably, we have little narrative material from that sanctuary that can usefully be compared with the other stories given here. However (although there are, of course, other dream oracles not mentioned by Tertullian, which have less impressive 'origin-stories' than those discussed in this section), looking at the material given here there are suggestive hints that the deities or heroes connected with dream-oracles have somehow bypassed death: they are translated by lightning, they are taken alive into the underworld, they pass on in their sleep, or accompanied by personified Sleep (Hypnos), the twin-brother of Death. This, of course, reminds us very much of Endymion, eternally asleep in his cave, whether that sleep is accompanied by Selene or Hypnos.

---

22 Pausanias, 9.37.7 (1935: Vol. 4, pp.339-341).

23 Cicero, *Tusculan Disputations*, 1.47 (114) (1945: Vol. 18 p.137).

24 Rohde 1925 (Rpt. 1966): p.162. Strabo: Geography 8.6.12 (C373) (1927: Vol. 4, p.171).

There is one further, tangential point here. Cicero, discussing the way Agamedes and Trophonius passed on in their sleep, compares it to the story of Cleobis and Biton. This story, the classic source of which is Herodotus, tells how these youths were sons of a priestess of Hera at Argos. At a particular festival their mother was supposed to be carried to the temple in an ox-drawn cart. The oxen being lacking, Cleobis and Biton pulled the cart themselves for six miles. Their mother then prayed to Hera that they should be rewarded with the greatest blessing that man could receive. As a result the youths fell asleep in the temple and, like Agamedes and Trophonius, never woke up.[25] There is, of course, nothing oracular here, but A.B. Cook discusses, and reproduces a drawing of, a Roman sarcophagus from Venice. The reliefs on this show the story in four consecutive scenes, almost like a comic-strip. In the first, Cleobis and Biton (shown as boys, rather than youths) replace the oxen of their mother's cart. In the second, they lie down to sleep in the temple while their mother performs the rites. In the third, they journey to heaven, and in the fourth they are reunited with their mother in the afterlife. It's the third scene that is of interest here, for the journey to the otherworld shows the boys accompanying the chariot driven by Selene, her iconography easily recognisable from the Selene and Endymion sarcophagi to be discussed below in Chapter 14.[26] While it's true that this may represent, and be influenced by, the same Roman sentiment which makes Endymion's eternal sleep with Selene an acceptable surrogate for death, the connection of Selene with this otherworld translation, so similar to that of Trophonius and other dream-oracle heroes, is at least worthy of remark.

10.3.2 Cave Deities. In the last section it was pointed out that Amphiaraus and Trophonius (in one version of the story)

---

25 Cicero, *Tusculan Disputations*, 1.47 (113) (1945: Vol. 18, p.137). Herodotus, 1.31. (1920: Vol. 1, pp.35-37).

26 Cook 1914: Vol. 1, p.449.

were swallowed up by the earth, while the other oracular figures made unusual transitions to the after-life. For the Greeks, of course, the after-life was passed in the underworld, and it should be remembered that the concept of the 'underworld' was taken very literally, particularly in those days when the Earth was still conceived to be flat. We've seen that the underworld was also very close at hand: thus sacrifices could be offered to the chthonic deities by simply digging a trench, then sacrificing an animal and letting the blood pour into the pit. The trench was, in effect, a door through the 'skin' of the earth that gave direct access to the underworld.[27] Unsurprisingly, there were a number of *ploutonia* throughout the classical world: caves, chasms or 'bottomless' lakes that were thought to be entrances to the underworld, and through which heroes such as Heracles and Orpheus were able to descend and return. Hermione, mentioned by Tertullian, was one such place.[28]

As Rohde pointed out in a groundbreaking (both literally and figuratively) chapter on 'cave deities', figures such as Amphiaraus and Trophonius were *made* immortal by these translations below the ground, and continued to exist there. However, they continued their existence not in the geographically generalised and relatively non-specific Hadean underworld, along with the swarming dead, but in their own underground chambers; and these chambers were actually sited in Greece, at their cult-sites where dream-incubation took place.[29] Even more interestingly, the subterranean chambers were known, in Greek, as *megara* (singular *megaron*). And *megaron*, apart from its usual meaning of 'large room or chamber', can also mean 'a woman's apartment', or 'a bed-chamber'. Perhaps more tellingly still, Ustinova quotes Euripides as referring to the oracle of Trophonius as *thalamai Trophoniou*, 'the bed-chamber of

---

27 Rohde 1925 (Rpt. 1966): p.104.
28 For a detailed survey of *ploutonia*, see Ogden 2001: particularly chapters 3-5.
29 Rohde 1925 (Rpt. 1966): p.89-91.

Trophonius'[30], which would seem to indicate that the terms were perhaps interchangeable, and is particularly interesting when we consider the known incubatory practice at the oracle of Selene at Thalamae. While we have no evidence of a subterranean chamber at Thalamae itself (but equally there is no physical evidence of a subterranean chamber at the Amphiareon), the correspondence is notable and suggestive. Immortal figures such as Amphiaraus and Trophonius live on and send oracular dreams from underground 'bed-chambers'; Selene appears to preside over a similar dream-oracle at another 'bed-chamber'; and Endymion sleeps forever with Selene in a cave. Endymion, though asleep, is also immortal. We've seen above (1.5.2) that the reasons why he is both immortal and asleep are far from clear, and that the explanations that were put forward are less than convincing. We might conjecture from this evidence that those attempting to 'explain' are looking at the question from the wrong angle. It is *not* that Endymion was put to sleep and made immortal, and *then* taken to a cave; it's *because* he passes his existence in a cave ('below the earth') that he is immortal. Again, we may suppose that the prolonged sleep of Epimenides (and his subsequent lengthy life) is not to be seen as 'he slept for a long time, and it just happened to be in a cave', but rather that his actually *being in the cave* (and so removed from the normal passing of time in the upper world) caused the prolongation of his sleep and life.

The oracle of Trophonius at Lebadea, in Boeotia, was, perhaps, the most obviously 'cave-like' of oracles, but it is difficult to know precisely what occurred there, in spite of another eye-witness account from Pausanias, who consulted the oracle. In brief, he describes it as follows:

The consultant (who is generally referred to as a man) spent some days in a special building dedicated to Good Spirit and Fortune, purifying himself by bathing in the river Herkyna

---

30 Ustinova, 2002: p.270.

*Selene*

(named after a Nymph associated with Trophonius) and using no hot water. He ate the meat from frequent sacrifices, which were offered to Trophonius, Zeus, Apollo and other deities, and the priests examined the entrails of each for omens. On the night of the actual consultation, a ram was sacrificed at a pit to Agamedes, the brother of Trophonius, and if the entrails of this provided good omens, the consultation could go ahead. After being bathed in the Herkyna by two boys with the title of Hermae ('Hermeses'), he was taken to drink from a spring called Lethe (Forgetfulness), to forget everything currently in his mind, and then from a spring called Mnemosyne (Memory), so that he'd remember what he saw in his consultation. Dressed in a linen tunic and wearing heavy local boots, he was then taken to the shrine itself, which was on the mountainside above the sanctuary. There, with the aid of a light ladder, he descended into an artificial, stone-lined, kiln-shaped chamber, some 10 feet in diameter and 20 feet deep. There he found an opening between the wall and the floor some 2 feet wide and 1 foot high. Laying on his back and holding honey-cakes in his hand, with which to appease the sacred snakes said to live in the cave, he inserted his booted feet into the opening and pushed forward until his knees were in as well, after which he was immediately dragged through the opening as if something was sucking him down. After that, arriving in the 'second place', the procedure remains unclear; some heard the oracle, others saw as well. The consultant returned feet first through the same mouth, and when he came up out of the shrine, the priests took him and sat him on the throne of Memory, not far away, and questioned him about what had occurred. He was then turned over to his friends, who took him back to the building where he began his preparations. At this point he was still possessed by terror and hardly knew himself or anything around him, but some time afterward he came to his senses and could laugh again.[31]

---

31 Pausanias, 9.39.1-14 (1935, pp.347-355). For lengthy commentary on this

Amongst other features, we can note here the presence of two springs; it may be pure coincidence that two springs are also found at present near the shrine of Thalamae, particularly as Pausanias only mentioned one in his description of Pasiphae's shrine. However, it should also be noted that springs by the name of Lethe and Mnemosyne were thought to be present in the underworld, and were drunk from by the souls of the dead (see below, 13.3.4). The consultant of Trophonius, then, appears to have literally entered the 'underworld' by descending into the cave; but at the same time, he also seems to have crossed the border between life and death. The oracle of Trophonius is the only one where we have actual evidence that the springs were named Lethe and Mnemosyne, but the presence of springs appears to be widely-attested, as does the presence of a Nymph (in this case Herkyna). It's also apparent that, at Lebadea, although the 'cave' is an artificial construction, it's actually positioned on the side of a mountain; in this, then, it has some correspondence to our 'archetypal model' of Endymion's cave on the mountain. This 'cave' appears to have been found by archaeologists, though at 'four metres deep and two in diameter' it is slightly smaller than described by Pausanias. The fact that, from its bottom, a small hole extends out in a south-west direction would seem to clinch the identification, but when found the hole was blocked by a large stone. As Ogden remarks, the oracle may have been destroyed by earthquake, though he speculates that it may have consisted of a worked natural cave.[32] There is also some evidence that Trophonius was thought to continue to inhabit the very chamber in which consultants received their oracles: certain obscure commentators say that Trophonius constructed the chamber himself, retreated into it, and prophesied until he died of hunger, after which a 'demon', perhaps his ghost, continued to give oracles.[33]

---

passage by Sir James Frazer, see Pausanias 1898: Vol. 5, pp.196-204.
32 Ogden 2001: p.81.
33 Ogden 2001: p.85.

However, precisely what form of divination occurred here remains unclear. As we've seen at the beginning of this chapter, Tertullian listed Trophonius among the dream-oracles, and he is the only surviving ancient source to address the problem directly. However, a passage in Plutarch's discussion of the 'Demon (or Sign) of Socrates' suggests that this might also be the case. Plutarch wrote in a mythologising format to introduce a discussion of souls and the afterlife, etc., but used a consultation of the Trophonian article as a vehicle for this; this would be quite appropriate, of course, considering what was said above about the consultant passing into the 'underworld' at Lebadea. His hero, Timarchus, is said to have performed the usual rites and descended into 'Trophonius' cave', where he lay in darkness not certain whether he was awake or dreaming, before his soul seemed to depart through the top of his head and embark on a voyage of otherworldly exploration that included hearing voices explaining to him the particularly Pythagorean tenet of metempsychosis.[34] This sounds suspiciously like a fictionalised version of an incubatory dream. Ogden believes incubation to be the form of divination practiced there;[35] so also does Detienne, who compares the experience to an initiation.[36] The alternative hypothesis is that when the consultant emerged from the shrine and was sat on the throne of Memory, the priests constructed the oracle from his confused remarks.[37] This is a possible conjecture, but still does nothing to explain the nature of the experience in the shrine itself. Ultimately, we simply do not know what occurred, in spite of the usual conjectures about hallucinogenic drugs, disguised priests and peculiar machines, and speculation without evidence seems pointless.

---

[34] Plutarch, *On the Sign of Socrates* 21-22 (590A-592E) (1959: Vol. 7, pp.461 477).
[35] Ogden 2001: p.82-83.
[36] Detienne 1996: pp.63-64.
[37] Parke 1967: p.94.

There's also an interesting, if highly legendary, tale about the oracle of Trophonius that's worth mentioning here. It's contained in the hagiographic life of the Pythagorean sage Apollonius of Tyana, written by Flavius Philostratus in the 2nd century CE.[38] Apollonius visited the shrine but was refused entry by the priests on the basis that they would never allow a 'wizard' like him to enter and test the cave. He thereupon entered the cave secretly, dressed as a philosopher (an action said to be approved by the God, who appeared to his priests to tell them so) and asked Trophonius what he considered the most complete and purest system of philosophy. Apollonius is said to have emerged from the cave after seven days, bearing with him a volume containing the tenets of Pythagoras (with the obvious implication that this book was given to him by Trophonius). It might seem fairly obvious that a Pythagorean sage would find such a confirmatory volume, but there seems to be a connection between such subterranean oracles and initiatory traditions and the Pythagorean and Orphic traditions (see Chapters 8 and 13), and the length of time Apollonius spent underground places him firmly in the 'cave-sleeper' tradition.

We shall have more to say of the oracle of Amphiaraus in the following section. Here we can note that, while there is no evidence of any physical representation of a cave at his sanctuary at Oropus, there is some suggestion that Amphiaraus was thought to continue his existence in an underground chamber. Philostratus the elder, describing a painting showing Amphiaraus driving his chariot down below the earth, adds a couple of interesting details about the background. Oropus is shown personified as a youth, 'and it depicts also the place used by Amphiaraus for meditation, a cleft holy and divine. Truth clad all in white is there and the gate of dreams – for those who consult the oracle must sleep – and the god of dreams himself is depicted in a relaxed attitude.'[39]

---

38 Philostratus, *The Life of Apollonius of Tyana* 8.19. (1912: Vol. 2, pp.379-383).
39 Philostratus (the elder): *Imagines*, 1.27 (332-333K) (1931: p.105-107).

10.3.3 Sheep Skins. We have seen, in the last section, that it was customary to sacrifice a ram before consulting Trophonius, and this was also commonplace with other dream-oracles. As Ogden points out, the purpose of this was probably purificatory.[40] However, there are other practices that go beyond this simple act of purification, where the ram is not only sacrificed but skinned, and the consultant of the dream-oracle then sleeps wrapped up in the fresh fleece. This was the procedure at the oracle of Amphiaraus, often mentioned in the same breath as that of Trophonius; and these two oracles were, perhaps, the most famous in Greece, outside of the Apolline tradition at Delphi and elsewhere.

For the shrine of Amphiaraus, at Oropus, on the borders of Attica and Boeotia, we have rather fewer details than we do for that of Trophonius. Incubation was practiced here, mainly for the cure of disease, in much the same way as at the Asclepian temples. Originally, it appears, Amphiaraus' shrine was at Knopia in Boeotia, which was believed to be the site where Amphiaraus drove his chariot into the underworld; but another tale has it that he descended at a place called Harma (literally, 'Chariot'). It seems that the oracle was moved to Oropus at the end of the 5th century BCE, probably on instruction from the Delphic Oracle.[41] Given this migration, it's perhaps not surprising that we find no mention of an underground chamber at the site. Pausanias provides us with a description of the shrine and its numerous altars to various deities and heroes, including members of Amphiaraus' immediate family, and of the Nymphs in general. He makes no mention of a specific Nymph associated with the shrine, though it appears from other sources that the Halia Nymph (the 'Sea Nymph') was worshipped at Oropus; whether she had any specific relation to the shrine of Amphiaraus is unclear, however.[42] There was also a sacred spring

---

40 Ogden 2001: p.174.
41 Pausanias, 9.8.3, 9.19.4 (1935: Vol. 4, pp.207, 253).
42 Larson 2001: p.143.

near the shrine, but this was not used for purifications; instead patients who had been cured at the shrine would cast silver or gold coins into it, as this was said to be where Amphiaraus rose up from the underworld as a God (quite how this squares with the moving of the shrine is unclear). For the consultant, preparatory purificatory rites consisted of offering sacrifice (usually a piglet) to Amphiaraus and the other deities presiding over the numerous altars mentioned above. After this, the consultant sacrificed a ram and slept on its fleece in the temple, the oracle then responding with a dream.[43] Frazer gives an extensive commentary on the passage from Pausanias, including a description and plan of the site, and the rules of consultation preserved on inscriptions.[44] The sanctuary appears to have been open only during the summer months, and was open to both men and women, who had separate bathing establishments. Consultants then slept in a south-facing stoa or colonnade, 360 feet long, separate from the temple itself, men on the east and women on the west.[45]

While the Oropus shrine appears to date only from the late 5th century, we recall that this was actually transferred from Knopia, where consultations appear to have begun at an uncertain date. Interestingly, the name 'Amphiaraus' has been read on Linear B tablets from Knossos, as has that of Mopsus.[46] The name 'Mopsus' also appears in early Hittite, Lydian, Cilician and Phoenician texts,[47] which provide an interesting link back to Asia Minor, although not specifically back to Caria where our primary Endymion myth is set. These may well be ordinary male names that have nothing to do with oracular seers, but the mere fact that the name-forms can be traced back to the same period as Thalamae is of some interest.

---

43 Pausanias, 1.34.1-5. (1918: Vol. 1, pp.183-187).
44 Pausanias 1898: Vol. 2, pp.4632-477.
45 For a very detailed archaeological/architectural examination of this stoa, see Coulton 1968: pp.147-184.
46 Ventris & Chadwick 1973: pp.99, 104.
47 Burkert 1992: p.52.

This practice of sleeping on sheep-skins extended to other dream-oracles, including temples of Asclepius in Attica.[48] Thus Strabo tells us of two temples in southern Italy (which, before the expansion of Roman power, would have been in Magna Graecia): 'In Daunia, on a hill by the name of Drium, are to be seen two hero-temples: one, to Calchas, on the very summit, where those who consult the oracle sacrifice to his shade a black ram and sleep in the hide, and the other, to Podaleirius, down near the base of the hill, this temple being about one hundred stadia from the sea; and from it flows a stream which is a cure-all for diseases of animals.'[49]

Calchas was another famous seer, involved with the Greeks during the Trojan War. It was foretold by an oracle that he would die when he met a diviner greater than himself; when he was defeated in a divinatory contest by Mopsus (who had a Cilician dream oracle of his own, as listed by Tertullian) he died of a broken heart.[50]

When we turn to the almost incomprehensibly elaborate poem of Lycophron, the *Alexandra*, we find him attributing the same practice to the temple of Podaleirius (who was one of the sons of Asclepius, and of whom we shall have more to say in 13.5): 'And near the Ausonian [Italian] false-tomb of Calchas [Calchas is elsewhere said to be buried in Colophon] one of two brothers [Podaleirius and Machaon] shall have an alien soil over his bones and to men sleeping in sheepskins on his tomb he shall declare in dreams his unerring message for all.'[51] Whether consultants in search of dreams slept on sheepskins at the shrines of *both* Podaleirius and Calchas, or whether one or other of our sources is in error here, is impossible to tell.

---

48 Ustinova 2002: p.269.
49 Strabo, 6.3.9 (1917-1932: Vol. 3, p.131).
50 Apollodorus, *The Library*, 6.2-4 (1921: Vol. 2, pp.243-245).
51 Lycophron, *Alexandra*, 1047-1050 (1955: pp.407-409).

A similar practice existed with the Romans, who consulted the dream oracle of Faunus, near the Tiber, by sleeping on the skins of sacrificed rams. This will be discussed more appropriately, and in more detail below, in Chapter 12.

Admittedly, this is a fairly short list of dream-oracles where we know that it was the practice to sleep on sheepskins: Asclepius, Amphiaraus, Calchas, Podaleirius and Faunus (although obviously there are a number of known oracles where we have so little information we simply do not know what the practices were). Obviously sleeping on sheepskins was not universal; however, equally obviously, it was not rare.

Our next step is to pull this material together, and see how it applies to the myth of Selene and Endymion.

Chapter Eleven

# Selene And Endymion: A Reprise

## 11.1 Introduction

It's now time to reconsider the Selene and Endymion myth, in the light of the material that has been gathered up in the last few chapters, on dream oracles, cave-sleepers and the like; and to formulate some sort of tentative hypothesis about the sort of ideas the myth refers to. If this provides us with insights into the Endymion myth, the next step will be to try using it as a key to unlock the mysteries of other Selenic myths; and if it proves to be useful in these further cases also, then its broader applicability would seem to validate and strengthen the original hypothesis. Our first task, then, is to summarise the important points from the previous chapters and, discussing their relevance to the Endymion myth, formulate our preliminary hypothesis.

## 11.2 Sleeping On The Edge Of The World

While any attempt to categorise the different stories and material we have to deal with would necessarily be crude and of limited applicability, such an attempt may help us get to grips with things more easily; and so, bearing in mind the limitations, seems worth the effort. A first approach might be to compare facets of the mythical, legendary and real worlds. Looking at the material gathered so far, we can see much the same 'story-line' being acted out on all three differing levels of reality.

We can begin by placing the story of Selene and Endymion on the 'mythical' level. Endymion, in the Carian version of the tale, appears to have no family, or any ties with the real world at all; he is a 'purely mythical figure' in that he is nothing more than what he does and represents. We've seen (6.3) how Endymion's cave, although nominally on Latmos, is hardly on this side of the world's-edge at all. His sleep is eternal and he doesn't age; effectively he's outside of time completely. And he is in eternal and presumably blissful interaction with a loving, nocturnal Goddess.

On the 'legendary' level, we have Epimenides and, as we've seen, others like him (Chapters 7 & 8). Epimenides is on the borderline between the real and unreal: he may be entirely legendary, but he's been provided with a genealogy and a set of separate actions and functions that suggest a life-history beyond the mere fact of sleeping in a cave. Whether he was actually a living person is a moot point; but he was *thought* to have been a real man. He too sleeps in a cave, but it is the Cave of Zeus, a very special and sanctified spot which, while it has known geographical coordinates in this world, certainly seems to intersect with the otherworld also. His sleep, however long it may be, is of a limited period, and similarly his life, also unnaturally lengthened, eventually comes to an end. In his sleep (apparently during dream), he meets 'Gods', gains wisdom and, eventually, is responsible for written 'oracles'. His relationship with Selene is that he is said to be her 'son', although this may well be more figurative than literal.

At the 'real-world' level, we descend the mountain to Thalamae and, by association, the other dream-oracles that have been examined. Here the consultant is, quite obviously, a real person and, while he may not sleep in a cave, he is at least sleeping in a sanctified place: either the temple itself or a part of the temple-complex designated for the practice. This, effectively, puts the spot where he sleeps 'at the edge of' or 'outside' the real world, if only artificially and temporarily. His lifespan is natural, and his sleep is restricted to a single night, though this too is sanctified and purposeful, in that it is specifically undertaken in order to obtain an oracular dream. He may meet Selene in dream (assuming she was, in fact, the presiding deity at Thalamae), or receive meaningful dreams thought to have been sent by her. Similarly, the same would apply to the other dream-oracles and their presiding deities. As we've seen in Chapter 7, other men withdrew to underground chambers ('pseudo-caves') in order to receive visions and gain wisdom.

Here we might revert, for a moment, to the 'Sanctuary of Endymion' on Mount Latmos, discussed above at 6.2. As stated there, the identification is hardly certain, and even if this is the shrine of Endymion, there is no evidence of what occurred there. However, with the rounded back of the shrine being built into outcrops of rock, and the suggestion that perhaps the rear chamber of the shrine represented Endymion's cave, the thought cannot help but occur that perhaps this too was a dream-oracle, the consultant emulating Endymion by sleeping in 'his cave' on the very slopes of Latmos, and presumably encountering Selene herself in dream. Attractive as this idea may be, however, it has to be emphasised that it is no more than speculation.

If to sleep in a cave effectively removes one from the flow of time itself, eternally in the case of Endymion, pretty much the same in such cave-dwelling deities as Trophonius and Amphiaraus, and for an extended period with Epimenides, the other aspect of this non-temporal experience is that it puts one in touch with the Gods or their wisdom. Endymion's intercourse with Selene is eternal and, ultimately, outside the real world, for he never wakes and we have no record of what he may have learned. Epimenides benefits from his intercourse with the deities, in that when he wakes he has received sufficient initiatory wisdom to become a purificatory priest and a composer of written oracles. The consultant of a dream oracle interacts with the deity concerned for the single night that the particular consultation lasts, and receives a meaningful dream in answer to his question, or some form of healing.

There is, of course, the matter of the sheep to consider as well. We are told that Endymion was a shepherd, but by the time we 'meet him' in the story he is generally already asleep in his cave, and the sheep make no active or physical appearance. And yet it is quite obvious that they must have had at least some part to play, if only in that if Endymion had not been a shepherd, he wouldn't have had cause to be on Mount Latmos in the first place. 'Coming down one level' to Epimenides, who has a more fully constructed life-history, we find sheep once more. Here Epimenides is searching for his sheep when he enters the cave. While still not physically present in the action of the story (except as an absent object searched for), effectively it is the sheep that 'leads' Epimenides to the cave, and so is the 'vehicle' by which, ultimately, he comes into communion with the deities. And lastly, descending further to the 'real world', we find that it is commonplace to sacrifice a sheep before consulting a dream-oracle and, in a number of cases, such as those of Amphiaraus, Calchas and Podaleirius, to sleep wrapped up in the skin of the sacrificed sheep. Again there is a common thread here, from mythical down to real worlds, where an approach to deity through sleep and dream appears to be made with the aid of a sheep. In all three cases, no matter how near or far from the forefront of the action, it is the sheep that is the vehicle leading to communion with deity: either as ritual practice in the dream-oracle, as story-element with Epimenides, or by implication with Endymion.

Naturally, the fragmentary state of the surviving evidence, and our inability to make an 'on-the-spot' investigation at the precise times and places where these practices were carried out or these stories were told, means that it is impossible to make a perfect fit of all the aspects to the stories, or to argue a case that would 'stand up in a court of law'. However, it seems possible to detect at least some form of pattern that, vague or imperfectly-fitting as it may be, seems to be reproduced at all three levels.

## Steve Moore

We might argue, then, that on an archetypal/mythical level, the story of Selene and Endymion represents ultimate 'intercourse' with the deity of night and dreams, and a gaining of knowledge which, told in the myth, is symbolically represented in the physical and Biblical sense of the word 'knowing' Selene (even if Endymion's part in the process often appears to be entirely passive). From the emanations of the story on lower planes, it seems reasonable to imagine that this knowledge is gained through dream and vision coming from an unconscious level, represented by caves, the underworld and liminal areas in general. However, this is a 'lunar', imaginative knowledge, unlike the rational, solar knowledge represented by the Apolline tradition and oracles such as Delphi. The story of Epimenides appears to represent the same thing on a somewhat less exalted level, although this is still considerably higher than that of the everyday human-being; Epimenides, after all, leads a legendary life, with a legendary knowledge. On the lowest level, we have the human individuals consulting dream-oracles; they are in quest of the same 'lunar' variety of knowledge arising from the unconscious through dream, but in 'real-world' terms.

Thus we might say that the Selene and Endymion story reflects down into the dream-oracles, and provides them with a mythical archetype and a functioning rationale. But at the same time, the process works both ways, and those who consult dream-oracles can be seen as re-enacting the story of Selene and Endymion. And this, in turn, suggests a function of Selene as a purveyor of that 'lunar knowledge' discussed above, which takes her a considerable distance from the usual interpretations of the Goddess, as an astronomical deity, or as a 'Goddess of women'.

This, then, is the skeleton of our working hypothesis. Before seeing if such an idea has any relevance to other stories from Selenic mythology, there are a couple of points we need to flesh out to back up the hypothesis. The first is to look at the evidence for Endymion as a recipient of dreams, and Selene as a sender of the same. The second point would be, if we propose that Selene is a Goddess sending oracular dreams, to see if we can find a story that illustrates the hypothesis with a fair degree of exactness.

## 11.3 The Dreamer And The Dream-Sender

It was implied above that the 'intercourse' of Endymion and Selene while asleep was not necessarily to be taken in a purely figurative sense; but nor should it be regarded as purely symbolic. As Rohde points out, in early authors such as Homer and Pindar, it is apparent that the psyche was to a certain extent regarded as a 'second self', and that while the person is conscious, the psyche is asleep while the body is awake. Contrariwise, when the body is asleep, the psyche or dream-self is awake and interacts with those figures met in dreams as if they were realities. Thus in Homer when Achilles dreams of the dead Patroclus, it is not said that he *thought* he met him while dreaming, but that he *met* him.[1] While it's obvious that later and more sophisticated Greek authors made a distinction between 'reality' and 'dream', it's apparent that this was not always the case. It's thus possible to conceive of Endymion's relationship with Selene as taking place entirely in dream while also being real ... or at least so apparently real as to be indistinguishable from reality. We are in that same world where 'Selene' is both the name of the physical Moon and of the Moon's Goddess: a world of delightful ambiguity where a single concept can represent two completely separate things at the same time, and yet also be both those entirely separate things at once. If Endymion dreams of a relationship with Selene, it is effectively a real relationship; yet similarly if Endymion has a relationship with the Goddess, it effectively has to occur in dream. If these ideas are seen as compatible, it may go some way to explain why we have the variant stories from Nonnos and the like, given above in 1.5.2, where Endymion is said to be the conscious, rather than the sleeping lover of Selene. He *can* be her conscious lover, and still be lost in dream.

---

1 Rohde 1925 (Rpt. 1966): p.7.

This notion may well be the key to understanding the various ways our ancient sources handled the concept of Selene making love to Endymion in his sleep, an idea which is often thought to present certain problems regarding masculine physiology (to put it delicately) and reflects the notion that a man cannot be raped by a woman. This is not actually the case,[2] though there is a strong folklore tradition that it is, which is probably of greater interest to us here than the physical facts. It may thus have been believed to be impossible, in physical terms, for Selene to make love to a passive Endymion (perhaps still less possible if he was also asleep). As we've seen above, at 1.5.2, the rationalising Cicero gets round the difficulty by having Selene do no more than kiss Endymion in his sleep. If the previously-mentioned stories, by Nonnos and the like, of Selene and Endymion as conscious, active lovers originally referred to their intercourse in dreams, and the reference to dream then failed to pass on with the stories of love-making, we may have an explanation for the apparent contradictions between the stories' variants.

That said, specific references to Endymion dreaming are not common. However, Sheila McNally points out that the quotations from Hesiod about Endymion being the 'steward (or keeper) of his own death' (1.5.2) and Athenaeus about Hypnos putting Endymion to sleep with his eyes open (1.5.3) imply 'some tradition of a remaining consciousness in his sleep/death'.[3] This is not quite evidence of dreaming, but we might infer the thought that he dreamed from Cicero, when he says: 'The prospect of the most delightful dreams would not reconcile us to falling asleep for ever; Endymion's fate we should consider an exact image of death.'[4] In other words, not to wake is effectively the same as death, no matter how delightful Endymion's dreams may have been.

---

2 Brookesmith 2013, pp.32-33, 37, with collected medical references.
3 McNally 1985: p.190.
4 Cicero, *De Finibus Bonorum et Malorum*, 5.20 (55) (1914: pp.455-457).

Plutarch, writing in a Platonic context where the Moon is seen as the lowest of the Celestial Spheres above the material Earth, discusses the notion that, of the three parts of the human being, the Earth provides the material body, the Moon the soul (*psyche*) and the Sun the mind; after death, the soul returns to the Moon.[5] Very interestingly, a little further on, while apparently referring to the same entities, but changing the terminology from 'soul' (*psyche*) to 'spirit' (*daimon*), he remarks: 'Yet not forever do the Spirits tarry upon the moon; they descend hither to take charge of oracles ...' (and carry out various other functions).[6] While the *type* of oracle is not specifically mentioned here, the connection between oracles and the Moon may be seen as going some way toward backing up the hypotheses presented here. In this section the final item of interest to us is that Plutarch then goes on to refer to souls in further need of purification before rebirth (a notion deriving from the Pythagoreans), some of which 'pass their time as it were in sleep with the memories of their lives for dreams as did the soul of Endymion'.[7] It is far from clear precisely what Plutarch intends by using Endymion as an example here, unless he's comparing the extended stay of the souls in the Moon to the extended sleep of Endymion: if he was under the impression that Endymion, asleep, relived his former life in dreams, there seems to be no other corroboration of this view in ancient literature. For our purposes, though, it seems to be sufficient to use this reference to illustrate that Endymion was, at least, thought to dream, whatever the subjects of his dreams might have been.

Similarly, we're not overwhelmed with material suggesting Selene to be the Goddess of dreams, though as she is very much

---

5 Plutarch, *Concerning the Face which Appears in the Orb of the Moon*, 28 (943A-E) (1957: Vol. 12, pp.199-205).

6 Plutarch, *Concerning the Face which Appears in the Orb of the Moon*, 30 (944D) (1957: Vol. 12, p.211).

7 Plutarch, *Concerning the Face which Appears in the Orb of the Moon*, 30 (945B) (1957: Vol. 12, p.217).

a Goddess of the nocturnal hours it would seem to be an obvious connection to make. What we do have, though, connects Selene with both dreams and oracles. Once again our source is Plutarch and, again, he's concluding one of his Platonic dialogues with an exemplary mythical tale. Here a certain Thespesius is said to have fallen into a coma for three days (again, an extended sleep) and, effectively, to have had what would now be called a Near-Death Experience. Travelling into the otherworld as far as Orpheus did in search of the soul of his wife Eurydice, he saw a giant goblet tended by three *daimons*, who combined three rivers which flowed into it, one white, one purple and one vari-coloured. His spirit-guide told Thespesius that, not understanding what he saw, Orpheus had spread a false report that the Oracle at Delphi was held in common by Night and Apollo. But, the guide told him, '... Night has partnership in nothing with Apollo. "This is instead," he pursued, "an oracle shared with Night and the Moon; it has no outlet anywhere on earth nor in any single seat, but roves everywhere throughout mankind in dreams and visions; for this is the source from which dreams derive and disseminate the unadorned and true, commingled, as you see, with the colourful and deceptive".'[8] Thespesius goes on to hear the voice of a Sibyl, singing prophecies from the face of the Moon; but we shall have more to say of this below, at 13.3.2.

Our next item has to be treated with some caution and reservation, as it derives from a Graeco-Egyptian magical papyrus of the 3rd or 4th centuries CE. It appears among a collection of spells for obtaining oracular dreams, is entitled 'Lunar Spell of Claudianus', and is addressed to 'Mistress Selene the Egyptian'. This is, effectively, the Egyptian Goddess Hathor, identified through her lunar attributes with Selene. Instructions for making an image of Selene are given; offerings are to be made; and then a dual-purpose spell follows, partly for the sending of dreams, and

---

8 Plutarch, *On the Delays in Divine Vengeance*, 28 (566C) (1959: Vol. 7: p.289).

partly for a form of erotic binding-magic, in which the Moon is asked to send forth the appropriate angel from a list of twelve who watch over the twelve hours of the night.[9] This is, of course, a late text from a period of extreme syncretism; the fact, though, that the dream-sending Egyptian Hathor was thought to correspond with the Greek Selene may imply that Selene, too, was thought to send dreams.

Perhaps, because in both cases under discussion here the implication would have seemed obvious (that the sleeping Endymion would dream, or that the nocturnal Moon-Goddess Selene would be associated with dreams), such things hardly seemed worth mentioning. So the evidence here is admittedly slim; but that some exists should at least show that we're not entirely on the wrong track, particularly taken with the rest of the material assembled here.

A form of Selene as oracular dream-sender, however, does appear in our next story.

## 11.4 Brutus The Trojan And The Oracle Of Diana

The following material may seem so remote in time and space from the ancient Greek world as to be inadmissible: it is written in Latin, by an author from the borders of Wales, in the first half of the 12th century CE. It is, though, of enormous interest and well worth examining; but first we need to establish some background and context.

Our source is Geoffrey of Monmouth's *Historia Regum Britanniae* (*History of the Kings of Britain*),[10] a work widely regarded as combining equal measures of history and romantic invention. Fortunately we have long ago abandoned such questions of 'reality' or 'truth' in favour of looking at 'story-content' instead, and

---

9 *PGM* VII.862-918 (Betz 1986: pp.141-142).
10 Geoffrey of Monmouth 1966.

Geoffrey certainly has some extremely interesting and entertaining stories to tell.

Regardless of its historicity or otherwise, Geoffrey's work was a literary masterpiece, inventively combining sources (some now lost to us), such as old chronicles, traditions and tales, to provide a marvellous and continuous history of Britain, from pre-Roman times, through the age of Arthur and Merlin, to the Saxon domination. It is the material from the beginning of the work, providing us with a history of Brutus, the eponymous founder of Britain, which concerns us here (such eponymous foundation-tales being popular and commonplace from ancient to mediaeval times).

This story is both broadly based on, and an imitation of Virgil's material from the Latin *Aeneid*, which tells the story of the Trojan Aeneas' flight from Troy, his wanderings and settlement of Italy, and his establishment of a line which eventually led to the foundation of Rome. Aeneas, of course, is a figure from the Greek legends of Troy; Virgil gave him a son, Ascanius, who in Geoffrey has a grandson called Brutus. Brutus frees several thousand Trojans held captive in Greece and then, after consulting an oracle of Diana, leads his people, via Africa, France, and so on, to the island of Albion, which is promptly renamed Britain, after Brutus.

Geoffrey claimed to have translated his work from an ancient Welsh chronicle, which remains untraced; this may perhaps be one of those subterfuges whereby 'quoting from an unknown source' allows the author to indulge in a little fictioneering of his own. What does seem clear, though, is that the basics of this pseudo-Virgilian tale of Brutus, but without any mention of the oracle of Diana, go back at least to the fragmentary and variant tales collected in the *British History* of Nennius, written about 800 CE.[11] In this context, the name 'Brutus' has a rather more interesting prehistory. Early

---

11 Nennius 1980. The Brutus material appears in *British History* sections 7, 10, 15, 17, 18, pp.18-22.

*Selene*

in the 7th century CE Isidore of Seville explained that the British were so-called because they were *bruti*, 'stupid', and two or three decades later the Irish annalist Cuana, accepting the British were 'odious', personalised their founder as 'Brutus'.[12]

This leaves us with the problem, of course, of where, exactly, Geoffrey got the story of Brutus consulting the oracle of Diana, to be discussed below.[13] It doesn't appear in any surviving source dating before Geoffrey, such as Nennius, and considering what we now know about the origin of the name Brutus, it hardly seems likely to be ancient. As Geoffrey's putative 'ancient Welsh chronicle' doesn't appear to have survived either (*pace* authors such as W.M. Flinders Petrie and William R. Cooper,[14] to whom we'll return below, who believe the *Tysilio Chronicle* to be the said original, rather than a translation of Geoffrey's work into Welsh, as is the common view) we are left in a position where we can only say, with safety, that we don't know the story's origin. Whether Geoffrey or *Tysilio* has priority, it is more commonplace to make Geoffrey the original author, and so we'll continue to refer to him as such; but it appears the Diana story can't be traced before his time. Nonetheless, as Flinders Petrie point outs, there are certain details in the 'voyage of Brutus' story which seem to indicate that Geoffrey had access to classical geographical sources no longer available to us, and which may well date as early as the first half of the 1st century CE.[15] There is thus the *possibility* that Geoffrey may have had access to an ancient source on which to model the Diana story; alternatively, we may be looking at a pastiche on Geoffrey's part, in a determinedly Virgilian style. This is, perhaps, rather by the way; more important is the content of the story itself, which can be summarised as follows:

---

12 Morris 1973: p.420.

13 For a general discussion of Geoffrey's sources, see Fletcher 1906: pp.43-115.

14 Petrie 1917-1918: pp.251-278. Cooper 1995: Web version, Chapter 4.

15 Petrie 1917-1918: pp.258-260.

Steve Moore

Brutus, having freed the captive Trojans from Greece, assembled a fleet and, after sailing for two days and one night, arrived at a deserted island called Leogetia, uninhabited since a pirate attack some time before. Landing, Brutus sent 300 men to explore. Coming to a deserted city, they found a temple of Diana in which was a statue of the Goddess that gave answers if it chanced to be questioned by anyone. Impressed by this miracle, the party returned to the ships and persuaded Brutus to go to the temple, offer sacrifice, and question the Goddess regarding where they should make their permanent home. Brutus, accompanied by an augur and twelve elders, went to the temple and offered sacrifice to Jupiter, Mercury and Diana. Then, holding a vessel of wine and of the blood of a white hind, he addressed Diana nine times, beginning as follows: 'Oh powerful goddess, terror of the forest glades, yet hope of the wild woodlands, you who have the power to orbit through the airy heavens and the halls of hell, pronounce a judgement which concerns the earth ...' and followed this with his question. Then he lay down before the altar on the skin of a hind (presumably one that he had offered in sacrifice), and slept until the third hour of the night. Then it seemed the Goddess stood before him and told him to sail beyond the setting Sun (and so eventually to Britain) and establish a second Troy. When he woke, Brutus was uncertain whether it had been a dream or whether the living Goddess had prophesied to him, but on further discussion with his comrades the voyage was undertaken.[16] The *Tysilio Chronicle* is substantially the same, allowing for differences in translation, adding only the detail that Brutus slept on the skin of a *white* hind, suggesting that both skin and blood came from the same white hind, which was presumably the object of sacrifice.[17]

This may seem a fairly surprising tale for a Christian ecclesiastic like Geoffrey to be promoting, but it has to be remembered that

---

16 Geoffrey of Monmouth, 1.11 (1966: pp.64-66).
17 Cooper 2002: pp.5-6.

certain classical authors, such as Virgil, remained popular in the mediaeval period for their literary qualities, and Geoffrey is undoubtedly attempting to write a 'Brutus story' to match that of Aeneas. In effect, Brutus' consultation of Diana's dream-oracle is equivalent to Aeneas' consultation of the Cumaean Sibyl and the ensuing necromancy carried out at Lake Avernus, in Book 6 of the *Aeneid*, and this, in turn, derives from Odysseus' consultation of the dead in Book 11 of the *Odyssey*.[18]

The 'question-answering statue of Diana', not mentioned after its first appearance, is presumably merely a literary link to provide a reason for Brutus to visit the temple himself. As for Diana the Goddess, we seem here to be dealing with precisely that late-antique 'Triple Moon-Goddess' described by Servius (but not by Graves!) and discussed above in the Introduction. So the Goddess is addressed as Diana (of the forest), as Luna (orbiting through the airy heavens) and Proserpine (in the halls of hell).

This becomes even more apparent when we turn to the Latin verse version of Geoffrey's *History*, the *Gesta Regum Britannie*, written in Brittany between 1235 and 1254 CE, perhaps by William of Rennes. The passage is substantially the same in content. Leogetia has become Loegencia and the answering statue has disappeared from the temple where now Diana simply 'gives answers to those who consult her'. Brutus builds three altars and sacrifices the entrails of an ox to Jupiter, of a hind to Diana, and of a dog to Mercury, and invokes as follows: 'Threefold goddess, whose names are Proserpina, the Moon [Luna], and Diana, you enter the prisons of the Styx, you shine bright in the sky, and with your javelin you hunt boar in the woods. You survey the present, the past, and the future ...' Then he asks his question, sleeps on the skin of the hind, and the story proceeds as in Geoffrey.[19]

---

18 Virgil, *Aeneid*, 6 passim. (1934: Vol. 1, pp.507-571). Homer, *Odyssey*, 11 passim (1919: Vol. 1, pp.387-431).

19 *Gesta Regum Britannie*, 1.260-270 (1991: Vol. 5, p.17).

Steve Moore

At this date, and in this language, we cannot reasonably expect either author to refer to Luna (Selene) alone; the process of syncretisation is too far advanced. For Geoffrey and William, the Moon is Diana, and to think of Diana is to embrace all the associations listed here. However, as Diana/Artemis, taken alone, is not noted as an oracular Goddess, it seems unlikely that our authors are thinking primarily of the huntress deity as she who is consulted. Instead, given the nocturnal setting, it seems reasonable to suppose that we are here dealing with a 'dream oracle of the Moon', and that is sufficient for our purposes.

We are, of course, dealing with an 'artistic production' in this story, rather than a factual narrative of dream oracle practice, and it's obviously this artistry that has shaped some of the factors here. Brutus doesn't sleep on the skin of a sheep, but on that of a hind, because the hind is the animal specifically sacred to Diana. It is a white hind for two reasons. Firstly because white is appropriate to a celestial deity while, as we've seen, black animals are offered to underworld/underground deities such as Trophonius. The second is that white is a running motif throughout this episode. Cooper, in his otherwise unconvincing revisionist interpretation of early British history, has perhaps interpreted 'Leogetia' correctly as 'Leucadia', an alternative name for the island of Leucas (modern Lefkas), off the Epirote coast of Greece.[20] The name derives from the Greek *leukas*, 'white', and refers to the island's white rocks. Thus, on the 'white island', the Goddess of the white Moon directs Brutus to sail to the island of Albion, a name which, deriving from Latin *albus* this time, likewise means 'white island'. For Brutus to sleep on the skin of a white hind is thus entirely appropriate.

Unfortunately, there appears to be no trace of any temple or large-scale cult of Artemis/Diana or Selene on Leucas, and so we perhaps have to conclude that the story has no historical basis. Rather it seems that Geoffrey has either transferred another story,

---

20 Cooper 1995: Web version, Chapter 4.

now lost to us, to a location on Leucas, where it fits better with the artistic construction discussed above, or invented the story himself, perhaps combining two Virgilian motifs: the consultation of the Cumaean Sibyl, mentioned previously, and the dream oracle of Faunus,[21] to be discussed in the following chapter. This oracle of Faunus, as mentioned by Virgil, is placed in the forest of Albunea, similarly deriving from the Latin *albus*, 'white'; this may also be an influence on Geoffrey's construction of the story. Nonetheless, this tale, late, distant and 'in disguise' as it may be, does provide us with another piece of the puzzle, and goes some way to build up the emerging pattern of Selenic dream-oracle practice.

Before leaving the subject of Brutus, there is one last, fascinating aside. The Tudor dynasty, originating in Wales, claimed direct descent (admittedly based on one of those largely-fictitious genealogies so popular in Mediaeval and Renaissance times) from Brutus the Trojan, and the last of the Tudor monarchs, of course, was Elizabeth I, the 'Virgin Queen'. She, in turn, was frequently portrayed and referred to as Diana, or other lunar titles, such as Cynthia, Phoebe, and so on.[22] And so Diana appears at both the beginning and the end of the alleged Tudor line, from Brutus to Elizabeth. And more, it's undoubtedly the queen herself who's portrayed as Cynthia in John Lyly's contemporary play, *Endymion*...[23]

## 11.5 A Virgilian Folktale

There is one more tale we can add here, though it comes from a very late source whose reliability is questionable. It comes from a collection of folktales about Virgil, who, as we've seen above (8.7), was widely regarded in mediaeval times as a sorcerer. The

---

21 Virgil, *Aeneid*, 7.81ff (1934: Vol. 2, p.9).

22 See, *inter alia*, Wilson 1939: *passim*.

23 Lyly 1996.

story was collected from an unnamed north Italian source by Charles Leland,[24] a late 19th century folklorist whose reputation has rather suffered in recent times, particularly as he's suspected of making his source material rather more literary and readable than it might originally have been. Nonetheless, it's not without interest.

It features an unidentified 'Emperor of Rome' who, after a day's hunting with his courtiers, is informed by one of them: 'Now, there is near by an ancient grotto, long forgot by men, wherein if you will sleep you may have significant dreams, even as people had in the olden time.'

The Emperor is led to the cave where he falls asleep, but is soon said to be awakened by the barking of a dog, and sees before him a beautiful woman or Goddess clad in white, with a star on her forehead. Leland would 'correct' this star to a crescent, and given the hunting context, the white clothing and the barking dog, his supposition that this is Diana would seem to be a reasonable one. The woman then releases two doves, a white one that settles on the Emperor's shoulder, and a black one that flies away. Then both woman and doves disappear. The following morning the Emperor tells the courtier of his 'vision', and the latter then recommends Virgil as a person who could interpret the omen for him.

Unsurprisingly, given the Italian origin of the story, we are once again dealing with Diana, rather than Selene, and the story is late and unreliable. Taken with everything else we've gathered, however, it may add a little more evidence to our interpretation of Selene as an oracular Goddess.

---

24 Leland 1899: pp.11-14

Chapter Twelve

# Selene And Pan

## 12.1 Introduction

It's now time to turn our attention to the tale of Selene and Pan, as outlined in section 1.4 above. As was noted there, the story survives only in Latin sources, through Virgil and his later commentators, although Macrobius and Phylargyrius tell us that the story originates with the Greek Nicander of Colophon, of the $2^{nd}$ century BCE. Colophon, interestingly, is no more than 50 miles to the north of Mount Latmos, though as we'll see it appears that the setting of the story, and quite possibly its origin, lies in Arcadia, in the central Peloponnese. From what survives of Nicander's works, he appears to have been more of an adapter of others' works than an original talent, so it seems quite likely that Nicander is merely transmitting an Arcadian tale here, rather than being the 'originator of the story'.[1]

Our Latin sources for this story refer to the Goddess as Luna, the direct equivalent of the Greek Selene, but seem generally to regard the story as scandalous. The reason for this would obviously be that to a Latin author, Luna was identified with Diana/Artemis, the virgin Goddess. A story of a sexual encounter between virginity-personified and the goat-like Pan, willing or unwilling, could thus hardly be seen as anything else but scandalous and defamatory

---

1 Such is the view of Borgeaud 1988: p.56.

to the Goddess' reputation. If the original story is Greek and the Goddess concerned Selene, of course, such difficulties disappear.

It's now time to examine those sources in a little more detail, and then to see if the hypothesis formulated in the previous chapter can provide us with any meaningful referents or interpretations.

## 12.2 Sources Of The Pan Story

12.2.1 Virgil. The earliest surviving source we have for this story (ignoring for the moment the attribution to Nicander) is Virgil (70-19 BCE), in the third book of his *Georgics*, a poem about country pursuits and works. Nicander is also known to have written a *Georgics*, now lost, and it seems quite possible that Virgil may have drawn more from Nicander than just the passage under discussion here. Let's look at the entire passage, including its context. Virgil says:

'If wool be your care, first clear away the prickly growth of burs and caltrops; shun rich pastures, and from the first choose flocks with white, soft fleeces. But the ram, however white be his fleece, if he have but a black tongue under his moist palate, cast out, lest with dusky spots he tarnish the coats of the new-born lambs; and look about for another in your teeming field. 'Twas with gift of such snowy wool, if we may trust the tale, that Pan, Arcadia's god, charmed and beguiled thee, O Moon, calling thee to the depths of the woods; nor didst thou scorn his call.'[2]

It's obvious here that Virgil's primary interest in this section is giving instruction on how to get the best (whitest) fleece, and that the tale of Pan and Selene is pretty much a secondary, illustrative feature. This may go some way to provide us with a reason for the unusual features in our second source.

12.2.2 Probus. Marcus Valerius Probus was a Latin grammarian who wrote in the latter part of the 1st century CE;

---

2 Virgil, *Georgics*, 3.384-393 (1978: Vol. 1, pp.181-183).

however, the commentary on Virgil's *Eclogues and Georgics* attributed to him is thought to be by another, later hand. The other Virgilian commentators, to be discussed below, show a fair amount of consistency in their handling of the story, and probably all refer to a version derived from Nicander where Pan either offers, or wraps himself in the fleece of, a single sheep. 'Probus', however, has a different story to tell:

'Pan, son of Mercury, desired Luna and had the best flock of sheep. When she asked for them, he offered to divide his flock with her if she would lie with him. He divided the flock into two parts, where one of the two was whiter but the wool more coarse. Luna, deceived by the whiteness, took the worse flock.'[3]

The emphasis here is very much on the quality of the fleece, and so seems to refer equally, if not more so, to the beginning of Virgil's paragraph, than to the latter half. Virgil, referring to the quality of the fleece, refers to a single preferred quality of white *and* soft; 'Probus' on the other hand divides this into two: there is white, as opposed to dark, and coarse as opposed to soft. This is combined with a typical (for the ancient world) misogynistic notion that 'women are easily tricked by appearances' and Virgil's reference to a gift. It is possible, of course, that 'Probus' is the only surviving example of a broader interpretational tradition. But equally one might conjecture that 'Probus' (or perhaps his immediate source) was simply unaware of Nicander's story, and invented an explanation based on nothing more than the words of Virgil and his own imagination. It is, perhaps, dangerous to write off a story because it doesn't fit with the rest of the surviving material; but this tale is particularly aberrant in context of the rest of the material assembled here. It's undoubtedly worthy of record, but perhaps not of too much emphasis.

12.2.3 Servius, Macrobius, Philargyrius, 'Interpretes Virgilii'. Our remaining sources for this story are all comparatively

---

3 Probus, commentary to *Georgics*, 3.391 (1826: Vol. 2. p.369-369).

late (4th-5th centuries CE) and derive from the commentatory tradition on Virgil. Macrobius merely tells us that the author of the story is Nicander, a 'writer of myths', but says little else of any use.[4] The comment of the anonymous 'Interpretes Virgilii' is fragmentary, but implies that Virgil's 'gift of snowy wool' refers to a ram's fleece, with which Pan deluded Selene.[5] Servius is of the opinion that the story has been changed, and should refer to Endymion's love for Luna/Selene rather than to Pan's, then tells us: 'As a despicable, trembling white sheep he seduced her to his embrace. The mystics find a secret meaning in this story.' Unfortunately he doesn't tell us what this 'secret meaning' might be, but merely states that the story is a 'profanation of Luna'.[6] Philargyrius gives us the most complete version. After remarking on the fact that the story is 'impious to the Goddess', he continues: 'Pan burned with love for Luna, so in order to appear beautiful to her he surrounded himself with a snowy fleece, and in this way seduced her to the act of love. The originator of this story is Nicander. Only a Greek would think of such a thing.'[7]

In essence, then, it appears that Nicander's story was that Pan, seeking to seduce Selene, wrapped himself up in a white fleece and drew her to the deep woods, where the act of love took place.

## 12.3 Interpretations

Unsurprisingly, this story has not been well-understood, thus leaving it open to further elaboration in an attempt to add sufficient material to make sense of it. So Graves tells us that Pan accomplished his seduction of Selene 'by disguising his hairy black goatishness with well-washed white fleeces. Not realising who he

---

4 Macrobius, *Saturnalia*, 5.22.9-10 (1969: pp.383-384).
5 *Interpretes Virgilii*, commentary to Georgics, 3.391 (1826: Vol. 2, p.309).
6 Servius, commentary to *Georgics*, 3.391 (1826: Vol. 2, p.281).
7 Phylargyrius, commentary to *Georgics*, 3.392 (1826: Vol. 2: pp.338-339).

was, Selene consented to ride on his back, and let him do as he pleased with her.' To put it mildly, this can hardly be justified by the sources quoted above (one wonders where Pan washed the fleeces, why Selene didn't see through such an obvious disguise, and what riding on his back has to do with anything), and Graves then goes on to explain this as referring to 'a moonlight May Eve orgy, in which the young Queen of the May rode upon her upright man's back before celebrating a greenwood marriage with him.'[8] As the Greeks used a lunar calendar which wouldn't have included May Eve (a solar calendrical date) one can only regard this as another fantasy on Graves' part.

Considering the material presented in the last chapter, there is one key to interpretation here that is quite obvious: the fact that Pan wraps himself in a fleece. Thus we appear to be back in dream-oracle territory once more and, as remarked above, the fact that the fleece is white is again appropriate to a celestial rather than a chthonic deity. Our next step, then, will be to look for other connections between Pan and Selene, between Pan and dream oracles, and so on, in hope of rounding out the picture.

12.3.1 Arcadia. Pan's origins, both mythologically and in terms of religious cult, lie in Arcadia, the land-locked state in the central Peloponnese; it is really only after the 5th century BCE that his cult begins to spread out into the Greek world at large.[9] As we've seen above (3.2.2) there were tales suggesting that Selene might perhaps have been born in Arcadia, and so to have her own Arcadian genealogy and mythology. We've also seen (1.5.3) that there was a version of the Endymion story placed in Arcadia, and while we lack details of this, its presence may suggest common modes of thinking between Caria and Arcadia; or at least that the Arcadian Selenic mythology was strongly developed enough that it became natural to attach Endymion to it also.

---

8 Graves 1960: Vol. 1, pp.102-103.
9 The most comprehensive recent treatment of Pan is Borgeaud 1988.

## Selene

Arcadia was considered a 'backward' and under-developed part of Greece, a land of mountains and forests, caves and herdsmen, in contrast to the urbanised city-states with their well-developed religious cults and literate societies. It has been pointed out above (6.3) that such a non-urban landscape is a typically liminal one, and this applies very much to Arcadia as a whole. It is 'Greece', but it is not 'civilised Greece'; it is a land (at least in early times) lacking major cities and social structures; a land, indeed, where the River Styx bursts up from the underworld to flow above ground (3.2.3). This is a land that has barely achieved a state of stability, where anything could happen: an archetype of liminality.

Pan himself was very much a pastoral deity whose name, as Borgeaud points out, appears to derive from a root meaning 'shepherd' or 'goatherd'; the connection with the word *pan* meaning 'all' being a result of later etymological speculation.[10] This, in itself, gives us a simple connection between Pan and fleeces, but one suspects there must surely be more to the story than this. Pan, too, is very much a liminal God. There are no fewer than 14 different versions of his parentage, but usually he is the son of a God and a human woman or a Nymph; in the most common, and most quintessentially Arcadian version, the son of the Arcadian God Hermes and an unnamed 'daughter of Dryops'[11] (which puts her in the same lineage as Pallas and Lycaon and thus, conjecturally, as the Arcadian Selene). Other variants differ both in the father (usually Hermes but sometimes Apollo or Zeus) and mother (Penelope features in a scandalous story whereby she is the mother and the 'father' is 'all' (*pan*) her suitors on Ithaca, during Odysseus' absence); the point is that his half-divine, half-human parentage plants him firmly in the liminal borderland. Similarly, in form he is half-human and half-animal, and he is a God who walks

---

10 Borgeaud 1988: pp.181-182, 185-187.
11 *Homeric Hymn XIX–To Pan, passim* (in Hesiod 1914: pp.443-447).

the Earth ... his domain is the wild places of nature, rather than the celestial realm or Olympus.

Indeed, when Hermes first took the infant Pan to Olympus to show him to Zeus and the other Gods, special measures were necessary, and he wrapped Pan in the skins of mountain hares.[12] As Layard remarks, the hare was almost universally associated with the Moon,[13] and also known to the Greeks as a symbol of winter, because the alpine hare's coat turned white at that season.[14] This wrapping in white skin would thus seem to function as a mode of transport to the celestial realm. Furthermore, Xenophon tells us that the hare sleeps with its eyes open, though the eyes do not move.[15] Inevitably we are reminded here of the story of Endymion loved by Hypnos and sleeping with his eyes open (above at 1.5.3). This is liminal, once again: the sleep that is not a sleep, but rather bordering on trance. Indeed, Borgeaud, describing a person in an ecstatic state, says: 'He is asleep with his eyes open, somewhere else. He is taken beyond the limits of the social world [...] he is drawn to caves, wild thickets, springs'.[16]

This material on Pan and the hare may not be directly applicable to the story of Pan and Selene, but it is suggestive of the measures necessary for Pan to interact with the celestial Goddess: the enfolding white skin and the ecstatic dream-sleep.

There is another aspect of Pan, suggestive at once of his liminality but also tying him in with further material that has been gathered above. This is the 'Hour of Pan', when it is dangerous to disturb him, because he is thought to sleep at this time.[17] The Hour of Pan is noon. So Theocritus tells us that it is not fit for shepherds

---

12 *Homeric Hymn XIX– To Pan*, 1.40-44 (in Hesiod 1914: p.445).
13 Layard 1988. For lunar-hare connections, see index, *s.v.* 'Moon'.
14 Layard 1988: p.220.
15 Xenophon, *Cynegeticus* 5.11 (1857: p.343).
16 Borgeaud 1988: p.113.
17 Borgeaud 1988: p.111.

to play the syrinx at Noon, for that's when Pan is tired and rests.[18] Similarly this is the time when Pan can also appear to those who are asleep, sending them dreams and visions. So, in Longus' novel *Daphnis and Chloe*, an offended Pan appears to the captain of some pirates when he falls asleep at high noon, and berates him for his outrages against the flocks and Nymphs.[19] As we've seen above (at 7.3), noon is one of those liminal points when 'time stands still'; the Sun is neither rising nor declining and, effectively, a 'gateway' opens up between the worlds of time and timelessness. It is also, one might note, an 'unnatural' time to sleep; the very opposite of night itself. It is, thus, hardly surprising that this is a time when contact with the otherworld is particularly likely to occur, and an apt time for Pan to cross over from the supernatural to the natural realm and appear in dream. It is also, as we've seen above, the same 'timeless instant' when Epimenides withdrew into the Cretan cave, to begin his lengthy sleep and interaction with the deities.

12.3.2 The Oracle of Faunus. Our search for specific connections between Pan and dream oracles (and then to Pan and dreams more generally) takes us first to Italy and the Latin literature concerning Faunus. This is not quite as risky a procedure as it might appear, as from the beginning of the 2$^{nd}$ century BCE Faunus was, whatever his origins as a local woodland deity, almost completely identified with the Arcadian Pan. The sources we have to handle here are considerably later than that, and so refer to 'Faunus identified with Pan'; and it hardly needs reiterating that we are dealing with ideas and the contents of stories, rather than 'facts'. Besides, there was thought to be a connection between Rome and Arcadia, in that some time before the Trojan War an expedition of Arcadians was said to have arrived in Latium, led by Evander, and given permission to settle by Faunus (here euhemerised as the local king of the aborigines). Evander was said to have the

---

18 Theocritus 1.15-20 (1853: p.2). Borgeaud 1988: p.111.
19 Longus: *Daphnis and Chloe* 2.26. (1916: p.105).

familiar-sounding parentage of Hermes and an Arcadian Nymph; and is said to have introduced the worship of Lycaean Pan.[20] Our source here, Dionysius of Halicarnassus, was writing a historical work, so it's perhaps not surprising that the tale is couched in these terms; beneath the stuff of euhemerised legend it's possible to see an explanation for the identification between Roman Faunus and Arcadian Pan. As we'll see, Ovid actually refers to Faunus as the God of the Arcadian Mount Maenalus, which, being a title of Pan himself, means that for Ovid the identification is absolute.

We have two tales of the dream-oracle of Faunus, by Ovid and Virgil, each set in early times and featuring the legendary Roman kings Numa and Latinus. Ovid, giving a story that explains why the Romans sacrificed a pregnant cow to the Earth on the 15th of April, tells us that the land was barren in the reign of the legendary sage-king Numa: 'There was an ancient wood, long unprofaned by the axe, left sacred to the god of Maenalus [*i.e.,* Pan/Faunus]. He to the quiet mind gave answers in the silence of the night. Here Numa sacrificed two ewes. The first fell in honour of Faunus, the second fell in honour of gentle Sleep [Somnus]: the fleeces of both were spread on the hard ground. Twice the king's unshorn head was sprinkled with water from a spring; twice he veiled his brows with beechen leaves. He refrained from the pleasures of love; no flesh might be served up to him at table; he might wear no ring on his fingers. Covered with a rough garment he laid him down on the fresh fleeces after worshiping the god in the appropriate words. Meantime, her calm brow wreathed with poppies, Night drew on, and in her train brought darkling dreams. Faunus was come, and setting his hard hoof on the sheep's fleeces uttered these words on the right [lucky] side of the bed: "O King, thou must appease Earth by the death of two cows: let one heifer yield two lives in sacrifice." Fear banished sleep: Numa pondered the

---

20 Dionysius of Halicarnassus: *Roman Antiquities,* 1.31.1-1.32.3 (1937: Vol. 1, pp.99-103).

vision, and revolved in his mind the dark sayings and mysterious commands.'[21] Numa's wife, the Nymph Egeria, then explained the oracle as referring to a pregnant cow, and when this was offered the land became fruitful.

In Virgil's *Aeneid*, King Latinus, pondering the question to whom he should give his daughter in marriage, resorts to the oracle of Faunus in the forest at Albunea. Here, according to Virgil, it was the custom of the priestess to make offerings and then 'as she lies under the silent night on the outspread fleeces of slaughtered sheep and woos slumber, she sees many phantoms flitting in wondrous wise, hears voices manifold, holds converse with the gods, and speaks with Acheron in lowest Avernus [*i.e.*, the underworld]'. Latinus himself comes to the shrine and, perhaps with the excessiveness of kings, slaughters a hundred sheep and himself sleeps on the skins; in the night he hears Faunus giving him oracular instructions.[22]

Quite obviously, both these stories provide us with further evidence of the practice of consulting dream-oracles by sacrificing sheep and sleeping on their skins, and so should be added to the material assembled above at 10.3.3. Whether they are merely 1st century BCE literary reproductions, or actually record a cult practice still extant in the authors' day, is rather more difficult to determine.[23] Ovid gives no location for the oracle; Virgil places it at Albunea and implies that this is close to Lavinium. However, 'Albunea' (a name deriving from *albus*, 'white') was also the name of a Nymph with a fountain and a grotto at Anio on the river Tiber; more, she was also confused with, or said to be, a Sibyl of the same name. Lactantius, in his *Divine Institutes*, not only describes Albunea as a Sibyl, but says she was worshipped as a Goddess whose statue, holding a book, was found in the Anio;

---

21 Ovid, *Fasti* 4.629-676 (1951: pp.235-239).
22 Virgil, *Aeneid*, 7.81-106. (1978: Vol. 2, p.9).
23 For discussion, see: Parke 1992: p.49. Ogden 2001: pp.91-92.

her oracles were then transferred to Rome to become part of the Sibylline books.[24]

Further on, Lactantius, discussing Faunus, again refers to the deity as if he was a historical person who deified his father and grandfather (Picus and Saturn), and also 'consecrated his sister Fatua Fauna, who was also his wife; who, as Gabius Bassus relates, was called Fatua because she had been in the habit of foretelling their fates to women, as Faunus did to men.'[25] Again, we are in the slightly confusing world of curious connections and overlapping motifs; of Nymphs, Goddesses, caves, springs, fleeces, prophecies and dream-oracles.

**12.3.3 Pan and dreams.** Back in Greece, we find a case of Pan sending oracular dreams, although the context and details are missing. Pausanias tells us that on the way down from the acropolis at Troezen was a sanctuary of Pan Lytirius ('of Release' or 'the Redeemer'), who revealed to the local magistrates, in dreams, the cure for a plague that had beset both that country and Athens.[26] Roscher talks of this as likely to be an incubation oracle, similar to that of Faunus mentioned above; this may well be the case, but there seems little evidence to back up the assumption.[27]

A Greek inscription, found at Rome and dating from the 2nd century CE, describes a healing, noon-day vision of Pan:

> 'To you, o flute-player, hymnist, benevolent God
> Pure leader of the naiads pouring bath waters,
> Hyginis, whom you yourself healed of severe illness
> By coming near him, presents this oblation.
> For you have appeared to all my sheep,
> Not as a dream vision but in the middle of the day.'[28]

---

24 Lactantius, *Divine Institutes*, 1.6 (1871: p.17).
25 Lactantius, *Divine Institutes*, 1.22 (1871: p.66).
26 Pausanias, 2.32.6 (1918: Vol. 1, p.425).
27 Roscher 1972: pp.74-75.
28 Roscher 1972: p.41.

As Roscher points out, that Pan (who, from his titles in the first two lines is obviously the deity concerned) appeared to 'all the sheep' is simply a way of indicating that Hyginis is a shepherd, while the vision is obviously seen by Hyginis, not his sheep; but yet again we have a connection between sheep and dreams. Also (as in the story from Longus, given above at 12.3.1), we find the vision appearing at noon, the Hour of Pan and, while Hyginis claims that it was *not* a dream vision (although one rather suspects it was), the fact that he makes this claim rather suggests that Pan appearing in dream was certainly the more common form of experience. We might also note that both these stories are examples of cures given through dreams that, while they are not said to actually occur at dream-oracles, are very much the type of dream that such oracles normally provided.

However, Pan was known just as much as a sender of nightmares in their classic form, particularly when identified as, or with, the somewhat demonic figure of Ephialtes.[29] So Artemidorus tells us: 'Ephialtes is identified with Pan but he has a different meaning. If he oppresses or weighs a man down without speaking, it signifies tribulations and distress. But whatever he says on interrogation is true.'[30] As Pan is the originator of *panic*, this rather more negative and aggressive aspect of dreams attributed to him is perhaps not surprising; we should note, though, the oracular aspect at the end of the quotation from Artemidorus. Later, the Christian Augustine identifies Pan with the *incubus*, that nightmare demon specifically thought to have sexual intercourse with sleeping women.[31] Roscher collects a number of other ancient testimonia of Pan's connection with dreams, such as this from the lexicon of Hesychius: 'the emanations of Pan cause nightly visions'.[32]

---

29 On this identification, see Roscher 1972: pp.59-60.

30 Artemidorus, *Oneirocritica*, 2.37 (1975: p.118).

31 Augustine, *City of God*, 15.23 (quoted in Roscher 1972: p.60).

32 Roscher 1972: p.61.

Steve Moore

12.3.4 Caves and Nymphs. It's become customary, since the publication of Borgeaud's work on Pan, to present a picture of the development of the God's cult roughly as follows. Before the 5th century BCE, Pan was mainly a local deity of Arcadia (or at most of the Peloponnese), worshipped in sacred groves or sanctuaries, but not in caves. After Pan's alleged intervention on behalf of the Athenians at the battle of Marathon in 490 BCE, the cult spread first to Athens and then throughout the Greek world generally. Outside Arcadia, Pan was usually worshipped in caves, which he commonly shared with the Nymphs, and it's thought that this type of 'primitive' cave-sanctuary was chosen to reflect the 'rustic' nature of the Arcadian God.[33]

However, a careful reading of Borgeaud's text reveals a more interesting state of affairs. Borgeaud's discussion of Pan's *heira* (a general term referring to any sort of sacred place) in Arcadia centres mainly on the account of Pausanias, who mentions numerous sanctuaries and temples, none of which are caves; and it is simply the lack of references to caves in Pausanias which (circumspectly presented) forms the basis of Borgeaud's rather tentative conclusions. These tentative conclusions, unfortunately, swiftly passed into quotation by other authors, largely presented as the established state of our knowledge about the cult of Pan. However, as we've seen, and Borgeaud also mentions this, there is one, brief reference to an Arcadian cave of Pan, and this was actually shared with Selene. This comes from the 3rd century CE work, *On the Cave of the Nymphs*, by the Neo-Platonist philosopher Porphyry:

'Before they invented temples for the gods, the earliest men consecrated caves and grottoes to them. The Couretes in Crete consecrated a cave to Zeus as did people in Arcadia to Selene and to Lycaean Pan, and in Naxos to Dionysus. Likewise, wherever they recognised Mithras they propitiated the god in a cave.'[34]

---

33 Summary based on Borgeaud 1988: p.48-52.
34 Porphyry, *On the Cave of the Nymphs* 20 (70) (1983: p.32).

Borgeaud's discussion of this passage, in a lengthy footnote,[35] is of some interest. Porphyry mentions these caves as survivals from an earlier age (and this is particularly appropriate, given that Selene's Arcadian myth appears to place her 'birth' at the beginning of Arcadian history), whose cult goes back to a time before the invention of architecture allowed the building of temples. But Borgeaud also points out that the other deities listed by Porphyry have one thing in common: not that their cult was usually practised in caves, but that one particular cave plays a crucial part in the myth of each of them. So Zeus was hidden in the Cretan cave by the Couretes, to protect him from his father Kronos; the young Dionysus was tended in the cave on Naxos by Nymphs; and Mithras sacrificed the bull (a scene appearing so frequently in Mithraic reliefs) in a cave. Borgeaud then returns his attention to the myth of the love affair of Pan and Selene, and continues: 'That there should be a cult connection between these two divinities in a district that claimed to be the birthplace of them both seems not at all improbable. I [...] think it possible that the Arcadians would have wished to identify the particular place that sheltered this famous and delusory love affair.'[36]

If the affair of Pan and Selene, which, it's been suggested, has some connection to dream-oracles through the fact that Pan wraps himself in a fleece, took place in a cave, this would be of considerable interest; but it appears to contradict what Virgil says about the seduction taking place in 'the depths of the woods'. Virgil and his commentators, of course, provide no identification, not even of a country, of where the affair took place. However, if the cave mentioned by Porphyry is connected with the story, and Porphyry mentions 'Lycaean Pan', the most obvious setting would be on Mount Lycaon; even more so, perhaps, given the

---

35 Borgeaud 1988: pp.208-209.

36 Borgeaud (or perhaps his translators) appears to be using 'delusory' here to refer to Pan's deluding of Selene, rather than to suggest that the seduction itself was in some way a delusion.

close connection between the mountain and the man Lycaon who we have tentatively identified (above at 3.2.2) as the possible grandfather of the Arcadian Selene. We might thus expect a 'compromise solution' where the cave is to be found in the deep woods on Mount Lycaon.

When we turn to Pausanias' description of Mount Lycaon, we do indeed find mention that 'there is on Mount Lycaeus (Lycaon) a sanctuary of Pan, and a grove of trees around it' but, frustratingly, absolutely no mention of a cave. However, a few lines before mentioning Pan's sanctuary, Pausanias has a curious tale to tell of Mount Lycaon: 'Some Arcadians call it Olympus, and others Sacred Peak. On it, they say, Zeus was reared. There is a place on Mount Lycaeus (Lycaon) called Cretea, on the left of the grove of Apollo surnamed Parrhasian. The Arcadians claim that the Crete, where the Cretan story has it that Zeus was reared, was this place and not the island. The nymphs, by whom they say that Zeus was reared, they call Theisoa, Neda and Hagno.'[37] The standard versions of the rearing of Zeus, of course, are placed in a Cretan cave (either the Idaean or the Dictaean); one might suspect, then, the presence of a cave in the Cretea area of Mount Lycaon, and one is reminded that the cave of Zeus was also the scene of Epimenides' lengthy sleep, and Minos' 9th-yearly consultation with Zeus. Such a cave would, then, be a particularly appropriate scene for the encounter between Pan and Selene ... but, again, the evidence of a cave is lacking. Once again, we are in the realm of suggestive hints and almost-perceived patterns, but the remains are too fragmentary for absolute proof.

If the encounter between Pan and Selene is, in some way, connected to oracles, then further evidence of Pan having an oracular connection would, naturally, help to strengthen the case. The evidence, however, tends to show Pan's oracular functions rather more associated with the Nymphs than with Selene. This

---

37 Pausanias 8.38.5 and 8.38.2-3 (1935: pp.93, 91-93).

*Selene*

perhaps should not surprise us. We have seen above that the presence of a Nymph is a common attribute of dream oracles; and Nymphs, besides, are the most common object of Pan's sexual attentions.

In Arcadia itself, we find a sanctuary of Pan on the hillside just below Lycosura, not far from Mt Lycaon, and here, Pausanias tells us: 'It is said that in days of old this god [Pan] also gave oracles, and that the Nymph Erato became his prophetess, she who wedded Arcas, the son of Callisto. They also remember verses of Erato, which I too myself have read.'[38] Borgeaud implies that this is the sanctuary of Pan on Mt Lycaon, and refers to a scholiast on Theocritus who mentioned a *manteion* (oracular shrine) of Pan on Mount Lycaon;[39] however, it's quite obvious that the oracular shrine mentioned by Pausanias is at Lycosura ... the sanctuary on Lycaon is discussed separately, on a succeeding page. It appears that either Borgeaud or the scholiast (or both) have confused the two sanctuaries. This is unfortunate; to place Pan's oracular sanctuary on Lycaon, where we have posited the cave sanctuary of Pan and Selene to be, would have been satisfyingly tidy.

Little is known of this Erato, although Pausanias tells us that she was married to Arcas, from whom Arcadia derives its name, himself a grandson of Lycaon;[40] once again, the family connections are very close. It's also of some interest that Erato's verses are recorded, and that Pausanias refers to the oracle in the past tense. Whether this means that oracles to individual queries were given in verse, or that we're dealing here with a collection of less consultant-specific prophetic verses from 'olden times', similar to those attributed to Musaeus, Epimenides and others (see 13.3.3-4) is a moot point.

There is further evidence of an association with divination. The Corycian Cave on Mount Parnassus, near Delphi, was

---

38 Pausanias, 8.37.11-12 (1935: p.91).
39 Borgeaud 1988: pp.43, 205.
40 Pausanias, 8.4.2, 8.37.11-12 (1933: Vol. 3, p.359; 1935: Vol. 4, p.91).

dedicated to both Pan and the Nymphs (though perhaps more to the latter). Here the excavators of the cave found 23,000 *astragaloi* ('knucklebones' of sheep and goats), which were used like dice for both gaming and divination. It appears that divination, probably centred on questions with simple yes/no answers, took place here on a large scale and for a long period of time. Once the Nymphs had answered the question, the *astragaloi* were then deposited in the cave as votive offerings.[41] Again, at the Nymphaeum at Apollonia, in Illyria, the Nymphs gave yes/no answers to querents who cast grains of incense on a fire.[42] However, generally the Nymphs were more likely to inspire nympholeptic seers, such as Bakis, to produce oracular verse, a subject to which we will return at 13.3.1.

## 12.4 Summary

As usual, we have a collection of suggestive hints here, that seem to fall into the same developing pattern that we have seen in relation to Selene and dream oracles in general. Pan is a deity who sends oracular dreams, and who is particularly approachable (or likely to approach) at liminal times and places: noon, caves, deep woods and so on. We have seen him presiding over his own dream oracles, where the consultants wrapped themselves in the fleece of sacrificed sheep. In the same way, Pan wraps himself in a fleece in order to approach Selene, and their encounter is described in sexual terms, similarly to the encounter between Endymion and Selene. If as has been suggested, both Selene and Pan are deities responsible for sending dreams, and a method for approaching both appears to be to wrap oneself in a fleece, it's perhaps natural that Pan, wishing to make a connection with Selene, should also wrap himself in a fleece.

---

41 Larson 2001: pp.11-12, 234-238.
42 Larson 2001: pp.12, 162-163.

## Selene

There would, however, seem to be a difference in emphasis between the stories of Selene and Endymion, and Selene and Pan. Although both appear to be related tales of dream-oracle interaction, portrayed in sexual terms, Endymion would seem to remain entirely passive; Pan, on the other hand, is at least the instigator, if not the aggressor, in the interaction. This may not be surprising, given Pan's aggressively masculine sexuality; but we have also seen that he was regarded as the sender of nightmares, and also of the female-oriented sexual nightmare, that of the incubus (there seems, though, to be no evidence that the ancients regarded Selene as connected with the succubus). One might speculate that in this case, Selene and Endymion represents the oracular dream that is sought, while Selene and Pan represents the oracular dream that comes of itself; but, as usual, there is insufficient evidence for this to be more than speculation.

There remains the question, though: if both Selene and Pan are senders of oracular dreams, why should it be necessary to connect them in a story like this? One simple answer would be that they were deities of similar function, though opposite sex, originating in the same mytho-geographical Arcadia; a relationship between them might thus have seemed natural, and the story to have been constructed using elements (such as the fleeces) common to both.

There is another possibility, however. We have seen that Pan, when not being solely responsible for sending oracles and oracular dreams, was associated with oracular Nymphs. Nymphs were also the normal object of his lusts. Selene, in fact, is the only Goddess with whom he was said to have had a sexual relationship. Although Selene is not normally connected with Nymphs, we may have another case of 'mythical enhancement' here, similar to that we saw when dealing with the Endymion material. Pan normally has relationships with Nymphs, and the Nymph-oracles we have discussed tend to be of a fairly simple

## Steve Moore

nature (*astragaloi*, incense, etc.); the story of his relationship with Selene may thus provide a 'superior archetype' which illuminates the more everyday practices. She is a Goddess, and the oracles of dreams are infinitely superior in scope, flexibility and personal relevance to a simple yes/no oracle.

Chapter Thirteen

# Selene And The Oracle-Mongers

## 13.1 Introduction

The material assembled so far has suggested, at the minimum, a putative connection between Selene and certain ancient Greek oracular and divinatory practices, mostly centred, thus far, on dream-oracles. If we discover a Selenic presence in other, similar Greek practices, our previous theorising may explain elements of Selene's relationship with those practices, while at the same time further reinforcing and validating the theories already put forward. Our attention next turns, then, to the chresmologues, or 'oracle-mongers', known from at least as early as the 6th century BCE, who were itinerants who specialised in quoting oracles that they knew and which seemed relevant to prospective clients, in the hope of gaining a reward. The oracles they quoted derived from books, and among the authors of these we will find some familiar names awaiting us. Naturally, space demands that we can only cover the relatively small area of Selenic involvement in chresmology, and readers interested in pursuing this fascinating subject in greater detail are referred to those works mentioned in the notes.

## 13.2 The Oracle-Mongers And Their Wares

To talk of 'oracles' here is to speak of them in a special sense. What we have to deal with here is unlike the dream-oracles previously discussed, the oracle of Apollo at Delphi or even the astragaloi used at caves of Pan and the Nymphs: *those* oracles were all designed to provide specifically-tailored answers to a specific and individual question, whether the answer was yes-or-no, a dream, or inspired hexameter verse. The 'oracles' under discussion here are quite different, in that they are literary, 'prophetic' texts, usually describing how this world came to be, what will happen in it (but most frequently in terms of large-scale political events, rather than the fate of individuals) and, sometimes, what will happen to us when we leave it. The 'questions' answered are thus universal and general rather than specific, although they do share some common features, such as claiming to be inspired texts, and often being written in hexameters, which allowed the Greeks to class them as 'oracles' in company with the other varieties. The original Sibylline Books, as they existed in the Roman Republic (rather than the surviving text of the *Sibylline Books* we have today, which is largely a Christian forgery) provide an example which seems to cross over the boundaries of the two varieties, in that they were formed of a prophetic, literary text which could be consulted (somehow; the procedure is not clear) when advice was needed on the interpretation of, or the best response to, prodigious events. From the surviving examples we have, preserved by Phlegon of Tralles, the Sibyl seems to have usually prescribed certain forms of sacrifice to specified deities in response to particular situations.[1] It seems less likely that the Greek oracular texts were intended for consultation, and more that they claimed to deal with the prediction of future events, although, unfortunately, the texts survive in such fragmentary form it's hard to be certain. If we wanted to place the material in a modern context, we would probably be looking at something like a cross between the *I Ching* and the *Revelation of St. John*.

These texts, circulating from at least as early as the 6$^{th}$ century

---

1 Phlegon of Tralles, *Book of Marvels* 10 (1996: pp.40-43).

BCE and continuing into Roman imperial times, were usually attributed to famous seers of the distant past, and were often found to contain 'prophecies' of catastrophic events occurring relatively recently to the time of their circulation. Modern academic scholarship, unable to accept the existence of veritable predictive abilities, regards such 'prophecies' as fictions, written after the event, either as entirely new works or as passages inserted into earlier, previously existing, oracles. Fortunately, such matters of historical veracity, or otherwise, are of no concern to us here: we are simply interested in the *idea* that such prophecies were possible, in the stories of the personnel involved, and in the deities with whom they were associated. And, as mentioned, some of the personnel are already familiar to us: the main authors to whom such oracular texts were attributed were Bacis, the Greek Sibyls, Orpheus, Musaeus and Epimenides.[2]

However, before we look at these individuals in more detail, we might note a couple of observations by Jan Bremmer.

## 13.3 The Prophets

13.3.1 Bacis. The first problem we have to confront when dealing with Bacis and the Sibyl is that, even to the ancients, these 'names' were not regarded as those of individuals, but rather as titles, in the same way that 'The Pythia' was the title of successive prophetic priestesses of Apollo at Delphi. Thus there were thought to be as many as ten Sibyls, and three prophets called Bacis, at various times and places, to the point that the plural 'Bacides' became a collective noun both for 'individuals called Bacis' and 'persons emulating Bacis'. It is possible, of course, that such a multiplicity of individuals arises from the fact that the continuing publication of new prophecies attributed to 'Bacis' or 'The Sibyl' made it

---

2 For general discussion see Parke 1988: *passim* for the Sibyls; for the other prophets, 'Appendix 1: The Theologoi', pp.174-189. See also: Fontenrose 1978: Chapter 5 'Chresmologues and Oracle Collections', pp.145-165.

obvious that they could not *all* be attributed to a single ancient individual, unless that individual lived an extraordinarily long life; thus inviting the alternative and more obvious solution that there must have been more than one of them. However, as we'll see, particularly with the Sibyl, some of these prophets *were* attributed an extraordinary longevity, which takes us back once more to that borderland area between life and death. And it has to be said that, just as often as our sources refer to multiple figures using the same name, they also refer to 'Bacis' or 'The Sibyl' as if they *were* single individuals. As usual, what is said about them is more important than who were they were, or whether they 'really lived'.

Of all the prophets discussed here, Bacis seems to have the least immediate connection with the Moon. However, there is a reference to him by Cicero that puts him in an extremely interesting context. Discussing the differences between divination by art (such as lots) and inspiration, he defines operators of the latter variety as those who 'forecast the future while under the influence of mental excitement, or of some free and unrestrained emotion. This condition often occurs to men while dreaming and sometimes to persons who prophesy while in a frenzy – like Bacis of Boeotia, Epimenides of Crete and the Sibyl of Erythraea.'[3] Thus we have Bacis grouped together with both Epimenides and the Sibyl; but we also have an implied connection drawn between dreaming and divine inspiration. Interestingly, Wardle remarks of these types of divination that 'there is a direct impact on the human mind by the gods so that no interpretation or application of rational faculties is required to understand the message.'[4]

The oracles of Bacis (which, from the surviving fragments quoted in ancient authors, seem to have centred mainly around the prediction of wars, battles, political events and other 'real-world' matters) appear to date at least as far back as the 6th century BCE,

---

3 Cicero, *De Divinatione* 1.18 (34) (1923: Vol. 20, p.263).
4 Wardle 2006: p.196.

and the earliest Bacis was thought to have originated in Boeotia. He is said to have been possessed and prophetically inspired by the Nymphs,[5] and Parke points out that there was known to be a cave of the Nymphs, called the Sphragidium, which was also an oracle-centre, on the Boeotian Mount Cytharon. Plutarch tells us, relative to this Nymph cave, that 'many of the natives were possessed of the oracular power, and these were called *nympholepti*' ('nymph-possessed'). Although this cave hasn't been specifically connected with Bacis, it at least provides a reasonable geographical background context for his story.[6] Again, the constellation of mountain, cave, Nymphs/Goddesses and oracles is extremely interesting, particularly in view of Cicero's connection of inspiration and dream, mentioned above.

As Parke points out, although the 'original' Bacis may have been Boeotian, around the time of the Peloponnesian War (in the 5th century BCE) the Athenians found it politically expedient to claim an Athenian Bacis of their own, whose oracles were more specific to their own particular and local situation.[7] Finally, we hear of an Arcadian 'Bacis' of the 4th century BCE and although Parke, with his usual rationalising approach, provides a political motive for his 'invention', there are circumstantial details that suggest the possibility of a real figure at the root of the story. For this 'Bacis' *didn't* assume the name, but kept his; in fact he had two, the first being Cydas, which sounds like a real personal name, and the second Aletes, meaning 'Wanderer'. We also know his place of birth, Caphye, and so it sounds as if this 'Bacis' may well have actually been 'Cydas the wandering prophet, from Arcadian Caphye'.[8] More than this we know nothing regarding him; but given the material discussed above, of Boeotian Trophonius and

---

5 Pausanias, 10.12.11 (1935: Vol. 4, p.437).

6 H.W. Parke, 1988: pp.180-181. Pausanias 9.3.9 (1935: Vol, 4p.187). Plutarch *Aristides* 11.4 (1914: Vol. 2 p.147).

7 Parke 1988: p.183.

8 Parke 1988: p.183.

Arcadian Pan and Endymion, the fact that we have Bacis traditions from both areas is, at least, both of some interest and another piece that fits into the same pattern that we've seen developing throughout this study. As Fritz Graf remarks,[9] both Bacis and the Sibyl 'belong to the world of rather shadowy, non-official ecstatic prophecy known since the late Archaic age.' The fact that this world with which we have to deal here is shadowy and non-official is a valuable insight, for the figures under discussion here are, unlike the official Apolline oracle tradition, very much of the margin.

13.3.2 The Sibyl. Discussion of the Sibylline tradition is complicated, particularly by the fact that the most well-known aspects of it relate to Rome and the Sibylline Books.[10] These books were said to have been written by the Cumaean Sibyl (Cumae being a Greek colony in southern Italy) and brought to Rome in the reign of the king Tarquinius Priscus (616-579 BCE); they were destroyed by a fire on the Capitol in 83 BCE and replaced with a miscellaneous collection of 'Sibylline Oracles'; these in turn were destroyed c.400 CE and the surviving text of the *Sibylline Oracles* that we have today is a *mélange* of largely Christian and Jewish material.

Virgil devoted the sixth book of the *Aeneid* to an imitation of book ten of the *Odyssey* (Odysseus' necromantic consultation of the dead), in which Aeneas consults the Cumaean Sibyl and she, in turn, takes him through a cave into the underworld to consult his dead father Anchises.[11] Virgil has it that the Sibyl is inspired by Apollo; Greek sources, however, are rather less clear on this, suggesting the possibility that she either spoke of her own volition, was inspired by the Nymphs, or had a connection to the Moon.

Pausanias has a lengthy discussion of the Sibyls,[12] and the

---

9 In Hornblower & Spawforth 1999: *s.v.* 'Bacis'.
10 Again, the major discussion is Parke 1988.
11 Virgil, *Aeneid* 6.*passim*. (1978: Vol. 1, pp.507-571).
12 Pausanias 10.12.1-11 (1935: Vol. 4, pp.431-437).

fact that he only appears to know of four suggests, according to Levi, that he was using a Hellenistic source, rather than a later Roman one, where the Sibyls are usually ten.[13] Pausanias mentions an 'original' Sibyl, a daughter of Zeus and Lamia the daughter of Poseidon. He then continues by discussing a 'younger' Sibyl, still believed to have lived before the Trojan War and to have made prophecies about it, called Herophile (a name which seems to have been borne by several of the Sibyls, meaning the friend or lover of a hero, or heroes; an interesting name considering that Nymphs are frequently to be found in relation to oracular heroes such as Amphiaraus and Trophonius [10.3.2]). On Delos, apparently, was preserved a *Hymn to Apollo* written by her, in which she called herself not only Herophile but Artemis as well, the wedded wife of Apollo or, again, either his sister or his daughter. Given the strongly Apolline traditions associated with Delos, it's perhaps not surprising that here the Sibyl is tied in with the Apolline prophetic tradition; however, if Pausanias was using a source of the Hellenistic period, by that date Artemis would also have lunar connections.

However, Pausanias then goes on to say that 'elsewhere in the oracles' Herophile (this time the Sibyl of Marpessos in the Troad) said that her mother was a Nymph of Mount Ida, while her father was a man; this Herophile was said to have interpreted a dream of Hecuba, wife of the Trojan king Priam, and prophesied her fate from this. Her memorial, in the temple of Apollo Smintheus at Alexandria-in-the-Troad, bore an epitaph referring to her as Apollo's wise woman, but also associating her with the Nymphs, who also had statues nearby, as well as a spring of water.

Not far from Marpessos, the town of Erythrae also claimed Herophile, with considerable competition between the two places for the title of her true birthplace. Pausanias tells us that the Erythraeans 'adduce as evidence a mountain called Mount

---

13 Pausanias 1971:Vol. 2, p.435.

Corycus with a cave in it, saying that Herophile was born in it, and that she was a daughter of Theodorus, a shepherd of the district, and of a nymph.' He also tells us that the Erythraeans claimed that the only reason the Nymph was referred to as Idaean (*i.e.*, from another Mount Ida, nearer Marpessos) rather than Korykonian, was because places that were 'thickly wooded' were called *idai*. This final piece of forced etymology shouldn't distract from the interest of a familiar conjunction, of mountains, caves, shepherds, Goddesses or Nymphs, and oracles or prophecy. We may also mention another observation of Bremmer's here: that the Sibyls are mostly situated in places, such as Erythrae, Marpessos and Italian Cumae, that are on the edge of the Greek world, and the importance of such liminal areas has been discussed above, at 6.3; and also that female seers were often believed to be in a sexual relationship with the deities that provided their oracles.[14]

Another aspect of the Sibyl that ties in with the material under discussion here is her extreme longevity, usually given as a thousand years, or ten full lifetimes. Ovid, in his *Metamorphoses*, gives a speech to the Cumaean Sibyl, when she's visited by Aeneas, which explains this longevity. In her youth, she tells him, she was wooed by Apollo (who, for Ovid, is presumably the source of her prophetic talent). Again, we notice the sexual element in the relationship. Apollo told her to choose what she wished, and he would grant it; she pointed at a heap of sand and asked for as many years of life as there were grains of sand in the heap, which was, in effect, a thousand ... but she forgot to ask for eternal youth. Apollo offered this as well if she would submit to his desires, but she rejected him. At the time of her meeting with Aeneas, she claimed to be seven lifetimes old, and with another 300 years to live. And, she told him, before the end of her life she expected to become a tiny, feather-light creature with shrunken limbs, although her voice would still remain.[15]

---

14 Bremmer 1993 [2]: p.152.
15 Ovid: *Metamorphoses* 14.130-153 (1916: Vol. 2, pp.309-311).

That Ovid's treatment of this story has parallels with that of Tithonus is quite obvious, and we have seen some interesting comparisons between the stories of Tithonus and of Endymion, in terms of 'half-given immortality'. It would be tempting to draw conclusions from this that place the Sibyl, Tithonus and Endymion in a group combining semi-immortality with the oracular function. But it has to be said that there is a problem with Ovid's story, in that it is extremely ill-constructed: why does Apollo offer her the gift of longevity without exacting any promise of submission, and then only ask for such a promise in return for the corresponding gift of eternal youth? One is tempted to think that Ovid, faced with a pre-existing tradition of a long-lived but hag-like Sibyl, constructed an explanation for this from a knowledge of the Tithonus story and a certain poetic license, while not making a very good job of it. Again, one cannot be certain, but the story's defects should perhaps caution us against giving it too much weight.

Nonetheless, Ovid is not the sole source for this notion of the Sibyl's extreme longevity. Phlegon of Tralles preserves the text of an oracle apparently spoken by the Erythraean Sibyl, in which she claims to have lived almost a thousand years (ten lifetimes) and now to be grievously old-aged, and talks of her expectation that soon Apollo, jealous of her divinatory skills, will dispatch her with an arrow. Thereafter, her voice will remain in the wind, while she expects her blood to soak into the ground and feed the grass that is eaten by the sheep, which in turn, are sacrificed so that omens can be taken from their livers (haruspicy), while her flesh will feed the birds from whose flight omens will be drawn (augury).[16] There is no mention here of *how* the Sibyl obtained her longevity, and one might infer, from Apollo's resentment of her prophetic talent, that perhaps it does not originate from him either. Such an interpretation can only be speculative, however.

---

16 Phlegon of Tralles, *Long-Lived Persons* 5.2.99 (1996: p.55).

*Selene*

However, what is obviously the same story was also known to Plutarch, who uses it in his philosophical dialogue, *The Oracles at Delphi No Longer Given in Verse*, and extends it to something rather more interesting. When the participants in the dialogue have arrived at the rock at Delphi where the 'first Sibyl' was said to have sat after arriving from Mount Helicon, where she had been raised by the Muses, one of their number, Sarapion: 'recalled the verses in which she sang of herself: that even after death she shall not cease from prophesying, but that she shall go round and round in the Moon, becoming what is called the face that appears in the Moon; while her spirit, mingled with the air, shall be for ever borne onward in voices of presage and portent; and since from her body, transformed within the earth, grass and herbage shall spring, on this shall pasture the creatures reared for the holy sacrifice, and they shall acquire all manners of colours and forms and qualities upon their inward parts, from which shall come for men prognostications of the future.'[17] The birds have dropped out here, but the phraseology is so similar that we are obviously dealing with variants of the same original story, with the very interesting addition that after her death the Sibyl becomes identified with the Moon herself, and does not cease to prophesy.

Plutarch returns to the subject in another dialogue, *On the Delays in Divine Vengeance*, where, in a mythologising passage, he describes the journey of one Thespesius into the world after death (mentioned above at 11.3). Thespesius has a Guide, who tells him: '... Night has partnership in nothing with Apollo. "This is instead," he pursued, "an oracle shared with Night and the Moon; it has no outlet anywhere on earth nor in any single seat, but roves everywhere throughout mankind in dreams and visions; for this is the source from which dreams derive and disseminate the unadorned and true, commingled, as you see, with the colourful and deceptive."

---

[17] Plutarch, *The Oracles at Delphi No Longer Given in Verse* 9 (398C-D) (1936: Vol. 5, p.281).

'But he [Thespesius] did hear, as he passed by, a woman's high voice foretelling in verse among other things the time (it appears) of his own death. The voice was the Sibyl's, the daemon said, who sang of the future as she was carried about on the face of the moon. He accordingly desired to hear more, but was thrust back, as in an eddy, by the onrush of the Moon, and caught but little.'[18]

Here we have, succinctly, a discussion of the entire 'nocturnal lunar oracular tradition', of dreams, visions and prophecies, in which we are interested, distinctly stated to be non-Apolline, and also to be tied in with the Sibyl.

There is obviously a contradiction running through all this discussion (too briefly given here, admittedly) of the Sibylline tradition: on the one hand, we hear that the Sibyl's inspiration comes from Apollo; on the other hand, that she has nothing to do with Apollo, and is rather more in the Lunar/Nymph/Muse tradition. This contradiction perhaps arises from her overlapping position: she was *both* said to be an ecstatic prophetess, and to have produced non-question-specific books of oracles. As an ecstatic seeress she was, of course, in the same tradition as the Pythia, Apollo's priestess at Delphi, and thus an 'explanation' of her inspiration as deriving from Apollo is hardly surprising. Being responsible for written oracle-books, however, places her in the same tradition as Orpheus, Musaeus and Epimenides who, the remainder of this chapter will argue, were in the Lunar/Nymph/Muse tradition. Given the widespread and multiplicitous traditions about the various Sibyls, such an overlap may not be seen as surprising.

13.3.3 Epimenides. Epimenides has, of course, been discussed at some length above (7 *passim*), particularly as a cave-sleeper, in relation to the story of Endymion. Although we'll find the cave-

---

18 Plutarch, *De sera numinis vindicta* 28-29 (548A-568A) (1959: Vol. 7, pp.181-299).

sleeping theme continues to be important in the discussion to follow, this aspect of Epimenides' story has already been dealt with in detail (7.3) and here it will be sufficient to remind ourselves of a number of other aspects of the story.

First, we may mention Epimenides' extreme longevity, a trait he shares in particular with the Sibyl. Like her, also, we've seen that Epimenides is quite strongly connected with Nymphs, a trait he shares both with the heroes presiding over dream oracles and the other chresmologues discussed here. Plutarch makes him the son of a Nymph (7.2), while Diogenes Laertius tells us that he received special food from the Nymphs, and was building a temple to the Nymphs when a supernatural voice told him to dedicate it to Zeus instead. All this at least suggests that Epimenides might be considered a nympholept in the same way as Bacis obviously was, and both were credited with the production of oracle texts; as Parke argues, there is some evidence that as well as being inspired by the Nymphs, he was also hostile to Apollo, one quotation from his writings contesting the Delphian claim to possess the *omphalos* or navel of the world.[19] Huxley also mentions this, while adding an interesting remark about the so-called 'Epimenides paradox'.[20] This, preserved by St. Paul in his Epistle to Titus (1.12), says that 'the Cretans are always liars,' a saying usually attributed to Epimenides (though Paul says no more than that the saying comes from a Cretan prophet). As Epimenides was, of course, Cretan, he'd therefore be lying about his countrymen being liars. However, Huxley points out that the Greek text of this is actually a fragment of hexameter verse, the form in which Delphic pronouncements were made. He goes on to speculate that Paul has misattributed the quote, and that it is actually part of a Delphic riposte to Epimenides. This would explain the paradox, in that it's no longer Epimenides who's calling the Cretans liars. It may also suggest

---

19 Parke 1988: p.177.
20 Huxley 1969: p.81-82.

that Epimenides was a proponent of a non-Apollonian tradition of seership.

We've also seen, though (1.3.6-7), that in one of the verses attributed to Epimenides, he claimed to be a son of Selene, although whether that claim is to be taken literally or figuratively (perhaps in terms of being an adherent of Selene rather than an actual son) is hard to determine. Parke (perhaps influenced by his apparent belief that Epimenides was a historical figure) conjectures that Aelian, in quoting this 'son of Selene' verse has mistakenly attributed the quotation to Epimenides when it should have been attributed to Musaeus, elsewhere said to be the son of Selene.[21] This is always possible, but the conjecture seems unnecessary; it would appear just as likely that *both* Epimenides and Musaeus should claim to be 'sons of Selene' as that one should be mistaken for the other. Indeed, if 'son of Selene' is simply a coded way of saying 'purveyor of oracles in the "lunar" tradition' it would be perfectly appropriate for both to claim the same. Furthermore, as M.L. West points out, the quote from Aelian actually begins 'For I *too* am...' thus meaning that Epimenides is claiming to be a son of Selene in the same way that someone else has claimed to be; West speculates that this other person is Musaeus, and that what links them is oracles.[22] It might also be suggested, though very hesitantly, that the claim to lunar descent might derive from a pun: if the second epsilon of Epimenides' name was replaced with an eta, this could be read as meaning that he was 'descended (offspring, rather than fallen) from the Moon (*Mene*)'. The tentativeness of this suggestion cannot be overemphasised, however.

As we've seen (7.2), Diogenes Laertius lists a number of works attributed to Epimenides: an *Argonautika*, a *Theogony* and three works on matters of Cretan rites and religion: *On the Birth of the Curetes and Corybantes, On Sacrifices and the Cretan Constitution*

---

21 Parke 1988: p.187.
22 West 1983: pp.47-48.

and *On Minos and Rhadamanthus*. Although Diogenes mentions, and gives a couple of examples of, Epimenides' 'superhuman foresight' he makes no mention of actual oracle-texts. However, it appears that the *Oracles* of Epimenides was actually a theogony presented as an oracular revelation, and so probably corresponds with the *Theogony* mentioned by Diogenes Laertius. Aristotle, too, tells us that Epimenides 'used to divine, not the future, but only things that were past but obscure'.[23] This could be taken two ways. Firstly, it might imply that Epimenides divined about the *causes* of problems, and then would have prescribed rituals appropriate to them (such as in his purification of Athens); if such was the case, his *Oracles* could have been similar to the Roman *Sibylline Books*. However, the quotation from Aristotle could equally apply to the *Theogony*, which would reveal how 'obscure' past events occurred, and how things came to be. From the few surviving fragments we have of the *Oracles*, the latter interpretation would seem to be the most likely. Those fragments suggest a theogony very similar to, or 'in the same school' as, those of Orpheus and Musaeus, with an origin of the world from Aer and Night, a Cosmic Egg, and so forth.[24] We'll return to these teachings, then, in the next section.

13.3.4 Orpheus and Musaeus. As Musaeus is often said to be the son or disciple of Orpheus, it's convenient to take the two together here, though we will, of course, begin with Orpheus himself. It hardly needs to be said, though, that Orpheus and the Orphic tradition are very large subjects, and ones about which academic opinion seems to be constantly mutable;[25] we'll therefore only have the room to concentrate on a few aspects here which seem most relevant to our subject matter. The first of these is found in the mythic story of Orpheus himself.

---

23 Parke 1988, p.175. Aristotle: *Rhetoric* 3.17.10 (1418a21) (1926: p.455-457).
24 West 1983: p.48.
25 The main academic works consulted here have been: Guthrie 1935; West 1983; Graf 1987: pp.80-106, and Graf's entries in Hornblower & Spawforth 1999: *s.v.* 'Orpheus', 'Orphic Literature' and 'Orphism'.

The fullest treatments we have of the story are comparatively late, and in Latin, being by Ovid and Virgil.[26] Orpheus is always said to be a Thracian, and usually the son of Oeagrus and the Muse Calliope; in one source, Oeagrus is in turn said to be the son of the Nymph Methone.[27] For a singer (*i.e.*, both poet and musician) of such magical abilities as Orpheus, it's natural that his mother should be a Muse, and Calliope was herself the Muse of epic poetry. We've also seen, though, that Muses can be viewed as a specialised form of Nymph, and when we find that Orpheus' wife Eurydice was a Dryad Nymph, the connection with the Nymphs (grandmother, mother and wife) that we've seen elsewhere among our oracle-purveyors continues to be very strong in his case. Of additional interest here is a reference in the *Orphic Argonautica*, that Calliope conceived Orpheus with Oeagrus in a Thracian cave.[28]

Eurydice, of course, trod on and was bitten by a snake (on her wedding day, according to Ovid), and died; Orpheus thus descended into the underworld where, with his magical singing, he charmed Hades and Persephone into releasing her on condition that he didn't look at her before returning to the upper world. Although there are indications that in some variants Orpheus succeeded in bringing Eurydice back, the canonical version of the story is the well-known one where he looks back at the last minute, and his wife dies a second time and is then lost forever.

That Orpheus is said to be Thracian does not, necessarily, mean that the stories about him are anything else than Greek; it's quite possible that, once again, we're dealing with a powerfully magical figure whose place of origin is said to be in a liminal area, at the edge of the Greek world; and that, furthermore, in Graf's

---

26 Ovid, *Metamorphoses* 10.1ff; 11.1ff (1916: Vol. 2, pp.65-71,121-125). Virgil, *Georgics* 4.453-527 (1978: Vol. 1, pp.229-231). See also Apollodorus, 1.3.2 (1921: pp.17-19).
27 *Contest of Homer and Hesiod* 314 (in Hesiod 1914: p.571).
28 Guthrie 1935: p.27.

words, he was 'experienced as a stranger'[29] (similarly, Crete, where Epimenides originated, could be seen as on the fringe of the Greek world). Orpheus' trip to the underworld has also been seen as an example of Greek 'shamanism', a notion popular in the latter half of the 20th century, but more recently falling into disrepute; Graf gives the notion of a 'shamanic Orpheus' short shrift and finds the origin of his stories in masculine secret societies.[30] Be that as it may, what does seem obvious is that like the stories of so many of the figures discussed here, the tale of Orpheus and Eurydice once again takes us into that borderland area of the living and the dead, and the (some might say impossible) tensions between mortality and immortality.

Virgil tells us that, after the final loss of Eurydice, Orpheus spent seven months in a cave, though Ovid and others tell us that he spent three years wandering, charming the birds and beasts, and even the trees and rocks, with his singing; and also eschewing the company of women. He was ultimately torn apart by Thracian women (sometimes said to be Dionysiac Maenads) who were offended at the slight, and while some variants have him buried in Thrace, one major form of the story has his lyre and head, still singing, floating down the Hebrus river, then out to sea and eventually arriving, washed up on the shore, at Lesbos. Here the head continued to give oracles, in one version in a cave, until Apollo, deciding that it was usurping his prerogative, commanded it to stop. Guthrie reproduces illustrations from vase paintings and Etruscan mirrors where a young scribe (sometimes thought to be Musaeus) is writing down, on tablets, the oracles spoken by the severed head.[31] Graf, in his discussion of the same material, makes two interesting points: one is that there are passages in the (admittedly late) Greek Magical Papyri which instruct the

---

29 Graf 1987: n.22, p.100-101.

30 Graf 1987: n.22, *passim*.

31 Guthrie 1935: pp.35-39.

performer of the ritual to have a tablet at hand to take down what the God reveals during the ritual, or in the dream provoked by the ritual, and the resulting writing is known as a *pharmakon*, an oracle or a recipe (often medical). He also quotes a passage from Euripides' play, *Alcestis*, discussing the overwhelming power of 'Necessity', which says: 'Nor is there any remedy either in the Thracian inscriptions written down from the voice of Orpheus, or in all the salves and simples which Apollo gave to the priests of Asclepius to heal the many hurts of mankind.'[32] From there he goes on to make the obvious links: that Apollo is the God of healing as well as of oracles; that Asclepius heals through dream oracles, as does Amphiaraus.[33] Orpheus' dictated oracles would then seem to be very much in the same area; an area with which the reader should be feeling some considerable familiarity by now.

Before moving on to discuss the main body of Orphic writing, the theogonies, we should make brief mention of the other surviving literature attributed to 'Orpheus' or the Orphics. There is an Orphic version of the *Argonautika*, with the tale of Jason and the Argonauts here centring on Orpheus, who was one of the crew; there is also a *Lithica*, on the virtues of gemstones. More interesting are the works ascribed to him which have not survived: astrological works, including one known as the *Sphaera*, and poems on divination by birds, eggs, entrails, earthquakes and, most interestingly, dreams.[34]

Opinions have varied as to whether there was ever an 'Orphic religion' as such, with rites and a priesthood. The notion was popular earlier in the 20th century, but has faded even more than that of 'Greek shamanism'. What we do know for sure is that there were a number of poems attributed to 'Orpheus', or 'the Orphics',

---

32 Euripides, *Alcestis*, l. 966-971 (1974: p.73). I use the Penguin edition here, as the Loeb translation, being done into English verse is, unusually, much less satisfactory. See Euripides 1912:Vol. 4, p.489.

33 Graf 1987: n.22, p.94.

34 West 1983: p.33.

which survive in fragmentary form; and that there were a number of figures called *Orpheotelestai*, 'Orphic initiators' who purveyed rituals, prescriptions and oracles. Fortunately, it's precisely these two areas that interest us most here.

There were a number of poetic theogonies attributed to Orpheus, the most important being a collection of 24 poems known as the *Rhapsodic Theogony*, though we have testimony of, and fragments of, a number of variant versions.[35] Regrettably, nothing more than fragments have been preserved of any of these poems. They provide an alternative 'history of the universe' to the 'standard' one of Hesiod (discussed above at 1.2.1 and 3.2), where Ouranos and Ge (Sky and Earth) give birth to Kronos and the Titans, who are in turn overthrown by Zeus and the Olympians.

Condensing the theogonies together (though mainly following the Rhapsodic version) to give a very brief summary, the universe began with Chronos (Time), together with Ananke (Necessity). Chronos generated Aither (Ether) and a bottomless Chasm or Chaos, along with Nyx (Night). Chronos then made a shining egg from Aither and Chaos, in which developed Phanes, a hermaphroditic being with wings and multiple heads, and at his appearance the universe was filled with radiance. By self-fertilisation he gave birth to a number of Gods, and also mated with Night to give birth to Ouranos and Ge. Phanes also created the Sun and Moon (treated in one of the surviving fragments more as a world, rather more than a Goddess, which suggests a relatively late date for the poem as we have it[36]), places for Gods and men to live, and so forth, producing these from his seat in the cave of Night. Phanes was first king of the world, but abdicated in favour of Night, who passed the title on to her son Ouranos. Thereafter

---

35 Discussed at length by West 1983.

36 Orphic fragment 91 (Kern), preserved by Proclus and translated by Guthrie 1935: p.138: 'And he [Phanes] devised another world, immense, which the Immortals call Selene and the inhabitants of Earth Mene, a world which has many mountains, many cities, many mansions.'

the theogony mostly parallels that of Hesiod, though when Zeus is born, he was not hidden in a Cretan cave, but in the cave of Night, who had now become prophetic (we have seen above, 13.3.2, that according to Plutarch, Night shares her oracle with the Moon). She predicted that Zeus would become king of the Gods and instructed him in the methods by which he could do so, ultimately resulting in Zeus swallowing Phanes and all the universe he had created, then bringing it forth again so all the universe was created anew from Zeus. Night continued to advise Zeus, and to prophesy from her cave. Zeus, in the form of a snake, fathered Dionysus on Persephone (here said to have two faces, four eyes and horns), but the Titans tore apart the boy and ate him, except the heart. Zeus destroyed the Titans with thunderbolts and Dionysus was revived, from his heart (and then became the major deity in the 'Orphic pantheon'), but from the ashes of the Titans was born the race of men. Later (Neoplatonic) speculation had it that, as the ashes of the Titans contained some part of the body of Dionysus that they had eaten, so men contain an immortal spark; but it seems that the soul was immortal in Orphic thinking without this embellishment. For mankind in general, after death Hermes led the soul to the underworld, where the good had a more pleasant fate than the bad. After 300 years, souls are said to be reborn, though their ambition is to break this cycle, and Zeus has prescribed various purification ceremonies to assist in this.[37]

It would, undoubtedly, be unsafe to draw any firm conclusions from all this, when the Orphic literature we have is in such a fragmentary state. What we can note, though, is that, while *containing* much of the standard theogony and cosmogony of Hesiod and others, this is a 'description of the world' that very much adds a 'nocturnal' dimension. The universe originates in darkness, light only coming into being with Phanes, and the 'standard' theogony, commencing with Ouranos and Ge, only comes about from the

---

37 Summarised mainly from West 1983: pp.70-75.

mating of Phanes and Night. The Gods are much more strangely formed than the anthropomorphised deities of the Olympian pantheon, and there is much chthonic symbolism here, of snakes, and bottomless gulfs and cosmic eggs. The process seems to be largely guided by Nyx/Night, prophesying from her cave and consulted even by Zeus. And finally, there is much emphasis on the underworld and the afterlife, and reincarnation, which is perhaps not surprising, given the mythic tale of Orpheus as one who crosses and recrosses that borderline between life and death. We also know, from archaeological discoveries of inscribed gold tablets found with burials in Italy, Crete and elsewhere, that Orphic teachings offered advice on how to behave in the underworld; to avoid drinking from the fountain of Lethe (forgetfulness) in favour of the fountain of Mnemosyne (memory), and how to ensure a happy future state.[38]

What few fragments we possess of the *Theogony/Oracles* of Epimenides, and writings attributed to Musaeus, are quite obviously in the same tradition. Epimenides is credited with saying that all things came from Aer (here implying mist and darkness, rather than the 'air' we think of at present) and Night, who produced Tartarus, from which two Titans were produced, and who mated to give birth to the cosmic egg; Musaeus apparently said things originated with Tartarus and Night.[39] Obviously the correspondences are not precise in their terminology, but they show distinctly similar thinking.

This mention of Musaeus brings us to the *Orpheotelestai*, or 'Orphic initiators', mentioned above. Once again, we are in fairly murky water here, and it may be wrong to think of anything so specific as 'ordained Orphic priests'. Instead, the *Orpheotelestai* seem to have been part of a larger class of itinerant freelance religious specialists, who purveyed purifications, rituals, oracles,

---

38 West 1983: pp.23ff. Guthrie 1935: pp.171ff (with translations).
39 Kirk & Raven 1957: pp.21, 44.

magic spells, and so forth, who ranged from the authentically religious to the outright charlatan; some of these wanderers were Orphic, some not. Some of the Orphics used the written texts and oracles attributed to Orpheus and Musaeus, and some didn't; but similarly, some of the wanderers who made no claim to be Orphic used the oracles of Orpheus and Musaeus as well. In this case, there are two questions we need to concentrate on here. Firstly, who is the Musaeus whose name was important to these wanderers? And secondly, what was the content of the oracle-texts attributed to him and Orpheus?

As West aptly remarks, Musaeus is classed as a mythical person, in that there seems to be no basis for his historical existence, but equally there are no myths or stories about him either.[40] His life is effectively blank and even his name is obviously artificial, meaning 'Belonging to the Muse'. He is said to be one of the oldest poets (only Orpheus being older), and in this role is said to have written about the Gods, so once again we probably have to deal with a theogony.

However, his first appearance on the historical stage is as a poet of oracles, known to Athenian chresmologues in the 6th century BCE. His oracles were said to have been collected together by a chresmologue called Onomacritus (himself a seer of whom, as Aristotle tells us, it was said that he 'first arose as an able lawgiver, and that he was trained in Crete, being a Locrian and travelling there to practise the art of soothsaying'[41]), who was duly banished from Athens when he was caught interpolating one of his own prophecies among them. The oracles of Musaeus (like those of Bacis) continued to circulate throughout the Persian and Peloponnesian Wars, and (also like those of Bacis) seem to have dealt, to a certain extent, with political events; they were

---

40 This and the following material is summarised largely from West 1983: pp.39-44.

41 Aristotle, *Politics* 2.9.5 (1274a26) (1932: p.167).

## Selene

still available to Pausanias in the 2nd century CE. We also hear of cures attributed to Musaeus, poems about medicinal plants, and an astrological *Sphaera*.

In the 5th century BCE, Musaeus was attached to the Eleusinian Mysteries, and was said to be the father (by a wife called Deiope) of Eumolpus, the eponymous ancestor of the Eleusinian priestly clan of the Eumolpidae (thus West,[42] and the references gathered there; however, we've seen above at 1.3.7 that Philochorus makes Musaeus the *son* of Eumolpus, by Selene). As such, he became the author, or co-author with Eumolpus, of the theological and eschatological poetry the Eumolpidae sang (Orpheus was later joined to the mysteries as well; perhaps not surprising in that both Orphism and the mysteries offered personal salvation in the afterlife). Among these works, the fragments we possess of the *Eumolpia* suggest that it was a theogony, and that it seems to have combined elements of both the Orphic and standard theogonies, with particular emphasis on material relevant to Eleusis.

Material about the relationship between Orpheus and Musaeus (as usual) survives in fragmentary and variant form. That there was thought to be a close relationship between them is obvious from the fact that the introductory prayer that precedes the collection of *Orphic Hymns* (probably compiled in the early centuries CE) is addressed from 'Orpheus to Musaeus', though we have no indication here as to what the relationship was thought to be (son or disciple).[43] The *Suda* (10th century CE) provides us with an Attic genealogy for Musaeus, which makes him the son of Kerkyon and his wife 'Helene' (which looks rather like a euhemeristic fudge for 'Selene'), and makes him a student of Orpheus.[44] Diodorus Siculus states that Musaeus

---

42 West 1983: p.41.

43 *Orphic Hymns* 1977: p.3.

44 *Suda s.v.* Mousaios.

is the son of Orpheus.⁴⁵ The Christian Clement of Alexandria quotes an Orphic fragment that begins, presumably in the voice of Orpheus: 'My words shall reach the pure; put bars to ears all ye profane together. But hear thou, Child of the Moon [*i.e.*, Mene], Musaeus, words of truth ...'⁴⁶ Athenaeus quotes from a poem of the Alexandrine period by Hermesianax of Colophon, the *Leontion*, which catalogues a series of love affairs. Here we have a narrative of Orpheus' journey to the underworld in search of his dead wife (here called Agriope), and in this version he successfully restores her to life. Immediately after this, we read: 'Nor did the son of Mene, Musaeus, master of the Graces, cause Antiope to go without her meed of honour. And she, beside Eleusis's strand, expounded to the initiates the loud, sacred voice of mystic oracles, as she duly escorted the priest through the Rarian plain to honour Demeter. And she is known even in Hades.'⁴⁷ Unsurprisingly, this is rather confusing. The Antiope best known to us is a figure of Theban myth, the mother by Zeus of Amphion and Zethus. Amphion was another famous poet and lyrist, who was said to be able to make stones move with his playing; it would thus obviously be fitting to bring Amphion and Antiope into the same lineage as Orpheus. However, the rest of the quotation makes it obvious that this is an Attic story, referring to Musaeus' connection with the Eleusinian Mysteries. Perhaps Antiope is here being confused with Deiope, on whom Musaeus is said to have fathered Eumolpus. We can only speculate on such matters; here the points to note are that Musaeus is said to be the son of Mene/Selene, and that Antiope, whatever the precise nature of her relationship with Musaeus, expounded 'mystic oracles'.

---

45 Diodorus Siculus, 4.25.1 (1935: Vol. 2, p.425).

46 Orphic fragment 5 (Abel), in Clement of Alexandria, *The Exhortation to the Greeks* 7.63p (1919: p.167).

47 Athenaeus, *Deipnosophistae*, 13.597 [13.71] (1937: Vol. 6, p.219). For a more modern translation, see Lightfoot 2009, p.165.

## Selene

We thus have stories where Musaeus is, on the one hand, the son of Orpheus, and on the other the son of Selene, although we have no explicit tale that says he is the son of Orpheus *and* Selene. If Orpheus is Musaeus' father, it seems unlikely that Eurydice would be his mother, as she appears to have died on her wedding day; unless we had to deal with a story of her successful return to the upper world, where Musaeus is conceived after that event; no such story survives. One is tempted, then, to infer a variant telling of an amour between Orpheus and Selene, particularly if to be 'loved by', or to be 'the son of' Selene is symbolic of an oracular function. Such a reading would certainly be fitting in the context of the material discussed here; but it has to be emphasised that this is an inference, and that the hard evidence that would clinch the matter is, unfortunately, lacking.

Parke is of the opinion that 'Musaeus son of Selene' is the oldest version of the story, and that this was dropped when Attic genealogies were produced to bring him into line with Eleusinian tradition. However, he adds another element of confusion by quoting a papyrus containing a fragment of Philodamus, 'with a quotation of Musaeus, stating that he was the son of Pandia, daughter of Zeus and Semele'.[48] We've already seen that the confusion of Semele and Selene was (and remains) commonplace, and as we know from the *Homeric Hymn to Selene*, Pandia was the daughter of Zeus and Selene (1.3.1, 3.3.1); Musaeus here becomes the grandson of Selene, but the lunar connection is still quite apparent.

One of our main sources for material about the *Orpheotelestai* is Plato, who seems to have rather mixed feelings about them. In the *Protagoras*, he tells us that 'sophistry is an ancient art', often presented in disguise, sometimes as poetry, sometimes as 'mystic rites and soothsayings, as did Orpheus, Musaeus and

---

48 Parke 1988: pp.180, 188.

their sects'.[49] It's true that Plato may here be referring more to the *writings* of Orpheus and Musaeus, but this fairly benevolent attitude contrasts with that shown in the *Republic*. In a discussion of the fate of the just and unjust in the afterlife, we hear that: 'And Musaeus and his son [presumably Eumolpus] have a more excellent song than these of the blessings that the gods bestow on the righteous. For they conduct them to the house of Hades in their tale and arrange a symposium of saints, where, reclined on couches and crowned with wreathes, they entertain the time henceforth with wine, as if the fairest meed of virtue were an everlasting drunk.' Considering the exceptionally important part that Dionysus plays in Orphic teaching, this is perhaps a rather slanted and unjust portrayal, though it once again points out the emphasis on the afterlife in the teachings of Orpheus and Musaeus. Then, continuing the discussion of the just and unjust, a little later we find that: 'Begging priests and soothsayers go to rich men's doors and make them believe that they by means of sacrifices and incantations have accumulated a treasure of power that can expiate and cure with pleasurable festivals any misdeed of a man or his ancestors, and that if a man wishes to harm an enemy, at slight cost he will be able to injure just and unjust alike, since they are masters of spells and enchantments that constrain the gods to serve their end. [...] And they produce a bushel [literally: a 'noise, hubbub, babel'] of books of Musaeus and Orpheus, the offspring of the Moon [Selene] and of the Muses, as they affirm, and these books they use in their ritual, and make not only ordinary men but states believe that there really are remissions of sins and purifications for deeds of injustice, by means of sacrifice and pleasant sport for the living, and that there are also special rites for the defunct, which they call functions, that deliver us from evils in that other world, where terrible

---

49 Plato, *Protagoras*, 316d (1937: Vol. 4, p.117).

things await those who have neglected to sacrifice.'⁵⁰ These are obviously the oracle-mongers, purifiers and 'magical technicians' among whom the *Orpheotelestai* were numbered and, whether we agree or not with Plato's stance about their ethics, this is probably our fullest description of their activities. Our interest here, of course, lies in the fact they dealt in oracles and prophecies, and were obviously trading under the aegis of the Moon; that they dealt also with the otherworld and with magic only adds to the picture already built up.

The geographer Strabo seems, however, to have attributed similar behaviour to Orpheus himself, telling us: 'At the base of Olympus is a city Dium. And it has a village near by, Pimpleia. Here lived Orpheus, the Ciconian, it is said – a wizard who at first collected money from his music, together with his soothsaying and his celebration of the orgies connected with mystic initiatory rites, but soon afterwards thought himself worthy of still greater things and procured for himself a throng of followers and power. Some, of course, received him willingly, but others, since they suspected a plot and violence, combined against him and killed him.'⁵¹ This is a rather rationalising account of the legendary Orpheus, but elsewhere Strabo discusses prophets and the honour they were held in, both alive and dead, singling out the seer Tiresias, who was necromantically consulted after his death by Odysseus in Book Ten of the *Odyssey*. He continues: 'Such, also, were Amphiaraus, Trophonius, Orpheus, Musaeus and the god among the Getae, who in ancient times was Zalmoxis, a Pythagorean.'⁵² This quotation, of course, puts Orpheus and Musaeus in some very interesting company, and once again emphasises the links between the Orphic and Pythagorean traditions.

---

50 Plato, *Republic* 2.6 (363C-D), 2.7 (364B-C), 2.7 (364-E-365A) (1930: Vol.1, pp.129, 133, 135).

51 Strabo. 7. fr.18 (C330) Strabo, Geography 8.6.12 (C373) (1917-1932: Vol. 3, p.339).

52 Strabo: 16.2.39 (1917-1932: Vol. 7., p.289).

## 13.4 Summary

As is so often the case, the evidence discussed above is fragmentary and inconclusive, though it is suggestive. What we have here is a collection of 'oracle' literature circulating throughout the Graeco-Roman world, attributed to various famous seers. This literature is very varied in content. It contains (apparently) predictive prophecies about events in the real world; ritual prescriptions for dealing with prodigies and unforeseen events; works on various forms of divination; spells and incantations; alternative cosmologies and theogonies; and speculations and ritual instructions about the afterlife. All this material is very much 'non-official'. It falls outside the Olympian religion and the Apolline oracle tradition, was looked down on by philosophers and, at least as far as magic was concerned, was often prohibited by law. Divorced from the Apolline tradition, it can also be seen as a 'nocturnal' and Lunar, as opposed to a Solar, collection of material.

Much of this material, particularly the parts of it that we would understand more specifically as oracles and prophecies, was believed to be the product of divine inspiration, and this inspiration is frequently mentioned in the same context as such outright dream-oracles as those of Asclepius, Amphiaraus, and Trophonius. There appears, then, to be a continuity between these 'nocturnal' oracle traditions, whether they refer to answers to specific questions given in dreams, or to oracle-texts produced from the same inspired source.

We also find a similar continuity when we look at the 'life-stories' of the various seers concerned: there is much reference to time spent in caves on mountains, much association with Nymphs, extreme longevity that tests the boundaries between life and death, and outright crossings-over of those boundaries that validate a set of teachings about the nature of the otherworld. And over all of this is Selene, either as source of oracular inspiration, or as 'mother' (literally or figuratively) of seers and poets. In effect, then, we see the same pattern reflected here as has been explored in previous chapters, showing a continuity between the myth of Selene and Endymion, dream-oracles, oracular writings and 'non-official' religious practice. That same pattern will re-appear, with startling clarity, in the final section of this chapter.

## 13.5 Appendix: Alexander Of Abonoteichus And The 'Mysteries Of Selene'

13.5.1 Introduction. The $2^{nd}$ century CE saw the rise of a fascinating oracular cult in the town of Abonoteichus in Paphlagonia (now northern Turkey, on the shore of the Black Sea). There is a small amount of independent testimony for its existence, in terms of inscriptions, coins and statues of the cult's chief God, Glycon (meaning 'Sweetie'), a human-headed snake. For details of the history and practices of the cult, however, we are almost entirely reliant on a lengthy, contemporary essay by Lucian of Samosata (c.120-190 CE) called *Alexander the False Prophet*,[53] which is something of a mixed blessing. On the one hand, Lucian gives us a detailed and circumstantial account of the cult, apparently from first-hand experience, and one may well believe that Lucian met Alexander and carried out a personal investigation (whether Alexander actually tried to have Lucian murdered is another matter, of course); on the other, Lucian is an utterly hostile witness, a rationalist to whom all religion is error and, being a satirist, not in any way constrained to tell the truth. It thus becomes extremely difficult to answer even simple questions such as whether Alexander was the sincere founder of a religious cult or the charlatan portrayed by Lucian. In recent centuries it doubtless seemed that Alexander, being the prophet of a non-Christian God, was inherently 'false'; while modern, rational minds have generally

---

53 Lucian: *Alexander the False Prophet*. (1925: Vol. 4, pp.175-253). See also, for a much more even-handed treatment, Jones 1986: pp.133-148, and for a re-evaluation of Lucian's account, suggesting that it may be highly prejudiced, and that Alexander may not have been so 'false' a prophet after all, Moore 2011.

accepted Lucian's work of exposure on the basis that *any* religious phenomenon is inherently 'false' (and it has to be admitted that, *as presented by Lucian*, there are aspects of the cult which seem more than a little dubious). Once again, though, we are in the fortunate position of not having to judge such matters, for we are more interested in the content of the stories told, rather than their truth or otherwise. The point here is simply that Lucian is an unreliable witness, and if it's inadvisable to take him entirely at face value in matters of fact, it's even more inadvisable to accept his judgements and opinions. In all that follows, then, this proviso should be born in mind, including the presence of Selene in the rites of the cult.

13.5.2 Alexander and his Cult. Lucian provides us with a considerable amount of circumstantial and highly defamatory detail about the early life and career of Alexander which, as he was unlikely to learn it from any official source is probably, at best, based on scandal or, at worst, outright invention. It seems better, therefore, to summarise the essential features of his cult. Lucian tells us that Alexander began his career as an acolyte of a (nameless) follower of the 1$^{st}$ century CE Neo-Pythagorean wonder-worker and holy man, Apollonius of Tyana. Alexander's master, described by Lucian as a 'quack', sounds very much like the wandering religious specialists described above (13.3.4) who included the *Orpheotelestai*. Lucian describes him as specialising in 'enchantments, miraculous incantations, charms for your love affairs, "sendings" for your enemies, and successions to estates'; however, he's also said to have been a physician. This teacher died, though, just as Alexander was reaching manhood. Lucian tells us that he thereafter tied up with a Byzantine writer of choral songs called Cocconas and, after a visit to Macedon where they acquired a large tame snake, Cocconas began writing oracles, but died soon after. Alexander then returned to his home town of Abonoteichus and began to set up his cult, with its own temple. This we know, from coins, took place in the reign of Antoninus Pius (138-161 CE).

*Selene*

This cult combined many of the features we've come across before, specialising in oracles and healing. Alexander claimed to be a son of the oracular Podaleirius, the son of Asclepius, and his Snake-God Glycon was obviously cognate with the sacred snakes of the Healer-God, or even the snake-form of Asclepius himself; indeed, he claimed that Glycon was, in fact, the 'new Asclepius'. What was different about Glycon was that he had a human (or at least humanoid) head, and flowing locks of hair. Here we have some independent confirmation of Lucian's description, as some statues, coins and gems have survived which portray Glycon.

Lucian is rather like a modern sceptical investigator, who knows a way in which some effect *could* be achieved, and so roundly declares that that *is* how it's achieved. So he tells us that Glycon is that same Macedonian snake mentioned above (for which we only have his word), which was so tame and sleepy that it allowed Alexander to fit a human-shaped head made of linen over its own, after which, coiling the snake around his body, he displayed his God to the gullible Paphlagonians in a shadowy room. The gullibility of the locals appears to be a commonplace in such stories; we have seen Herodotus say much the same of the Thracians when discussing Zalmoxis (8.3) and it is, perhaps, to be taken with a pinch of salt. Next he tells us that Alexander announced he would give oracles (none too cheaply) and answer specific questions written on scrolls; these would be presented to him, sealed, and he would then withdraw into the sanctuary to consult the God (apparently to an underground chamber or *adyton*),[54] returning the scrolls with the seals unbroken, and with an appropriate answer. Lucian then gives us a lengthy explanation of the tricks used to open and read scrolls while leaving the seals intact. All this may be precisely what happened, or then again it may not; we only have Lucian's word. Alexander also prescribed medical treatment, including selling a patent medical ointment, claimed to find thieves, buried treasure,

---

54 Jones 1986: p.139.

and so on. Lucian, entirely for the purposes of ridicule, preserves some of Alexander's oracles, most of which were in hexameter verse, in common with other such pronouncements; unlike those of Orpheus and Musaeus, there is nothing theogonic among the oracles Lucian preserves, but this may just be an accident of choice or invention.

Alexander then began to give audible oracles 'through the mouth of Glycon' (called 'autophones'), and again, Lucian 'knows how it was done', proposing that Alexander manipulated Glycon's head like a glove puppet, while a speaking tube made of several cranes' windpipes led away in the shadows to a speaker in another room; simple ventriloquism sounds much more likely.

Despite Lucian's portrayal of Alexander as a sideshow huckster, the cult and oracle-shrine actually became extremely powerful and popular, with an immense revenue and a large staff to handle all the business involved; and its fame spread throughout the Roman empire (even being recognised by the emperor Marcus Aurelius, to whom Alexander offered oracular advice), largely due to the influence of one of its adherents, the aged P. Mummius Sisenna Rutilianus, consul in 146 CE, governor of Moesia around 150 and of the province of Asia between 161 and 163 (of whom more below). The cult appears to have survived Alexander's death sometime in the 170s, and inscriptions suggest it continued well into the 3rd, or perhaps the 4th centuries CE. If there was nothing more here than a con man with a glove puppet, this would be rather surprising.

There are other points, which may be mentioned briefly, which place Alexander and his oracle in the same context as other oracles discussed here. Alexander seems to have taught a Pythagorean doctrine of reincarnation, including producing oracular information on previous lives. Glycon, questioned directly, replied that he would stay and give oracles for 1,003 years, a similar span to that of the Sibyl. And, when the consultants of the shrine grew too numerous for autophone responses, Alexander took the scrolls away overnight to 'sleep on' (presumably in the same underground chamber as mentioned above), giving 'nocturnal responses' heard from Glycon in his dreams. This is not quite the incubation practised at the majority of other oracular shrines, such as those discussed in Chapter 8, in that it was Alexander who dreamed on the consultants' behalf, rather than the consultants themselves; but effectively it means that at least some form of dream-oracle was active at the shrine. It appears that a somewhat similar procedure may have been practiced at the dream-oracle of Amphilochus in Mallos;[55] and a similar procedure is suggested in Virgil's account of the dream-oracle of Faunus (12.3.2).

Alexander, although claiming that he would live for 150 years, died 'before reaching the age of 70', apparently from a poisoned and mortified leg. Whether the cult continued to be oracular after his death, or was simply devoted to worship of the God Glycon, is far from clear. As Jones remarks, we simply have no way of knowing whether Alexander was the deliberate charlatan portrayed by Lucian, or actually thought himself a prophet;[56] but we've now set the scene in which Selene will appear.

### 13.5.3 The Mysteries of Selene.

It's perhaps of some interest (though not anything that one would want to place too great an emphasis on) that Abonoteichus claimed to be founded by colonists from the city of Miletos, the nearest Greek city to Mount Latmos;[57] the tale of Selene and Endymion may thus, perhaps, have been more familiar to its inhabitants (including Alexander) than to those of other cities of the area. Be that as it may, Lucian has two tales to tell of Selene that are of considerable interest (with all the usual provisos about Lucian's reportage; and he does seem quite fond of the tale of Selene and Endymion, perhaps because by his day Selene was associated with the virgin Artemis/Diana, and thus the tale seemed more scandalous), and

---

55 Jones 1986: p.144.
56 Jones 1986: p.148.
57 Jones 1986: p.143.

both centre around the aged Rutilianus. Lucian is here worth quoting at length:

'When one time he [Rutilianus] enquired about getting married, Alexander said explicitly:

'"Take Alexander's daughter to wife, who was born of Selene."

'He had before given out a story to the effect that his daughter was by Selene; for Selene had fallen in love with him on seeing him asleep once upon a time – it is a habit of hers, you know, to adore handsome lads in their sleep! Without any hesitation that prince of sages Rutilianus sent for the girl at once, celebrated his nuptials as a sexagenarian bridegroom, and took her to wife, propitiating his mother-in-law, the Moon, with whole hecatombs and imagining that he himself had become one of the Celestials!'[58]

Obviously, Lucian's purpose in telling this story is to illustrate and condemn both Rutilianus' gullibility and the way that Alexander exploited his contacts; and the usual interpretation of the tale seems to be nothing more than this. However, we have noted above that 'marriage' to Selene, or another familial connection, such as 'son of Selene', is a commonplace feature in the stories of many seers, such as Epimenides, Orpheus and Musaeus. There should thus be nothing surprising in the fact that the prophet Alexander made a similar claim; it's certainly suitable to his role as seer, and Selene is certainly the appropriate deity with whom to claim the connection.

Nor might it have sounded as inherently unlikely to those of the 2nd century CE as it would to us today. C.P. Jones, discussing Lucian's apparently malicious claim that certain female admirers declared they had had children by Alexander, and that their husbands confirmed it, points out an inscription from Caesarea Troketta in Lydia. This recorded an oracle given by Apollo at Claros (a sanctuary with which Alexander cultivated good relations) and a statue of Apollo paid for by his priest, a Paphlagonian named

---

58 Lucian, *Alexander the False Prophet*, 35 (1925: Vol. 4, p.221).

Miletos son of Glycon; and as Jones points out, this conjunction of names and places suggest that the priest's father was thought to be the Snake-God himself.[59] Lucian, of course, regarding Glycon as a mere puppet, would fix the paternity on Alexander; which may well be the case; the point is, though, that to be the offspring of a deity (whatever that might mean, in precise terms, in the society of the time) was neither unheard of nor necessarily ludicrous, particularly for the priest of an oracular God. Besides, as Lane Fox points out[60], a frequently-asked question at oracles throughout the ancient world concerned the conception of children, and this could explain the inscription mentioning 'Miletus the son of Glycon.' Miletus' mother may have consulted the god about a fertility problem; if she then conceived, she perhaps attributed the paternity to Glycon. If such attributions were commonplace, this could explain Lucian's slanderous accusations of Alexander's extreme promiscuity and the placid acceptance of the offspring.

Alexander's other innovation was the three-day celebration of a mystery rite, similar to the Eleusinian Mysteries at Athens, which began with an 'expulsion' of any Christians or rationalist Epicureans, both of whom would be regarded as hostile and potentially disruptive to the proceedings. Lucian is once more our only source of information, so again he's worth quoting at length:

'He established a celebration of mysteries, with torch-light ceremonies and priestly offices, which was to be held annually, for three days in succession, in perpetuity. On the first day, as at Athens, there was a proclamation, worded as follows: "If any atheist or Christian or Epicurean has come to spy upon the rites, let him be off, and let those who believe in the god perform the mysteries, under the blessing of Heaven." Then, at the very outset, there was an "expulsion," in which he took the lead, saying: "Out

---

59 Jones 1986: p.143.
60 Lane Fox 1988: p.243.

with the Christians," and the whole multitude chanted in response, "Out with the Epicureans!" Then there was the child-bed of Leto, the birth of Apollo, his marriage to Coronis, and the birth of Asclepius. On the second day came the manifestation of Glycon, including the birth of the god. On the third day there was the union of Podaleirius and the mother of Alexander – it was called the Day of Torches, and torches were burned. In conclusion there was the amour of Selene and Alexander, and the birth of Rutilianus' wife. The torch-bearer and hierophant was our Endymion, Alexander. While he lay in full view, pretending to be asleep, there came down to him from the roof, as if from heaven, not Selene but Rutilia, a very pretty woman, married to one of the Emperor's stewards. She was genuinely in love with Alexander and he with her; and before the eyes of her worthless husband there were kisses and embraces in public. If the torches had not been numerous, perhaps the thing would have been carried even further. After a short time Alexander entered again, robed as a priest, amid profound silence, and said in a loud voice, over and over again, "Hail, Glycon," while, following in his train, a number of would-be Eumolpids and Ceryces [hereditary priesthoods in the Eleusinian Mysteries] from Paphlagonia, with brogans on their feet and breaths that reeked of garlic, shouted in response, "Hail, Alexander!" Often in the course of the torchlight ceremonies and the gambols of the mysteries his thigh was bared purposely and showed golden.'[61]

Before discussing the significance of this performance, we can clear up a couple of minor details. Firstly, it's probably not coincidence that the name 'Rutilia' should be similar to 'Rutilianus'; the steward's family may have been in a client-relationship with the aristocratic Rutilianus, and so would be likely to include a form of his family name in their own. And Alexander's golden thigh was obviously intended to remind the viewer of Pythagoras, who legend also said had a golden thigh. Given that Alexander's own

---

61 Lucian, *Alexander the False Prophet*, 38-40 (1925: Vol. 4, pp.225-227).

teaching included Pythagoreanism and reincarnation, this display presumably signified, if not that Alexander was a reincarnation of Pythagoras, at least that he shared the same essence and tradition.

So what are we to make of Alexander's mysteries? Obviously Lucian's description is rather slender: the rites he describes are hardly likely to have taken three whole days to perform and there's no discussion of any reasoning behind the performances, of accompanying teachings, or of the participation of the audience. If the rites were intended as an imitation of the mysteries of Eleusis, as Lucian claims and as is also suggested by the fact that both sets of mysteries lasted three days, we might expect them to share similar concerns. Although we know little of the precise nature of the Eleusinian Mysteries, their primary purpose (as with other mystery religions) appears to have been salvationary, and to have assured the participants a blessed existence in the afterlife. All we have with Alexander, however, is vague suggestions of Pythagorean reincarnation, and one suspects the record is almost certainly incomplete.

The performances that Lucian does mention, short of the conclusion, seem to be aimed at demonstrating and legitimating the history and lineage of Alexander and his God. So we have a lineage that refers to both oracles and healing traced back from Alexander through Podaleirius to his father Asclepius, to Apollo, with the birth of Glycon, the 'new Asclepius' included as well. All this is what we might expect.

There seems to have been very little discussion before now, though, of the presence of the Selene and Endymion story, and particularly it being the concluding tableau, which would seem to indicate that it was of considerable importance. This is hardly likely to have been a random choice of myth nor, given that the rites were intended to be celebrated in perpetuity, does it seem likely that it was merely intended to flatter Rutilianus on his marriage. Instead the primary purpose seems to have been to demonstrate and proclaim Alexander's connection with Selene; and this is performed through a re-enactment of the myth of Endymion and Selene.

Without the material already gathered so far, this performance would be difficult to interpret; in view of what we now know, however, Selene's presence here seems perfectly natural. At an oracular shrine with a sacred snake/snake-God, an underground chamber and dream-oracles, Alexander is proclaiming himself at one with Epimenides, Orpheus and Musaeus, by claiming the same Selenic connection, and thus legitimising his production of oracles, of teachings on reincarnation and the afterlife, of miracle-cures, and so forth. He proclaims himself worthy of, if not one of, the Gods themselves and, if only in a single symbolic case, by uniting his daughter, the offspring of the Goddess, with Rutilianus, he opens up a channel for others to interact with the deities through his good offices. In effect, he adds Selene to the Asclepiad lineage he has already claimed, and in doing so makes her just as much a Goddess of oracles as all his other deities, just as she's a Goddess of oracles to Epimenides, Musaeus and the like.

And if this is presented in terms of the story of Selene and Endymion, then one may well suspect that Selene was also thought to be taking the same role in that myth too: the Goddess of oracles visiting her sleeping lover. And that, in turn, may be seen as providing further confirmation for the interpretation of the Endymion story presented earlier.

Chapter Fourteen

# Mythical Afterlife: The Endymion Sarcophagi

## 14.1 Introduction

We've seen above that many variant versions have survived of the narratives referring to Selene, and particularly to her encounter with Endymion (1.5). In a similar way, there are variations in the way that the myth could be interpreted, and in the ways that it was put to symbolic use, even in the ancient world. Being both extremely well-known and fragmentarily brief, the story of Selene and Endymion was both resonant with meaning and easily adaptable, and during the Roman Empire it was used in an entirely new context. This was as decoration for the marble sarcophagi of the upper classes, where the story became redolent with funerary symbolism. Most popular in the 2$^{nd}$ and 3$^{rd}$ centuries CE, such sarcophagi, the main feature of which is the descent of Selene to the sleeping Endymion, have mainly been found in Italy, though examples also occur from various other parts of the empire. So far, no fewer than 110 of these 'Endymion sarcophagi' have been discovered, either complete or in fragmentary form. For the most part, the scene depicted contains a number of standard elements, though there are, of course, variants to be found.

## 14.2 The Endymion Sarcophagus In The Metropolitan Museum Of Art

Perhaps the most beautiful of these sarcophagi, and certainly one of the most complete, is to be found in New York's Metropolitan Museum of Art.[1] It dates from the early Severan dynasty (c.190-210 CE) and was discovered in 1825, in a funeral chamber at the Roman port of Ostia.[2] We'll take this elaborately carved version as our standard model in discussing the sarcophagi, while pointing out some of the major variants as we go along. Early examples of the sarcophagi tend to be fairly simple, while the later ones become more elaborately detailed. Although the story of Selene and Endymion is shown in its essentially Greek form, the work is Roman and relatively late, and this has some influence on the actual portrayal.

Such sarcophagi were obviously intended to be displayed in a funeral chamber or vault that would continue to be visited by the descendants of the deceased, rather than buried in the ground. As such, the main imagery is carved on the front side of the sarcophagus in high relief, although the Metropolitan casket is unusual in actually being carved on both sides, and both ends. The rear, with less relevance for public display, is only carved in low relief, and shows two herdsmen, one standing and the other reclining, with three horses, three cows, a sheep and a dog. Overall, this may simply represent a pastoral scene, corresponding to the similar setting for the encounter between Selene and Endymion on the front surface, which reflects the Carian, rather than the Elean version of the story. However, it's also been suggested that scenes such as this (and another appears on the front of the sarcophagus) may represent an image of the afterlife as a state of bucolic bliss.[3] Two Nymphs appear at the far right of this scene, on the rounded

---

1 Acquisition No. 47.100.4.
2 Koortbojian 1995: pp.63-84. Matz 1956-1957: *passim*. McCann 1978: pp.39-45.
3 Koortbojian 1995: p.80.

corner between rear and end, one pointing left to right, the other pouring water from a jug, and possibly representing a spring. We may note in passing, however, the prevalence of springs and Nymphs in relation to dream oracles, mentioned above (10.3.2-3).

Continuing in the same direction, we find that the main feature of this end of the sarcophagus (the left end when seen from the front), is a figure of Helios, also driving his four-horse chariot from left to right, and this would seem to give an indication of the direction in which the carved scene, which is now very much in high-relief, is intended to be 'read'. Such being the case, the pointing and pouring Nymphs would appear to be providing a link between the rear of the sarcophagus and the scenes on the end and front, and the poured water may represent more than merely a spring; the Nymph may in fact be 'pouring out' the imagery that follows.

Above Helios' chariot, a small, winged erote or cupid flies along, holding a torch pointed in an upward direction. This has been identified as the Morning Star (Venus), which in the sky is never far away from the rising Sun; however, this could also be thought of as the Evening Star (again, Venus), although, as we shall see shortly, both these identifications may be wrong. If we think of the sarcophagus having a reading order from left to right, the pastoral vista on the back may represent a day-time scene; Helios' chariot may then be reaching the end of its journey in the evening, while the front of the sarcophagus, with Selene and Endymion, is obviously set at night. At the far right end of the sarcophagus, Selene is shown once more, departing in her chariot at the end of the night. Beneath Helios' chariot horses a bearded figure reclines, representing the Ocean; if, as seems more likely, this represents the western ocean, this would be the end of Helios' journey.

The opposite end of the sarcophagus is pretty much a matching doublet of the first. There we see Selene driving her two-horsed chariot, again from left to right, while below the horses reclines the figure of the Goddess Ge or Gaia, the personification of Earth.

*Selene*

Above the horses, an erote bearing a torch plunges downward, and is thought to represent the Evening Star in a corresponding fashion to the 'Morning Star' erote (if such it be) above Helios' chariot. However, to have Venus appear as both the Morning and Evening Stars on the same night is an astronomical impossibility. An alternative explanation, therefore, might be that the 'rising' erote at the left hand may symbolise the stars beginning to appear in the sky, while the 'plunging' erote may represent the stars disappearing at the end of the night. Selene's horses are led by a winged, booted female figure that Robert identified[4] over a century ago as Aura, a personification of the Breeze. This identification seems to have been largely accepted ever since, despite the fact that Aura plays no part whatever in the mythical narratives of Selene; however, Jean Sorabella associates the figure with darkness, rather than air, and this would seem to make considerably more sense in this context.[5] This mysterious figure appears frequently on the sarcophagi, always leading Selene's horses, though more often she appears in the main scene on the front of the casket. The figure of Selene shown here is portrayed in identical fashion to that on the front of the sarcophagus, and we shall return to this shortly. These depictions of Helios and Selene in their chariots have been explained as framing the main scene within a cosmological context. As we've seen above, however (2.3.2), the times when the Sun and Moon appear together in the sky, at opposite horizons, are the dawn and dusk of the Full Moon, and it's possible that some such indication of the lunar phase is intended here also.

Turning to the front panel, we find that at either end, near the top, is a large lion's head. These fairly rare features have been explained by the fact that the sarcophagus itself is shaped similarly to a wine-vat, and the lion's heads may represent spouts

---

4 Robert 1900: p.83.

5 Sorabella 2001: p.79.

through which the new wine is expressed.⁶ It's been conjectured that there may be a symbolic reference to the 'wine of new life' and a connection to the Dionysiac mysteries, but this has no connection with the scene portrayed. As these lions also appear on other sarcophagi portraying quite different subject matter, we can assume they play no part in the symbolic narrative. They are best regarded, perhaps, simply as decorative features that need not really concern us, and any thought of a possible connection with the Nemean Lion would seem inappropriate here.

Immediately below the left lion's head are small figures of Eros and Psyche, embracing. Not only are these classical representations of true love, they also bridge the divide between deity and mortal in a similar way to Selene and Endymion and Psyche is, besides, a personification of the soul.

Moving toward the right, we next find the figure of a seated shepherd, surrounded by his flock, some of which are above him and appear to be lying on a rocky ledge. This figure appears on several, but by no means all of the Endymion sarcophagi, and again seems to have given commentators difficulty. Sometimes he is young and clean-shaven, at others a more mature, bearded figure; sometimes he appears to sleep, at others he's plainly awake. He has been explained as representing the bucolic afterlife, in similar fashion to the rear of the casket, or simply as setting the scene, in the Carian countryside; the fact that some of the sheep are above his head on a rocky ledge may indicate that the scene is mountainous, and so refer to Mount Latmos itself. On other Endymion sarcophagi we actually find the scene indicated by a personified form of Latmos as a mature, bearded man, but this figure is absent here; unless, the 'shepherd' being bearded in this case, the two have been combined. As we'll see, the figure of the sleeping Endymion is portrayed as a classically 'beautiful youth', so it seems unlikely that the shepherd is intended to be Endymion

---

6 Matz 1956-1957: p.127. McCann 1978: p.39.

## Selene

awake; unless we infer that the arrival of Selene casts a 'glamour' on the sleeping Endymion, portrayed further toward the right.

Next comes the same winged and booted female, identified as Aura, leading the prancing horses of Selene's chariot, which faces right to left. Below the horses is, again, a reclining figure of Ge, this time holding a snake. An erote stands in the car of the chariot as driver, while another stands on the back of the horses; other erotes, holding torches symbolic of a wedding procession, surround the figure of Selene as she steps down from the chariot, facing right toward the reclining figure of Endymion. In other sarcophagi she is occasionally accompanied by Hymenaeus, the God of marriage.

Selene bears a crescent on her brow and wears a long, diaphanous dress that exposes her right breast. In this, her portrayal may be influenced by the iconography of the Roman Goddess Diana, who was also frequently portrayed with one bare breast; however, it would also seem appropriate to the highly sexualised nature of an encounter portrayed as a marriage. Starting from beneath her right breast, a veil billows out in a circle over her head, the far end of which is held in her raised left hand, and she has a similar veil in the portrayal on the right end of the sarcophagus. Koortbojian[7] takes this veil as 'a traditional sign for the magical revelation of deity', but there are sarcophagi which also show Selene leaving the scene in her chariot (not present on the front of this sarcophagus, but perhaps implied by the image of Selene at the right end), where the veil billows in the same way, thus making the interpretation of 'revelation' somewhat problematical. An alternative solution might be found in representations of the Roman God Caelus, the personification of the sky corresponding to the Greek Ouranos. He is shown with a similar veil arcing above his head, and Cook argues that this is a representation of the over-arching sky.[8] Selene's veil

---

7 Koortbojian 1995: p.67.

8 Cook 1914: pp.59-60.

may thus indicate that she is a celestial Goddess whose natural habitat is the sky, here descended to earth.

Led on by the erotes, Selene steps down from the rear of her chariot toward the sleeping Endymion, who lies in a classic pose, reclining on his left elbow with his right arm thrown over his head, his cloak pulled away to reveal his naked body and genitalia. Obviously a sexual encounter is intended, although Endymion remains asleep. The face of Endymion was frequently carved as a portrait of the deceased, though this is not the case here. Above him the winged figure of Nyx (Night) holds a stalk of poppy seed pods, and pours a sleeping potion over him. In other sarcophagi, Nyx is frequently replaced by Hypnos (Sleep), with the same attributes. As has been argued above (10.2), there is no reason to think that this implies the use of drugs. Particularly in association with Hypnos, the presence of the poppy pods is perfectly explicable as symbolising sleep. Endymion's hunting dog reclines by his shoulder, and two more erotes stand beneath the right hand lion head, completing the scene before the other representation of Selene, possibly departing in her chariot, curves round the right end of the sarcophagus.

The cover of the sarcophagus has ten small pictorial vertical panels on either side of a central inscription. These ten panels form five symmetrical pairs. The outermost pair are, at far left, a personification of Mount Latmos, giving an indication of the scene less explicitly present here on the main face of the sarcophagus; and at far right, the woodland God Sylvanus, emphasising the rural setting. Moving in toward the centre, we next have two male Seasons: Spring at left, Autumn at right. The third pair shows Cupid and Psyche, the archetypal lovers, at left, and Aphrodite/Venus at right, also in a pastoral setting. The fourth pair is Ares/Mars, holding a spear, at left, and Aphrodite at right, this time standing and holding a wedding torch; the Goddess of love and her (preferred) second husband thus represent another pair of archetypal lovers suitable to a marriage. The inmost pair of panels show, at right, a portrait bust of the occupant of the sarcophagus, in this case revealed in the central panel's inscription to be, rather unusually, a woman: Arria, the mother of Aninia Hilara, who was responsible for placing her in the casket. At left, we see Selene and Endymion, sitting and embracing, both now awake and wearing crescents on their brows. This would appear to represent their married life together in heaven.

## 14.3 Interpretations

As previously mentioned, there are variants to be found among the multiple versions of the Endymion sarcophagi. Rarely, Selene is seen departing in her chariot as well as arriving (perhaps a rather over-literal interpretation of the Roman version of the myth, which saw Selene, identified with the virginal Diana, merely kissing Endymion in his sleep, rather than the celestial marriage implied by most interpretations), and Nyx and Hypnos seem to be interchangeable. There are also one or two examples where Endymion's eyes are open rather than closed, and others where Endymion is shown sleeping alone, apparently awaiting the arrival of Selene, whose part in proceedings is implied rather than shown. However, the encounter between Goddess and mortal remains the central symbol throughout.

It hardly needs pointing out that despite the additional symbolic elaboration on the sarcophagi, they really add nothing to the mythical narrative of Selene and Endymion. As Koortbojian points out, though, there was obviously a desire to 'expand' what was obviously a brief and fragmentary narrative even in antiquity, and the artists sculpting the sarcophagi seem to have chosen two ways of doing this.[9] The first was by attempting to extend the narrative itself, by showing Selene both arriving and departing in her chariot, thus implying both a beginning and an end to

---

9 Koortbojian 1995: pp.68-75.

the amorous encounter. The second, which we see exemplified in the Metropolitan Museum example described above, was by elaboration: increasing the number of characters shown and introducing elements that expanded the symbolic meaning. Thus the presence of the erotes, Cupid and Psyche, Hymenaeus and so forth all enriched the meaning of the sacred marriage, without actually adding anything to the story.

As mentioned above, the sleeping Endymion's face was frequently carved into a portrait of the deceased contained within the coffin, and the majority of Endymion sarcophagi appear to have been intended for masculine occupants. The parallel scene for women was that of the God Dionysus arriving to wake the sleeping mortal Ariadne, after her abandonment on Naxos by Theseus,[10] where Ariadne is shown in a very similar posture to the sleeping Endymion. One has to assume that Aninia Hilara bought the Metropolitan Museum sarcophagus 'off the shelf' for her mother Arria, rather than having one specially carved.

That Sleep (Hypnos) and Death (Thanatos) were brothers was a commonplace in antiquity and quite obviously this connection comes into play here. Identifying the deceased with Endymion suggests, at the most basic level, that he 'is not dead but sleeping'. The encounter with Selene, however, being portrayed as a wedding, suggests that she is actually waking him to a perpetual marriage in the afterlife; a suggestion made even more explicit by those sarcophagi where Endymion is portrayed with open eyes, and by the panel on the Metropolitan Museum example showing Selene and Endymion as full awakened lunar lovers. We might also point out that, as seen above (11.3), Plutarch had written shortly before these sarcophagi became popular, that souls resided in the Moon after death and, yet more explicitly, that 'some pass their time as it were in sleep with the memories of their lives for dreams

---

10 Koortbojian 1995: pp. 95-97.

*Selene*

as did the soul of Endymion.'[11] It is, perhaps, a short step from there to envisioning the soul of the dead man married to Selene and the promise of a blissful afterlife as eternal, in the end, as the circling Moon.

---

11 Plutarch, *Face in the Orb of the Moon* 945B (1957: Vol. 12, p.217).

Chapter Fifteen

# Conclusions: The Phases Of The Moon

## 15.1 Introduction

Having come this far, it's now time to try to sum up what we've learned about Selene and her mythology. As might be gathered from the title of this chapter, it seems impossible to decide on a simple, unitary 'meaning' that explains the whole range of Selenic mythology. Instead, we have a range of references to matters astronomical, genealogical, oracular, funereal, and so on, varying over both historical periods and geographical locations.

It should, however, be clear from our examination of the evidence that there is absolutely no sign of any connection between the mythology of Selene and 'Women's Mysteries' or even women's religion. Nor is there any evidence of a 'Triple Moon-Goddess' of the popular Maiden-Bride-Crone variety. These are merely modern constructs that, though they have become all-pervading on the internet, have no basis in ancient belief. This is not to deny outright that the Moon may have had some special meaning to ancient women. But there is simply no indication of it contained within the mythological stories relating to Selene. Identifications with other Goddesses believed to have lunar connotations, such as Artemis or Hecate, are the result of religious and philosophical speculation; they aren't mythological, and so lie outside the scope of this book. Let's summarise, then, what the evidence appears to indicate.

## 15.2 The Minor Myths

It should, perhaps, be pointed out once more that our source material is extremely fragmentary and, particularly with regard to the lesser tales related of Selene, that there's little in the way of systematic story-telling. Indeed, there's frequently so little narrative in these accounts that they hardly count as 'myths' at all.

Several of the minor stories, such as those naming Selene as mother of Ersa, the dew, of Pandia, the moonlight, and so on, appear to be poetic retellings of observed facts: for example, that dew is more likely to fall on bright, moonlit evenings than on cloudy ones. Similarly, the Seasons are said to be daughters of Selene and Helios because the Moon and Sun were the most obvious indicators of cyclical time in the ancient world. Although we know that 'Selene' refers to both the physical Moon and to the Moon-Goddess, these poetical phrasings seem quite obviously to refer more to the former than the latter. They are personifications of the physical Moon and phenomena associated with her, without narrative and, thus, without 'mythological' content as we have come to understand it.

That Selene and Helios, as Moon and Sun, were both 'visible deities' obviously influenced the way they were treated in the genealogical tradition. They could hardly be fitted in with the twelve Olympian deities as, quite plainly, they didn't reside on Mount Olympus, even if this were to be regarded as a celestial 'Home of the Gods' rather than the physical mountain on the border of Thessaly and Macedonia; instead, they were continually to be seen journeying across the sky. Rather than Olympians, they were described as offspring of the Titans and, considering the interpretation to be offered in the following section, it's of some interest that their 'relatives' among the Titans contain not only a number of obviously astronomical figures, but also several associated with magic and sorcery. The Titans were generally viewed as an 'earlier generation' of Gods, one of whose major functions seems to have been to define the Olympians by being what they were not. The Titans were essentially 'other' and so the story of their war with the Olympians, the Titanomachy, becomes understandable; by conquering the Titans, the Olympians also overcome the forces of chaos and establish the world of order over which they reign. Similar stories of wars with 'Former Gods' are to be found among the Hittites, Babylonians, Indians and elsewhere, and may well have been imported wholesale into the Greek tradition;[1] it's hardly necessary to suppose that they represent the non-Indo-European deities of the aboriginal inhabitants, 'overthrown' by invading Greeks, still less that they belonged to a suppositious 'matriarchal' period.

It's noticeable that Helios and Selene take no part in the Titanomachy. They could hardly be killed or imprisoned, like the other Titans, because it's necessary for them to continue to appear in the sky on a daily basis. Nonetheless, at a later period it seems to have been thought that, the Olympians comprising a 'complete set' of deities with a complete set of functions, they should also have included divinities of the obviously-important Sun and Moon, and this would appear to explain the identification of Apollo with Helios, and Artemis with Selene, with those deities taking on solar and lunar characteristics. As has been mentioned, these are *identifications* that have nothing to do with mythology; there are no solar or lunar narratives attached to Apollo and Artemis.

That Helios and Selene were visible deities also seems to have affected their handling by the mythical genealogists, who had to confront certain difficulties when faced with the question: if the solar and lunar deities had parents, while at the same time the Sun and Moon were plainly part of the physical world and could be presumed to have been present ever since the world began, what of the celestial lights before Helios and Selene were born? The answer was to make their parents, Hyperion and Theia, solar and lunar deities themselves; or more to the point, doublets of Helios

---

1 West 1997, pp.297-300. West 2007, pp.162-164.

and Selene under different names, and this equally applies to variants such as the 'far-shining' Euryphaëssa, an obviously lunar figure herself.

As always, there were variants, such as the tradition of the Arcadians, who claimed to have occupied their land since before the Moon was born and, indeed, claimed that that event had occurred in their territory. However, Arcadia was considered such a 'backwoods' country that its myths seem largely to have escaped the hands of mainstream genealogists and so the variant survived, obscure but intact, with a completely different lineage.

## 15.3 The Major Myths

Although we may describe the stories of Selene and Endymion and, to a somewhat lesser extent, of Selene and Pan as 'major' myths by comparison to the tales in the previous section, it has to be admitted that they don't contain a great deal of narrative content, and that references to them tend to be vague and fragmentary at best. In the case of Selene and Endymion, this may be because the story was so well known as to be a commonplace, to which it was only necessary to refer in passing. Even if this were the case, it would still have to be admitted that the lack of a single surviving 'long version' would remain puzzling. Given this, our attempts to understand to what these stories refer lead us to look beyond the simple narrative content.

The situation is complicated by the fact that we have two distinct versions of the Endymion figure. By far the most familiar is the Carian version, where he is a shepherd or herdsman loved by Selene, eternally asleep in a cave. The second is that from Elis, where Endymion is a king, firmly embedded within a semi-historical genealogical tradition, and a figure associated with the founding of the Olympic Games. Attempts have been made, from ancient times to the present, to associate the two figures; but the simplest answer is that they were different individuals with the same name. This is hardly stretching the imagination: one only has to glance at the *Oxford Classical Dictionary* to find 16 different, well-known persons from antiquity called Alexander and it would be more than a little foolish to try to argue that they were all identical with Alexander the Great. As the Elean tale appears to contain nothing that enhances our understanding of the story of Selene and Endymion, we can perhaps discount it. There are other versions, such as that of an Arcadian Endymion of whom we know very little, or others that place the encounter between man and Goddess in different locations from Caria; for the most part, though, these versions retain the same core elements as the Carian story, and this is what we'll concentrate on here.

Myths are, of course, mutable, and we have seen, in Chapter 14, that late antiquity reinterpreted the story of Selene and Endymion in a funerary context, where Endymion represented the soul asleep in death, yet married in the afterlife to Selene. This, of course, is symbolism rather than mythology; the use of a pre-existent story to provide comfort for the bereaved and the hope of salvation for the dead. It neither alters the original myth, nor does it explain it. However, we'll return to this below.

From an early date there were attempts to explain the story rationally, making Endymion an early astronomer who discovered the phases of the Moon, and so forth. Such rationalisations have been dealt with above at 5.4 and no longer need detain us. They are 'off-the-shelf' explanations applied to other figures besides, and a moment's thought reveals their patent absurdity: one can hardly make astronomical observations while asleep in a cave. It's only regrettable that such reductionism survives into the 21st century, with its quest to discover a rational and historical 'truth' behind ancient myths. On the other hand, it's also possible that the early dates of these rationalisations may indicate that the original referents for Selenic myths may, in fact, have been forgotten at a relatively early date.

*Selene*

Our quest to discover the resonances of the myths of Selene, Endymion and Pan have led us to three main areas: dream oracles, entering caves in search of visionary wisdom, and the oracular tradition of the chresmologues. Although these areas overlap, we'll look at them in turn.

We've seen above, in Chapters 9 and 10, that it was not uncommon to consult the deities directly in dream. There were dream oracles throughout the classical world, dedicated to different deities, and there are a number of common features found at such shrines, though not all are always present. The oracle is frequently consulted while sleeping in a cave, sometimes situated in a hill or mountain. There are often springs nearby and, regardless of the deity presiding over the shrine, a Nymph or minor Goddess is usually present as well; such oracles appear to require a female presence, despite the fact that the deities consulted are usually masculine. Also, the method of consultation frequently requires the sacrifice of an animal, most often a sheep or ram, though other animals are mentioned, after which the consultant usually sleeps on or wrapped up in the fleece or skin of the slaughtered animal.

We have at least one case where a connection can be shown between Selene and a dream oracle, that being at Thalamae, the place-name itself meaning bed-chamber; unfortunately we have little to indicate the exact procedures followed there, although it would seem that the oracle was both ancient and important. We do, though, have late literary stories of dream consultations with the Moon-Goddess, now identified as Diana, where the procedure is in line with other oracles (11.4-5). That Endymion is a shepherd or herdsman, asleep forever in a cave where, the evidence would seem to imply, he is loved in dream by Selene, is extremely suggestive; as is the fact that Pan, in a more aggressive fashion, has sexual intercourse with Selene while wrapped in a sheepskin. More, we have also seen that Pan and his corresponding Latin deity, Faunus, had connections with dreams and oracles, and that there was an Arcadian cave dedicated to both Pan and Selene together. One distinct referent for Selenic myth would, then, appear to be the dream oracle tradition.

It now seems fairly well established that there was also a tradition of descending into caves or underground chambers in order to commune with the deities and to obtain visions and wisdom, which is reflected in both the historical and legendary record. There is obviously a certain overlap with cave-centred dream oracles here; but while dream oracles were usually consulted with a simple overnight stay, the cave tradition seems to have involved lengthier stays underground, where the darkness and silence provoked visionary experience similar to that gained through the modern use of sensory deprivation tanks, as well as dreams. The archetype of this behaviour is, of course, Epimenides, whose protracted sleep of 40 years and upwards is said to have allowed intercourse with the deities, and to have given him sufficient sagacity to be numbered among the Seven Wise Men of Greece. However, we also have similar stories told of such figures as Pythagoras and Demosthenes, while memories of such gnostic activities, under the guise of 'black magic', appear to have survived into mediaeval Spain. It should, perhaps be emphasised that cave sleepers such as these were interrogating the 'otherworld', rather than the underworld; they interacted with deities, rather than the dead. The tale of Endymion's eternal slumber, engaged with Selene in dream, can thus be seen as a parallel to such cave-sleeping practices.

The connection is strengthened when we remember that Epimenides himself was claimed to be a 'son' of Selene, although the meaning of 'son' is open to different interpretations. Epimenides was, of course, credited with writing various 'oracles' of the type used by the chresmologues of the 6th century BCE onwards, as were Orpheus and Musaeus, both of whom were also said to have a close familial relationship to Selene. It's possible, however, that such relationships simply indicate that these oracles and teachings were given 'under the aegis' of Selene; in other words that they represent a 'lunar' wisdom tradition. Such a tradition seems to have been particularly associated with the Orphics and Pythagoreans, with its most startling emanation appearing in the Selenic 'mysteries' of the 2nd century CE Pythagorean Alexander of Abonoteichus. That the Orphics, in particular, taught a doctrine of salvation in the afterlife, may have some bearing on the choice of the Selene and Endymion myth in funerary symbolism, mentioned above.

Like Selene herself, who seems to have received little in the way of normal cult worship, this lunar-influenced wisdom tradition is a long way from the mainstream, urban-centred religion of the Greek city-states, growing as it does from dream-oracles, subterranean practices and unorthodox cosmologies. The evidence for its existence is fragmentary, and some might say that its reality is speculative. However, when faced with the question of 'what, exactly, is Selenic mythology all about?' this triple combination seems to provide an answer that covers more aspects of the material than any other prospective solution. If nothing else it may, perhaps, open the way to a new phase of research ...

Appendix

# Selene, Endymion And Incest

## 16.1 Introduction

We've seen above, at 1.5.2, a variant story from Nonnos, suggesting that Selene and Endymion might somehow be incestuous lovers. At first sight this may seem incomprehensible: how can a Goddess and a mortal man be siblings, after all? And yet, even though we have no more than a single reference to this tale, it is possible to make some sort of conjectures, at least as far as the time, place and circumstances of the story's origin, and to what it may have referred.

## 16.2 Nonnos' Tale

The story appears in Nonnos' epic at the point where Dionysus (Bacchos) is gathering his forces for an invasion of India, and mainly refers to the incestuous liaison between the Carian youth Caunos and his sister Byblis. The full passage is as follows:

'Asterios the father had gone with another band, but his son Miletos now in the flower of his age came in the company of Bacchos. With him came his brother Caunos to share his dangers. Although only a boy, he led the Carian people into the Indian War. Not yet had he conceived a passion for his innocent sister, and composed that tricking love song; not yet had he sung of Hera herself joined with her brother Zeus in a harmonious bed of love like his own, the song about the Latmian cowshed of the neversleeping herdsman, while he praised Endymion, the bridegroom of love-smitten Selene, as happy in love's care on a neighbouring rock. No, Byblis still loved maidenhood – no, Caunos was still learning to hunt, untouched by love for one so near. Not yet had the soft-haired brother fled, or the girl changed her body to water by her tears; she was still no sorrowing fountain bubbling up a watery stream.'[1]

The translator, W.H.D. Rouse, adds an explanatory footnote at this point, as follows: 'Miletos, founder of the city of that name, had two children, a son Caunos and a daughter Byblis. Byblis conceived an unholy passion for her brother, or he for her, or it was mutual. Finally they were separated, and she mourned so bitterly that she lost her human shape, and in some accounts, turned into a river or spring called after her. So much we know; this passage may serve to remind us how very little we really do know of Greek mythology and literature. We have no information about the song which Caunos sang, though plainly Nonnos knew it well, *i.e.*, it came in some poetical account of the story which we have lost, no doubt the work of an Alexandrian. The matter is rendered yet more obscure by the corruption or mutilation of the passage, which makes the connexion of the legend of Zeus and Hera with that of Endymion and Selene quite obscure.'

## 16.3 Interpretations

Miletos is the nearest major city to Heraclea-under-Latmos, so we are very much in the territory of the Selene and Endymion myth, if nothing else. There are two points that might be made about this footnote. Firstly, Rouse's views on the origin of the song that Nonnos knew may be too narrow. Writing in the 2nd century CE, Pausanias mentions that: 'The land of Miletus has the spring

---

1 Nonnos, *Dionysiaca*, 13.546-565. (1940: Vol. 1, pp.468-471).

Byblis, of whose love the poets have sung.'² This might seem to suggest the subject was one appearing frequently in popular Milesian song; not necessarily in the works of an Alexandrine poet. Popular tradition would seem just as likely a source here, or perhaps the 'Milesian Tale'. This literary form was named after the *Milesiaca* of Aristides of Miletos, a 2<sup>nd</sup> century BCE writer of amusing and salacious tales;³ the city of Miletos itself had a reputation in antiquity as being sybaritic and morally lax, and this would be an unsurprising location for a tale of sibling incest. Secondly, Rouse seems to assume that, because there is no other known reason for associating or paralleling the love of Zeus and Hera with that of Endymion and Selene, the passage must be corrupt or mutilated. This may possibly be the case, although it also has to be remembered that Nonnos' verse is in regular hexameters, which would seem to make obvious corruption more noticeable; it should be pointed out that Rouse's Greek text contains no critical notes here indicating lacunae or restored readings of the text. Given Rouse's own note on 'how very little we really do know of Greek mythology and literature' it would seem equally likely (if not more so) that, rather than corruption, we are dealing here, instead, with yet another variant tradition. That Zeus and Hera were incestuous was commonplace knowledge, though hardly given enormous emphasis. It has to be assumed, given that the story of Selene and Endymion was placed in the same sentence with this story, that it was somehow being used as a paradigmatic example to legitimise an act of sibling incest. The only reason for mentioning Selene and Endymion as exemplars for an attempted incestuous seduction is if there was, perhaps, some lost tradition regarding them as incestuous lovers themselves. Indeed, all this material may derive from one of those Milesian traditions of Byblis that are no longer extant. Unfortunately, as we have nothing more

---

2 Pausanias, 7.5.10 (1933: Vol. 3, p.197).

3 Hornblower & Spawforth (1999, *s.v.* 'Aristides (2)').

than this single reference from Nonnos, such inferences can be no more than speculation.

The story of the love between Caunos and Byblis was widely known in the classical world, its popularity doubtless reflecting the mingled Greek and Roman repulsion and fascination with incest, particularly as it occurred in other cultures. Recorded by authors as diverse as Conon, Pausanias, Parthenius, Antoninus Liberalis and Ovid,[4] we need to know little more here than the summary given by Rouse, above, except for a couple of interesting details. One of these is that Ovid, in a lengthy treatment of the story that makes Byblis the one to fall in love with Caunos, has her sleep with him in her dreams, with considerable pleasure;[5] the similarity to Selene and Endymion's somnial encounters hardly needs pointing out.

Although our sources generally treat Miletos, Caunos and Byblis as being of 'Greek' descent, they mostly agree that Miletos came originally from Crete, and founded the city named after him, thus reinforcing the connection between Crete, Caria and Arcadia. Regardless of this foundation myth, the city of Miletos was actually a Greek colony, and, as previously mentioned, the nearest Greek city to Heraclea-under-Latmos, the scene of Endymion's encounter with Selene. However, Conon[6] points out that the Greek city was founded by Ionians and Athenians at a later date than Miletos; when Miletos himself arrived, the region 'was inhabited by the large tribe of Carians, who lived in villages.' This is an interesting statement, as we know that the 'natural' state of Carian life before its Hellenisation was a village-dwelling one.[7] This might suggest that Conon's 1st century BCE narrative of the incestuous siblings

---

[4] Conon, *Narratives 2*, in Photius *Bibliotheca*, 186 (1994: p.177). Pausanias, 7.5.5, 7.24.5 (1971:Vol. 1., pp.243, 293). Parthenius, *Love Romances* 11 (1916: pp.293-295). Antoninus Liberalis, *Metamorphoses*, 30 (1992: p.89 [& commentary p.193-196]). Ovid, *Metamorphoses*, 9.451ff (1955: pp.215-221).

[5] Ovid, *Metamorphoses*, 9.451ff (1955: pp.215-221).

[6] Conon, *Narratives 2*, in Photius *Bibliotheca*, 186. (1994: p.177).

[7] Hornblower 1982: p.10.

may derive from original Carian sources. Conon also tells us that Caunus, fleeing from Byblis, arrived at the south-eastern seashore border of Caria, where either he, or his son, founded the city named after him (perhaps explaining the Caunians' claim to also be of Cretan origin[8]); Miletos is on the north-western coastal border of the same state. The tale thus, effectively, spans the whole of Caria, both in space and time. However, when Parthenius handles the tale, he lists his sources, all of which are Greek and date from the Hellenistic period.[9] This material seems to confirm, firstly, that the tale of the incestuous love between Caunus and Byblis was of Carian origin, and well-known in that country; and secondly that it either first became widely known in the Greek world, or that there was a renewed interest in it, in the early Hellenistic period. Indeed, Steven Jackson argues, with some justification, that Nonnos' probable source for the Caunus and Byblis story was Apollonius of Rhodes' *Caunou Ktisis*, a poem about the founding of the Carian city of Caunus.[10] Apollonius, of course, lived around the middle of the 3rd century BCE, and is included amongst Parthenius' list of sources.

In line with this idea, it's notable here that all our sources (surviving and lost) are said to be Hellenistic or later: in other words, they all post-date the Hecatomnid dynasty of the 4th century BCE, when Mausolus and his successors reigned over Caria as semi-independent satraps of the Persian empire. Mausolus, apart from refounding Heraclea-under-Latmos, was also responsible for the Hellenisation of the entire Carian state.

Mausolus was married to his sister Artemisia, while Mausolus' successor to the throne, his younger brother Idrieus, married his sister Ada.[11] Possible reasons for this marriage are discussed by

---

8 Herodotus, 1.171-172 (1972: p.110).
9 Parthenius, *Love Romances* 11 (1916: pp.293-295).
10 Jackson 2006: p.18.
11 Hornblower 1982: 'Appendix 2: Hekatmonid Sister-Marriage', pp.358-363.

Hornblower, and include keeping the property intact, ensuring the purity of the descent, the influence of Persian Zoroastrianism, and so on; but no definite conclusion seems possible. However, from the evidence, it would appear that incestuous marriage was restricted to the Hecatomnid rulers, rather than being practiced by the Carian population in general. Given the popularity of the tale of Caunus and Byblis and its pan-Carian setting, we may thus not be entirely off the mark in thinking that mythological references to incest have some relevance to, or originated in thoughts about, Hecatomnid sister-marriage.

Artemisia, of course, has a Greek name derived from the Goddess Artemis, who by this time was associated with the Moon. As Hornblower points out,[12] in the strange work falsely attributed to Plutarch, *De Fluviis* ('On Rivers'), there is a chapter devoted to the river Indus;[13] but this is not the familiar Indus river, anciently in India and now in Pakistan. From Livy, we know there was a Carian river Indus, mentioned in relation to the Carian 'Thabusium, a stronghold overlooking the river Indus, which takes its name from an Indian who was thrown from an elephant.'[14] Livy's rationalising etymology need not detain us over much; the importance of the quotation is simply that it establishes the presence of an Indus river in Caria, and Hornblower's assumption that this is the one referred to is made almost certain by the fact that, although the original author declares the Indus to be a river of India, he then goes on to say that 'it was first called Mausolus, from Mausolus the son of the Sun'.

From this, and a small amount of other fragmentary evidence, Hornblower argues for a separately existing mythical figure, 'Mausolus the son of Apollo/Helios', of whom we have no surviving narratives. Hornblower then goes on to argue, on the

---

12 Hornblower 1982: pp. 261, 271, 335-336.
13 (Pseudo-)Plutarch, *De Fluviis*, 25 (1870: Vol. 5, pp.508-509).
14 Livy, 38.14 (1976: p.346).

basis that Mausolan coins often featured the head of Helios, that the Mausoleum was surmounted by a quadriga similar to that driven by Helios, and may have contained a statue of the God, etc., for a deliberate, propagandist identification of the human king Mausolus with the mythical Mausolus, son of Helios.

That there was some sort of connection between Mausolus and Helios seems a reasonable assumption, and by this period, of course, Helios was identified with Apollo. Given, however, that Apollo and Artemis were brother and sister (likewise Helios and Selene), and that Artemisia derived her name from Artemis, it seems to me not too unlikely a speculation to suggest that Mausolus may have been identifying himself not with a mythical 'son of the Sun', but rather with the Sun himself, as Apollo/Helios, which would fit equally as well, if not better, with the propagandist iconography mentioned above. Such a direct identification of man and God, while reasonable enough in propaganda terms, is difficult to handle in mythical narrative, however; much easier is to refer to the man Mausolus as a son of the God.

Apollo and Artemis, of course, though brother and sister, were not incestuous; however, at least in some tales, Helios and Selene were [1.3.3]. So, although Artemisia may well have been connected with Artemis, if this propagandist imagery extended from identifications between rulers and deities to their incestuous marriage as well, it would perhaps be more logical to think of Artemisia identifying more with Artemis in her Selenic, Moon-Goddess aspect, rather than that of virgin-huntress. Is there, then, anything to connect Mausolus with Selene as well?

There is, though the connection is admittedly tenuous. It's found in the same chapter (25) of *De Fluviis*. Having started by telling us that the Indus was originally called Mausolus, our author then goes on to give the origin for the name of the nearby mountain, Lilaeus [see above, 1.6.2]. This is said to be named after a shepherd who worshipped the Moon alone, by night, and who, neglecting the other Gods, was torn apart by lions, animals which are particularly associated with the Sun;[15] after which Selene is said to have turned him into a mountain of the same name. The name Lilaeus may well derive from the Greek word *lilaiomai*, meaning 'to long for, to crave', an appropriate cognomen for one indulging in such obsessive devotion.

*De Fluviis* is a curious work, probably of the Roman period, containing much strange lore quoted from many books which are either lost or otherwise unknown (if, it must be said, some of these sources are not actually made up entirely). It discusses the names (past and present) of various rivers and mountains, and the stories behind the names; as well as discussing curious herbs and gemstones found associated with them. It's notable that a large number of these stories involve unwitting acts of incest between a man and his sister or daughter, or the misinterpretation of innocent acts as incest between the man and his sister, daughter or mother; with the ultimate result that the man often commits suicide, usually by drowning in the river that's named after him. As such, the whole work is imbued with a Graeco-Roman spirit of horror and hostility regarding the concept of incest.

We can note here that the mythical figures of Mausolus and Lilaeus are mentioned together in the same short chapter, and so we might conjecture that our author may perhaps be referring to the historical Mausolus through both figures. King Mausolus loved only his sister, the Moon-Lady Artemisia; the mythical Lilaeus loved only Selene. Lilaeus could thus be seen as a mythical doublet of Mausolus. In the mythical story, of course, Lilaeus is duly punished for his neglect of the other Gods. And if King Mausolus was not quite punished in the same way for his neglect of exogamous marriage, one gets the feeling that the author of *De Fluviis* would certainly think he deserved to be; which may explain the suitably ironic destruction of Lilaeus by solar lions.

---

15 Ptolemy, *Tetrabiblos*, 1.17 (1940: p.79).

There is one last aspect to discuss, which draws the circle to a close. Besides the correspondence between Mausolus and Helios, we have conjectured that Lilaeus is a doublet of Mausolus; the fact that Lilaeus is a shepherd, worshipping the Moon alone on a mountain and 'performing her mysteries in the dead time of the night', allows us to see him as a doublet of Endymion as well. We thus have a simple syllogism: 'Mausolus = Lilaeus = Endymion; therefore, Mausolus = Endymion'. And if Mausolus = Endymion, and Artemisia = Selene, and if Mausolus and Artemisia are incestuously married, then thus we have a basis for portraying Endymion and Selene as incestuous partners also.

This is, confessedly, highly speculative; and yet it is suggestive. Combined with the tale of Caunus and Byblis, with its similar Carian references, Hecatomnid propaganda identifying Mausolus and Artemisia with the Sun and Moon at least provides a possible key for unlocking a very obscure variant tale from Nonnus. One still would like to know exactly what the song was that Caunus is alleged to have composed, but that probably being gone forever, this is perhaps as much as we can hope for.

# Bibliography

Aelian: *On the Characteristics of Animals* [Trans. A.F. Scholfield]. Cambridge, MA & London: Harvard/Heinemann, 1958-1959.

Alcman fr.57P, quoted in Plutarch: *Quaestiones Conviviales*, 3.10.3 (in Deborah Boedeker, *Descent from Heaven*. Chico, CA: Scholars Press, 1984).

Allen, Thomas W. & E.E. Sikes: *The Homeric Hymns*. London: Macmillan, 1904 [via *Perseus Project* web-page].

Anon: *De Incredibilibus (Peri Apiston)*. *(Mythographoi: Scriptores Poeticae Historiae Graeci)* [Ed. Antonius Westermann]. Brunswick: 1843.

Anon: *The Wonderful History of Virgilius the Sorcerer of Rome*. London: David Nutt, 1893.

Antoninus Liberalis: *The Metamorphoses of Antoninus Liberalis* [Trans. Francis Celoria] London & NY: Routledge, 1992.

Apollodorus: *The Library* [Trans. Sir J.G. Frazer]. Cambridge, MA & London: Harvard/Heinemann, 1921.

Apollonius Dyscolus: *Historiae*. [Ed. Guilielmi Xylandri & Joannis Meursii & Ludovicus Henricus Teucherus]. Lipsiae: Bibliopolio Gleditschiano, 1792.

Apollonius Rhodius: *The Argonautica* [Trans. R.C. Seaton] Cambridge, MA & London: Harvard/Heinemann, 1912.

Aristides, P. Aelius: *The Complete Works* [Trans. Charles A. Behr]. Leiden: E.J. Brill, 2 vols. (Vol. 1, 1986, Vol. 2, 1981 – *sic*).

Aristophanes: *Pax* (Aristophanes: *Clouds, Wasps, Peace* [Trans. Jeffrey Henderson]. Cambridge, MA & London: Harvard, 1998).

Aristotle: *Nicomachean Ethics* [Trans. H. Rackham]. Cambridge, MA & London: Harvard/Heinemann, 1926.

Aristotle: *Politics* [Trans. H. Rackham]. Cambridge, MA & London: Harvard/Heinemann, 1932.

Aristotle: *Rhetoric* [Trans. John Henry Freeze]. Cambridge, MA & London: Harvard/Heinemann, 1926.

Arkwright, W.G.: 'Lycian and Phrygian Names'. *JHS*, Vol. 38, 1918.

Artemidorus: *The Interpretation of Dreams* [Trans. Robert J. White]. Park Ridge, NJ: Noyes Press, 1975 (Facsimile reprint: Largs: Banton Press, 1992).

Athenaeus: *The Deipnosophists* [Trans. Charles Burton Gulick]. Cambridge, MA & London: Harvard/Heinemann, 1937.

Bachofen, J.J.: *Myth, Religion & Mother Right*. Princeton, NJ: Princeton University Press, 1967.

Barton, Tamsyn: *Ancient Astrology*. London & NY: Routledge, 1994.

Bean, George E.: *Aegean Turkey*. London: Ernest Benn Ltd., 1979.

Bean, George E.: *Turkey Beyond the Maeander*. London: John Murray, 1989.

Betz, Hans Dieter [Ed.]: *The Greek Magical Papyri in Translation. Vol. One: Texts.* Chicago & London: University of Chicago Press, 1986.

Boardman, John: *Athenian Red Figure Vases: The Classical Period.* London: Thames & Hudson, 1989.

Boedeker, Deborah: *Descent From Heaven.* Chico, CA: Scholars Press, 1984.

Boer, Charles [trans.]: *The Homeric Hymns.* Irving, TX: Spring Publications, 1979.

Borgeaud, Philippe: *The Cult of Pan in Ancient Greece.* Chicago & London: University of Chicago Press, 1988.

Bremmer, Jan N.: 'The Skins of Pherekydes and Epimenides'. *Mnemosyne*, Fourth Series, Vol. 46, Fasc. 2 (May, 1993[1]), pp. 234-236.

Bremmer, Jan. N.: 'Prophets, Seers and Politics in Greece, Israel and Early Modern Europe'. *Numen*, Vol. 40, No. 2 (May 1993[2]), pp.150-183.

Brookesmith, Peter: '50 Shades of Grey'. *Fortean Times*, No. 296, January 2013, pp.30-37.

Burkert, Walter: *Structure and History in Greek Mythology and Ritual.* Berkeley: University of California Press, 1979.

Burkert, Walter: *The Orientalizing Revolution.* Cambridge, MA & London: Harvard University Press, 1992.

Buxton, Richard: *Imaginary Greece*. Cambridge University Press, 1994.

Casson, Lionel: *Libraries in the Ancient World*. New Haven: Yale University Press, 2002.

Cicero: *De Divinatione* (*Cicero* Vol. 20) [Trans. William Armistead Falconer]. Cambridge, MA & London: Harvard/Heinemann, 1923.

Cicero: *De Finibus Bonorum et Malorum* [Trans. H. Rackham]. Cambridge, MA & London: Harvard/Heinemann, 1914.

Cicero: *De Natura Deorum/Academica* [Trans. H. Rackham]. Cambridge, MA & London: Harvard/Heinemann, 1933.

Cicero: *Tusculan Disputations* (Vol. 18.) [Trans. J.E. King]. Cambridge, MA & London: Harvard/Heinemann, 1927.

Claudian: *De Raptu Proserpinae* [Trans. Maurice Platnauer]. Cambridge, MA & London: Harvard/Heinemann, 1922.

Clement of Alexandria: *The Exhortation to the Greeks* [Trans. G.W. Butterworth]. Cambridge, MA & London: Harvard/Heinemann, 1919.

Connor, W.R.: 'Seized by the Nymphs: Nympholepsy and Symbolic Expression in Classical Greece.' *Classical Antiquity*, Vol. 7, No. 2 (October 1988), pp.155-189.

Conon: *Narratives* (in Photius: *The Bibliotheca* [Trans. N.G. Wilson]. London: Duckworth, 1994).

Cook, A.B.: *Zeus. A Study in Ancient Religion*. Cambridge: Cambridge University Press. Vol. 1, 1914. Vol. 2, Part 1, 1925, Vol. 3, 1940.

Cooper, William R.: *After the Flood*. New Wine Press, 1995. Web version: http://www.ldolphin.org/cooper

Cooper, William R. (Trans.): *The Chronicle of the Early Britons*. Unpublished PDF file (2002), available at: http://homepage.ntlworld.com/mike.gascoigne.chronicle_of_the_early_britons.pdf

Coulton, J.J.: 'The Stoa at the Amphiaraion, Oropus'. *Annual of the British School at Athens*, Vol. 63, 1968, pp.147-184.

Davies, Owen: *Grimoires: A History of Magic Books*. Oxford: Oxford UP, 2009.

Del Rio, Martin: *Investigations into Magic* [Trans. P.G. Maxwell-Stuart]. Manchester: Manchester University Press, 2009.

Detienne, Marcel: *The Masters of Truth in Ancient Greece*. NY: Zone Books, 1996.

Dickins, G.: 'Thalamae'. *Annual of the British School at Athens*, Vol. 11, 1904-5, pp.124-136.

Dickins, Guy: 'The Growth of Spartan Policy'. *Journal of Hellenic Studies*, Vol. 32, 1912, pp.1-42.

Dicks, D.R.: *Early Greek Astronomy to Aristotle*. Ithaca, NY: Cornell University Press, 1970.

Diodorus Siculus: *Library of History* [Trans. C.H. Oldfather]. Cambridge, MA & London: Harvard/Heinemann, 1935.

Diogenes Laertius: *Lives of the Eminent Philosophers* [Trans. R.D. Hicks]. Cambridge, MA & London: Harvard/Heinemann, 1925.

Dionysius of Halicarnassus: *Roman Antiquities* [Trans. Earnest Cary & Edward Spelman]. Cambridge, MA & London: Harvard/Heinemann, 1937.

Dodds, E.R.: *The Greeks and the Irrational*. Berkeley, LA: University of California Press, 1951.

Dowden, Ken: *The Uses of Greek Mythology*. London: Routledge, 1992.

Dowson, John: *A Classical Dictionary of Hindu Mythology*. London: Routledge & Kegan Paul, 1972.

Edelstein, Emma J. & Ludwig Edelstein: *Asclepius*. Baltimore & London: Johns Hopkins University Press, (1945), 1998 (2 vols. as one).

Egan, Rory B.: 'Cicada in Ancient Greece'. *Cultural Entomology Digest* 3 (November 1994). Online version at: http://www.insects.org/ced3/cicada_ancgrcult.html

Eliade, Mircea: *Zalmoxis: The Vanishing God*. Chicago: University of Chicago Press, 1972.

Euripides: *Alcestis* (Euripides: *Alcestis, Hippolytus, Iphigenia in Tauris* [Trans. Philip Vallacott]. Harmondsworth: Penguin Classics, 1974).

Euripides: *Alcestis* (*Euripides* [Trans. Arthur S. Way] Cambridge, MA & London: Harvard/Heinemann, Vol. 4, 1912).

Euripides: *Iphigenia in Tauris* (*Euripides* [Trans. David Kovacs]. Cambridge, MA & London: Harvard/Heinemann, 1999.

Euripides: *The Phoenician Maidens* (*Euripides* [Trans. Arthur S. Way]. Cambridge, MA & London: Harvard/Heinemann, Vol. 3, 1912.

Euripides: *Rhesus* (*Euripides* [Trans. Arthur S. Way]. Cambridge, MA & London: Harvard/Heinemann, 1912.

Farnell, Lewis Richard: *The Cults of the Greek States*. Oxford: Clarendon Press, 5 Vols., 1896-1909.

Farnell, Lewis Richard: *Greek Hero Cults and Ideas of Immortality*. Oxford: Clarendon Press, 1921.

Fletcher, Robert Huntington: *The Arthurian Material in the Chronicles* (*Studies and Notes in Philology and Literature*, Vol. 10). Boston: Ginn & Co, 1906.

Flower, Michael Attyah: *The Seer in Ancient Greece*. Berkeley, CA: University of California Press, 2008.

Fol, Alexander & Ivan Marazov: *Thrace & The Thracians*. London: Cassell, 1977.

Fontenrose, Joseph: *The Delphic Oracle*. Berkeley: University of California Press, 1978.

Forster, E.S.: 'South-Western Laconia'. *Annual of the British School at Athens*, Vol. 10, 1903-4, pp.158-189.

Fox, Robin Lane: *Pagans and Christians*. London: Penguin Books, 1988.

Gantz, Timothy: *Early Greek Myth*. Baltimore & London, 1993.

Geoffrey of Monmouth: *The History of the Kings of Britain* [Trans. Lewis Thorpe]. Harmondsworth: Penguin Classics, 1966.

*Gesta Regum Britannie* (in *The* Historia Regum Britannie *of Geoffrey of Monmouth*, Vol. 5, *Gesta Regum Britannie* [Ed. & Trans. Neil Wright]. Cambridge: D.S. Brewer, 1991).

Godwin, Joscelyn: *Mystery Religions in the Ancient World*. London Thames & Hudson, 1981.

Graf, Fritz: *Greek Mythology: An Introduction*: Baltimore & London: Johns Hopkins University Press, 1993.

Graf, Fritz: *Magic in the Ancient World*. Cambridge MA & London: Harvard University Press, 1997.

Graf, Fritz: 'Orpheus: A Poet Among Men' in Jan Bremmer [Ed.]: *Interpretations of Greek Mythology*. London: Croom Helm, 1987.

Graves, Robert: *The Greek Myths*. Harmondsworth: Penguin Books, 1960.

Graves, Robert: *The White Goddess*. London: Faber and Faber, 1961.

Griffiths, Alan: "What Leaf-Fringed Legend ... ?' A Cup by the Sotiades Painter' *Journal of Hellenic Studies*, Vol. 106, 1986, p.58-70.

Grimal, Pierre: *The Dictionary of Classical Mythology*. Oxford: Blackwell, 1986.

Guazzo, Francesco Maria: *Compendium Maleficarum* [Ed. Montague Summers; trans. E.A. Ashwin]. NY: Dover Publications, 1988 (Rpt of 1929).

Guthrie, W.K.C.: *Orpheus and Greek Religion*. London: Methuen, 1935.

Halliday, W.R.: *Greek Divination*: Chicago: Argonaut Inc., 1967 (Rpt: 1913).

Haynes, Sybille: *Etruscan Civilisation*. London: British Museum Press, 2000.

Heraclitus: *De Incredibilibus (Peri Apiston). (Mythographoi: Scriptores Poeticae Historiae Graeci)* [Ed. Antonius Westermann]. Brunswick: 1843.

Herodotus: *History* [Trans. A.D. Godley]. Cambridge, MA & London: Harvard/Heinemann, 1920.

Herodotus: *The Histories* [Trans. Aubrey de Selincourt]. Harmondsworth: Penguin Classics, 1972.

Hesiod: *Theogony (Hesiod* [Trans. H.G. Evelyn-White]. Cambridge, MA & London: Harvard/Heinemann, 1914).

Homer: *Iliad* [Trans. A.T. Murray]. Cambridge, MA & London: Harvard/Heinemann, 1925.

Homer: *The Odyssey* [Trans. A.T. Murray]. Cambridge, MA & London: Harvard/Heinemann, 1919.

Homer: *The Odyssey* [Trans. E.V. Rieu] Harmondsworth: Penguin, 1946.

*Homeric Hymns* (in *Hesiod* [Trans. H.G. Evelyn-White]. Cambridge, MA & London: Harvard/Heinemann, 1914).

Hornblower, Simon: *Mausolus*. Oxford: Clarendon Press, 1982.

Hornblower, Simon & Antony Spawforth (Eds.): *The Oxford Classical Dictionary* (3rd edition). Oxford: Oxford University Press, 1999.

Huxley, G.I.: *Greek Epic Poetry*. London: Faber and Faber, 1969.

Hyginus: *Fabulae*. (Mary Grant: *The Myths of Hyginus*. Lawrence: University of Kansas Press, 1960).

Iamblichus: *Life of Pythagoras* (Kenneth Sylvan Guthrie: *The Pythagorean Sourcebook and Library*. Grand Rapids, MI: Phanes Press, 1987).

*Interpretes Virgilii*: commentary to *Georgics*. (*Commentarii in Virgilium Serviani* [Ed. H. Albertus Lion]. Göttingen, 1826.

Ions, Veronica: *Indian Mythology*. London: Paul Hamlyn, 1967.

Jackson, Steven: 'Apollonius of Rhodes: Endymion'. *Quaderni Urbinati di Cultura Classica*, New Series, Vol. 83, No. 2 (2006), pp. 11-21.

Jayne, Walter Addison: *The Healing Gods of Ancient Civilisations*. New Haven: Yale University Press, 1925.

Jones, C.P.: *Culture and Society in Lucian*. Cambridge, MA: Harvard UP, 1986.

Kedrenos, Georgios: *Hist. Comp.* 323c, quoted in A.B. Cook: *Zeus. A Study in Ancient Religion*. Cambridge: Cambridge University Press. Vol. 1, 1914.

Kerenyi, C.: *Asklepios*. New York: Pantheon Books, 1959.

Kerenyi, C.: *The Gods of the Greeks*. London: Thames & Hudson, 1951.

Kerenyi, C.: *Zeus and Hera*. London: Routledge & Kegan Paul, 1975.

Kirk, G.S.: *The Nature of Greek Myths*. Harmondsworth: Penguin Books, 1974.

Kirk, G.S. & J.E. Raven: *The Presocratic Philosophers*. Cambridge University Press, 1957.

Koortbojian, Michael: *Myth, Meaning, and Memory on Roman Sarcophagi*. Berkeley, Los Angeles & London: University of California Press, 1995.

Lactantius: *The Divine Institutes* (Rev. Alexander Roberts & James Donaldson, eds.: *The Works of Lactantius* Vol. 1 [Ante-Nicene Christian Library, Vol. 21]. Edinburgh: T. & T. Clark, 1871).

Larson, Jennifer: *Greek Heroine Cults*. Madison: University of Wisconsin Press, 1995.

Larson, Jennifer: *Greek Nymphs*. NY: Oxford University Press, 2001.

Layard, John: *The Lady of the Hare*. Boston & Shaftesbury: Shambhala, 1988.

Leahy, D.M.: 'The Spartan Defeat at Orchomenus'. *Phoenix* Vol. 12, No. 4 (Winter 1958) pp.141-165.

Lefkowitz, Mary R.: 'Predatory Goddesses'. *Hesperia* 71, 2002, pp.325-344.

Leland, Charles G.: *Aradia, or the Gospel of the Witches*. London: David Nutt, 1899.

Leland, Charles G.: *The Unpublished Legends of Virgil*. London: Elliot Stock, 1899.

Lempriere, J.: *A Classical Dictionary*. London: Routledge, n.d.

Levi, Peter: *Atlas of the Greek World*. Oxford: Phaidon Press, 1980.

Liddell-Scott (Henry G. Liddell, Robert Scott, Rev. Henry Stuart Jones, and Roderick McKenzie): *A Greek-English Lexicon*. Oxford: Clarendon Press, 1996.

Lightfoot, J.L. [Trans.]: *Hellenistic Collection*. Cambridge, MA: Harvard University Press, 2009.

Livy: *History of Rome* [Trans. B.O. Foster]. Cambridge, MA & London: Harvard/Heinemann, Vol. 1, 1919.

Livy: *Rome and the Mediterranean* [Trans. Henry Bettenson]. Harmondsworth: Penguin Classics, 1976.

Longus: *Daphnis and Chloe*. (*Daphnis & Chloe* + *Parthenius* [Trans. G. Thornley & J.M. Edmonds + S. Gaselee] Cambridge, MA & London: Harvard/Heinemann, 1916).

Lucian: *Alexander the False Prophet.* (*Lucian*, Vol. 4 [Trans. A.M. Harmon]. Cambridge, MA & London: Harvard/Heinemann, 1925).

Lucian: *Astrology*, (*Lucian*, Vol. 5 [Trans. A. M. Harmon]. Cambridge, MA & London: Harvard/Heinemann, 1936).

Lucian: *Dialogues of the Gods.* (*Lucian*, Vol. 7. [Trans. M.D. Macleod]. Cambridge, MA & London: Harvard/Heinemann, 1961).

Lucian: *The Dream* (*Lucian*, Vol. 2, [Trans. A.M. Harmon]. Cambridge, MA & London: Harvard/Heinemann, 1915).

Lucian: *The Lover of Lies* (*Lucian*, Vol. 3 [Trans. A M. Harmon]. Cambridge, MA & London: Harvard/Heinemann, 1921).

Lycophron: *Alexandra* (Callimachus, Lycophron, Aratus [Trans. A.W. Mair & G.R. Mair]. London & Cambridge, MA: Heinemann/ Harvard, 1955).

Lyly, John: *Endymion.* Manchester & NY: Manchester University Press, 1996.

MacKenzie, Norman: *Dreams and Dreaming.* London: Aldus Books, 1965.

Macrobius: *The Saturnalia* [Trans. P.V. Davies]. NY & London, Columbia UP, 1969.

Matz, Friedrich: 'An Endymion Sarcophagus Rediscovered'. *Bulletin of the Metropolitan Museum of Art* 15 (1956-1957) pp.123-128.

Maximus Tyrius: *The Dissertations of Maximus Tyrius* (1805), [Trans. Thomas Taylor] Rpt. Frome: Prometheus Trust, 1994.

McCann, Anna Marguerite: *Roman Sarcophagi in the Metropolitan Museum of Art*. New York: Metropolitan Museum of Art, 1978.

McNally, Sheila: 'Ariadne and Others: Images of Sleep in Greek and Early Roman Art'. *Classical Antiquity*, Vol. 4, No. 2 (Oct., 1985), pp.152-192.

Moore, Steve: 'Foam of the Moon'. *Fortean Studies*, Vol. 2 (1995), pp.216-245.

Moore, Steve: 'Magic Words: Virgil the Necromancer in Mediaeval Legend'. *Strange Attractor Journal* No. 3, 2006, pp.108-125.

Moore, Steve: 'The Men in the Moon', *Fortean Times*, No. 51, pp.58-61, Summer 1990.

Moore, Steve: 'The Fake, the Snake, and the Sceptic', *Fortean Times*, No. 276, pp.46-51, June 2011.

Morris, John: *The Age of Arthur* (1973). London: Phoenix, 1995.

Nennius: *British History & The Welsh Annals* [Ed. & Trans. John Morris]. London & Chichester: Phillimore, 1980.

Nicander: *The Poems and Poetical Fragments*. [Ed. and Trans. A.S.F. Gow & A.F. Scholfield]. Cambridge: Cambridge University Press, 1953.

Nilsson, Martin P.: *The Minoan-Mycenaean Religion and its Survival in Greek Religion*. Lund: C.W.K. Gleerup, 1950.

Nonnos: *Dionysiaca* [Trans. W.H.D. Rouse]. Cambridge, MA & London: Harvard/Heinemann, 1940.

Ogden, Daniel: *Greek and Roman Necromancy*. Princeton & Oxford: Princeton University Press, 2001.

Ogden, Daniel: *Magic, Witchcraft, and Ghosts in the Greek and Roman Worlds*. NY: Oxford University Press, 2002.

*Orphic Hymns* [Trans. Apostolos N. Athanassakis]. Missoula: Scholars Press, 1977.

Ovid: *Fasti* [Trans. Sir J.G. Frazer]. Cambridge, MA & London: Harvard/Heinemann, 1951.

Ovid: *Heroides and Amores* [Trans. Grant Showerman]. Cambridge, MA & London: Harvard/Heinemann, 1914.

Ovid: *Metamorphoses* [Trans. Frank Justus Miller]. Cambridge, MA & London: Harvard/Heinemann, 1916.

Ovid: *Metamorphoses* [Trans. Mary M. Innes]. Harmondsworth: Penguin Classics, 1955.

Page, D.L.: *Sappho and Alcaeus*. Oxford, 1955.

Palmer, L.R.: *The Greek Language*. London: Faber & Faber, 1980.

Parke, H.W.: *Greek Oracles*. London: Hutchinson, 1967.

Parke, H.W. (Ed. B.C. McGing): *Sibyls and Sibylline Prophecy in Classical Antiquity*. London & NY: Routledge, 1992.

Parthenius: *Love Romances* (Longus, *Daphnis and Chloe*/ Parthenius [Trans. George Thornley/J.M. Edmonds & S Gaselee]. Cambridge, MA & London: Harvard/Heinemann, 1916).

Patterson, Lee E.: 'An Aetolian Local Myth in Pausanias?' *Mnemosyne*, Fourth Series, Vol. 57, Fasc. 3 (2004), pp. 346-352.

*Pausanias* [Trans. J.G. Frazer]. London: Macmillan, 1898.

Pausanias: *Description of Greece* [Trans. W.S. Jones]. Cambridge, MA & London: Harvard/Heinemann, 1926 (Vol. 2), 1933 (Vol. 3).

Pausanias: *Guide to Greece* [Trans. Peter Levi]. Harmondsworth: Penguin, 1971.

Penglase, Charles: *Greek Myths and Mesopotamia*. London: Routledge, 1994.

Peradotto, John: *Classical Mythology: An Annotated Bibliographical Survey*. Chico, CA: Scholars Press, 1973.

Perrot, Georges & Charles Chipiez: *History of Art in Phrygia, Lydia, Caria and Lycia*. London: Chapman and Hall, 1892.

Perseus Project web-page: www.perseus.tufts.edu

Petrie, W.M. Flinders: 'Neglected British History'. *Proceedings of the British Academy*, Vol. 8 (1917-1918), pp.251-278.

Philostratus (the elder): *Imagines* (Philostratus: *Imagines*/ Callistratus: *Descriptiones* [Trans. Arthur Fairbanks]. Cambridge, MA & London: Harvard/Heinemann, 1931).

Philostratus: *The Life of Apollonius of Tyana* [Trans. F.C. Conybeare]. Cambridge, MA & London: Harvard/Heinemann, 2 Vols, 1912.

Phlegon of Tralles: *Book of Marvels* [Trans. William Hansen]. Exeter: University of Exeter Press, 1996.

Photius: *The Bibliotheca* [Trans. N.G. Wilson]. London: Duckworth, 1994.

Phylargyrius: commentary to *Georgics*. (*Commentarii in Virgilium Serviani* [Ed. H. Albertus Lion] Göttingen, 1826.

Pindar: *The Odes of Pindar* [Trans. Sir J.E. Sandys]. Cambridge, MA & London: Harvard/Heinemann, 1915.

Plato: *Charmides* (Plato, Vol. 8 [Trans. W.R.M. Lamb]. Cambridge, MA & London: Harvard/Heinemann, 1927).

Plato: *Laws* (Plato, Vol. 9 [Trans. R.G. Bury]. Cambridge, MA & London: Harvard/Heinemann, 1926).

Plato: *Minos* (Plato, Vol. 8 [Trans. W.R.M. Lamb]. Cambridge, MA & London: Harvard/Heinemann, 1927).

Plato: *Phaedo.* (Plato: *The Works of Plato* [Trans. Henry Cary]. London: Bohn, 1848).

Plato: *Protagoras* (Plato, Vol. 4 [Trans. W.R.M. Lamb]. Cambridge, MA & London: Harvard/Heinemann, 1937).

Plato: *Republic* [Trans. Paul Shorey]. Cambridge, MA & London: Harvard/Heinemann, 1930.

Pliny: *Natural History* [Trans. H. Rackham]. Cambridge, MA & London: Harvard/Heinemann, 1949.

Plutarch: *Aged Men* (Plutarch, *Moralia*, Vol. 10 [Trans. H.N. Fowler]. Cambridge, MA & London: Harvard/Heinemann, 1936).

Plutarch: *Agis* (Plutarch, *Lives*, Vol. 11 [Trans. Bernadotte Perrin]. Cambridge, MA & London: Harvard/Heinemann, 1921).

Plutarch: *Aristides* (Plutarch, *Lives*, Vol. 2 [Trans. Bernadotte Perrin]. Cambridge, MA & London: Harvard/Heinemann, 1914).

Plutarch: *Cleomenes* (Plutarch, *Lives*, Vol. 11 [Trans. Bernadotte Perrin]. Cambridge, MA & London: Harvard/Heinemann, 1921).

Plutarch: *Concerning the Face which Appears in the Orb of the Moon* (Plutarch: *Moralia*, Vol. 12 [Trans. Harold Cherniss & William C. Helmbold]. Cambridge, MA & London: Harvard/Heinemann, 1957).

Plutarch: *On the Delays in Divine Vengeance* (Plutarch: *Moralia*, Vol. 7 [Trans. P.H. De Lacy & B. Einarson]. Cambridge, MA & London: Harvard/Heinemann, 1959).

Plutarch: *Dinner of the Seven Wise Men* (Plutarch: *Moralia*, Vol. 2 [Trans. Frank Cole Babbit]. Cambridge, MA & London: Harvard/Heinemann, 1928).

Plutarch: *Demosthenes* (Plutarch: *Lives*, Vol. 7 [Trans. Bernadotte Perrin]. Cambridge, MA & London: Harvard/Heinemann, 1919).

Plutarch: *Numa* (Plutarch, *Lives*, Vol. 1 [Trans. Bernadotte Perrin]. Cambridge, MA & London: Harvard/Heinemann, 1914).

Plutarch: *Of Love* (Plutarch, *Moralia*, Vol. 9 [Trans. Edwin L. Minar jr, F.H. Sandbach & W.C. Helmbold]. Cambridge, MA & London: Harvard/Heinemann, 1961).

Plutarch: *On the Sign of Socrates (De Gen. Soc.)* (Plutarch: *Moralia*, Vol. 7 [Trans. Phillip H de Lacy & Benedict Einarson]. Cambridge, MA & London: Harvard/Heinemann, 1959).

Plutarch: *Oracles at Delphi No Longer Given in Verse* (Plutarch: *Moralia*, Vol. 5 [Trans. F.C. Babbit]. Cambridge, MA & London: Harvard/Heinemann, 1936).

Plutarch: *Solon* (*Plutarch's Lives*, Vol. 1 [Trans. Bernadotte Perrin]. Cambridge, MA & London: Harvard/Heinemann, 1914).

Porphyry: *On the Cave of the Nymphs* [Trans. Robert Lamberton]. Barrytown, NY: Station Hill Press, 1983.

Porphyry: *Life of Pythagoras* (Kenneth Sylvan Guthrie: *The Pythagorean Sourcebook and Library*. Grand Rapids, MI: Phanes Press, 1987.

Porphyry: *On Abstinence from Animal Food* [Trans. Thomas Taylor. Ed. Esmé Wynne-Tyson]. London: Centaur Press Ltd., 1965.

Porphyry: *Peri Agalmaton (On Images)*, fragments preserved in Eusebius: *The Preparation for the Gospel* [Trans. E.H. Gifford]: Eusebii Pamphili: *Evangelicae Praeparationis*. Libri XV. Tomus III. Pars Prior. Oxford University Press, 1903.

Probus: commentary to *Georgics* (*Commentarii in Virgilium Serviani* [Ed. H. Albertus Lion]. Göttingen, 1826).

(Pseudo-)Callisthenes: *The Life of Alexander of Macedon*. [Trans. Elizabeth Hazelton Haight]. New York: Longmans, Green & Co., 1955.

(Pseudo-)Plutarch: *De Fluviis*. [Trans. R. White] (in William W. Goodwin [Ed.]: *Plutarch's Morals*. Boston: Little, Brown & Co., 1870).

Probus: commentary to *Georgics*. (*Commentarii in Virgilium Serviani* [Ed. H. Albertus Lion] Göttingen, 1826).

Proclus: *Chrestomathia* (in *Hesiod* [Trans. H.G. Evelyn-White]. Cambridge, MA & London: Harvard/Heinemann, 1914).

Propertius: *Elegies* [Trans. C.P. Goold]. Cambridge, MA & London: Harvard/Heinemann, 1990.

Ptolemy: *Tetrabiblos* in Manetho + Ptolemy: *Tetrabiblos* [Trans. W.G. Waddell & F.E. Robbins]. Cambridge, MA & London: Harvard/Heinemann, 1940.

Quintus Smyrnaeus: *The Fall of Troy* [Trans. A.S Way]. Cambridge, MA & London: Harvard/Heinemann, 1913.

Rabinowitz, Jacob: *The Rotting Goddess*. NY: Autonomedia, 1998.

Reger, Gary: (reviewing Getzel M. Cohen: *The Hellenistic Settlements in Europe, the Islands, and Asia Minor*), *Bryn Mawr Classical Review*, 98.11.19.

Richer, Jean: *Sacred Geography of the Ancient Greeks*. Albany, NY: State University Press of New York, 1994.

Robert, C.: 'A Collection of Roman Sarcophagi at Clieveden'. *Journal of the Hellenic Society* Vol. 20 (1900), pp.81-98.

Rohde, Erwin: *Psyche*. New York: Harper and Row, 1925 (Rpt. 1966).

Roscher, Wilhelm: 'Ephialtes', in Wilhelm Heinrich Roscher & James Hillman, *Pan and the Nightmare*. Zurich: Spring Publications, 1972.

Rudgley, Richard: *The Alchemy of Culture*. London: British Museum Press, 1993.

Savignoni, L.: 'On Representations of Helios and of Selene'. *Journal of Hellenic Studies*, Vol. 129, 1899.

*Scholia in Apollonii Argonautica* (in *Apollonii Rhodii Argonautica* [Ed. Rich. Fr. Phil. Brunckii]. Lipsiae: 1810, 1813).

*Scholia in Lycophronis Alexandra* (in Lycophron: *Alexandra* [Ed. Eduardus Scheer]. Berlin, 1908).

Scholiast on Pindar: *Nemean Odes*, (quoted in A.B. Cook: *Zeus*. Cambridge: Cambridge University Press, 1914, Vol. 1, p.456).

Servius: commentary to Virgil's *Aeneid*. (*Commentarii in Virgilium Serviani* [Ed. H. Albertus Lion]. Göttingen, 1826).

Servius: commentary to Virgil's *Georgics*. (*Commentarii in Virgilium Serviani* [Ed. H. Albertus Lion]. Göttingen, 1826).

Shakespeare, William: *Henry IV, Part One*.

Simpson, R. Hope: 'Identifying a Mycenaean State'. *Annual of the British School at Athens*, Vol. 52, 1957, pp.231-259.

Smith, Cecil: 'Two Vase Pictures of Sacrifices'. *Journal of Hellenic Studies*, Vol. 9, 1888, pp.1-10.

Sorabella, Jean: 'A Roman Sarcophagus and its Patron'. *Metropolitan Museum Journal*, 36 (2001), pp.67-81.

Stannard, Jerry: 'Squill in Ancient and Medieval Materia Medica, with Special Reference to its Employment for Dropsy'. *Bulletin of the New York Academy of Medicine*, Vol. 50, No.6 (June 1974), pp.684-713).

Stark, Freya: *Ionia*. London: John Murray, 1956.

Statius: *Thebaid*. (*Statius* [Trans. J.H. Mozley]. Cambridge, MA & London: Harvard/Heinemann, 1928, Vol. 2.

Stephanus of Byzantium: *Ethnics* [Ed. Augusti Meinekii]. Berlin: 1849.

Stoneman, Richard: *Greek Mythology*. London: Aquarian Press, 1991.

Strabo: *Geography* [Trans. H.L. Jones]. Cambridge, MA & London: Harvard/Heinemann, 1917-1932.

Strataridaki, Anna: 'Epimenides of Crete: Some Notes on his Life, Works, and the Verse *"Kretes del Pheustal"'*. *Fortunatae*, (1991, No. 2), pp.207-224.

Tertullian: *De Anima*. (*Anti-Nicene Christian Library*, Vol. 15, *The Writings of Tertullian*. 2 vols. [Trans. Peter Holmes]. Edinburgh: T. & T. Clark, 1874.

Theocritus (*The Idylls of Theocritus, Bion and Moschus* [Trans. J. Banks]. London: Henry G. Bohn, 1853).

Thessalus of Tralles: *De virtutibus herbarum* (in Daniel Ogden: *Magic, Witchcraft, and Ghosts in the Greek and Roman Worlds*. NY: Oxford University Press, 2002).

Trendall, A.D.: *Red Figure Vases of South Italy and Sicily*. London: Thames & Hudson, 1989.

Trubshaw, Bob: 'Dream Incubation'. *3rd Stone*, 46, Spring/Summer 2003, pp.24-27.

Ustinova, Yulia: '"Either a Daimon, or a Hero, or Perhaps a God:" Mythical Residents of Subterranean Chambers.' *Kernos* 15 (2002), p. 267-288.

Valerius Maximus: *Memorable Doings and Sayings* [Trans. D.R. Shackleton Bailey]. Cambridge, MA & London: Harvard UP, 2000.

Varro: *On the Latin Language* [Trans. Roland G. Kent]. Cambridge, MA & London: Harvard/Heinemann, 1951.

Ventris, Michael & John Chadwick: *Documents in Mycenaean Greek*. Cambridge: Cambridge UP (2nd Ed.), 1973.

Vermeule, Emily: *Aspects of Death in Early Greek Art and Poetry*. Berkeley, Los Angeles, London: University of California Press, 1979.

Virgil: *Aeneid* [Trans. H.R. Fairclough]. Cambridge, MA & London: Harvard/Heinemann, 1934, Vol. 1.

Virgil: *Georgics* (*Virgil* [Trans. H.R. Fairclough]. Cambridge, MA & London: Harvard/Heinemann, 1978).

Walcot, Peter: *Hesiod and the Near East*. Cardiff: University of Wales Press, 1966.

Wardle, David [Trans. & Commentary]: *Cicero: On Divination, Book 1*. Oxford: Clarendon press, 2006.

Waxman, Samuel M.: *Chapters on Magic in Spanish Literature*. NY: 1916 [Kessinger Rpt. 2007].

West, M.L.: *The East Face of Helicon*. Oxford: Clarendon Press, 1997.

West, M.L.: *Hesiod, Theogony*. Oxford: Oxford University Press, 1966.

West, M.L.: *Homeric Hymns, Homeric Apocrypha, Lives of Homer*. Cambridge MA & London: Harvard UP, 2003.

West, M.L.: *Indo-European Poetry and Myth*. Oxford: Oxford UP, 2007.

West, M.L.: *The Orphic Poems*. Oxford: Clarendon Press, 1983.

Wilkins, W.J.: *Hindu Mythology*. (1882) Rpt. Calcutta: Rupa & Co, 1982.

Wilson, Elkin Calhoun: *England's Eliza* (1939). Rpt. NY: Octagon Books, 1966.

Wolkstein, Diane & Samuel Noah Kramer: *Inanna*. London: Rider, 1983.

Xenophon: *Cynegeticus* ('On Hunting') (Xenophon: *Minor Works* [Trans. Rev. J.S. Watson]. London: Henry G. Bohn, 1857).

Afterword

# At the Perigee

The book that you are holding in your hands is a more startling artefact than you might readily imagine, representing as it does the point at which classical scholarship comes closest to a physical embrace with its ethereal subject matter, or where the impassioned pressure of the nib tears through the page and into the still-live mythology beyond. Meticulous in its intelligent curating of the primary Selene myths and the great multiplicity of variant or otherwise related tales, the text herein is lucid and immediately comprehensible. And yet to understand the book itself, to fathom the extraordinary narrative surrounding it and how it came to be, will first require an understanding of its author and my dearest friend, the late Steve Moore.

His last completed work, the book's final pernickety adjustments were made sometime after 2.00 PM on the unseasonably sunny Friday afternoon of March 14th, 2014, meaning that its conclusion can be dated with some confidence. Its point of origin, however, is less certain. Although Steve considered this to be the most important thing that he would ever write, effectively a life's work, I imagine that most of the actual writing was accomplished in the 1990s and the opening decade of this current century, a true labour of love to be returned to in those periods without other pressing toil. That said, most of the heavy lifting in a strenuous intellectual endeavour of this nature lies in painstaking research and the discriminating gathering of materials; in the author's burgeoning

## Afterword

involvement with the object of his or her studies. Judged by these criteria, I think I can with some degree of certainty establish the October of 1976 as the most likely date for this volume's origination.

In the shabby autumn chill that followed Punk's fluorescent summer – which he personally hadn't noticed – Steve was running low on work and motivation. Comic strip commissions that had been his bread and butter for almost the last ten years were drying up save for occasional and unpredictable employment on such one-off items as his adaptation of *The Legend of the Seven Golden Vampires*, penned for Thorpe & Porter's *House of Hammer* monthly. There were text stories for children's annuals, a pseudonymous 'Sex-Secrets of Bangkok' for a soft-core rebranding of the venerable family weekly *Tit Bits* and, when even meagre opportunities like these were scarce, part time work at his friend Derek Stokes' world's-first comic-book emporium, Dark They Were and Golden Eyed in vanishingly narrow St. Anne's Court next to the brick wall that, reportedly, was Marianne Faithfull's primary residence during a 1960s low point. The intrepid crewmen of *The Fortean Times*, to which Steve had contributed since its inception, met at the shop regularly to sort their newsprint anomalies. Amongst all this, encouraged by a palm-reading that promised at the age of twenty-seven he would meet the woman he was meant for, a crush on a co-worker had flourished for a while before inevitably foundering in disappointment. This, then, was the largely dismal fabric of his life during that grey October forty years ago, sat restless in his room on Shooters Hill above the glittering city and attempting to find something meaningful amidst the safety pins and melancholy.

In an effort to encourage cheer by treating himself to some luxury long coveted, he'd blown a hefty portion of his wages for September in the purchase, on the first day of the new month, of an antique Chinese ritual coin-sword, with one hundred and eight cash coins bound together in a sword formation by red thread. Traditionally used for exorcism or for banishing, its provenance clearly unrecognised by the shop's owners, it had been his for a song. Near giddy with the prospect of owning a genuine magical artefact, on its first night in his possession he elected to make a preliminary and informal try at magic, pointing in the cardinal directions while requesting guidance and a confirmatory dream. Predictably, a dreamless night ensued but the next morning he was woken by an auditory hallucination, a male voice intoning the apparently meaningless word "Endymion" close to his ear. Over the next few days he realised that this was the title of a poem by John Keats retelling the Greek legend of the shepherd boy Endymion and his romance with pre-Olympian moon goddess Selene, a work that he'd previously heard referred to but had lacked sufficient interest to investigate.

That curiosity now piqued, his subsequent researches were conducted in a mounting atmosphere of numinous coincidence. Elusive and invaluable tomes of reference dived from library shelves to flutter at his feet and – hardly inappropriately given her dominion over the oneiric – the goddess herself or else pointed allusions to her were beginning to invade his as yet unrecorded dreams. Increasingly he perceived parallels between his lovelorn isolation there on Shooters Hill and that of mythical Endymion there in his solitary oracle-cave on the low slopes of Turkey's Mount Latmos. For my money, it would very probably have been around this time, while Steve was still surrounded by the thrilling aura of first contact with these new associations and ideas, that the first cloudy notions of perhaps one day writing a scholarly and serious account of this underreported and yet fascinating ancient lunar deity would have occurred to him. He was beginning, like Endymion, to fall in love with something silvery, and irresistible, and hardly there.

In a perhaps unprecedented fusion of the academic and erotic, the somehow more-than-just-philosophical relationship evolved into a thing that was more rarefied and yet more intimate over the course of the next twenty or so years. In April 1989, after further romantic failures, Steve felt compelled to fashion an exquisite miniaturist image of the goddess as he pictured her: naked and smiling; a chestnut Niagara spilling on her bare white shoulders. Offering a pin-sharp visual focus to his misty meditations, the creation of this graven image had the feeling, even to a close observer, of an almost matrimonial commitment. By this juncture he was certainly beginning to refer to his projected study of Selene in more concrete terms, as something more than just an exercise providing personal intellectual satisfaction, although he acknowledged that the work was going to take a long time to complete. Part of the problem lay in the fact that whatever aspect of the core Selene and Endymion story he investigated would inevitably turn up further aspects – other oracles said to have dreamed in caves, or the Selene/Helios-identified relationship between Mausolus and his sister Artemisia – that merited investigation in themselves. Nevertheless the book's sporadic progress, never quite forgotten or abandoned, would become a constant if infrequent subject of Steve's conversation over the next decade; a perpetual sense that something was accumulating, gradually and patiently increasing in its scope and depth as it moved at a stately, glacial pace towards its resolution.

By the middle 1990s, Steve's relationship with magic practice had become more serious in its intent, and so had the relationship between him and Selene. He'd been writing down his dreams, in which the goddess intermittently appeared, for several years by then. His still-evolving treatise, without forfeiting its intellectual distance or precision, seemed to take on undertones of the devotional, a sacred labour undertaken without expectation of financial reward or even academic recognition, something he was crafting as an offering to someone that he loved.

The onset of the current century delivered fresh romantic hopes in the material realm and just as quickly dashed them, which precipitated the emotional collapse and crisis that would prove to be a crucial turning-point in his unfolding story. He decided, perhaps recklessly given his psychological fragility during this period, to enter into a Selene-based retreat throughout the whole month of September, 2001, when he would be alone there in his hilltop house, during which time he would attempt to somehow manifest the goddess into visible appearance, or at least to his own satisfaction. Failure, I think, might have crushed him, but his unexpected and spectacular success, predictably, brought its own difficulties and dilemmas: a classical scholar with a justified pride in his own rigorous rationality who found himself in what amounted to a domestic relationship with what he knew to be, at least in one sense, an imaginary goddess. How he navigated these precarious rapids of ontology is documented elsewhere in the book/film/audio biography *Unearthing*, but suffice to say that very soon thereafter he appeared to reach a state of both creative and emotional equilibrium, perfectly comfortable in his developing relationship with an entirely immaterial entity and working on his masterpiece of lunar fiction, *Somnium*. This last had been conceived some time before his life-changing retreat, and prompted Steve to start a journal of the project's progress, journals which were as much diary entries as accounts of the vicissitudes of *Somnium* and which, coming to me after his death, provide some of the information here.

*Unearthing* was concluded at around this point, in 2005, and thus could not divulge the series of events that came after its publication – an extended sequel, *Earthing*, is intended for some yet to be determined future point – many of which seemed to result from *Unearthing*'s outing of Steve's inner life, and most of which were wholly beneficial. The love-object who'd unwittingly precipitated two of his most serious (and with hindsight valuable) emotional collapses understood him better after reading it and became a close, valued friend. His older brother Chris, with whom he'd shared his life and Shooters Hill address since the death of their mother around fifteen years before, also absorbed the piece and consequently formed a deeper and more fond relationship with the unworldly younger sibling whom Chris never really felt he'd known before. This closer union between the two would all-too-rapidly turn out to be of near incalculable human import.

During 2006, Chris Moore was diagnosed with Motor Neurone Disease of which Stephen Hawking is the world's most famous and, by still being alive, most atypical sufferer. Over the following three years as Chris's nervous system entered its cruelly protracted shutdown, starting with an irritating numbness in the fingertips before advancing inexorably towards the heart or lungs, Steve found himself increasingly responsible for his big brother's quality of life and simplest bodily functions, in the harrowing, heroic process gradually himself becoming a more grounded and substantial individual; a much better man than all the fictional adventure heroes he'd once secretly aspired to be. With Chris's death in 2009, having inherited the former's reasonably generous pension plan, Steve had become the sole owner and occupant of the hilltop abode and, lacking now for financial necessity, gave up what had become the drudgery of comic writing to fixate instead upon those projects that were closest to his heart. After a final polish, the completed *Somnium* was published in 2011 as a beautiful hardback by Strange Attractor, which left only the almost-completed study of Selene to revise, correct and bring into existence.

There remained the problem of the manuscript's ongoing mission-creep, with a few minor threads (such as the passages on nympholepsy, for example) that would still need to be tied into a tidy bow, but over those next two or three years came the growing sense that this decades-long magnum opus was just pages from its finish-line.

The last time that I heard his voice was Tuesday, March 11th in 2014, at around 6.00 PM. He'd called me to confirm my visit of ten days thereafter, and also to tell me that he seemed to be developing angina: he'd been given medication to assist with the attacks and had made an appointment with his regular GP for early the next week, following which he'd call to tell me how it went. By the next

Tuesday I still hadn't heard from him and my attempts to call were going to his answerphone. Being a stranger to the internet I sought remote assistance from my eldest daughter, Leah. She decided, sensibly, to contact the police in nearby Plumstead who immediately sent two officers up to the hilltop close to make sure all was well. It wasn't.

The policewoman – whose name was Clare, a lunar monicker that Steve would have appreciated – and her male companion drove to Steve's address and found it unlit save the bluish glow of a frozen computer screen that soaked into the outside night through Steve's thankfully open upstairs study window. Borrowing a ladder from a neighbour two doors down and setting it beside the front door, the male officer climbed up and entered to find Steve dead on the study floor, face down, his fall unbroken. The moon that night was a day or two past full, starting to pull a veil of shadow down across her top right quarter.

I immediately cancelled travel plans to visit Steve's place on that coming Friday and then, after a few moments' thought, cancelled the cancellation. I went down as planned, accompanied by my good friend the writer Ali Fruish and joined on the Saturday by the remarkable John Higgs, all of us trying to make sense of what had happened. We restarted his desktop computer and were able to determine a great deal about his final hours. The last thing he'd been working on had been a final edit and a proofreading of his Selene manuscript. Inspection of his emails told us that the last message he'd read, around 1.45 PM upon the afternoon of Friday, March 14th, had been from his *Fortean Times* colleague Val Sieveking telling him his health-related inability to attend a forthcoming meeting wouldn't be a problem. She also relayed a very rude and funny joke that punned upon the word 'angina' and would almost certainly have been the last thing that he laughed at. I read through his final fortnight of recorded dreams, concluding on the night of Thursday the 13th and marvelled at an entry only a few days before his death, about a man placing a ladder against Steve's house, by the front door, and then climbing up to seal the study window shut with plaster. On his desk, beside the half-drunk cup of coffee with a floating skin of mould and an uneaten finger of plain chocolate Kit-Kat, we discovered the handwritten notebook where he'd been recording his angina episodes, the last – or last recorded – having taken place just after 2.00 PM on that unusually balmy Friday afternoon.

As we construed it, then, at some point not long after that – the study window was still open and the lights not yet switched on – Steve had concluded work on his completed manuscript and risen from his chair, statistically the point at which cardiac incidents most typically occur. He'd stood up, had the heart attack and fallen forwards, his unbroken fall a merciful indicator that he was dead before he hit the study floor. I can't imagine any circumstances in which he could still be living after around five or six o'clock upon that Friday evening, and thus the heartfelt testimony of three separate neighbours who reported seeing and in one case speaking with Steve on the sunny Sunday morning following his death remains a glimmering mystery. It's perhaps worth remarking that that Sunday was the day of the full moon, just as the day of his birth in the June of 1949 had been.

John Higgs read the Selene manuscript and came to the conclusion, aided by a checklist of things yet to do that Steve had left, that this indeed was a completely finished and corrected version. When I'd read it for myself I readily concurred, and Strange Attractor was agreed upon as Steve's most likely choice of publisher. His funeral was in May, and his instructions that his ashes were to be strewn on the Bronze Age burial mound in Shrewsbury Lane by light of a full moon meant that this final ceremony had to wait until that August, when the skies were still and cloudless in the wake of an extreme tropical storm and when a glorious supermoon hung over Shooters Hill, the full moon at its perigee, the closest point in the approach between Earth and its lunar satellite.

Alan Moore

For the remainder of that year until the house was sold in March, 2015, I would make weekend visits every month or so, ostensibly to meet fellow executors and to recover various personal effects, but mostly just to eke out the last drops of his remaining presence. The framed image of Selene, obviously, was the first, most precious thing to be retrieved, but there were also something like a dozen ring-bound files containing all the private journal entries that he'd made since he began the diary as a record of his work on *Somnium* a decade-and-a-half before. When I could bear to, I began to read these from their painful, lovelorn start to their much happier conclusion, and began to understand my lifelong friend to a much greater and more intimate degree; began to understand what he was like when he was talking to nobody but himself, his diary, or his goddess.

The passage that I found the most arresting was related to a dreadful and heartbroken period at the start of the 21st century, in which Steve relates feeling so disheartened that he'd moaned, aloud or inwardly, 'Oh, please, Selene, take me home.' Inside his thoughts the goddess had replied by asking if he *really* wanted her to take him home. Knowing full well what being 'taken home' meant in this context, Steve was forced to reconsider. He'd replied, according to his journal, that if it should be the goddess's desire he would go with her straight away, but personally he hoped that he might have at least a little time before that happened. In his mind, Selene had at length announced that she would take him home only when his important book about her was completed.

Some fourteen years later, it appears that she fulfilled that obligation to the letter. To the instant. He'd have re-jigged the last awkward line, deleted the final extraneous comma, then he would have stood to stretch his legs. And then, embarking from the house that he'd been born in and had lived in all his life, he would have finally commenced his journey home.

The book you hold is an impeccable and flawlessly researched piece of classical scholarship, collecting for the first time in one

*Afterword*

place all that is known of this tremendously important and yet still largely undocumented goddess, and if that were all it was then that alone would be a thing worthy of celebration. It is so much more than that, however. It was compiled with a love for its subject that was human and immediate, stronger and warmer than religious adoration or consuming scholarly enthusiasm; written by somebody who, conceivably, was in himself the closest that the Earth and Moon had ever been, a kind of human perigee. There is no distance here between the author and his divine subject matter, nor between the author and his readers as he fathoms mythical antiquity as though it were a real and present thing and takes his audience perilously close to the peculiar reality of transcendent ideas. And of course the book's subject herself had overseen and guided the whole project as its unofficial supervisor, pointing the research in unexpected new directions and deciding on its literal, eventual deadline.

This book, that concerns one legendary being and was written by another, will transport you from the mundane world, through myth and mystery and deep into the shimmering moonlight that's behind it all. Please understand and treasure it for what it is, because you'll almost definitely never see another one: a message from between the Sea of Crises and the Sea of Dreams.

> Alan Moore
> Northampton
> January 24$^{th}$, 2017

# Index

Achilles, 89, 220
Actaeon, 85-6, 107
Acusilaus of Argos, 124
Ada, 313
Adonis, 4, 99-100
Aeëtes ('the terrible'), 67, 69
Aegyptians, see Egypt
Aegyptus, 126
Aelian, 19, 265
Aeneas, 97-98, 225, 228, 258, 260
*Aeneid* (Virgil), 225, 228, 242, 258
Aeolus, 125
Aer, 266, 272
*Aethiopis*, 89
Aethlius, 22, 24, 125
Aethra (possibly error for Theia, or for Aether), 14-15, 67-8
*Aetolica* (Nicander), 116
Aetolus, son of Endymion, 22, 122, 126
Agamedes, 201-2, 205
Agesarchus, 144
Agis, 174-175, 179
Agriope, wife of Orpheus, 275
Aigle ('light'), 67
Aither (Ether), 270
Akeso, 56
Albion, etymology of, 225, 229
*Alcestis* (Euripides), 269
Alcmaeon, 89
Alcman, 17, 78
Aletes (a name of Bacis), 257
Alexander, 29-30
Alexander of Abonoteichus, and Glycon cult, 280ff, 308
*Alexander Romance* (falsely attrib. Callisthenes), 29-30
Alexander the Great, 180, 305
*Alexandra*, The (Lycophron), 212
Alilat, 130
*alimon* (honey, cheese, seeds), 158
Allen, Thomas, 42, 76
Ammon (Amen), 175, 179-80
Ampelos, 18, 81
Amphiaraus, 89, and passim
Amphictyon, 22
Amphilochus, 89, 189, 200-201, 284
Amphion, 275
*amphiphon* cakes, 55
Amyclas, 175, 180
Ananke (Necessity), 270
Anchises, 96ff, 258
Andromeda, 99
Aninia Hilara, 298-299
Anius, 178
Anthana, founder of, 156
Antiochus and Antiochid phyle, 76
Antiope, 20, 275
Antiphates, 89
Antoninus Liberalis, 91, 312
Antoninus Pius, 281
Apesantus, 19
Aphrodite, 25-6, 38, 48, 55, 56, 88-9, 108-109, 297; Homeric Hymn to 41, 90; and Adonis, 99ff and Anchises, 105
*aphroselenos* ('Foam of the Moon'), 82-3, 140
Apollo, 3; and *passim*
Apollodorus and *Library* of, 14, 22, 60-67, 86; and *passim*
Apollonius Dyscolus, 147-9, 177
Apollonius of Rhodes (Apollonius Rhodius), 23, 28, 72, 107, 117, 119, 121-23, 139, 156, 313
Apollonius of Tyana, 195, 209, 281; Life of (Philostratus), 195, 209
Arcas, 22, 248

*Index*

Ares, 88, 100, 297
*Argonautika* (of Apollonius Rhodius), 23, 72, 107
*Argonautika* (attrib. Epimenides), 146, 265
*Argonautika*, Orphic version of, 267, 269
Aristides, Aelius Publius, 191, 196-8
Aristides of Miletos, 311
Aristophanes, 54
Aristotle, 23, 73, 266, 273
Aristoxenus, 177
Arrhephoria ritual, 77
Arria, 298-99
Artemidorus, 198, 244
Artemis, 3; and *passim*
Artemisia, 131, 313-317, 346
Arthur, King, 225
Ascanius, 225
Asclepius, 56; encountering in dreams 191ff; and *passim*
Astarte, 3
Asteria, 66
Asterios, 310
Asterodia, 22, 126
Astraeus ('Starry'), 66, 87
*astragaloi* (knucklebones), 249-50, 254
Athena, 55, 56
Athenaeus, 19, 30, 55, 158, 275
Athene, 34-5, 50, 85, 86, 96
Atlantis and Atlanteans, 15-16, 74
Atlas, 102, 175, 179
Attis, 104
augury, 261
Aura (a follower of Artemis), 79-80, 294, 295
Aurora (Eos; also Pallantis, 'daughter of Pallas'), 15, 70, 87

Babylon, and Babylonians, 43, 61, 150, 190, 303
Bacchos [Dionysus], 79, 309
Bachofen, J.J., 8
Bacis, 154, 255ff, and *passim*
Balte, a nymph, 144
Bardo Museum, 49
Basile or Basileia ('The Queen'), 15-16, 37; and Tethys 74ff
Bean, George E., 117-18, 132-3
Beleizis, see Zalmoxis
Berlin Museum, 44
Bithynians, 104
Biton, 202
Boedeker, Deborah, 93
Boer, Charles, 76
Boreas, 66, 87
Borgeaud, Philippe, 58, 72, 238-9, 245-6, 248
Bremmer, Jan, 156-7, 255, 260
Britain, etymologies of, 225-6, 224-6
*British History* (Nennius), 225-6
Brutus The Trojan, and Oracle Of Diana 224ff
Burkert, Walter, 2
Buxton, Richard, on caves, 135-6
Byblis, 26; and incest, 309ff

Caelos, 296
Calchas, a seer, 200, 212-13
Calliope, muse, 267
Callipus, and Callipic cycle, 150
Callisthenes, 29
Callisto, 248
Calyce, 22, 24, 125
Calypso, 91, 101-3, 109
Cassandra, 175, 180, 200
Caunos, 26, 310-12
*Caunou Ktisis* (Apollonius of Rhodes), 313

*Index*

Caves, crypts, and underground chambers, 159ff, 245ff; and cave deities, 203ff; and *passim*
Cecrops, 77, 88
Centaurus, and centaurs, 106, 120
Cephalos, 94-5
Cephalus, 46, 89, 91-2
Cephissus, 18, 78
Ceryces, 287
Chandra, Indian moon god, 8, 92
Chaos, 62, 270, 303
Chilon, 183
Chipiez, Charles, 130
Chresmologues, 253ff, 306-7
Chromia, 22, 126
Chronos, 270
Chryse, 71
Chrysothemis, 178
Cicero, 27, and *passim*
Circe, 63, 67, 69
Claudian, 16, 75
Cleitus, 89-90, 95
Clement of Alexandria, 20, 275
Cleobis, 203
Cleomenes, 156, 174
Clymene, 67
Clytemnestra, 180
Clytiadae, seers, 90
Cocconas, 281
Coeus, 66, 69
*Compendium Maleficarum* (Guazzo), 170
Connor, W.R., 154-5
Conon, 312-13
Cook, A.B., 48, 50-51, 82, 203, 296
Cooper, William R., 226, 229
Cornelius and Bebius, consuls, 105
Coronis, 199, 287
Cosmic Egg, 266, 272
Crius, 66, 70, 87

Cronos (Zeus), 75
Cuana, 226
Cumaean Sibyl, see Sibyl
Cybele, 15-16, 74
Cydas (Bacis), 257
Cylon, 145
Cynthia, 230

Danaus, 126
Daphne, 175, 180
*Daphnis and Chloe* (Longus), 240
Dardanus, 71
*De Fluviis*, see On Rivers
*De Incredibilibus* (anon.), 117
Deiope, 274-5
del Rio, Martin, 170
Delphi, Oracle of, 105, 177, 183, 192, 210, 219, 223, 254, 262-3
Demeter, 56, 100, 102, 161, 166, 275
Demetrius (possibly Demetrius of Phalerum), 157
Demodocus, 19
Demon (or Sign) of Socrates (Plutarch), 208
Demosthenes, and underground chamber, 167, 307
*Description of Greece* (Pausanias), 174
Detienne, Marcel, 208
Deucalion, 22, 125
Dia ('Goddess-like'), 106
Dia, wife or daughter of Lycaon, 72
Diana, see Artemis
Dickins, Guy, 182-6
*Dinner of the Seven Wise Men* (Plutarch), 158
Diodorus Siculus, 15; and *passim*
Diogenes Laertius, 144-63, 264-6
*Dionysiaca* (Nonnos), 43
Dionysius of Halicarnassus, 71, 105, 241

355

Dionysus (Bacchos), 55, 77, 79, 80-81, 96, 166, 246, 271, 277, 299, 310
Diphilus, 55
*Divine Institutes* (Lactantius), 242
Dosiadas, 144
Dreams and dreaming, wisdom through, and oracles, 143ff, 173ff, 189ff, 205ff; as interaction with numinous 171; and *passim*
Dryops, unidentified daughter of, 238
Dumezil, Georges, 7
Dysis, 31

Echelos, 75
Echo, 78
Edelstein, Emma and Ludwig, 191, 196-8
Egan, Rory B., 93-4
Egeria, goddess, 28, 86, 103-6
Egeria, nymph, 86, 103, 242
Egidius (later Giles), studies black arts in Toledo caves, 170
Egypt and Egyptians, 8, 29, 40, 104-5, 161, 163, 167, 169, 180, 190, 194, 223-4
Eileithyia, 5, 8
Eleusinian Mysteries, 19, 159, 194, 274, 275, 286-88
Elgin, Seventh Earl of, 50
Elgin Marbles, see Parthenon Marbles
Eliade, Mircea, 152, 160, 165
Elizabeth I, 230
Elysian Fields, 163
Emathion, 89
Empusae, 112
Endymion, 11, 111ff; and Selene, 21ff, 220ff, and *passim*; Elean version of (as prince or king), 22-23, 122ff; Carian version of (as shepherd) 23-28, 127 and *passim*; as 'cave sleeper', 114; and Hera, 119ff; sanctuary or shrine of, 131-33; as dreamer, 220ff and *passim*; as astronomer 117ff; and *passim*
*Endymion* (Lyly), 230
Engels, Friedrich, 8
*Enuma Elis*, Babylonian epic, 61
Eos (Aurora, the Dawn), 14; and her lovers, including Tithonus, 86ff; as nymphomaniac, 88ff; interpretations of, 91ff; and *passim*
Eosphorus (Morning Star), 66, 87
Epeius, 22
Ephialtes, 244
Ephorus, 70
Epicharmus, 189
Epimelides, class of nymphs, 148
Epimenides, 19, 143ff, 264ff; and Musaeus, 19ff; sleep of, 146ff; dream revelations of, 152ff; tattooed skin of, 156; diet of, 157ff; parallels with Endymion, 173 and *passim*; as nympholept 264; and I
Epione, 56
*Epistle to Titus* (St Paul), 264
Erato, nymph, 248
Ersa (or Herse; 'Dew', daughter of Selene), 17, 75, 77ff, 302
Ethiopia, 89
*Ethnica* (Stephanus), 18, 131
Etruria, Etruscans, 44, 57, 268
*Etymologicum Magnum* (Byzantine lexicon), 29, 116
Eucrates, sorcerer's apprentice, 169
euhemerism, defined, 15-16
Eumolpia, and Eumolpidae, 274
Eumolpids, 287

*Index*

Eumolpus, 19, 274-75, 277
Euripides, 15, 68, 166, 204, 269
Eurybia, 66, 70, 87
Eurycyda, 22
Eurydice, 223, 267-8, 276
Euryphaëssa ('far-shining'), 15, 68, 87, 304
Evander, 240
Evelyn-White, H.G., 39, 120

*Fabulae* (Hyginus), 14, 75-6
*Face which Appears in the Orb of the Moon* (Plutarch), 157, 222
Farnell, Lewis, 55
Fatua Fauna, 243
Faunus, 213, 230, 240ff, 284, 307; and dream oracle of, 240ff
feminist approaches to myth, 7ff
Ferdinand of Castile, 170
Festus, 51
*Fifth Isthmian Ode* (Pindar), 65
fleece, see sheep skins
Flood, Greek story of the, 125
Foam of the Moon, *see aphroselenos*
Forster, E.S., 182
Fox, Robin Lane, 286
Frazer, J.G., 51

Gabius Bassus, 243
Ganymede, 97, 99
Ge or Gaia (Earth), 14, 16, 53, 61, 66, 200, 293
Gebeleizis, see Zalmoxis
Geoffrey of Monmouth, 224-30
*Geography* (Strabo), 70, 132-33, 278
*Georgics* (Virgil), 20, 234-5
Germanicus Caesar, 117
*Gesta Regium Britannie* (William of Rennes), 228

Getae, Thracian tribe, 278, 162-4
Glycon and Glycon cult, 280ff
Gnosticism, 307
Goddesses and mortal lovers 85ff, and *passim*
God-man (anthropodaimon), 166
Gods and goddesses, encountering in dreams, 191ff, and *passim*
Graf, Fritz, 119, 159, 169, 258, 268-9
Graves, Robert, bad scholarship of, 4-8, 61, 111-13, 228, 236-7
*Great Eoiae* (Hesiod), 120
Grimal, Pierre, 70
Guazzo, Francesco Maria, 170
Guthrie, W.K.C., 160, 268

Hades, 16, 24, 94, 100, 120, 161, 267, 275, 277
Hagno, nymph, 247
Halia, nymph, 210
Halliday, W.R., 147, 152
Hares, 239
haruspicy, 57, 261
Hathor, 223-4
Haynes, Sybille, 57
Hecate, 3-6, 54-55, 66, 69, 301
Hecatomnid dynasty, 313-14
Hecuba, 259
Heira, sacred places, 245
Helen, 202
Helene, wife of Kerkon (possibly error for Selene), 274
Helios (the sun; sun god), 3, and *passim*
Hellanicus, 91, 93
Hemithea ('Half-Goddess'), as name of Parthenos, 179
Hera, 8, 17, 19, 24, 27, 55, 56; and Ixion, 106ff, 117; and Endymion, 119ff, 151, 203, 309-11

357

Herakles (Hercules), 13, 19, 72, 86, 96, 107, 164, 204; *History of Heracles* (Demodocus), 19, 83
Herkyna (nymph and river), 205-7
Hermae, 206
Hermes, 45, 63, 70, 88, 91, 95, 97, 102, 238-40, 271; as God of sleep and dreams, oneiropompos, 57; *Homeric Hymn to Hermes*, 15, 69
Hermesianax of Colophon, 19, 275
Hermione, and Oracle of, 189, 202, 204
Hermippus of Berytus, 189
Hero, 38
Herophile, 259-60
Herse, daughter of Cecrops, 77, 88, 91, 95
Hesiod, 14, and *passim*
Hesperides, 179
Hesperis, father of the Hesperides, 179
Hesperos, Evening Star, 47
Hestia, 96, 164, 165
Hesychios, *Lexicon of*, 244
*Historia Regum Britanniae* (Geoffrey of Monmouth), 224
*History of Plants* (Theophrastus), 158
Hittites, 61, 103
*Homeric Hymn to Aphrodite*, 41, 90, 96
*Homeric Hymn to Helios*, 15, 68, 76, 87
*Homeric Hymn to Hermes*, 15, 69
*Homeric Hymn to Selene*, 17, 38-9, 41, 76
Horae ('Seasons', daughter of Selene), 17-18, 78
Hornblower, Simon, 314
Horus, 161
Hour of Pan, 79, 239-40
Huxley, G.H., 151, 264
Hyades, 179
Hygeia, Hygieia, 56, 192-3
Hyginis, shepherd, 244
Hyginus, Roman author, 14, 67-8, 76
Hylas and the Nymphs, 107-8
Hymenaeus, God of marriage, 296, 299
Hyperion, 14-16; as father of Selene, 60-69; Carian and Latmian versions as separate figures with same name 304-5; and *passim*
Hyperippe, 22, 126
Hypnos, 30, 49, 80, 137, 201, 202, 221, 239, 297-99
Hyreus, treasury of, 201

I Ching, 254
Iamblichus, 163
Iamidae, seers, 90
Iamus, 90
Iapetus, 102
Iasion, 102
Idaean Dactyls, 152, 160
Idrieus, 313
Idyia ('knowing'), Oceanid, 67
Iliad (Homer), 60, 201
incubation ('temple-sleep'), 189-90, 195-6, 204, 208, 210, 243, 284
Indus river, 314-15
initiation in dreams 152; 159ff; and *passim*
Ino, 174-177, 181, 183-4
*Interpretes Virgilii* (anon.), 21, 235-6
Iphianassa, 22, 126
Iris, 19
Isabella, Queen, 170

*Index*

Ishtar (Inanna), 3, 41, 99-100, 108
Isidore of Seville, 226
Isis, 3, 40, 161, 169
Itonus, 22
Ixion, 24; and Hera, tale of, 106ff, 120-21, 123

Jackson, Steven, 116, 121, 124-125, 313
Jason, and the Argonauts, 23-4, 107, 269; poem on (Epimenides), 145-6
Jayne, Walter, 190
Jones, C.P., 284-6
Juan Manuel, Don, 170
Julian emperors of Rome, 98
Jung, Carl, 113
Jupiter, 77, 227-28

Kedrenos, Georgios, 56
Kerenyi, Carl, 36-7, 66-7, 76, 112-13, 149-51
Kerkyon, 274
Khonsu, Egyptian lunar deity, 8
Kirk, G.S., 7
Koortbojian, Michael, 296, 298
Kronos, 61, 163, 246, 270

Lactantius, 103, 105-6, 242-3
Lada, 130
Lamia, daughter of Poseidon, 259
Lampetia ('the illuminating'), 67
Lampus, 88
Laomedon, 90
Lars Porsena, 57
Larson, Jennifer, 74
Latinus, King, 241-2
*Laws* (Plato), 153-4
Layard, John, 239
L-dopa, 195
Leahy, D.M., 156-7

Leander, 38
Lefkowitz, Mary, 38
Leland, Charles, 231
Lempriere, J., 147
*Leontion* (Hermesianax), 275
Lethe, spring of (Forgetfulness), 206-7, 272
Leto, 56, 66, 287
Levi, Peter, 51, 126, 259
*Library* (Diodorus), 74
Licymnius, 30
*Life of Numa* (Plutarch), 28
*Life of Pythagoras* (Diogenes Laertius), 153
*Life of Pythagoras* (Porphyry), 152
Lilaeus, 30
liminality, liminal landscapes and states, 96, 101, 109, 133-41, 149, 153, 165, 219, 238-40, 260, 268, and *passim*,
Linear-B, 35, 60, 185, 211
Liriope, 18, 78
*Lithica* (attrib. Orpheus), 269
*Lives and Opinions of Eminent Philosophers* (Diogenes Laertius), 144
Livy, 103, 314
*Long-Lived Persons* (Phlegon), 150
Longus, 240, 244
*Lover of Lies, The* (Lucian), 169
Lozano, Cristóbal, 170
Lucian, 25-6, 117, 280-88
Lucina (Eileithyia, the birth-Goddess), 5
Luna (as Latin cognate of Selene/Mene), 5, 15-16, 20-21, 27, 34, 77, 228-9, 233-6
Lunar Spell of Claudianus, 223
Lycaon (possibly grandfather of Selene), 70-74, 238, 247-8; as werewolf, 71
Lycophron, 212
Lycurgus, 104-5

359

Machaon, 212
MacKenzie, Norman, 193-4
Macrobius, 20, 235-6
Maenads, 268
Manasses, Konstantinos, 82
Manes or Mannes or Men, Phrygian Moon-God, 37
Mantius, 89
Marduk, 61
Mars, 297
Marxism, 7-8
matriarchal society, as fantasy, 5, 8, 303
Mausolus, 13, 313-17
Maximus Tyrius, 148, 152-3
McNally, Sheila, 221
Medea, sorceress, 23, 67, 69, 139-40
Megamedes ('the very wise'), 15, 69-71, 102, 115
Melampid seers, Melampodidae, 90, 95
Melampus, 89-90
*melisponda* (libations of honey), 55
Memnon, 89, 168
Mene (moon), as name of Selene, 16, and *passim*
Menelaus, 202
Mercury, 21, 227-8, 235
Merlin, 225
Mesopotamia, Mesopotamian mythology, 41, 61
Metapontine Treasury, 126
Methone, 267
Meton of Athens, Metonic cycle, 149-51
Micyllus, 67
*Milesiaca* (Aristides of Miletos), and Milesian Tales, 311
Miletos, founder of city Miletos, 26, 312-13
Miletus, son of Glycon, 286

minions of the moon (Shakespeare), 138
*Minos* (possibly Pseudo-Platonic), 153-4
Minos, king of Crete, 104-5, 154, 165, 177, 184, 201, 247
*Mirabilia* (Theopompus), 148
Mitylene, 34
Mnaseas of Sicyon, 117
Mnemosyne (Memory), spring of, 55, 206-7, 272
Molpadia, 178-9
Mopsus, 189, 200-201, 211-12
Morgos, one of the Idaean Dactyls, 152
Musaeus, 19ff, and *passim*
Muses, 39, 41, 55, 93, 103, 262, 267, 277
Music, treatise on (Aristoxenus), 177
Mykene, putative city-Goddess of Mycenae, 35
Myrrha (or Smyrna), daughter of King Theias, 100
Myth, definition of, contrasted with fable, pp.1-2; monolithic theories of ('single key' fallacy) 7; method and scope of studying 11; and *passim*

Narcissus, 18ff, 78ff; as offspring of Selene 79-82; etymology of, 80
*Natural History* (Pliny), 80
Naxos (leader of Carians, possible son of Selene), 26
Neaira, 67-8
Near-Death Experience, 223
Nectanebos, Egyptian magician, 29-30
Neda, nymph, 247
Nemea, nymph, 18
Nemean Lion, 18ff, 82ff

*Nemean Odes* (Pindar), 18
Nemesis, 78
*nephalia* (wineless sacrifices), 55
Nephele, 24, 106
Nicander of Colophon, 20, and *passim*
Nike (Victory), 66-67
Nikosthenidas, 182
Nilsson, Martin P., 34
Nonacris, wife of Lycaon, 73
Nonnos, 15, 309ff, and *passim*
Notus, 66, 87
Numa, 28, 86, 104, 241-2; and Egeria, 103ff
Nymphaeum at Apollonia, 249
Nympholepsy, 108, 154-5
Nyx (Night), 48, 270-71, 297-8


Ocean (Okeanos), 16, 39-40, 45, 47, 66, 73, 75, 90, 134, 138, 293
Odysseus, 63, 86, 103, 166, 228, 238, 258, 278; and Calypso, 101ff
*Odyssey* (Homer), 40, 60, 67-8, 83, 86, 89, 106, 228, 258, 278
Oeagrus, 267
Ogden, Daniel, 207-8, 210
Oicles, 89
Oinopides, 151
Olympian Gods, 14; defined by being 'not-Titan', 62; and *passim*
Olympias, mother of Alexander, 30
Olympic Games, 22, 124, 126-7, 304
*omphalos*, 264
*On the Birth of the Curetes and Corybantes* (attrib. Epimenides), 145, 266
*On the Cave of the Nymphs* (Porphyry), 245
*On the Delays in Divine Vengeance* (Plutarch), 262

*On Divination* (Cicero), 174, 256
*On Images* (Porphyry), 34
*On the Incredible* (attrib. Heraclitus), 25
*On Minos and Rhadamanthus* (attrib. Epimenides), 146, 226
*On Rivers* (attrib. Plutarch), 19, 30, 83, 214, 314-16
*On Sacrifices and the Cretan Constitution* (attrib. Epimenides), 146, 226
*Oneirocritica* (Artemidorus), 198
Onomacritus, a chresmologue, 273
oracle at Delphi, see Delphi
oracle at Thalamae, see Thalamae
oracle-mongers (see chresmologues)
*Oracles at Delphi No Longer Given in Verse, The* (Plutarch), 262
Orion, 88-91, 95, 102
Oropus, as youth, 209
Orpheotelestai (Orphic initiators), 270, 272-3, 276, 278, 281
Orpheus, 19, 160; and Musaeus, 266ff; death of, 268; Strabo's account of, 278
*Orphic Argonautica*, 267
Orphic religion, question of, 269-70
Ouranos (Sky), 14, 16, 61, 270-71, 296
Ovid, 38, 48, 70, 78, 87, 91, 121, 241-2, 260-61, 267-8, 312
*Oxford Classical Dictionary*, 54, 305


Paeon, 22
Page, D.L., 123
Pallantis, 70, 87
Pallas, 66-7; plural identities

noted, 69; as son of Lycaon, 70-72; as Titan, 73-4; as son of Megamedes, 15, 69-70, 87, 115
Palmer, L.R., 80
Pan Lytirius, sanctuary of, 243
Pan, 20ff; 70; 234ff, 306; and Arcadia, 237ff; and *passim*
Pancrates, sorcerer, 169
Pandia (moonlight, 'All-bright', daughter of Selene), 17, 47, 75ff, 276, 302
Pandora, 41
Parke, H.W., 181, 257, 264-5, 276
Parker, Robert, 54
Parthenius, 312-13
Parthenon Marbles, 49-50
Parthenos, 178-9
Pasiphae (deity), 63; shrine of, 173ff; etymology, 177-78; distinguished from wife of King Minos of Crete, 177, 184; as name or title of Selene, 174, 186; as primarily title, 178, 181
Patroclus, 201, 220
Patterson, Lee, 122
Pausanias, 22, and *passim*
Pelasgus, 70-72
Penglase, Charles, 10, 41
Perrot, Georges, 130
Perseis, 67, 69
Persephone, 5, 13, 16, 56, 66, 100, 166, 207, 271
Perses and Perseis ('destroyers'), 66-7, 69+
Petrie, W.M. Flinders, 226
*Phaedrus* (Plato), 93
*Phaenomena* (Aratus), 117
Phaestius, 144
Phaethon ('The Brilliant', son of Helios), 63, 67, 88, 118
Phaethon (son of Cephalus), 88-9
Phaethon , a horse, 88

Phaethoussa, 67
Phanes, a hermaphroditic being, 270-72
Pheidias, 50-51, 56
Pherecydes of Athens, 124
Philargyrius, 2356
Philemon of Syracuse, 55
Philochorus, 19, 55, 189, 274
Philodamus, 77, 276
Philostratus, Flavius, 195, 209
Philostratus (the elder), 209
Phlegon of Tralles, 150, 254, 261
Phoebe, Titan goddess, 64, 66
Phoebe (Artemis, who takes epithet Phoebe), 64, 66, 230
Phoebe, Elizabeth I as, 230
Phoebus (Apollo as), 27-8
Phylarchus, 175, 180
Phylargyrius, 21, 233
Picus, 243
Pindar, 18, 65, 106, 121, 220
Pisander of Rhodes, 124
Plato, 23, 74, 93, 145, 153-4, 164, 277-78
Pleiades, 179
Pleione, 179
Pliny, 80, 117, 150
*ploutonia*, entrances to the underworld, 205
Plutarch, 28, and *passim*
Pluto, see Hades
Podaleirius, 9, 213, 218, 282, 287-88
Polybius, 180
Polyidus, 89
Polypheides, 89
Porphyry, 34, 56, 152, 157, 160, 164, 245-6
Poseidon, 55-6, 259
Priam, 126, 175, 180, 259
Probus, Marcus Valerius, 21, 234-5
Procris, 91

## Index

Propertius, 27-8
Proserpina (Persephone), 5, 16, 228
Protagoras (Plato), 276
Protogeneia ('Firstborn'), 22, 125
Ptolemaic dynasty, 124
Ptolemy, 43
Pyrrha, 125
Pythagoras, and cave or chamber initiation, 152-4, 160-62, 165, 209, 287-8, 307; and Zalmoxis, 162ff
Pythia (prophetic priestesses of Apollo), 192, 255, 263
*Pythian Ode, Second* (Pindar), 106
Python, snake deity, 192

Quintus Smyrnaeus, 17, 28-9, 68, 78, 193

*Revelation of St John*, 254
*Rhapsodic Theogony* (attrib. Orpheus), 270
*Rhapsodies, The* (Orpheus), 37
Rhesus, Thracian king, 166
*Rhesus* (Euripides), 166
Rhoeo, 178
Richer, Jean, 130
Rieu, E.V., 102
Robert, C., 294
Rohde, Erwin, 158, 176, 200, 202, 204, 220
Rouse, W.H.D., 310-12
Rudgley, Richard, 194
Rutilia, 287
Rutilianus, P. Mummius Sisenna, 283-9
*Sacred Tales* (Aristides), 191, 196
Sandys, J.E., 65
Sappho, 9, 25
Sarapion, 262

sarcophagi, 291ff
Sarpedon, Oracle of, 189, 201
Satyrus, an actor, 167
Savignoni, L., 44-5, 50, 75
Selenaeus, as earlier name of Apesantus, 19
Selene, 13, 33ff, 301ff, and *passim*; major myths of, 13ff, 304ff; descent and offspring, 14ff, 60ff, 75ff; and Pan, 20ff, 234ff, and *passim*; and Endymion, 21ff, 129ff, 215ff, 219, 309ff, and *passim*; iconography of, 38ff; in Greek religion, 54ff, 70; minor myths of, 59ff; and the Nemean Lion, 82ff; and sarcophagi, 144ff, 291ff; as goddess of dreams, 222-3; and chresmologues, 253ff; and Alexander of Abonoteichus 280ff; and incest 309ff
Semele, 85, 98, 276; as error for Selene and v.v., 77, 276
Servius, 5, 42, 91, 93, 228, 236; and Triple Moon-Goddess, 228
Seven Wise Men of Greece, 307
Severan dynasty, 292
Severus Alexander, 52
Shakespeare, William, 138
Shamanism, 268, 270
sheep skins, and dream oracles, 21, 153, 160, 210ff, 234-8, 241-3, 246, 249-50, 306, and *passim*
Sibyl, Sibyls, 258-63; Cumaean Sibyl, 228, 230; Sibyl of Erythraea, 154
Sibylline Books, 254-55
Sikes, E.E., 42, 76
Sillene spring, 57
Simpson, R. Hope, 184
Sin, Sumerian lunar deity, 8
Smith, Cecil, 45-7, 50
snakes, sacred, 45-7, 50, see also Glycon, Python

Sorabella, Jean, 294
Sorcerer's Apprentice, tale of, 169
Sosias, 44
*Sphaera* (attrib. Orpheus), 269, 274
Paul, Saint, 264
Staphylus, 178
Stark, Freya, 130, 132-3, 140
Statius, 30
Stephanus of Byzantium, 18, 131
Stoneman, Richard, 130
Strabo, 54, 131-133, 163-5, 202, 212, 278
Strataridaki, Anna, 152, 156
Strymon, 166
Styx, river and daughter of Ocean, 66, 73-4, 228, 238
*Suda*, 147, 156, 164, 274


Tammuz (Dumuzi), 99-100, 108
Tarquinius Priscus, 258
Tartarus, 62, 272
Taurus, 29, 43, 51
Tegean War, 183
Telestrion, 'House of Initiation', 166
Tellias and Telliadae, 90
Terpsichore, 166
Tertullian, 146, 176, 189, 199-202, 204, 208, 212
Tethys, 16-17, 745
Thalamae, and oracle at, (Shrine of Pasiphae), 173ff, 205, 207, 211, 216-17, 306
Thalassa (Sea), 53
Thanatos, 137, 201, 299
Theia, 14, 60-62, 64-5, 68, 87, 100, 303
Theias (or Cinyras), king of Syria, 99
Theisoa, nymph, 247
Themis, 18, 56

Theocritus, 239, 248
Theodorus (historian), 72
Theodorus (shepherd), 260
*Theogony* (attrib. Epimenides), 146, 266, 272
*Theogony* (Hesiod), 14, 41, 65-66
*Theogony* (Musaeus), 273-4
*Theogony* (Orpheus), 270-72
Theon of Alexandria, 23
Theophrastus, 158
Theopompus, 144, 147-51, 155
*Theriaca* (NIcander), 29, 116
Theseus, 15, 299
Thesmophoria, festival of, 8
Thespesius, 223, 262-3
Thessalus, physician, 167-68
Tiamat, 61
Timarchus, 208
Tiresias, 86, 107, 278
Titaea, mother of the Titans (Gaia), 16
Titans, 14 and *passim*; overthrow of, 61
Tithonus, 85-6, 89-101, 108, 157, 261
Tiur, Etruscan Moon-God, 57
Toledo, caves beneath 169-171
Triple-moon goddess, as 20th century invention, 4-6, 228, 301; see also Servius
Trophonius, 164-5, 190, 201-210
Troy, Trojan War, 29, 71, 89-90, 97, 99, 108, 124, 126, 166, 180, 199, 201, 212, 224-30, 240, 259
Tudor dynasty, 230
Tysilio Chronicle, 226-7


Universe, Orphic account of, 270-71
Ushas, Vedic Dawn Goddess, 91-2
Ustinova, Yulia, 204

*Index*

Valerius Maximus, 150
Valerius Probus, 21, 234
Varro, 146
Venus, 38, 98, 293-4, 297
Vermeule, Emily, 46-7, 51, 84-5, 99
Virgil, 20, and *passim*
*Virgilius Romance*, 170


Wardle, David, 256
West, M.L., 37, 265, 273-4
Wilkins, W.J., 92
Winds, 55, 66, 87


Xenophanes of Colophon, 150


Zaleucus, 104
Zalmoxis (also Zamolxis, Salmoxis), 162ff, 278, 282; bearskin etymology of, 164
Zechis, 29
Zephyrus, 66, 87
Zethus, 275
Zeus, 14, and *passim*
Zoroaster, 104

Strange Attractor Press 2019

www.ingramcontent.com/pod-product-compliance
Lightning Source LLC
Chambersburg PA
CBHW021148230426
43667CB00006B/306